CRAZY FOOD TRUCK

1

STORY AND ART BY **ROKUROU OGAKI**

#1 BLT SANDWICH

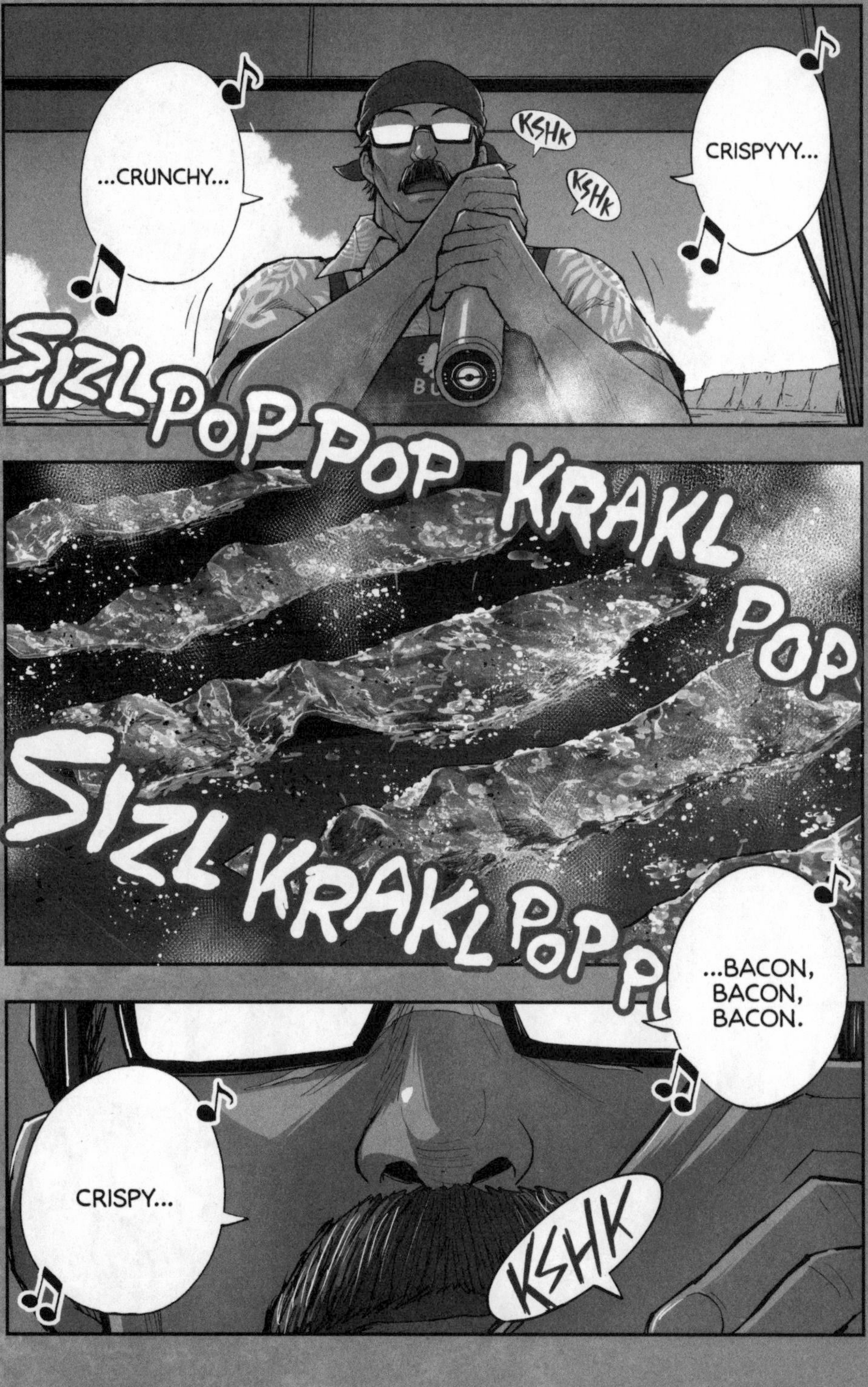
CRISPYYY...
KSHK
KSHK
...CRUNCHY...
SIZL POP POP KRAKL
POP
SIZL KRAKL POP
...BACON, BACON, BACON.
KSHK
CRISPY...

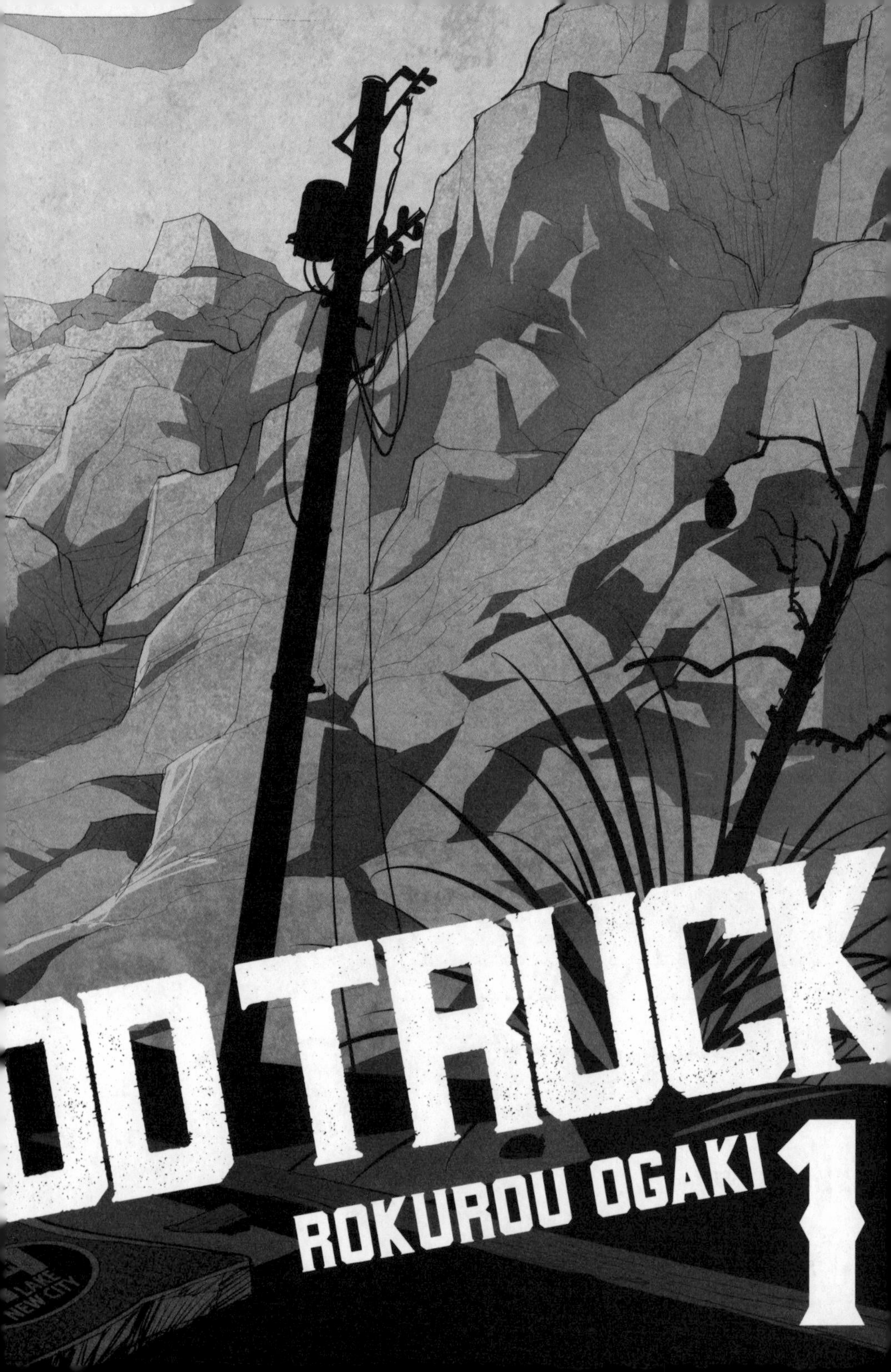
OD TRUCK
ROKUROU OGAKI
1
LAKE
NEW CITY

#1 BLT SANDWICH
...BLACKENED, CRUNCHY, CRISPY...
...BUH-BUH-BACON!
CRAZY FO

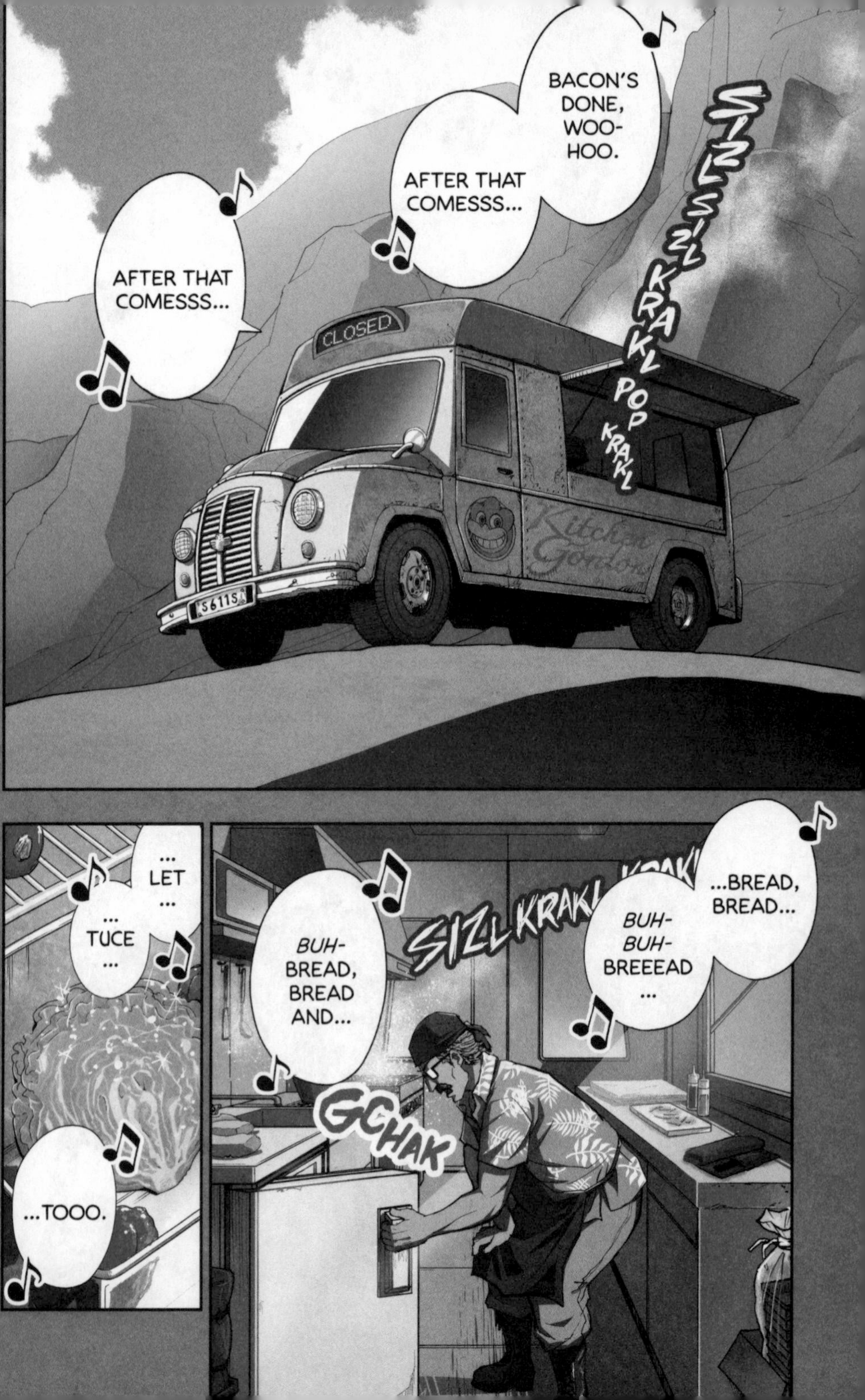
BACON'S DONE, WOO-HOO.
SIZLSIZL KRAKL POP KRAKL
AFTER THAT COMESSS...
AFTER THAT COMESSS...
CLOSED
Kitchen Gordon
S611S
...BREAD, BREAD...
BUH-BUH-BREEEAD...
SIZL KRAKL
BUH-BREAD, BREAD AND...
GCHAK
...LET...
...TUCE...
...TOOO.

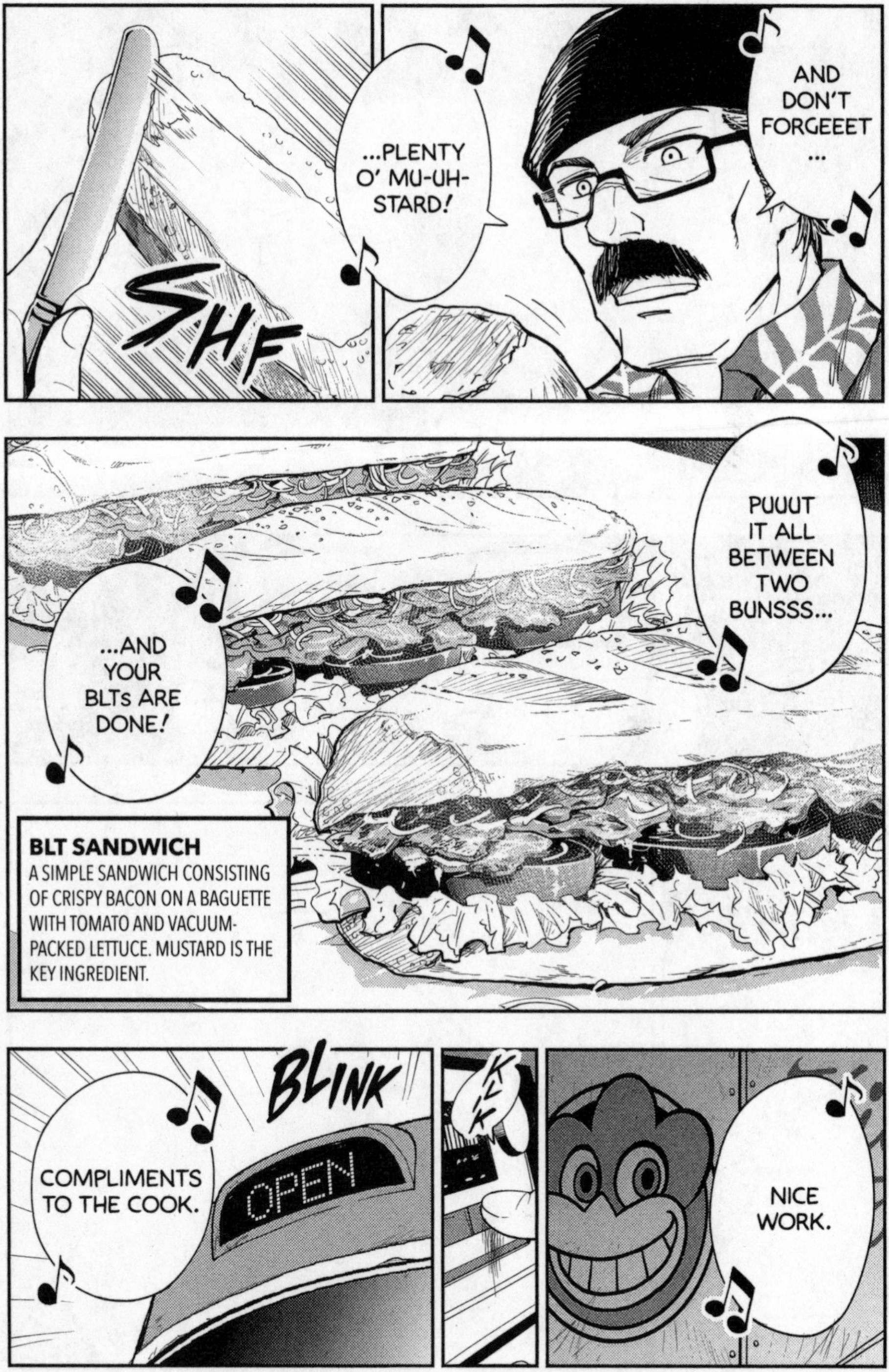
AND DON'T FORGEEET ...
...PLENTY O' MU-UH-STARD!
SHF
PUUUT IT ALL BETWEEN TWO BUNSSS...
...AND YOUR BLTs ARE DONE!
BLT SANDWICH
A SIMPLE SANDWICH CONSISTING OF CRISPY BACON ON A BAGUETTE WITH TOMATO AND VACUUM-PACKED LETTUCE. MUSTARD IS THE KEY INGREDIENT.
NICE WORK.
BLINK
OPEN
COMPLIMENTS TO THE COOK.

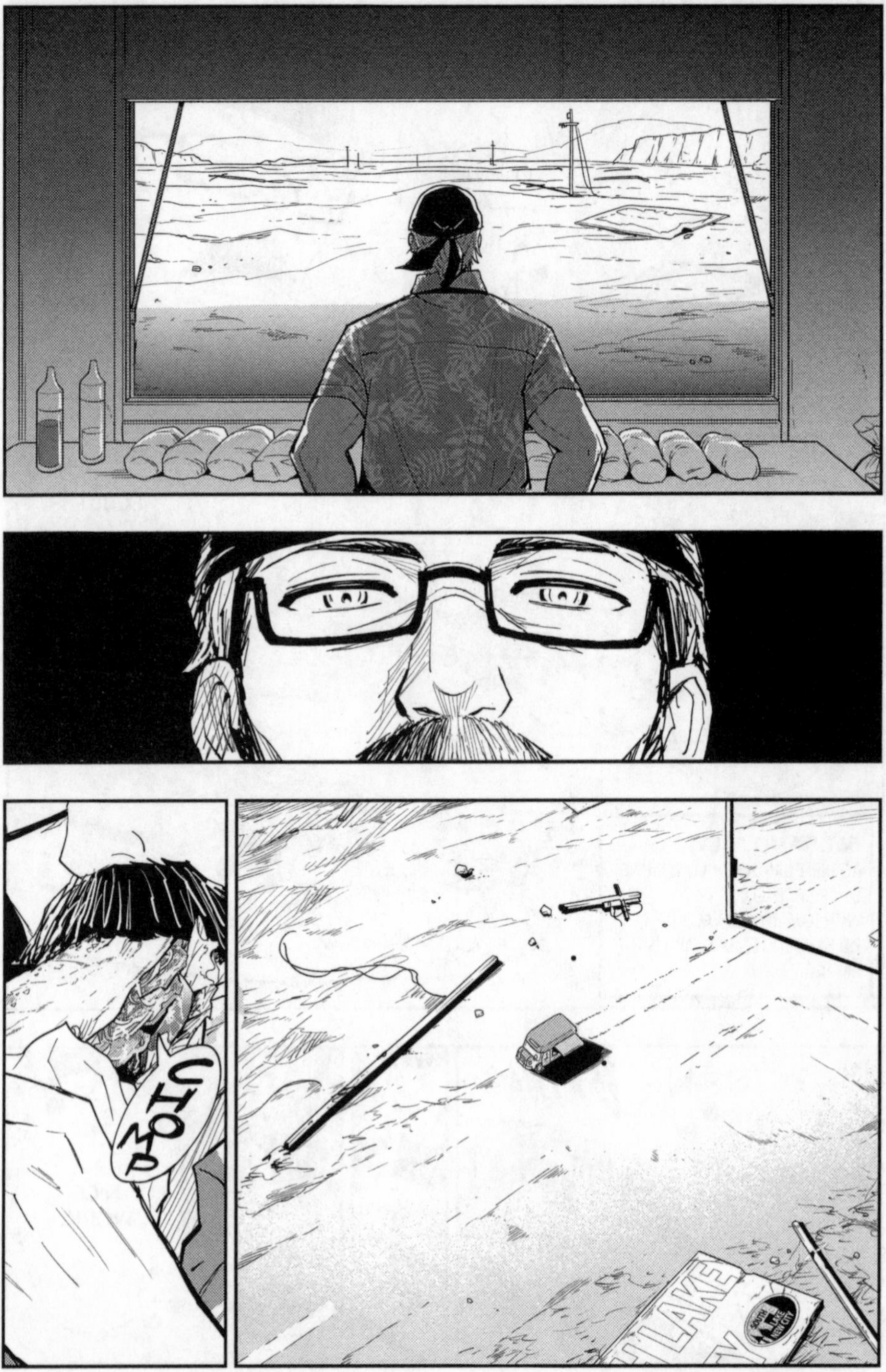
LAKE
CHOMP

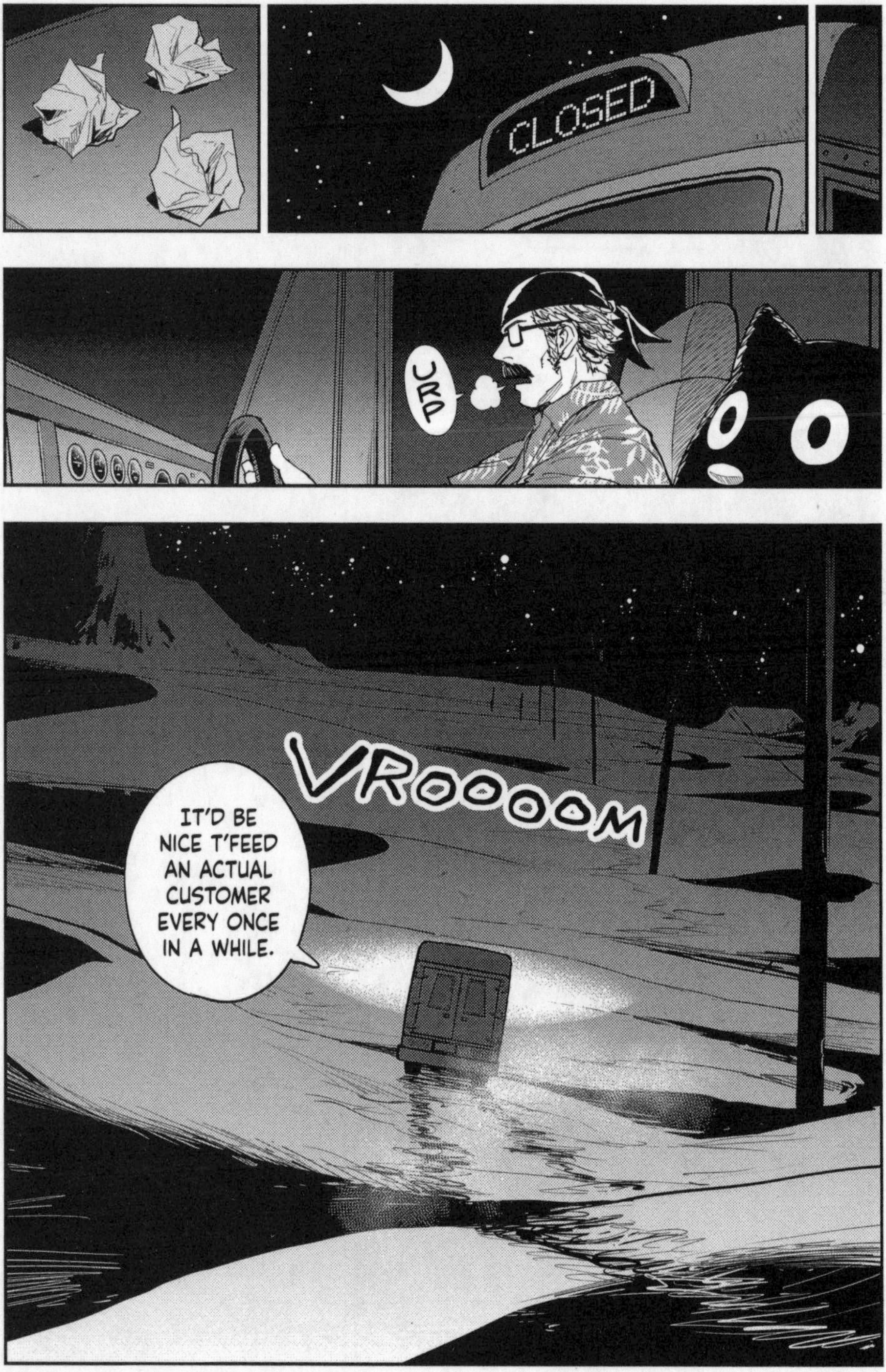
CLOSED
URP
VROOOOM
IT'D BE NICE T'FEED AN ACTUAL CUSTOMER EVERY ONCE IN A WHILE.

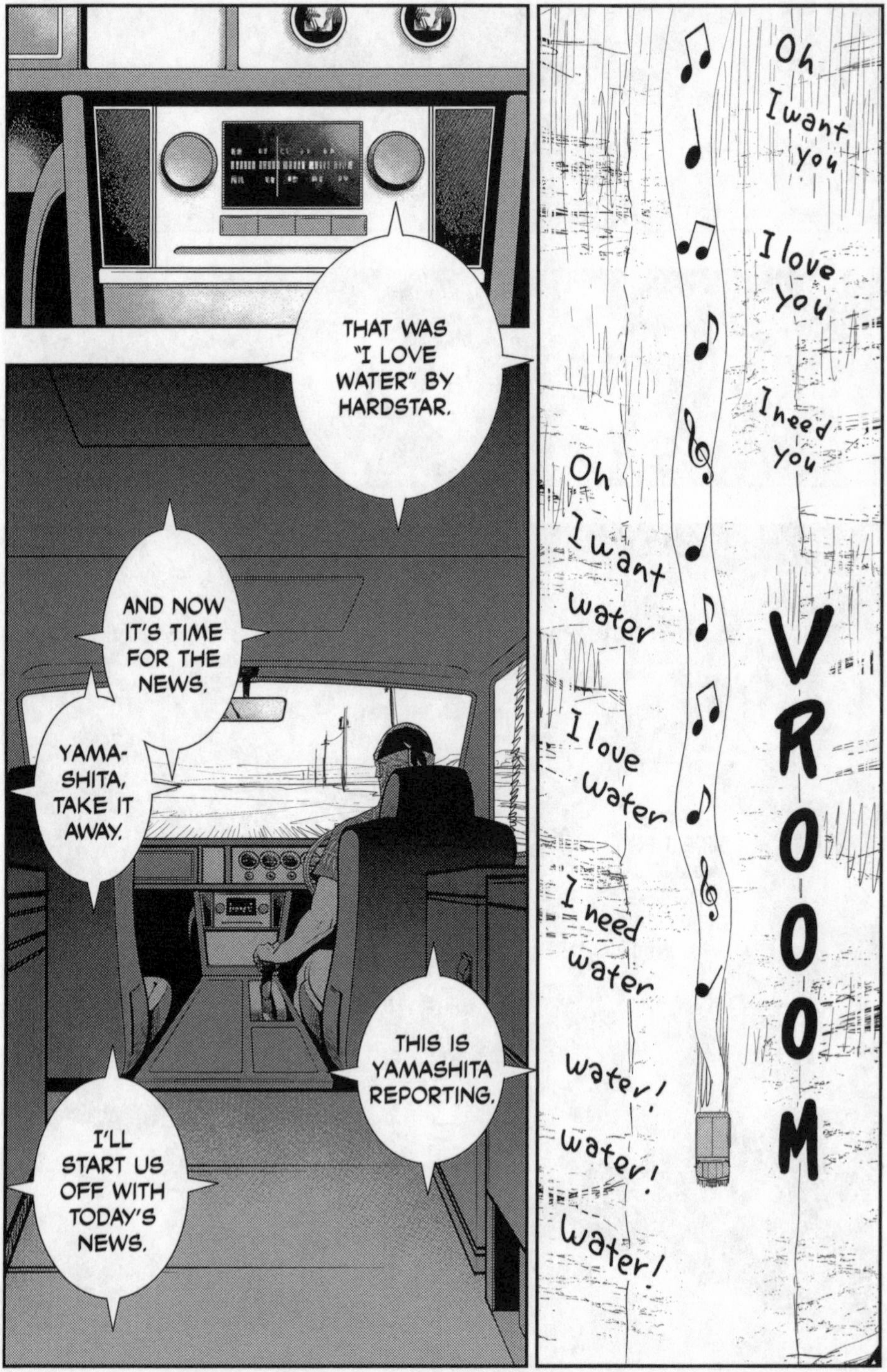
Oh I want you
I love you
I need you
VROOM
Oh I want water
I love water
I need water
water! water! water!
THAT WAS "I LOVE WATER" BY HARDSTAR.
AND NOW IT'S TIME FOR THE NEWS.
YAMA-SHITA, TAKE IT AWAY.
THIS IS YAMASHITA REPORTING.
I'LL START US OFF WITH TODAY'S NEWS.

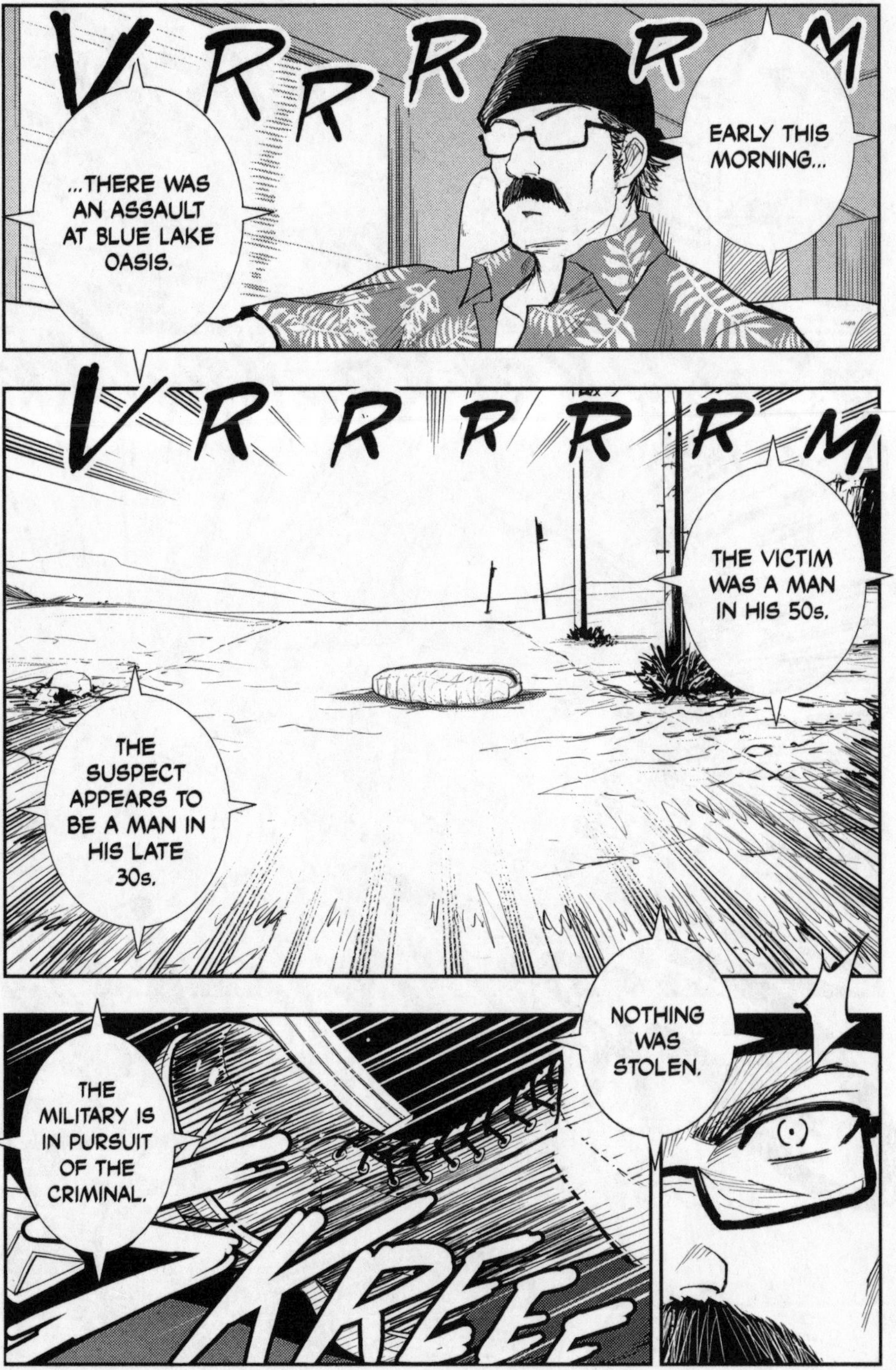
VRRRRM
EARLY THIS MORNING...
...THERE WAS AN ASSAULT AT BLUE LAKE OASIS.
VRRRRRRM
THE VICTIM WAS A MAN IN HIS 50s.
THE SUSPECT APPEARS TO BE A MAN IN HIS LATE 30s.
NOTHING WAS STOLEN.
THE MILITARY IS IN PURSUIT OF THE CRIMINAL.
KREEE

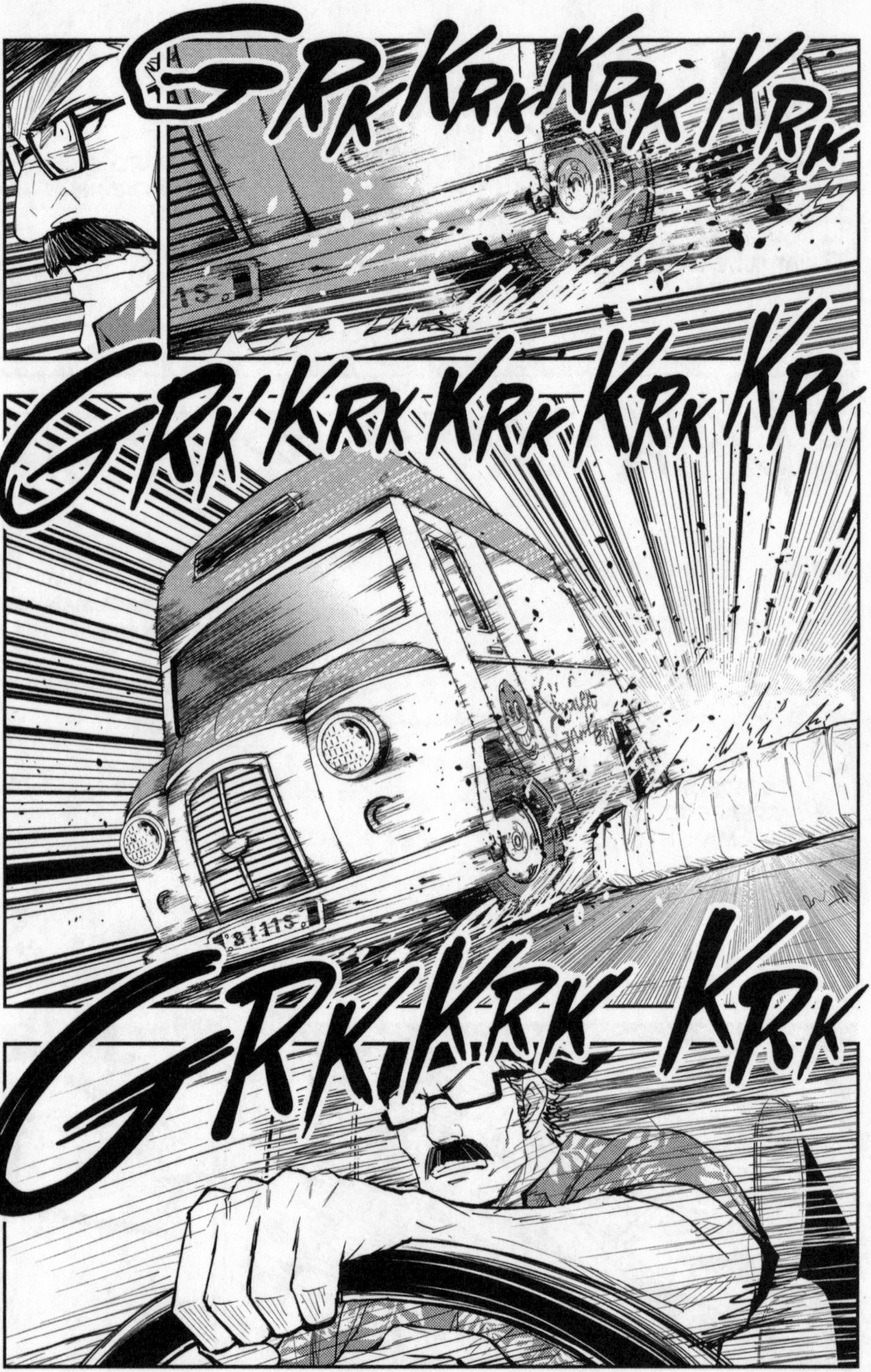
GRK-KRK-KRK-KRK
GRK-KRK-KRK-KRK-KRK
GRK-KRK-KRK

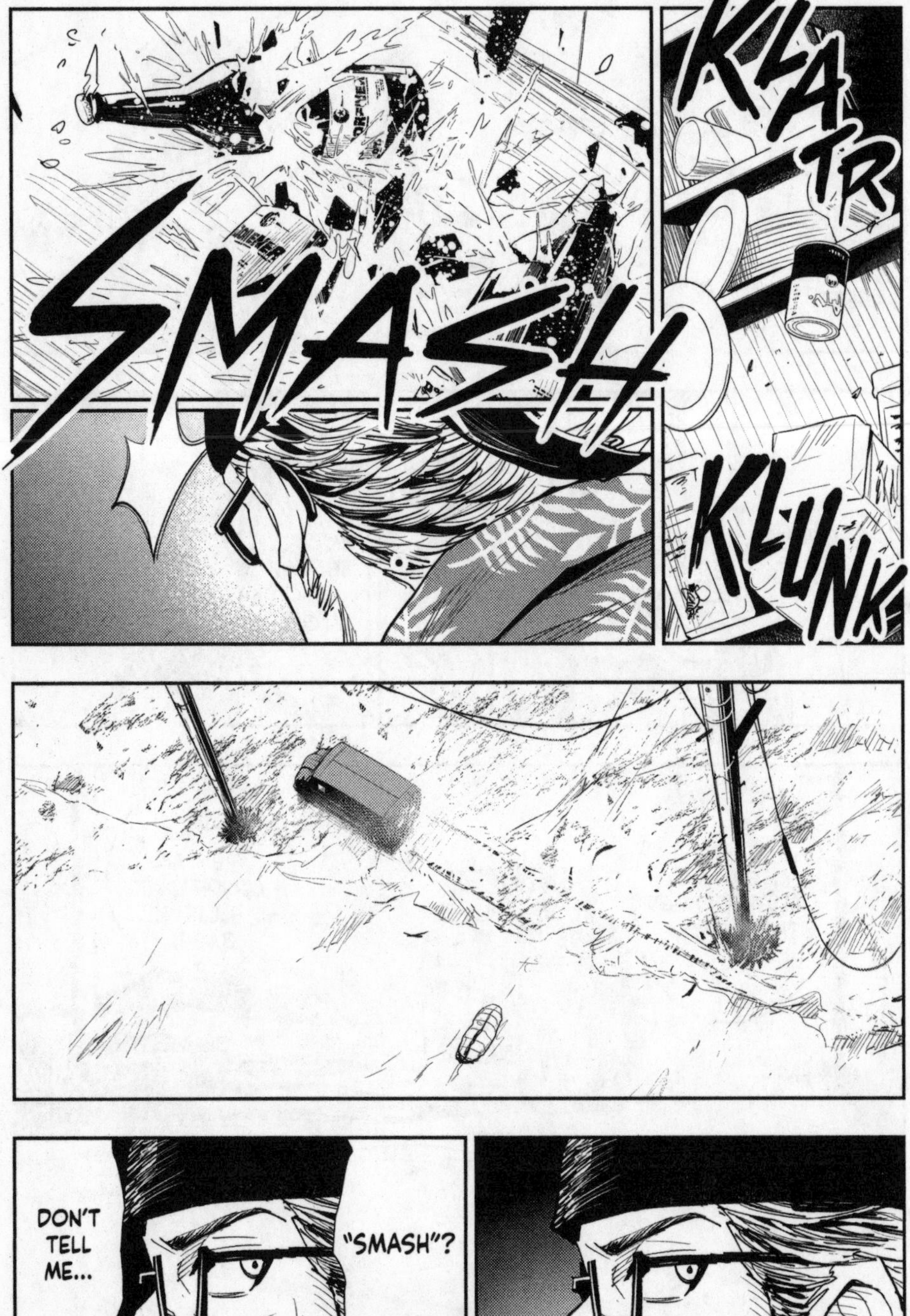
KLATR
KLUNK
SMASH
DON'T TELL ME...
"SMASH"?

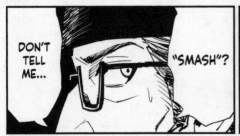

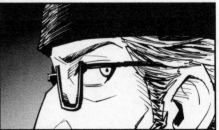

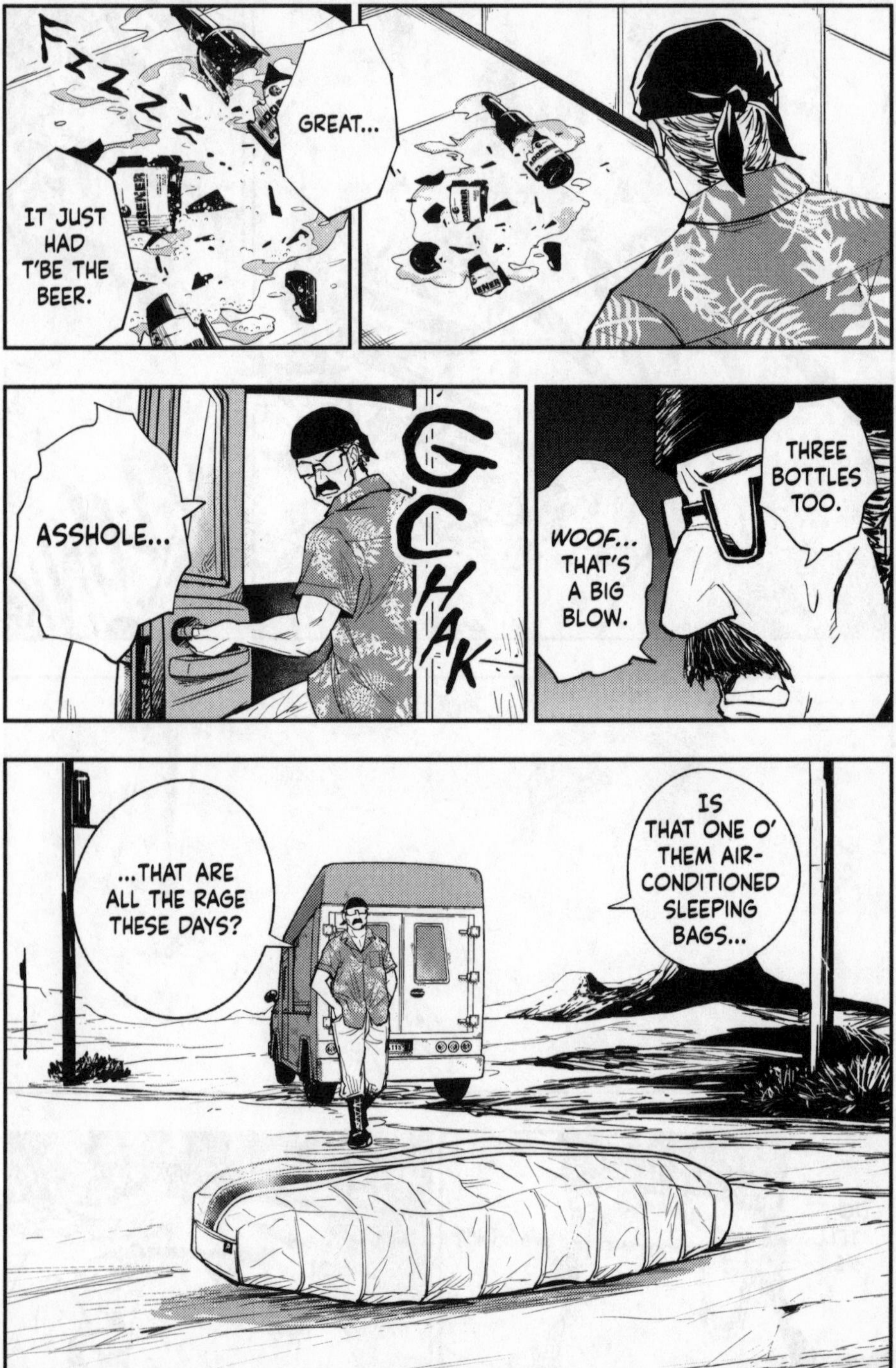
GREAT...
FZZZZ
IT JUST HAD T'BE THE BEER.
THREE BOTTLES TOO.
WOOF... THAT'S A BIG BLOW.
GCHAK
ASSHOLE...
IS THAT ONE O' THEM AIR-CONDITIONED SLEEPING BAGS...
...THAT ARE ALL THE RAGE THESE DAYS?

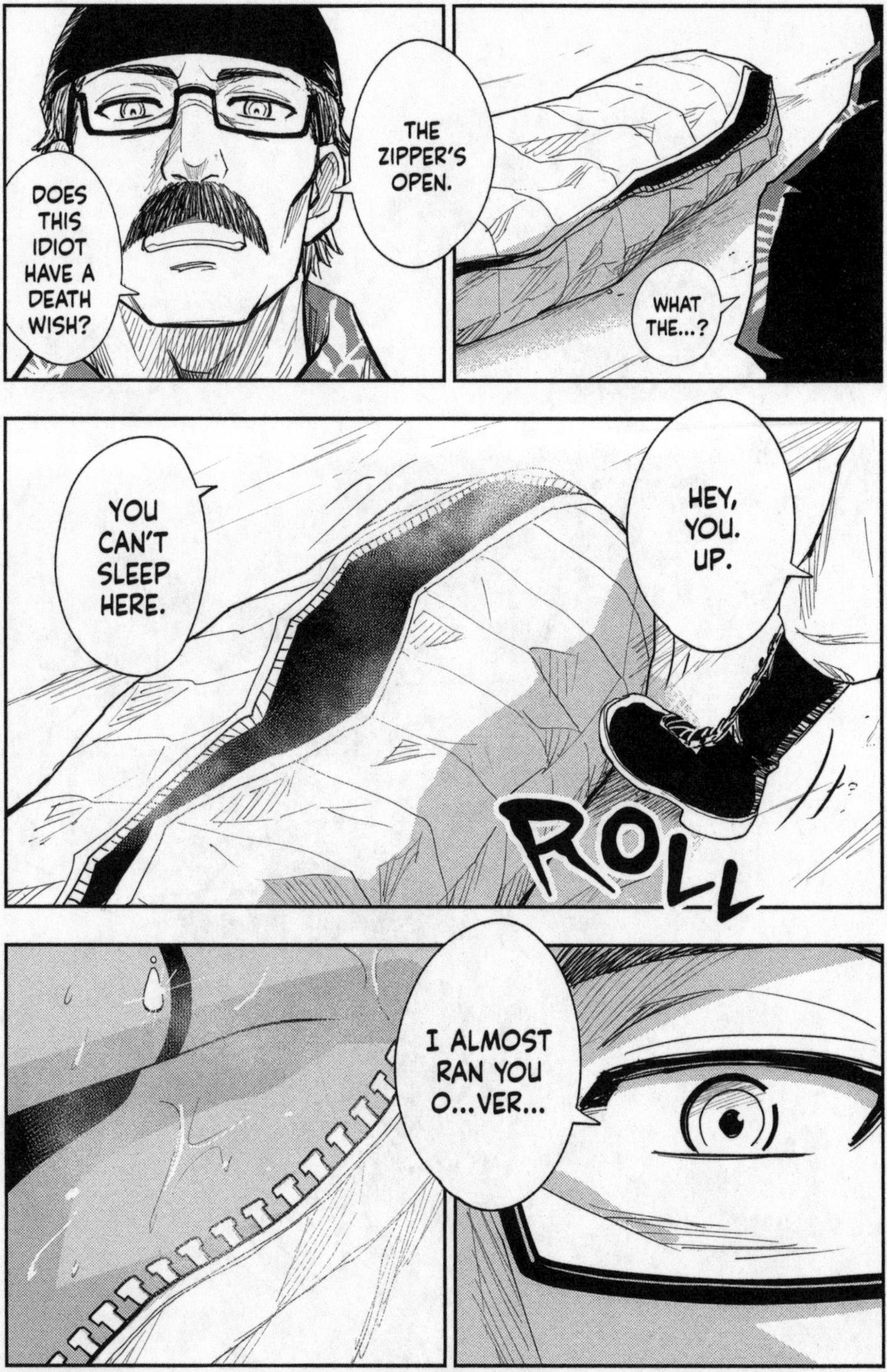
WHAT THE...?
THE ZIPPER'S OPEN.
DOES THIS IDIOT HAVE A DEATH WISH?
HEY, YOU. UP.
YOU CAN'T SLEEP HERE.
ROLL
I ALMOST RAN YOU O...VER...

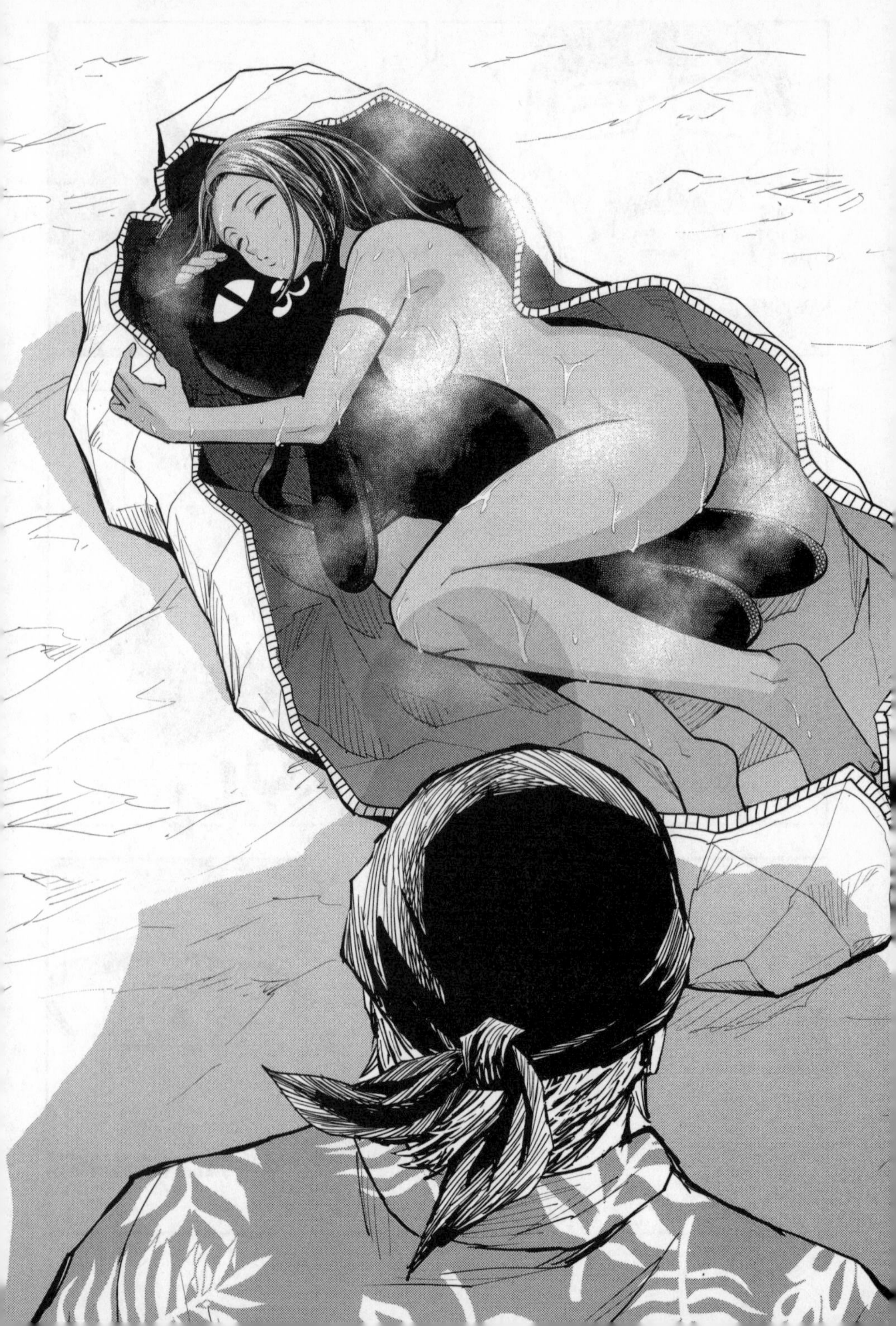

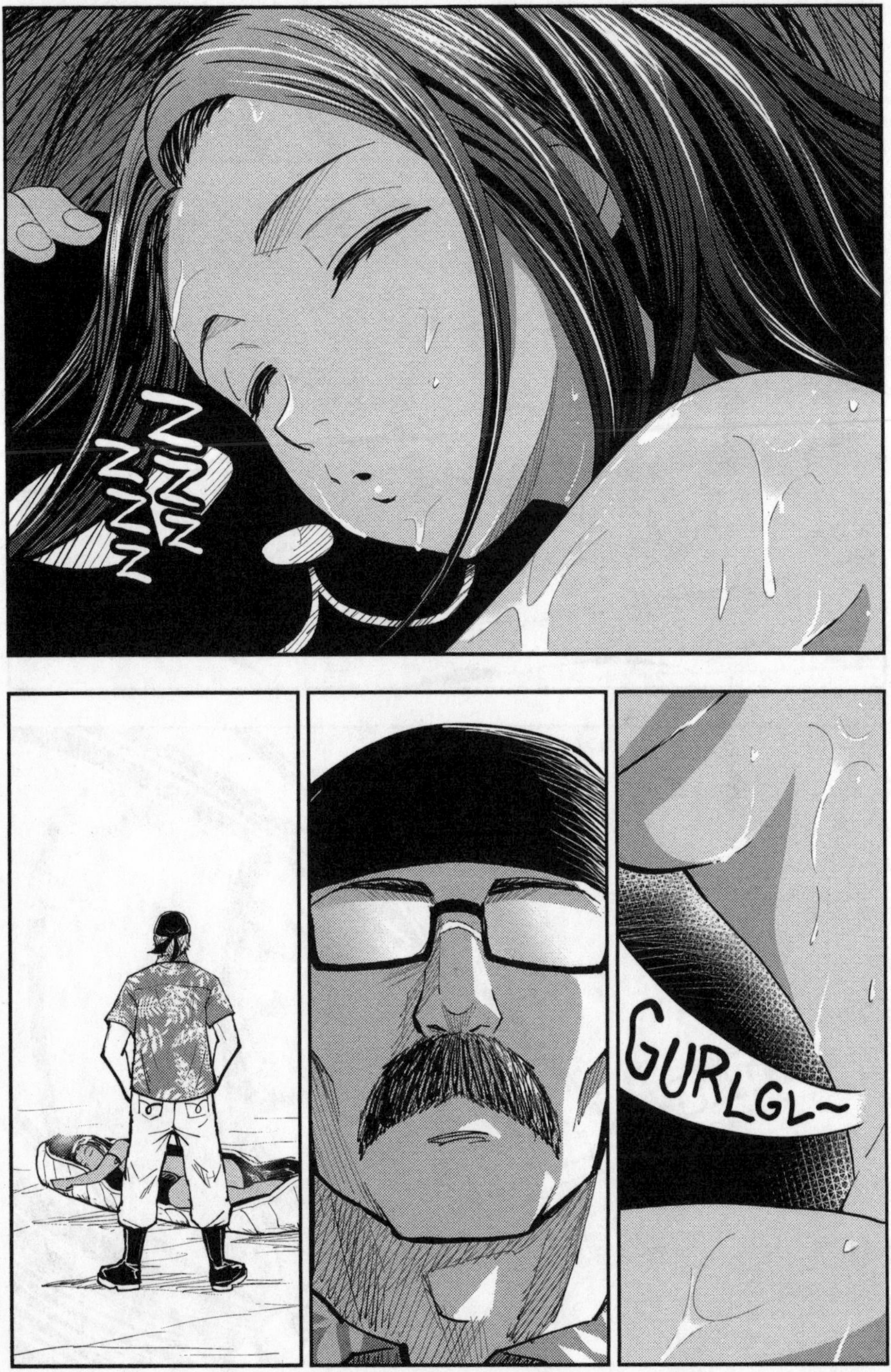
ZZZZZ
GURLGL~

SNIFF
SNIFF

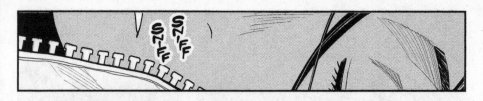

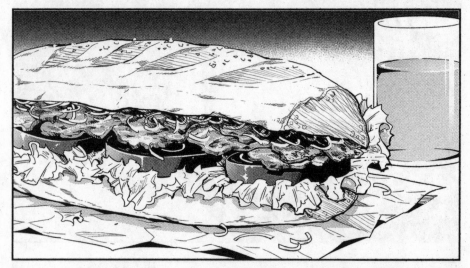

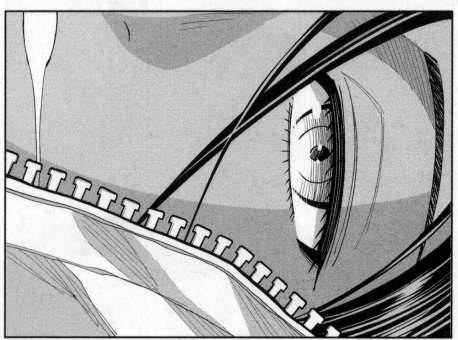

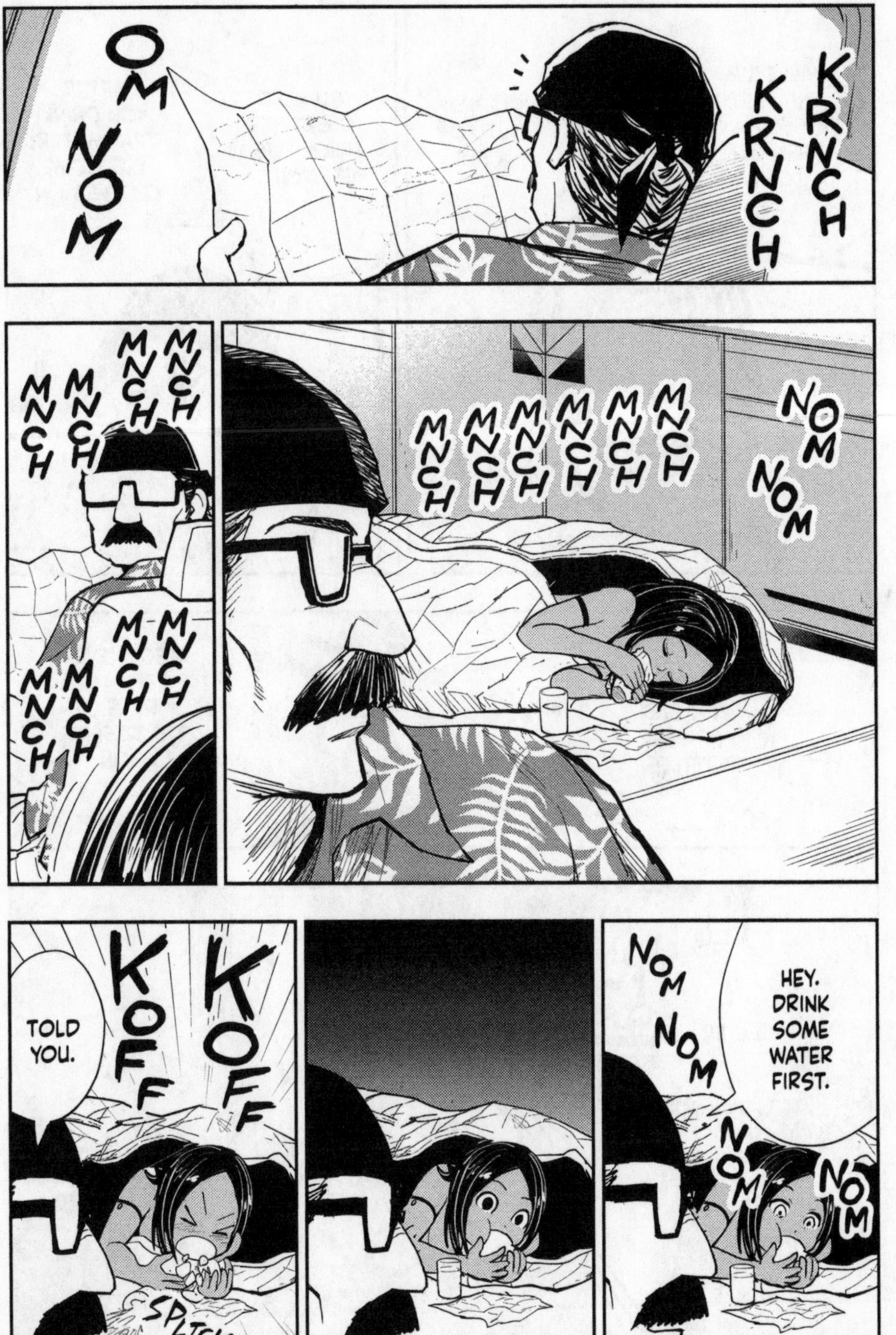
KRNCH KRNCH
OM NOM
NOM NOM
MNCH MNCH MNCH MNCH MNCH MNCH
MNCH MNCH MNCH MNCH
MNCH MNCH MNCH MNCH
HEY. DRINK SOME WATER FIRST.
NOM NOM
NOM NOM
KOFF KOFF
TOLD YOU.
SPLTCH

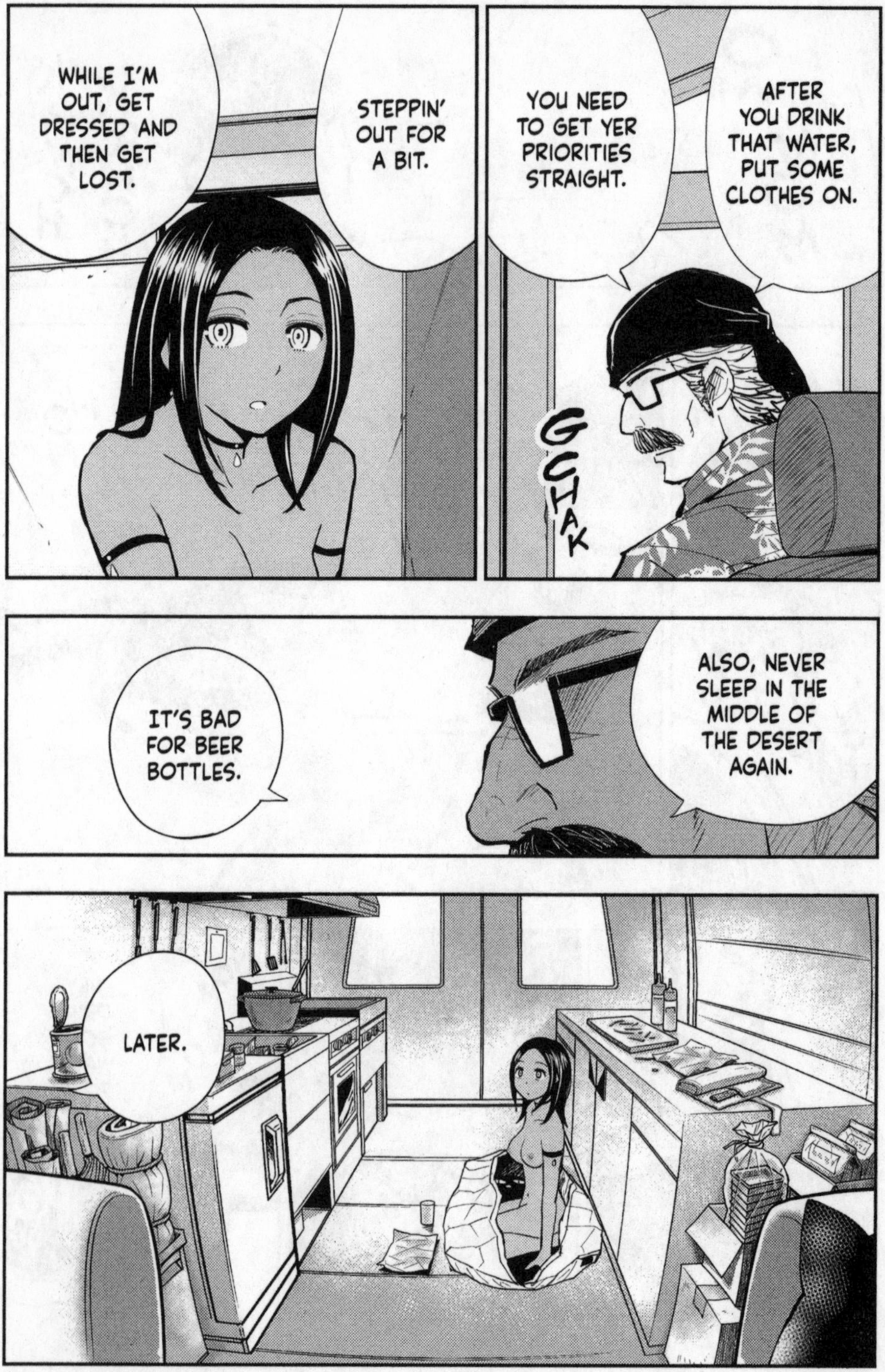
AFTER YOU DRINK THAT WATER, PUT SOME CLOTHES ON.
YOU NEED TO GET YER PRIORITIES STRAIGHT.
GCHAK
STEPPIN' OUT FOR A BIT.
WHILE I'M OUT, GET DRESSED AND THEN GET LOST.
ALSO, NEVER SLEEP IN THE MIDDLE OF THE DESERT AGAIN.
IT'S BAD FOR BEER BOTTLES.
LATER.

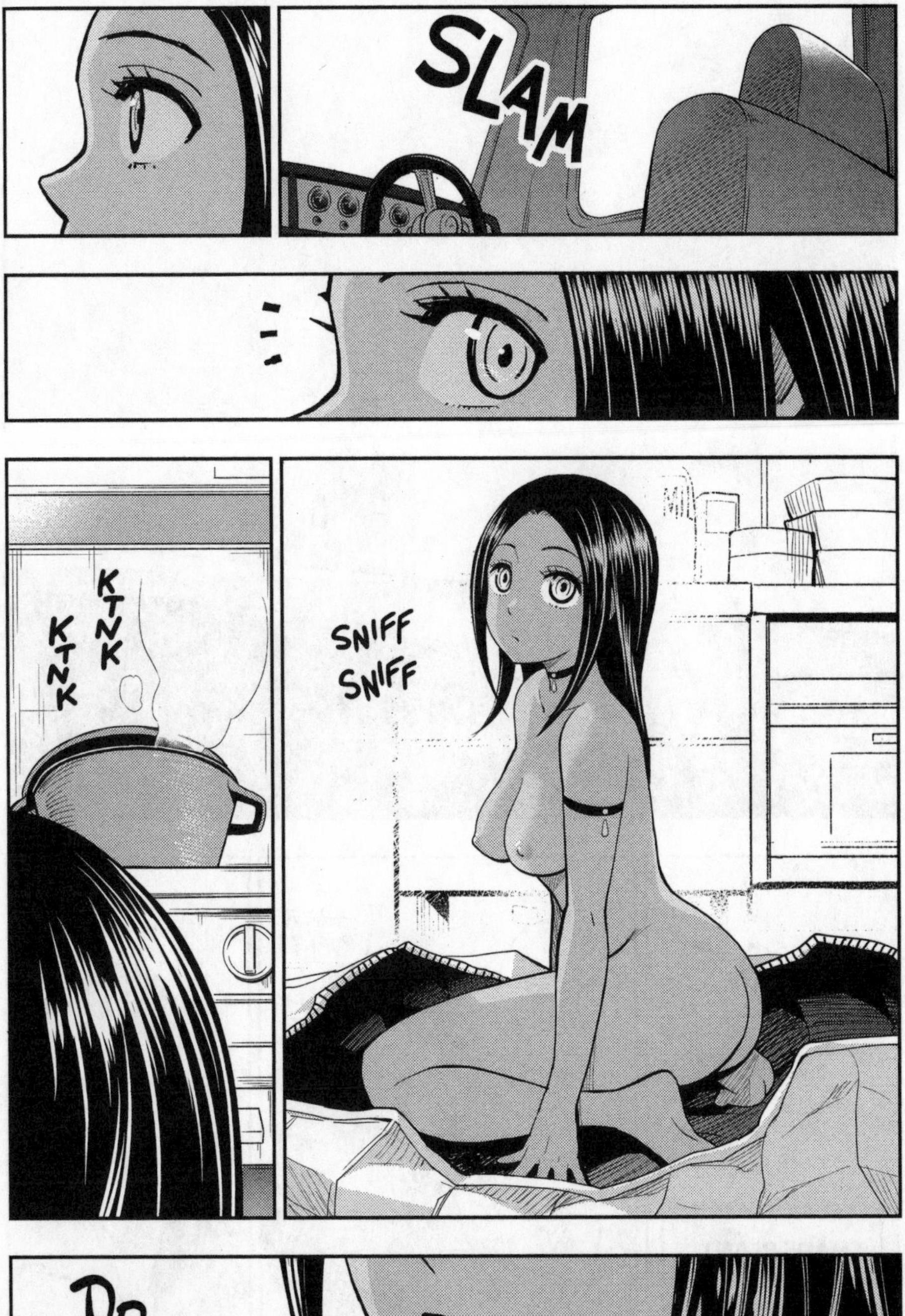
SLAM
SNIFF SNIFF
KTNK KTNK
DROOL

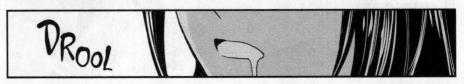

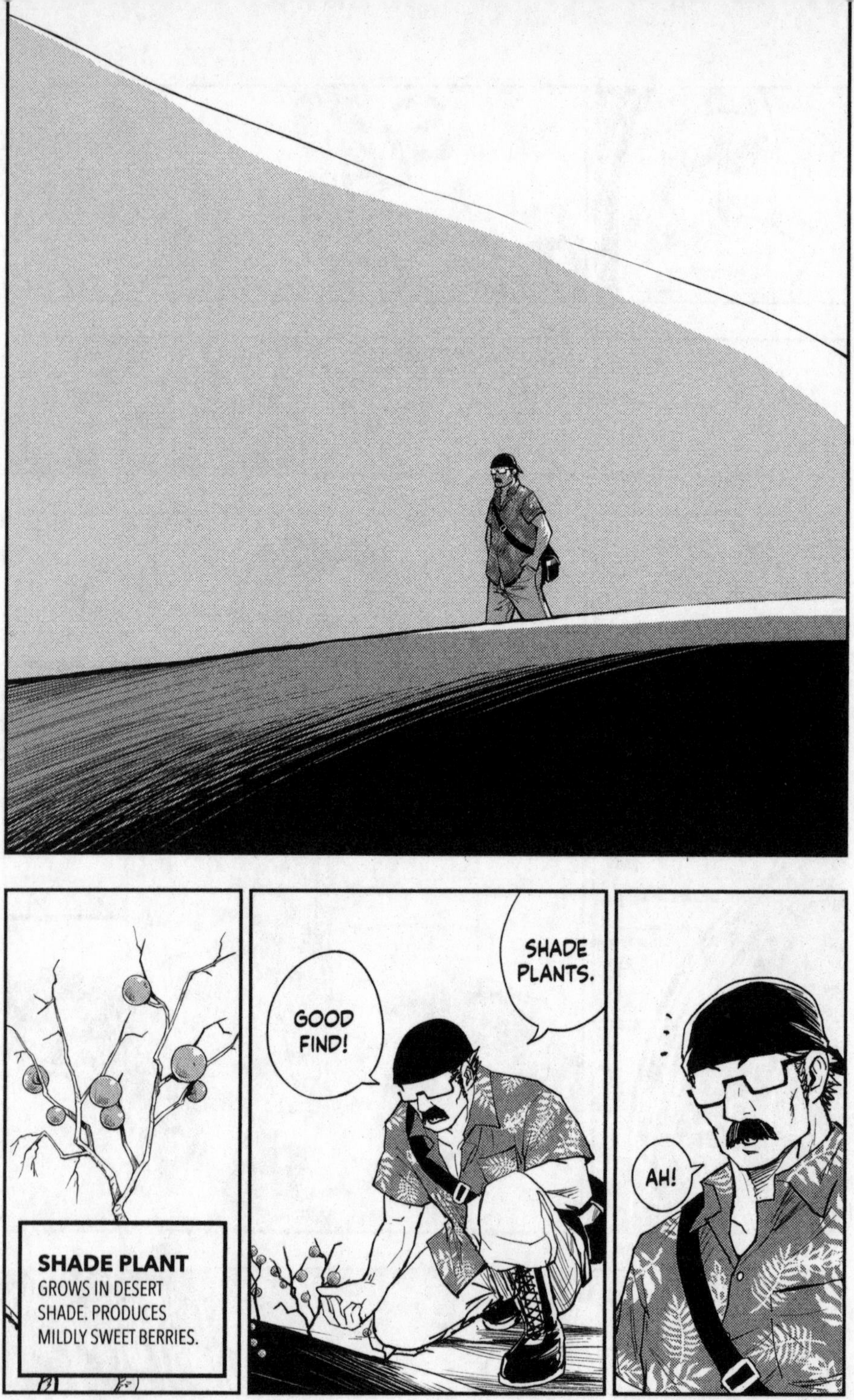
...
AH!
SHADE PLANTS.
GOOD FIND!
SHADE PLANT
GROWS IN DESERT SHADE. PRODUCES MILDLY SWEET BERRIES.

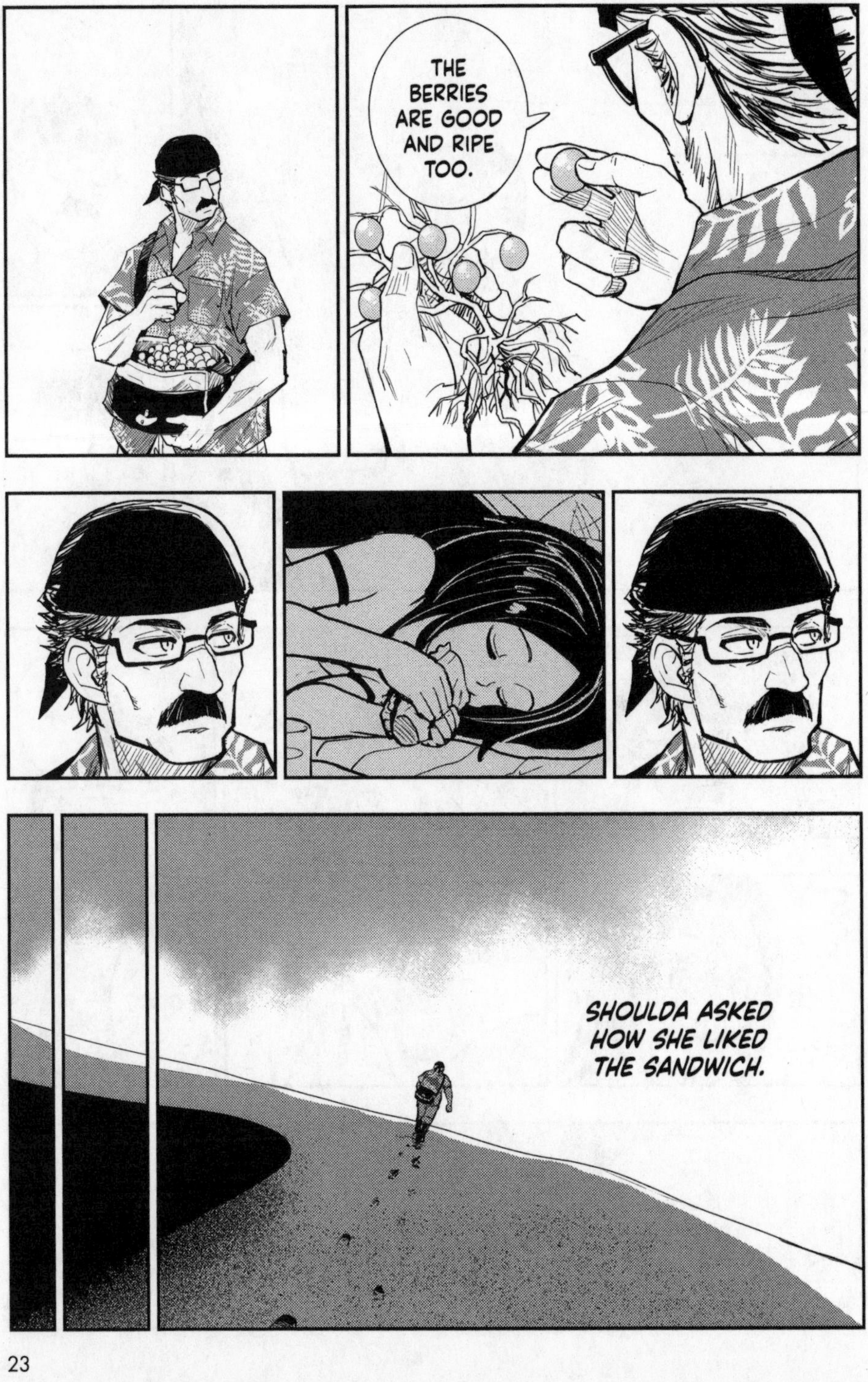
THE BERRIES ARE GOOD AND RIPE TOO.
SHOULDA ASKED HOW SHE LIKED THE SANDWICH.

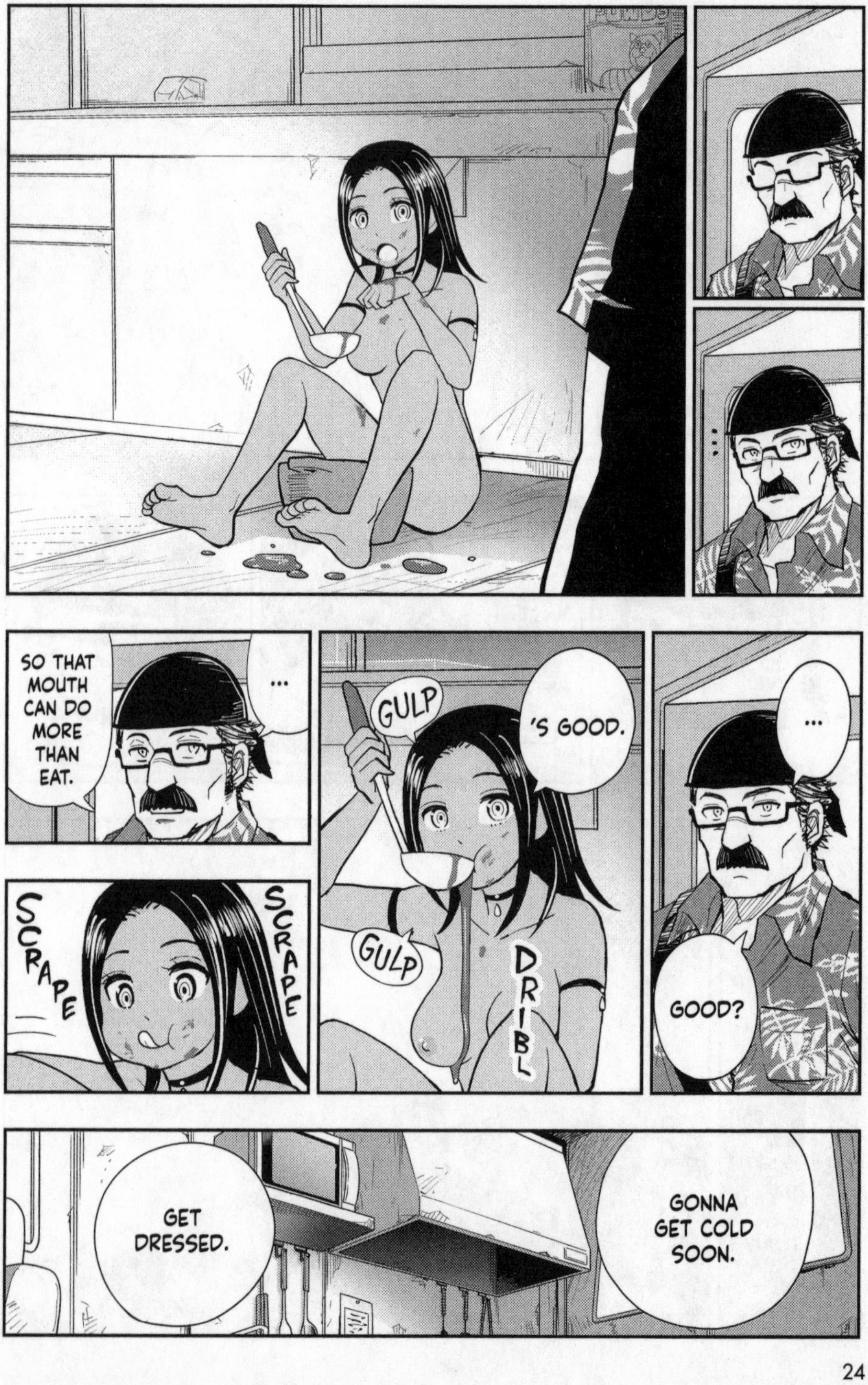
...
GOOD?
GULP
'S GOOD.
GULP
DRIBL
...
SO THAT MOUTH CAN DO MORE THAN EAT.
SCRAPE
SCRAPE
GONNA GET COLD SOON.
GET DRESSED.

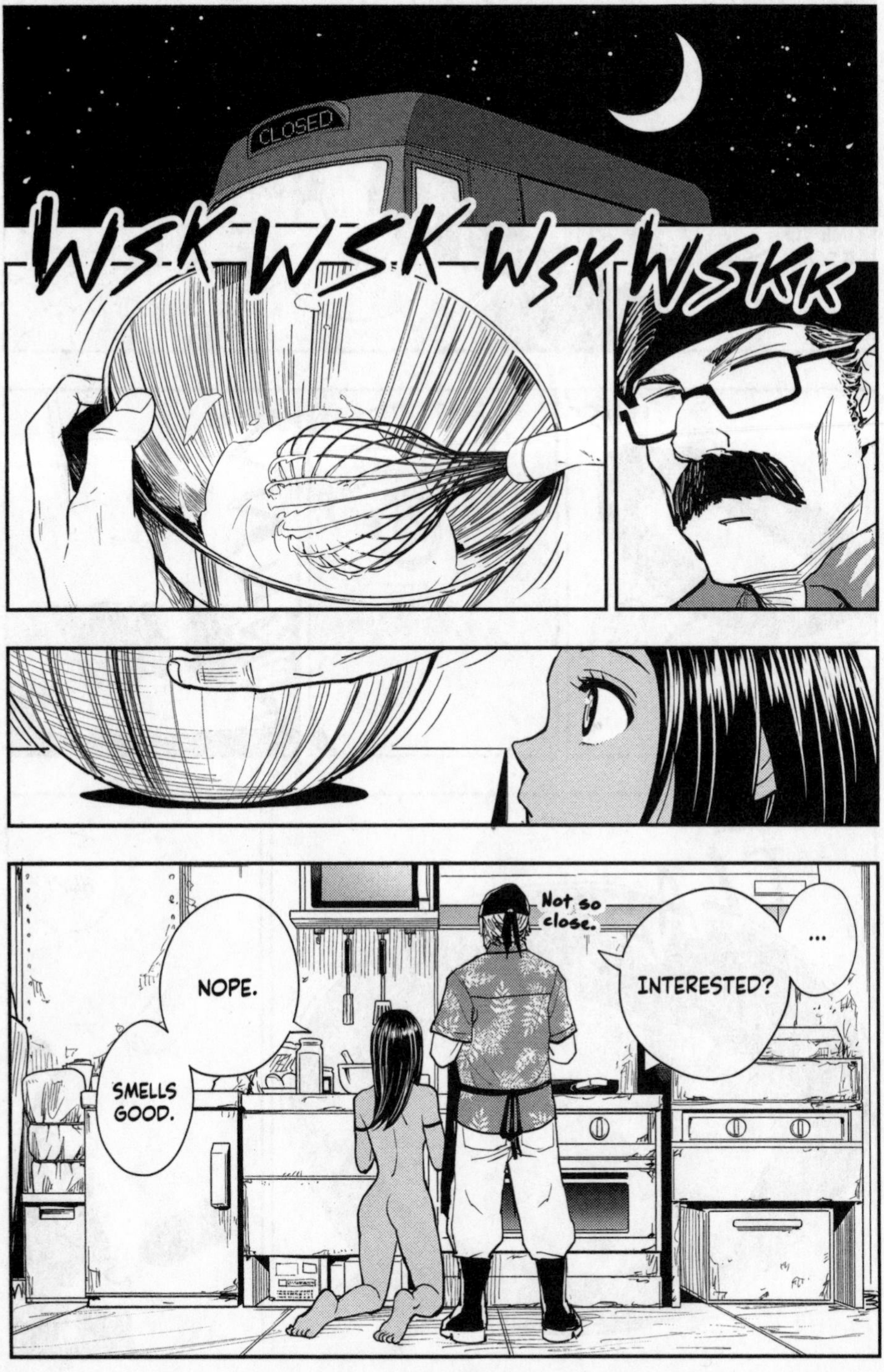
CLOSED
WSK WSK WSK WSKK
...
INTERESTED?
Not so close.
NOPE.
SMELLS GOOD.

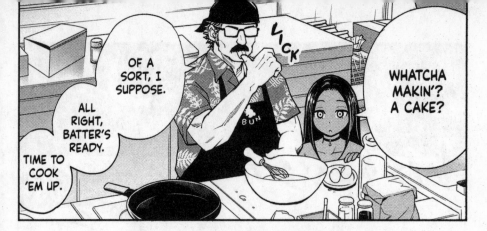

WHATCHA MAKIN'? A CAKE?
LICK
OF A SORT, I SUPPOSE.
ALL RIGHT, BATTER'S READY.
TIME TO COOK 'EM UP.
TWIST
TWIST
HUP!
FLAP

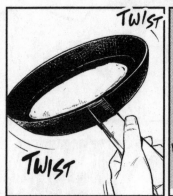

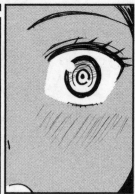

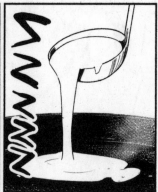

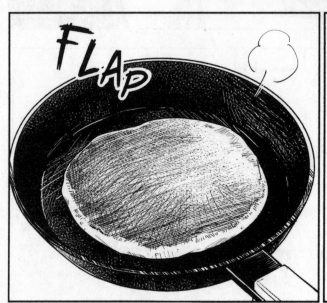

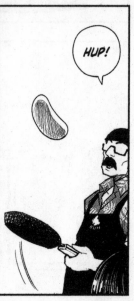

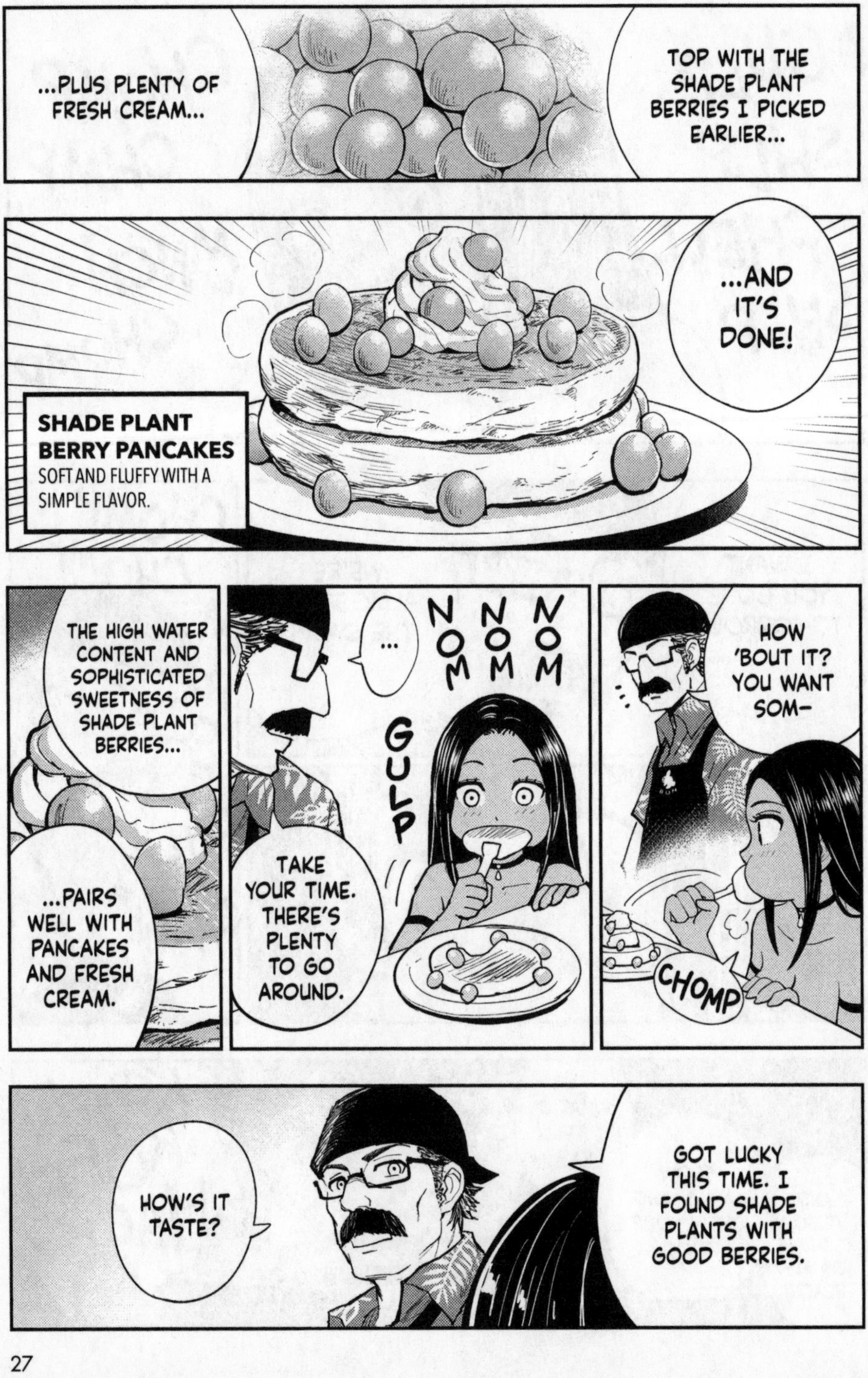
TOP WITH THE SHADE PLANT BERRIES I PICKED EARLIER...
...PLUS PLENTY OF FRESH CREAM...
...AND IT'S DONE!
SHADE PLANT BERRY PANCAKES
SOFT AND FLUFFY WITH A SIMPLE FLAVOR.
HOW 'BOUT IT? YOU WANT SOM–
CHOMP
NOM NOM NOM
GULP
...
TAKE YOUR TIME. THERE'S PLENTY TO GO AROUND.
THE HIGH WATER CONTENT AND SOPHISTICATED SWEETNESS OF SHADE PLANT BERRIES...
...PAIRS WELL WITH PANCAKES AND FRESH CREAM.
GOT LUCKY THIS TIME. I FOUND SHADE PLANTS WITH GOOD BERRIES.
HOW'S IT TASTE?

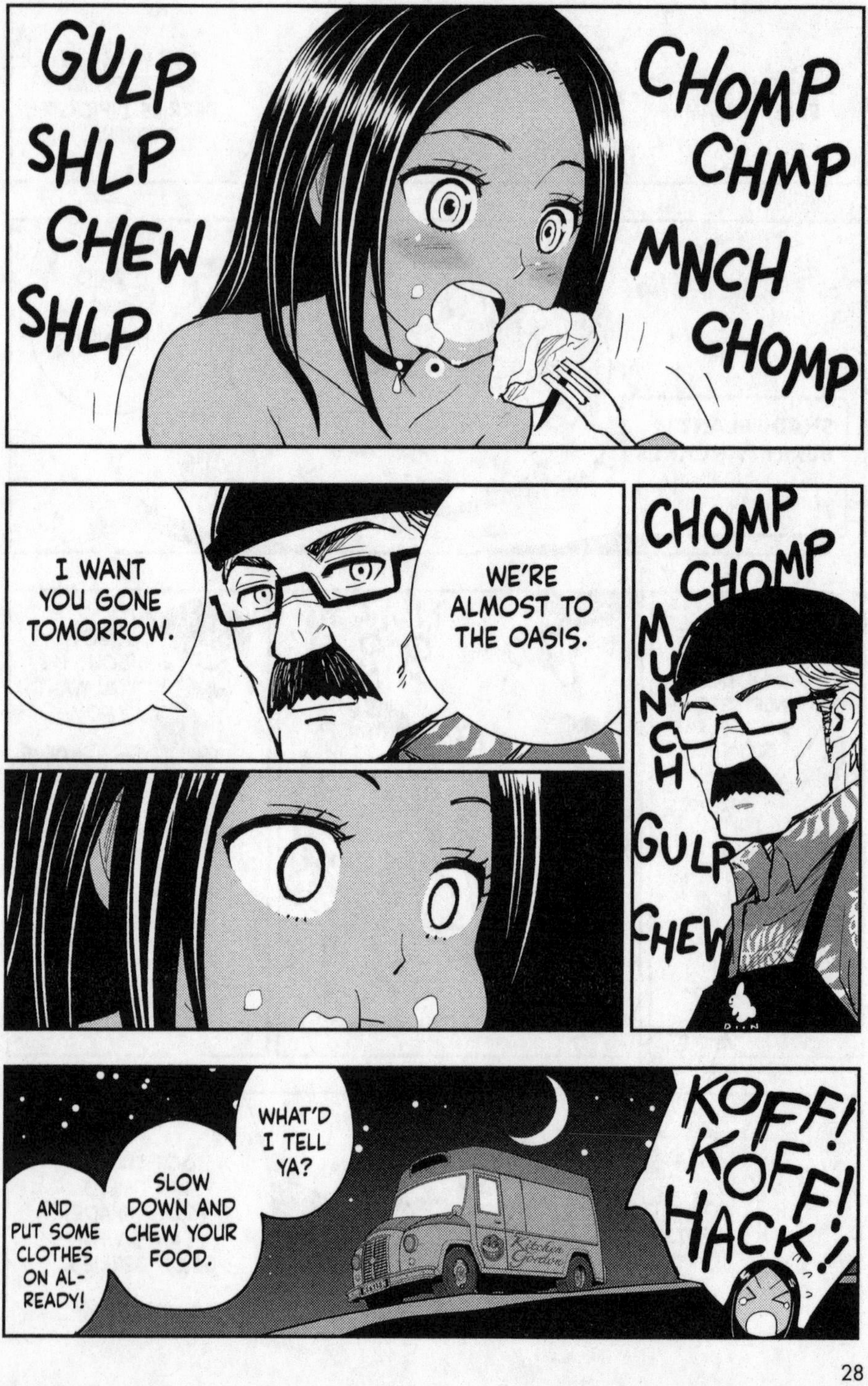
CHOMP CHMP MNCH CHOMP
GULP SHLP CHEW SHLP
CHOMP CHOMP MUNCH GULP CHEW
WE'RE ALMOST TO THE OASIS.
I WANT YOU GONE TOMORROW.
KOFF! KOFF! HACK!
WHAT'D I TELL YA?
SLOW DOWN AND CHEW YOUR FOOD.
AND PUT SOME CLOTHES ON AL-READY!

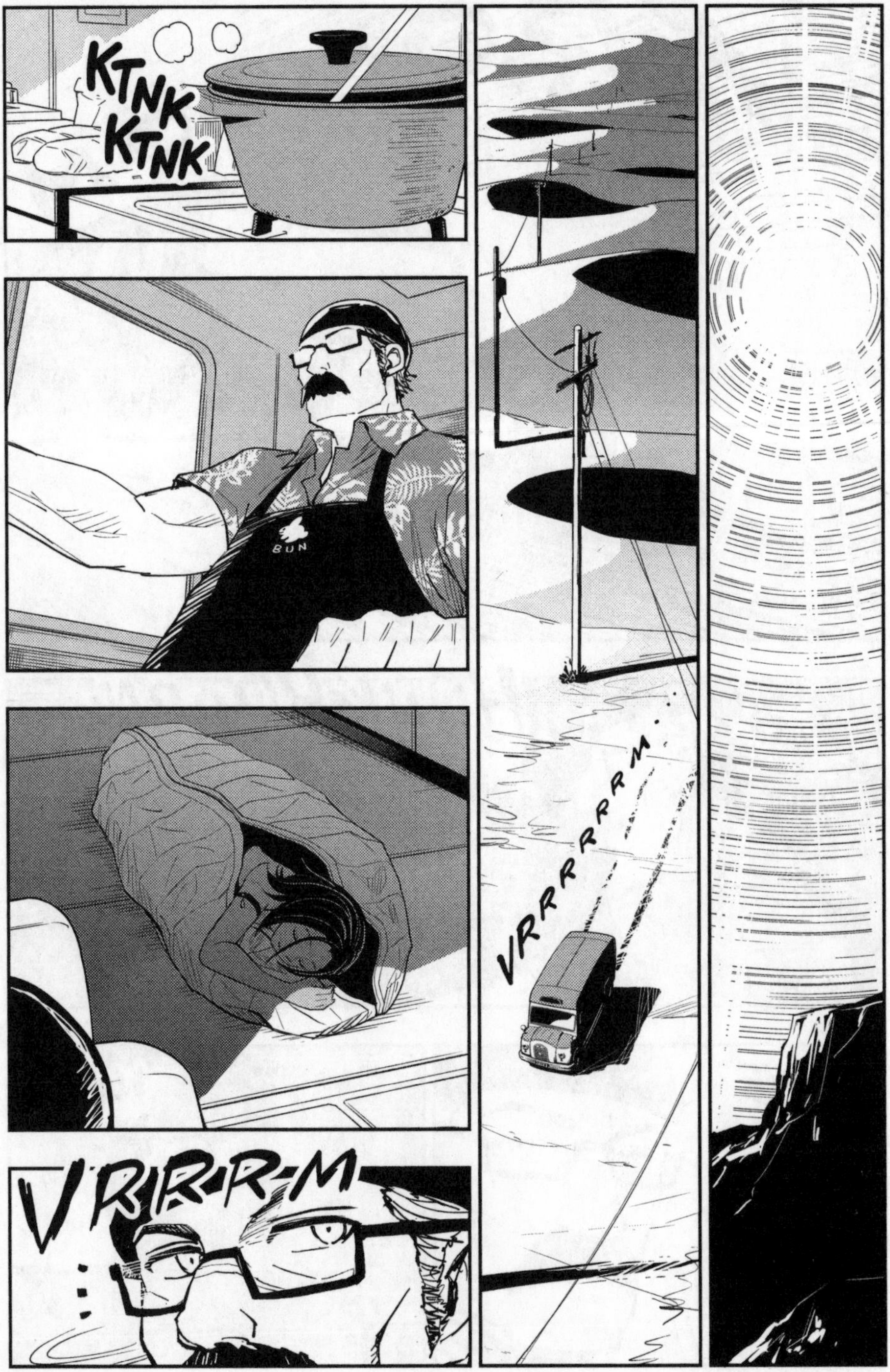
VRRRRRRM..
KTNK
KTNK
VRRR-M
...

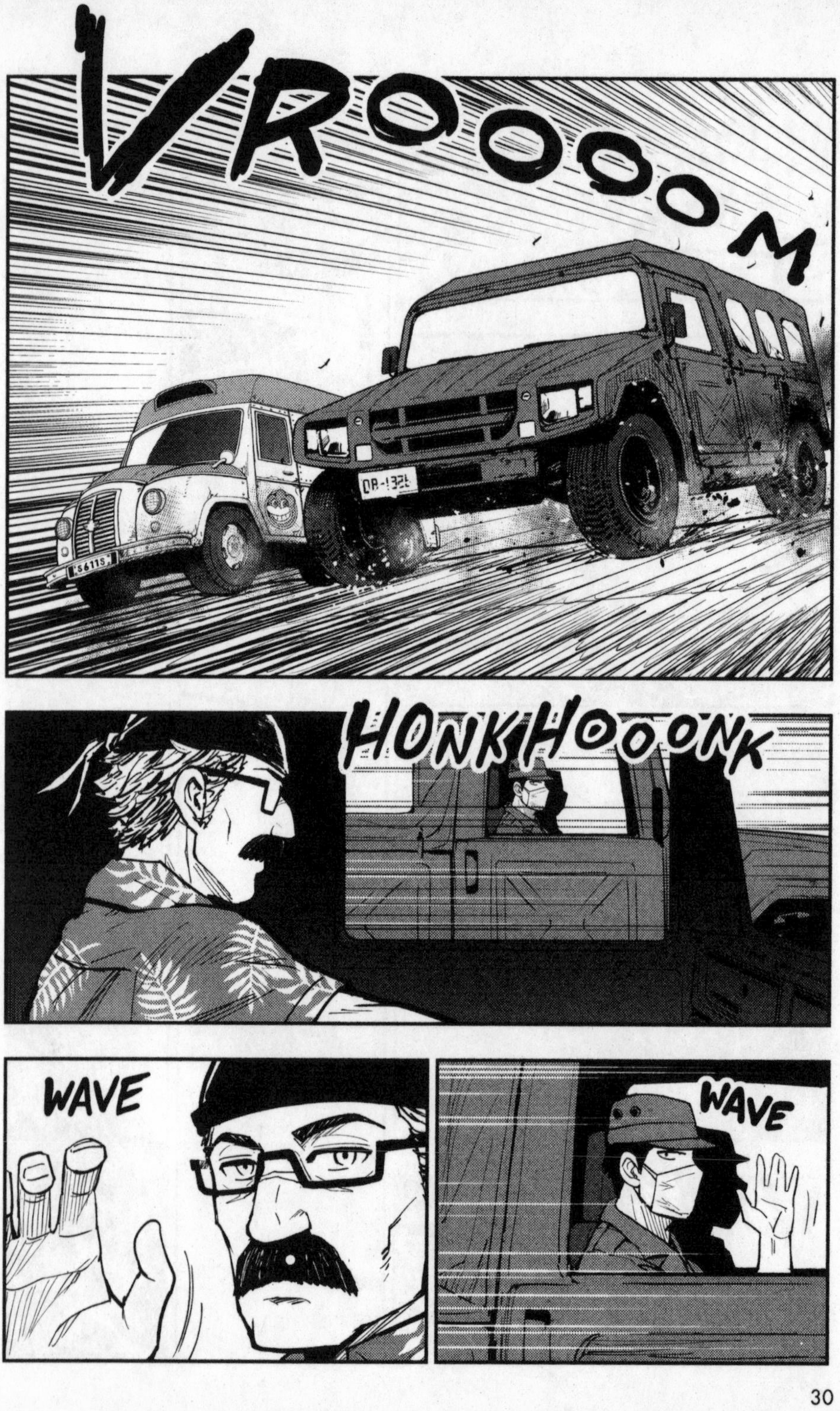
VROOOOOM
HONK HOOOONK
WAVE
WAVE

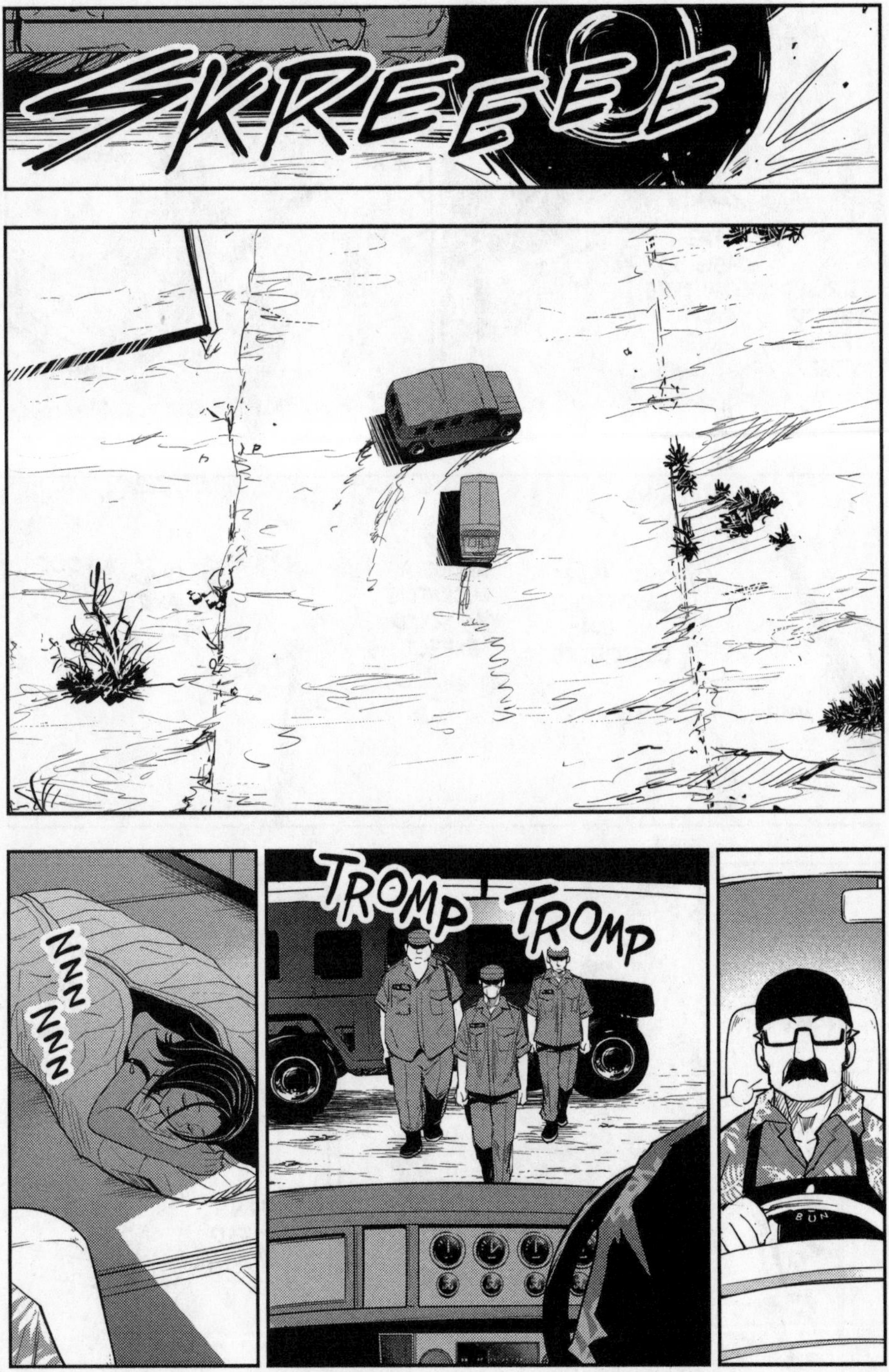
SKREEEE
BUN
TROMP TROMP
NNN NNN

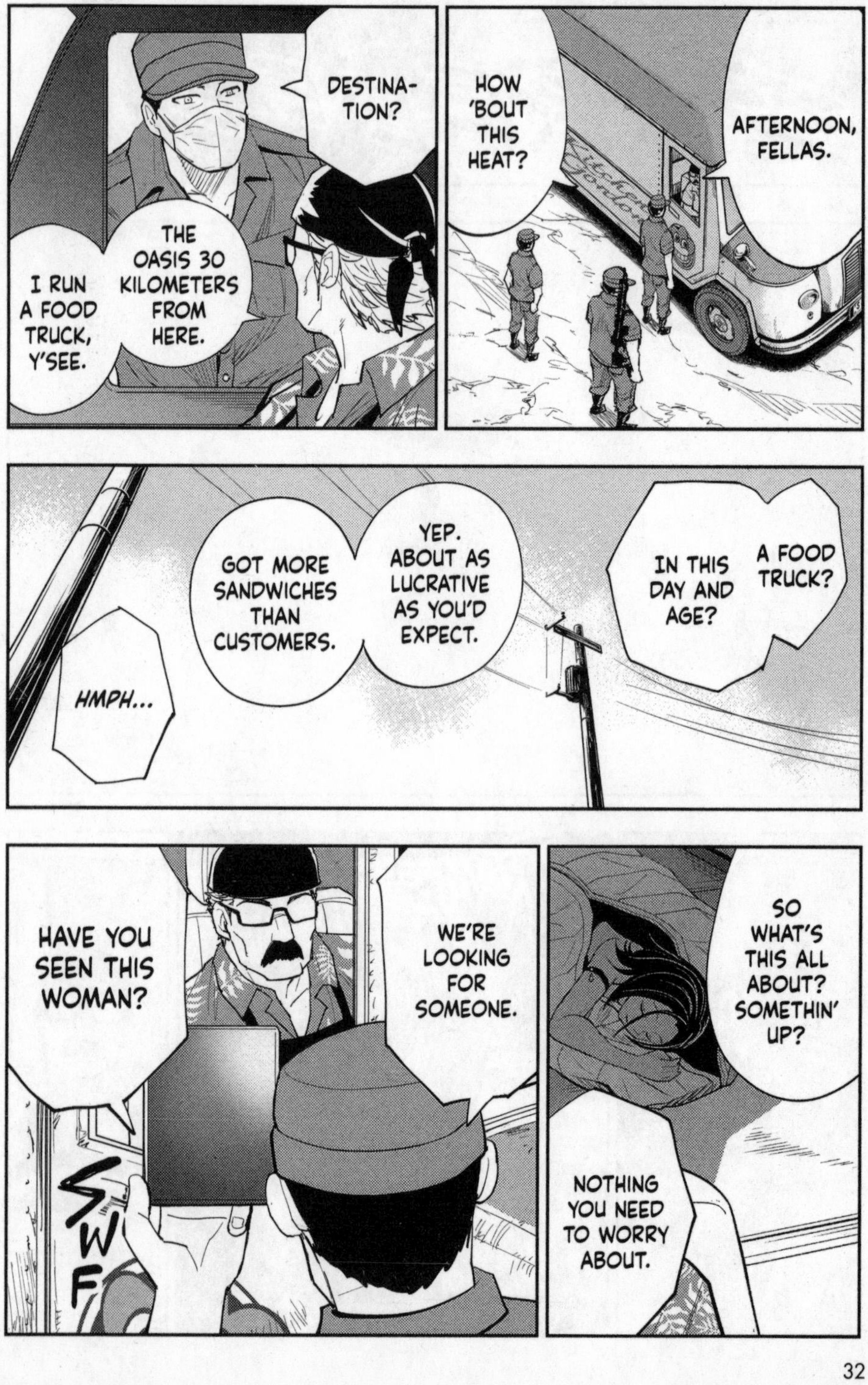
AFTERNOON, FELLAS.
HOW 'BOUT THIS HEAT?
DESTINA-TION?
THE OASIS 30 KILOMETERS FROM HERE.
I RUN A FOOD TRUCK, Y'SEE.
A FOOD TRUCK?
IN THIS DAY AND AGE?
YEP. ABOUT AS LUCRATIVE AS YOU'D EXPECT.
GOT MORE SANDWICHES THAN CUSTOMERS.
HMPH...
SO WHAT'S THIS ALL ABOUT? SOMETHIN' UP?
NOTHING YOU NEED TO WORRY ABOUT.
WE'RE LOOKING FOR SOMEONE.
HAVE YOU SEEN THIS WOMAN?
SWF

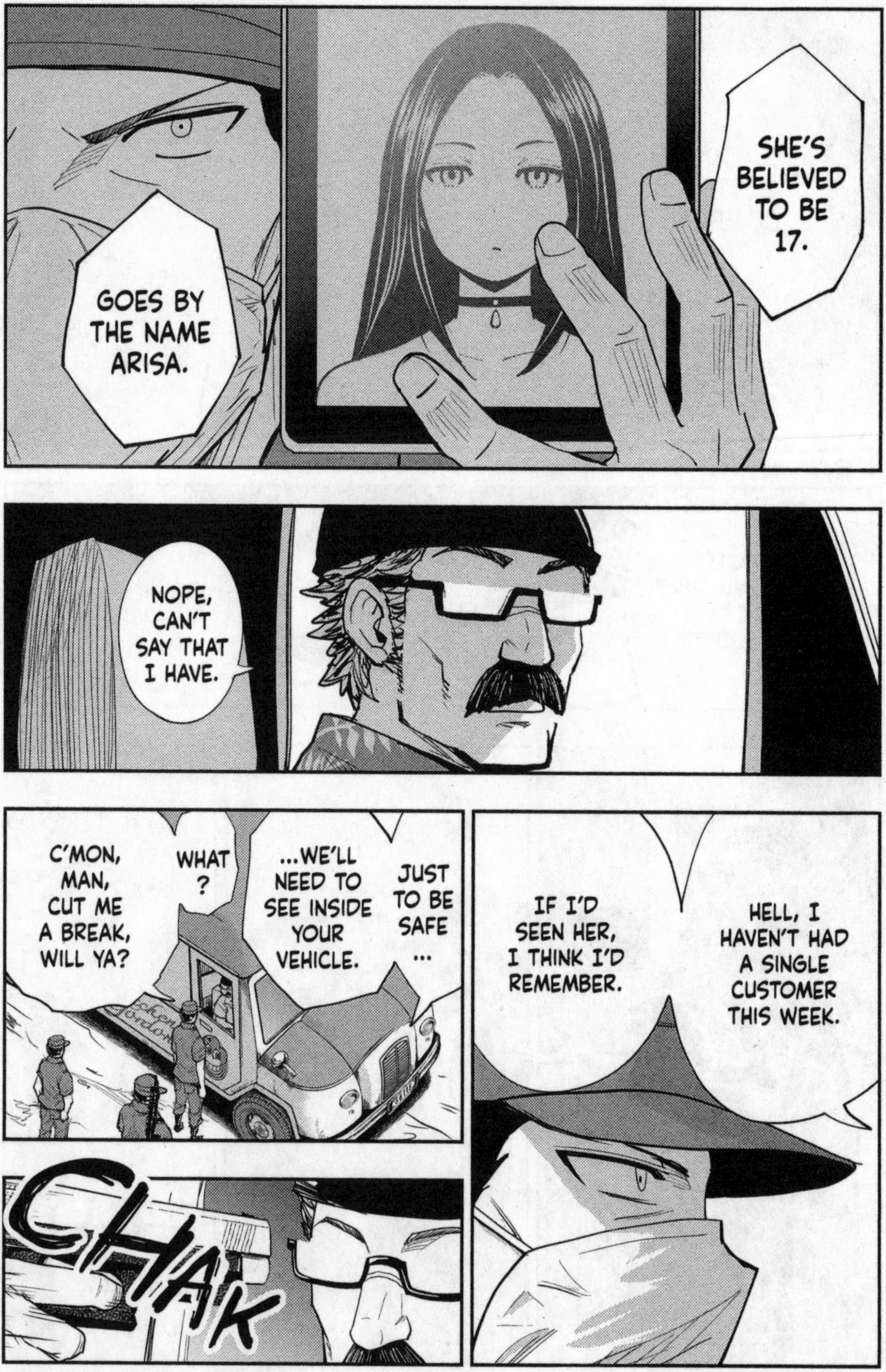
SHE'S BELIEVED TO BE 17.
GOES BY THE NAME ARISA.
NOPE, CAN'T SAY THAT I HAVE.
IF I'D SEEN HER, I THINK I'D REMEMBER.
HELL, I HAVEN'T HAD A SINGLE CUSTOMER THIS WEEK.
JUST TO BE SAFE ...
...WE'LL NEED TO SEE INSIDE YOUR VEHICLE.
WHAT ?
C'MON, MAN, CUT ME A BREAK, WILL YA?
CHAK

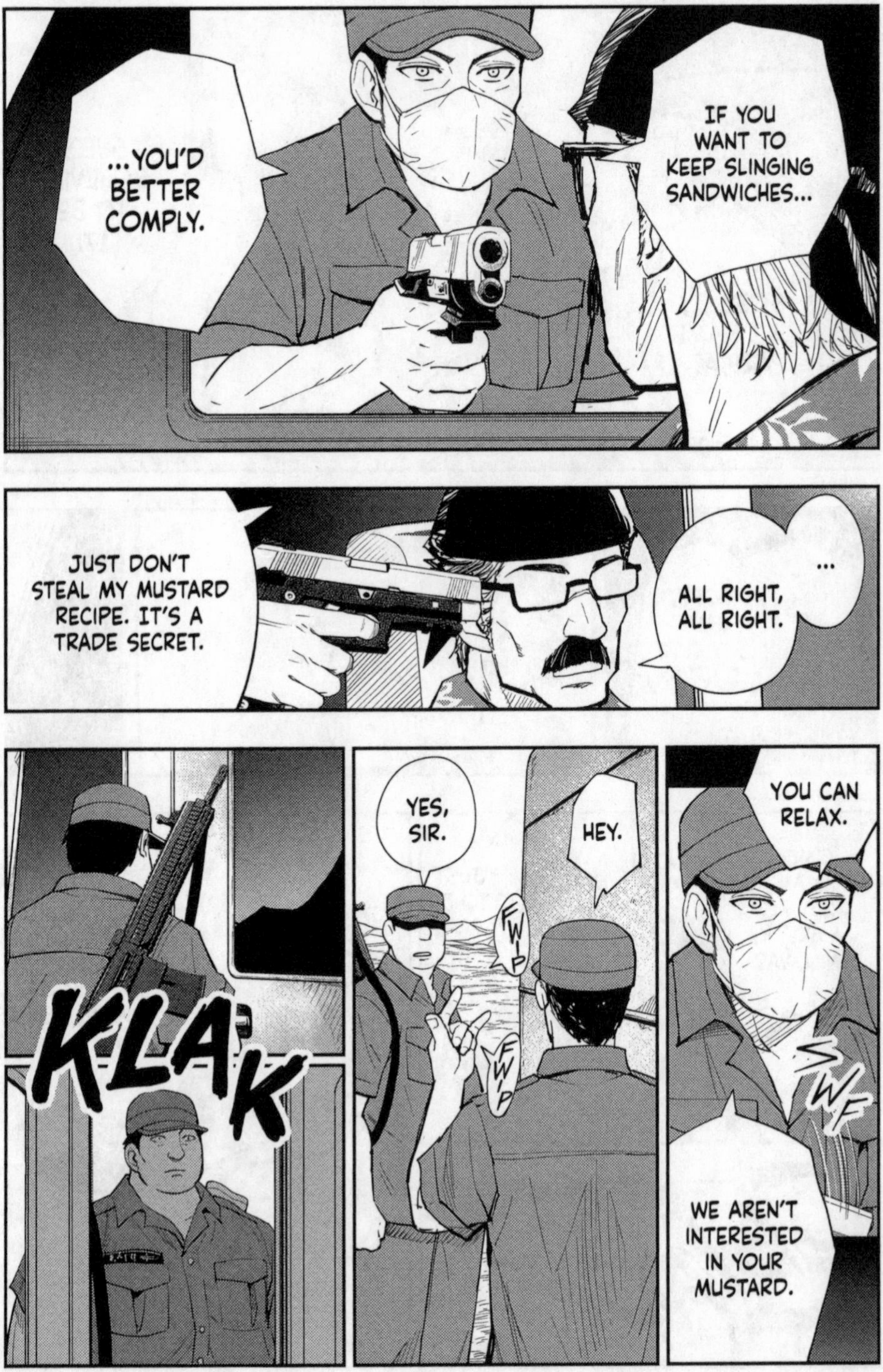

IF YOU WANT TO KEEP SLINGING SANDWICHES...
...YOU'D BETTER COMPLY.
...
ALL RIGHT, ALL RIGHT.
JUST DON'T STEAL MY MUSTARD RECIPE. IT'S A TRADE SECRET.
YOU CAN RELAX.
SWF
WE AREN'T INTERESTED IN YOUR MUSTARD.
HEY.
YES, SIR.
FWIP
FWIP
KLAK

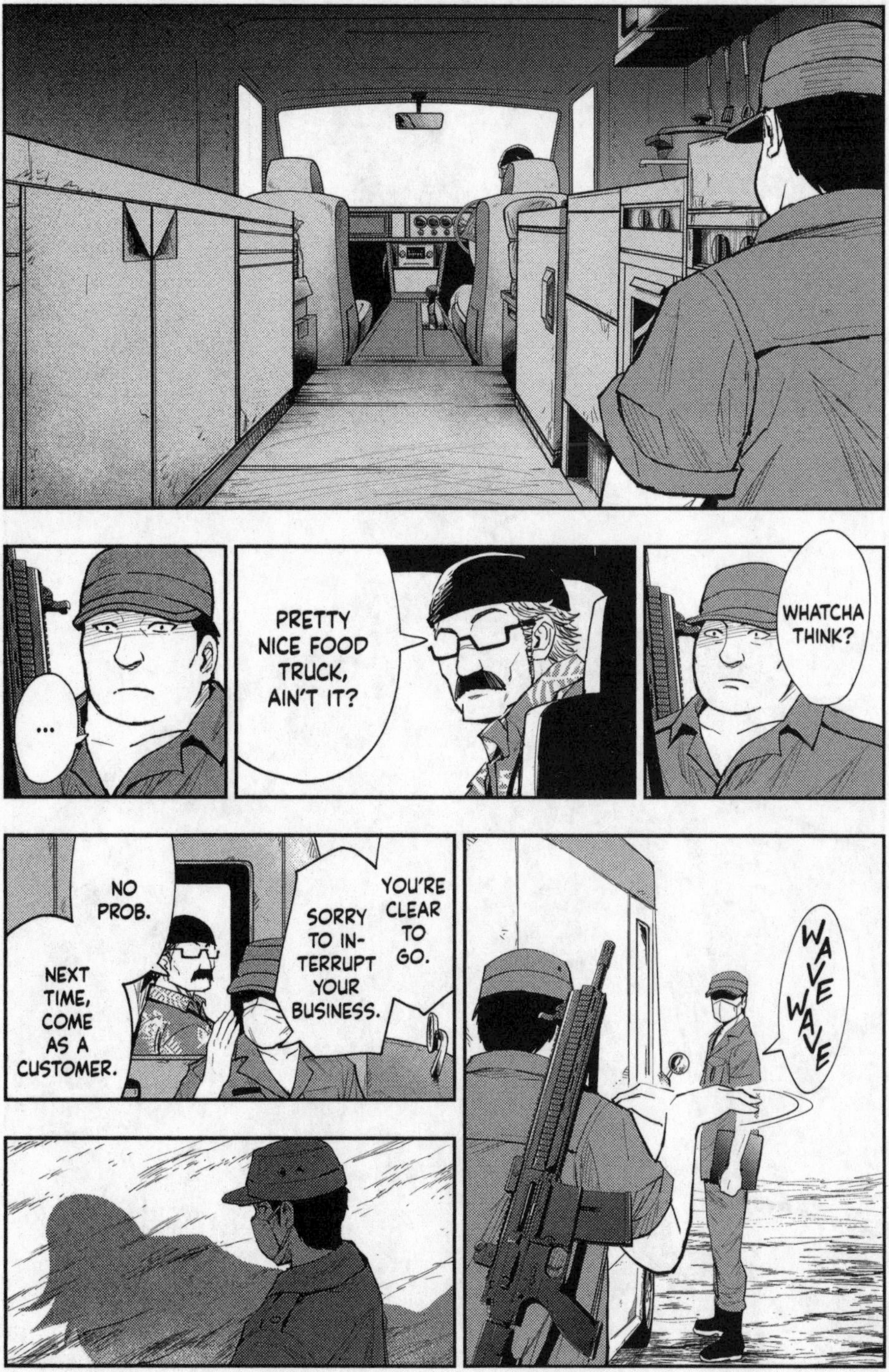
WHATCHA THINK?
PRETTY NICE FOOD TRUCK, AIN'T IT?
...
WAVE WAVE
YOU'RE CLEAR TO GO.
SORRY TO IN-TERRUPT YOUR BUSINESS.
NO PROB.
NEXT TIME, COME AS A CUSTOMER.

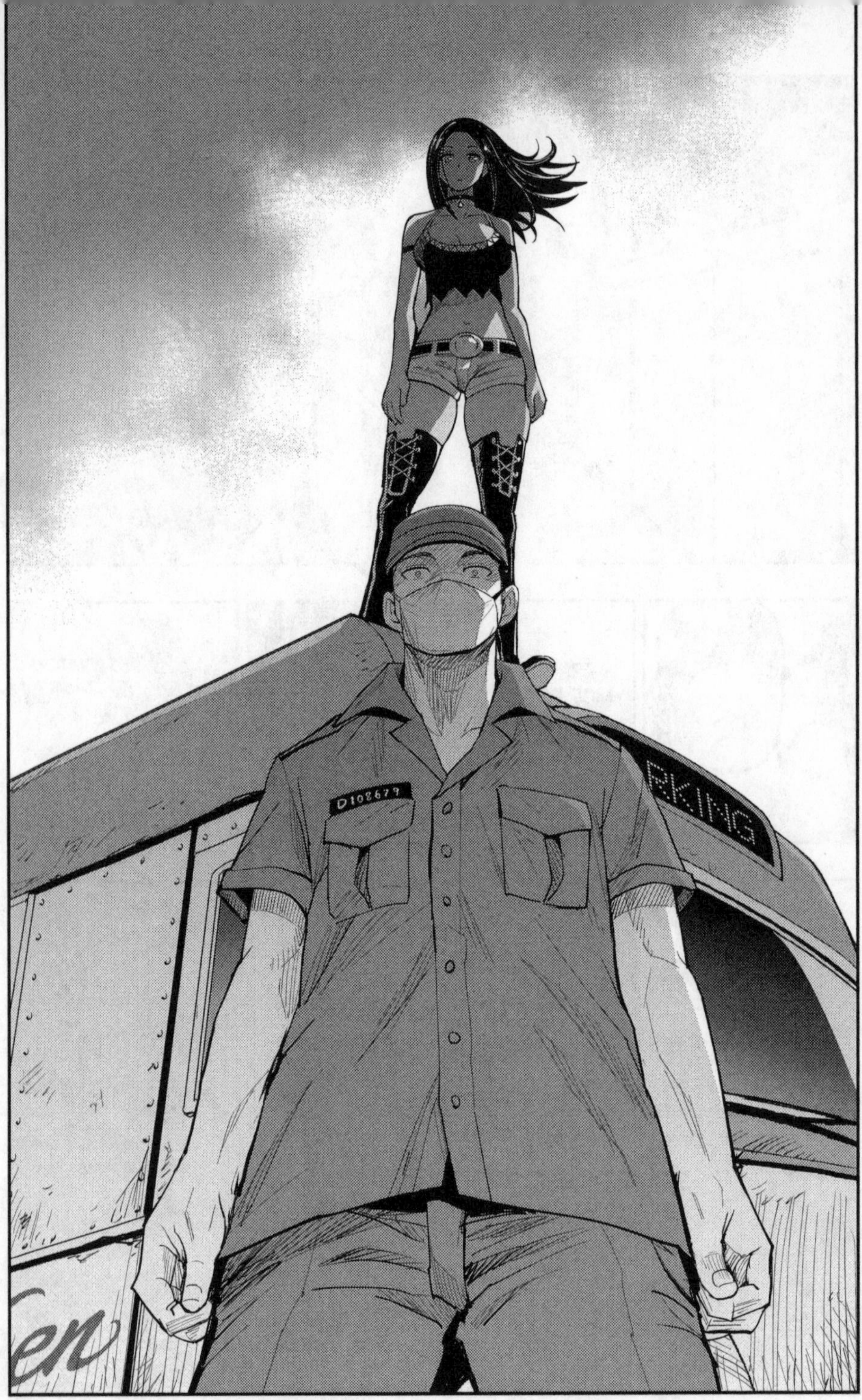
D108679
RKING

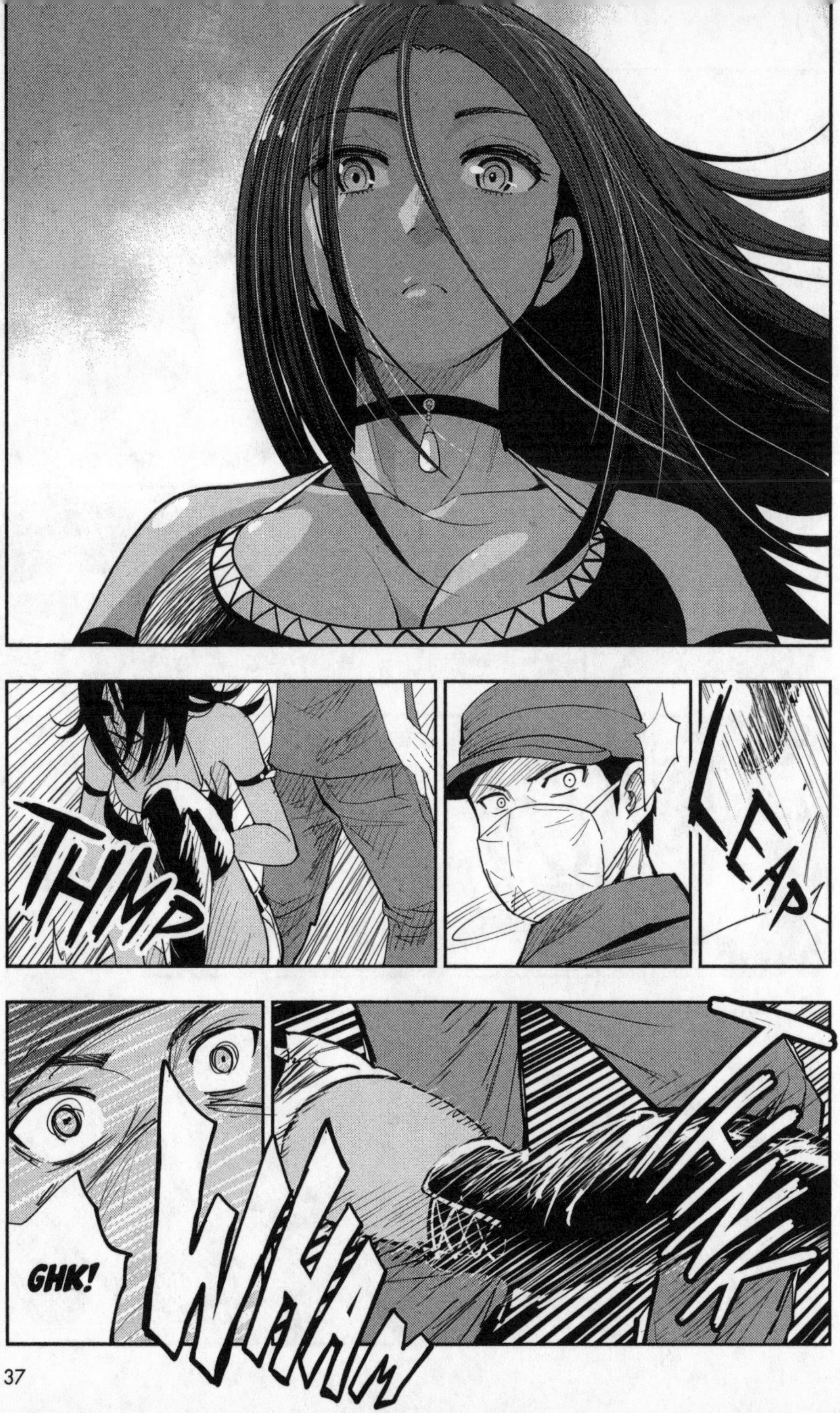
LEAP
THMP
THNK
WHAAM
GHK!

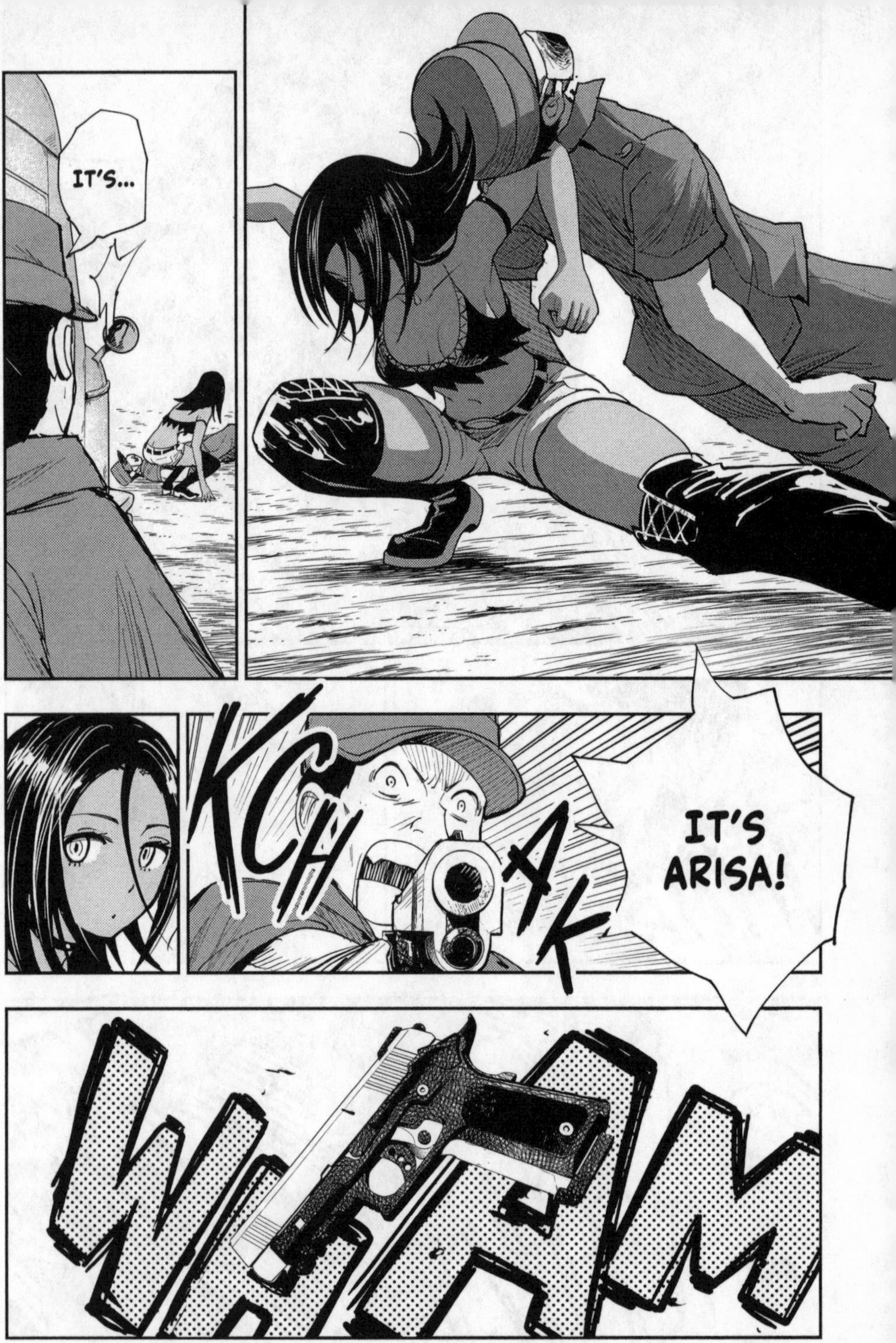
IT'S...
IT'S ARISA!
KCHAK
WHAM

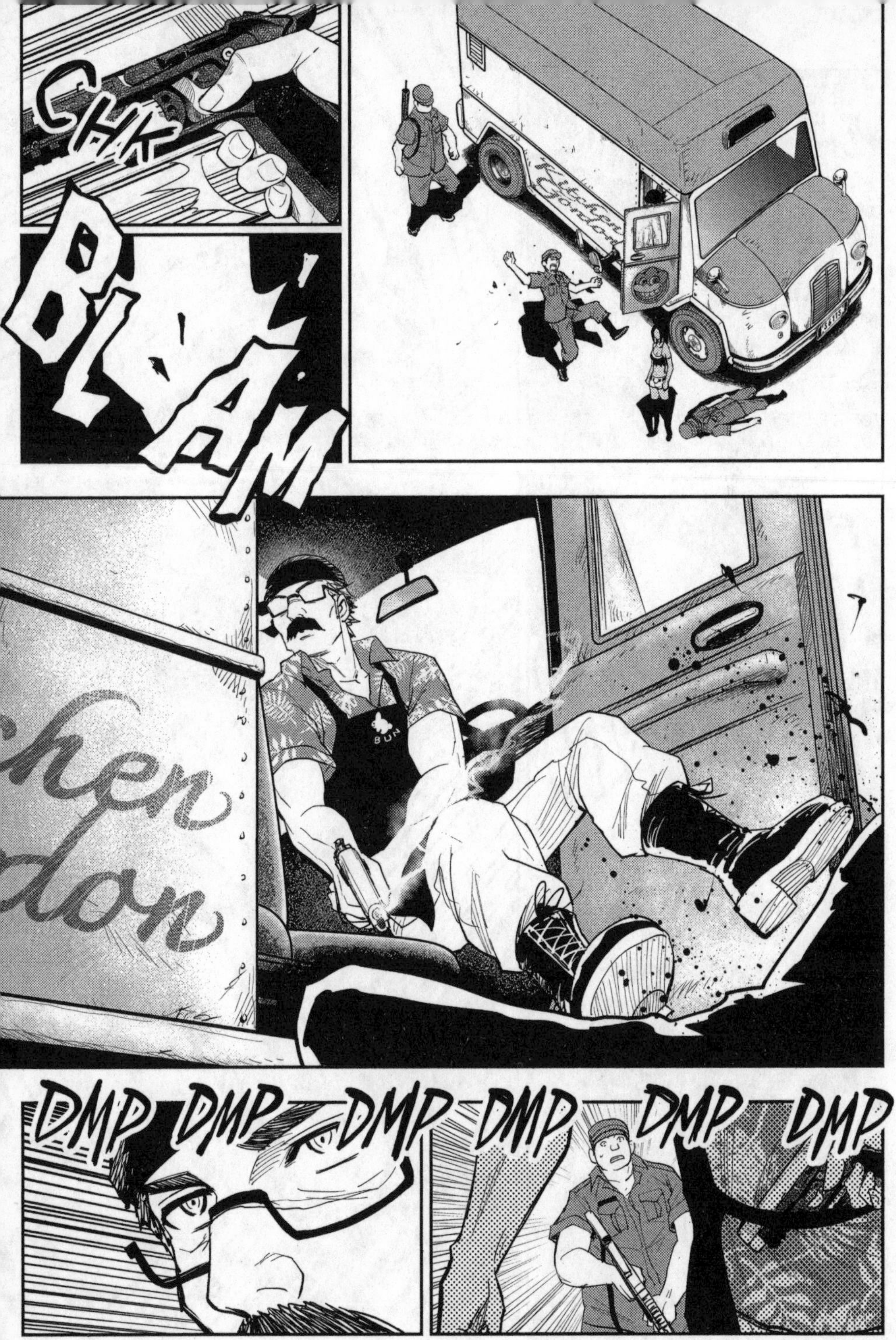
CHK
BLAM
DMP DMP DMP
DMP DMP DMP

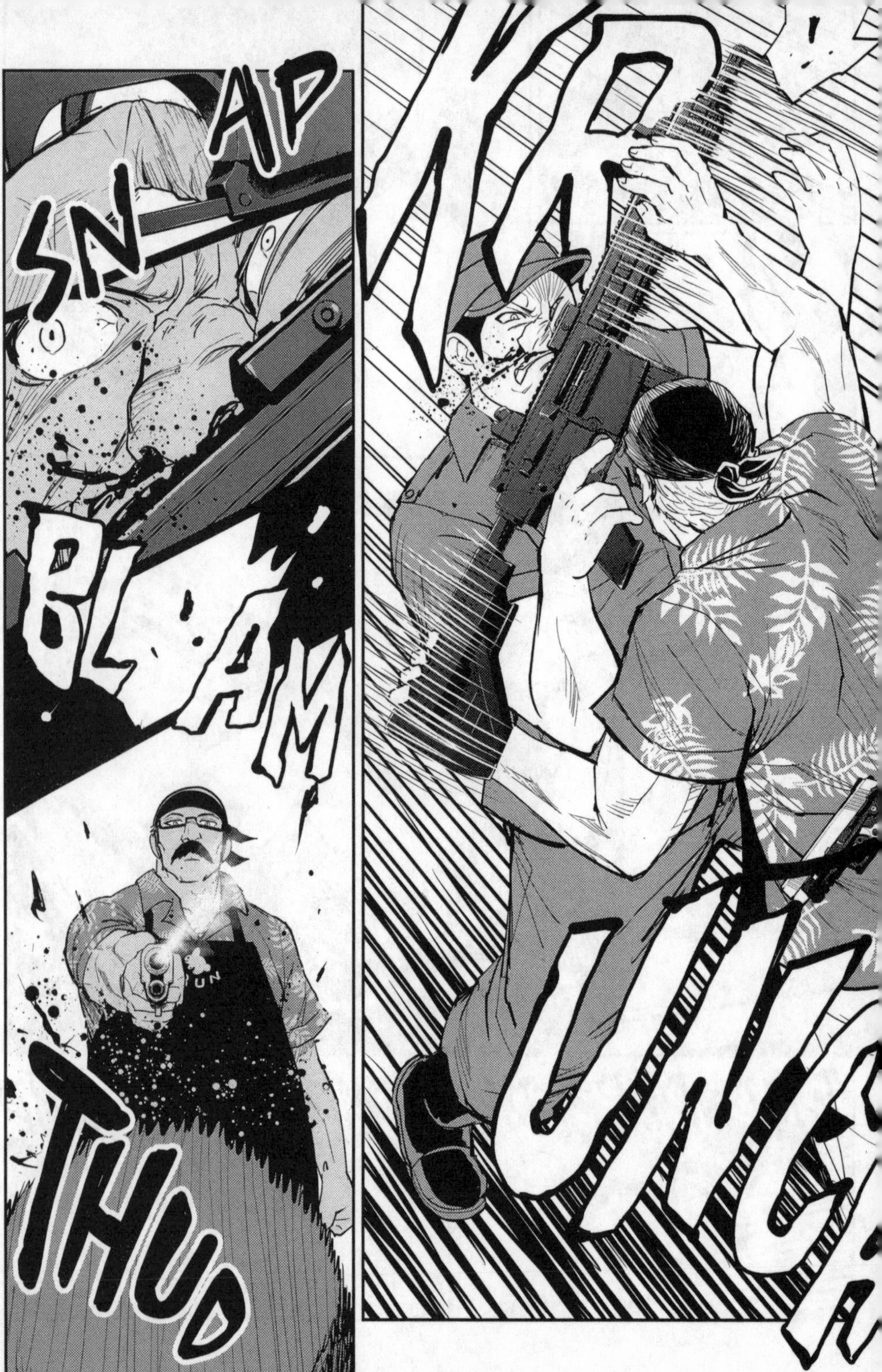
SNAP
BLAM
THUD

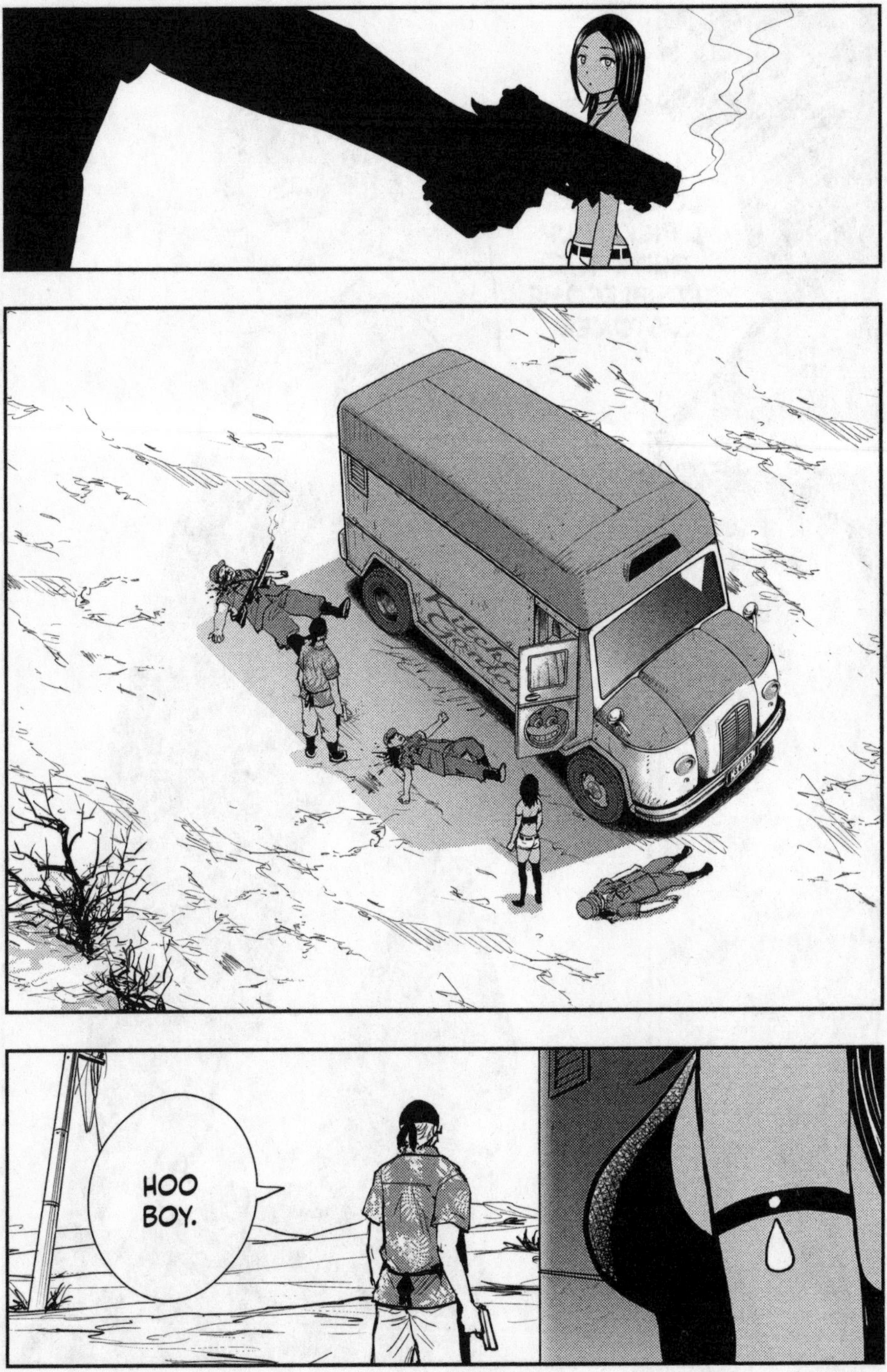
HOO BOY.

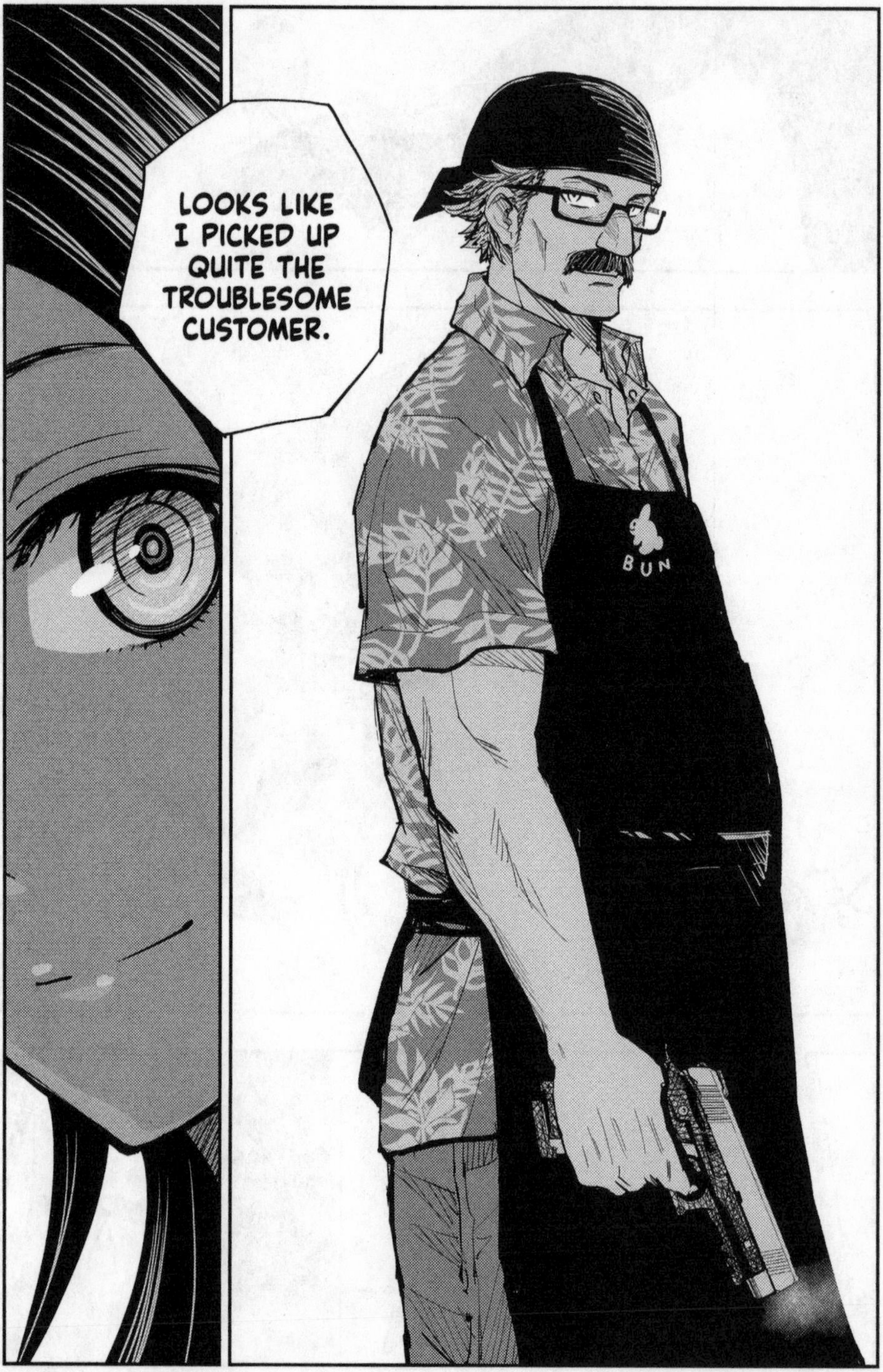
LOOKS LIKE I PICKED UP QUITE THE TROUBLESOME CUSTOMER.
BUN

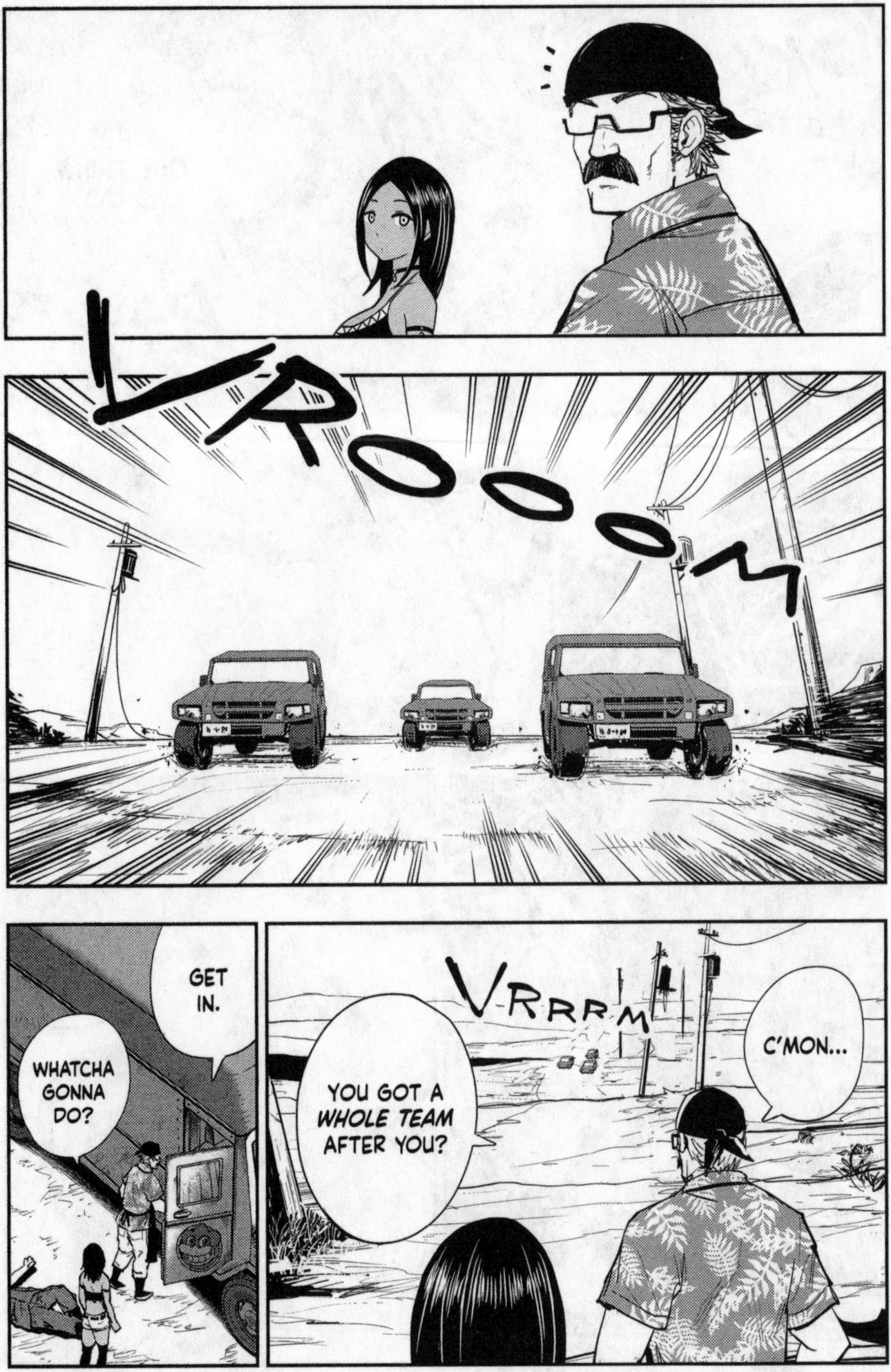
VROOOOM
VRRRM
C'MON...
YOU GOT A *WHOLE TEAM* AFTER YOU?
GET IN.
WHATCHA GONNA DO?

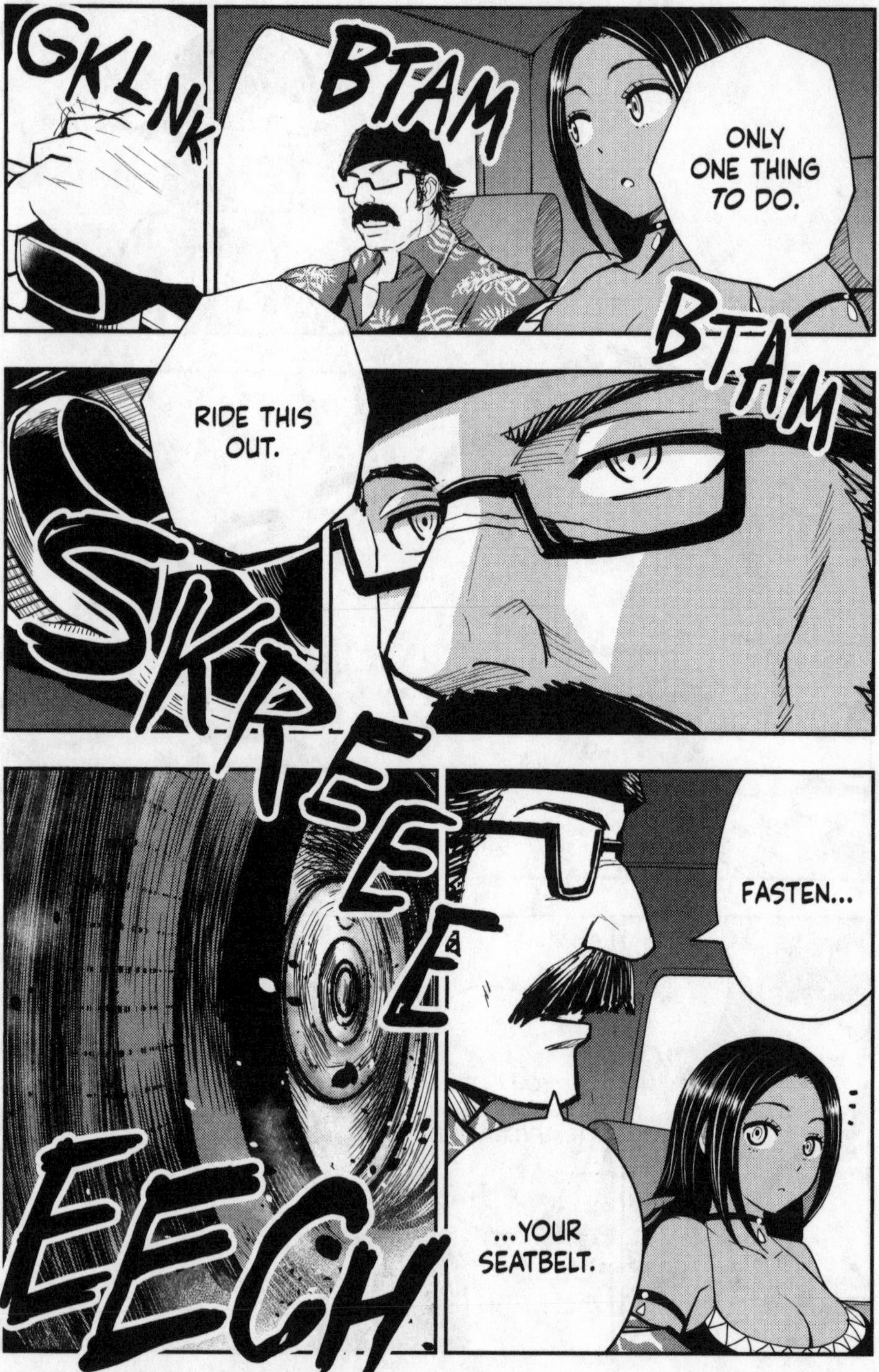
BTAM
ONLY ONE THING TO DO.
BTAM
GKLNK
RIDE THIS OUT.
SKREEEEEECH
FASTEN...
...YOUR SEATBELT.

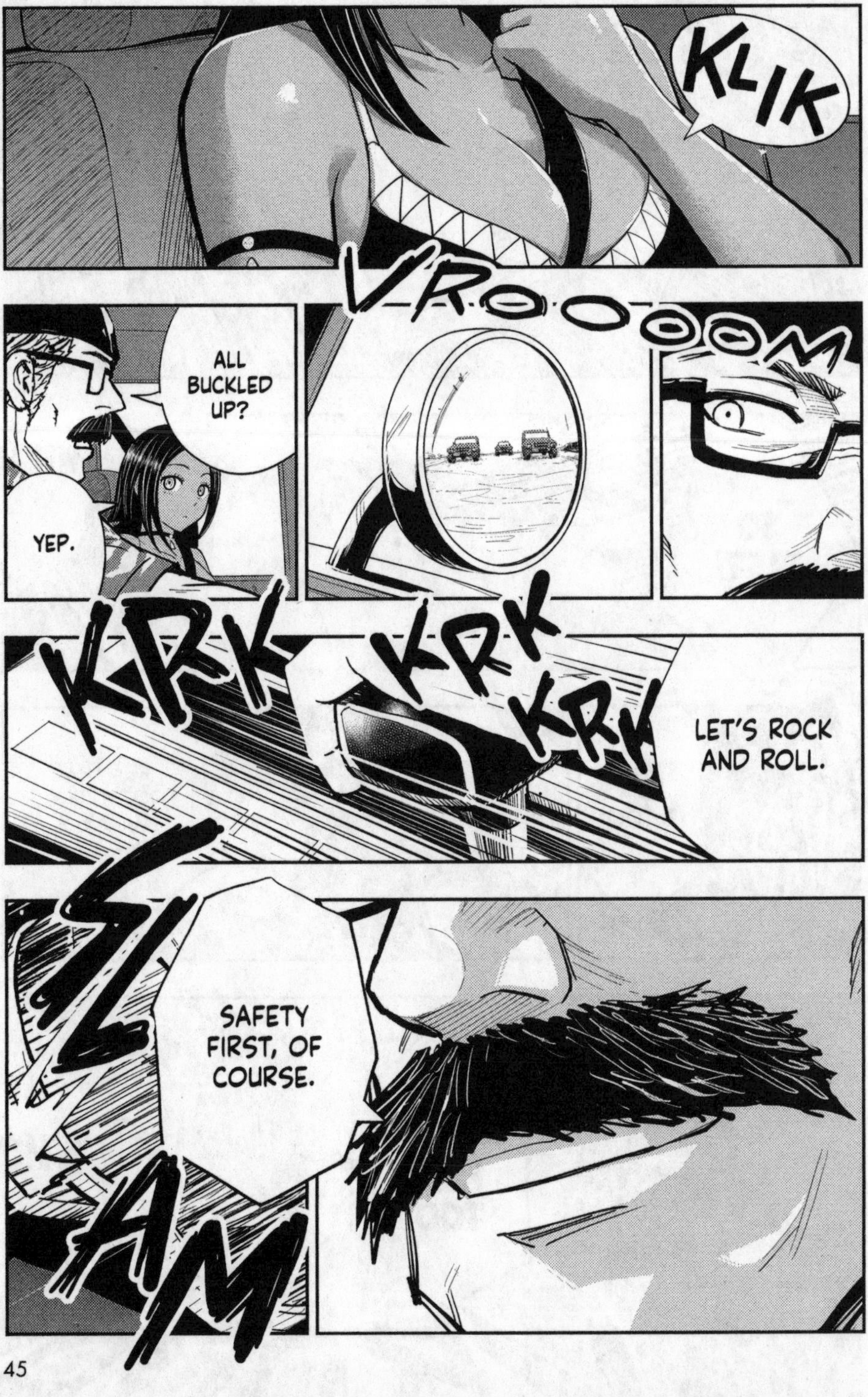
KLIK
VROOOOOM
ALL BUCKLED UP?
YEP.
LET'S ROCK AND ROLL.
KRK
KRK
KRK
SAFETY FIRST, OF COURSE.
SLAM

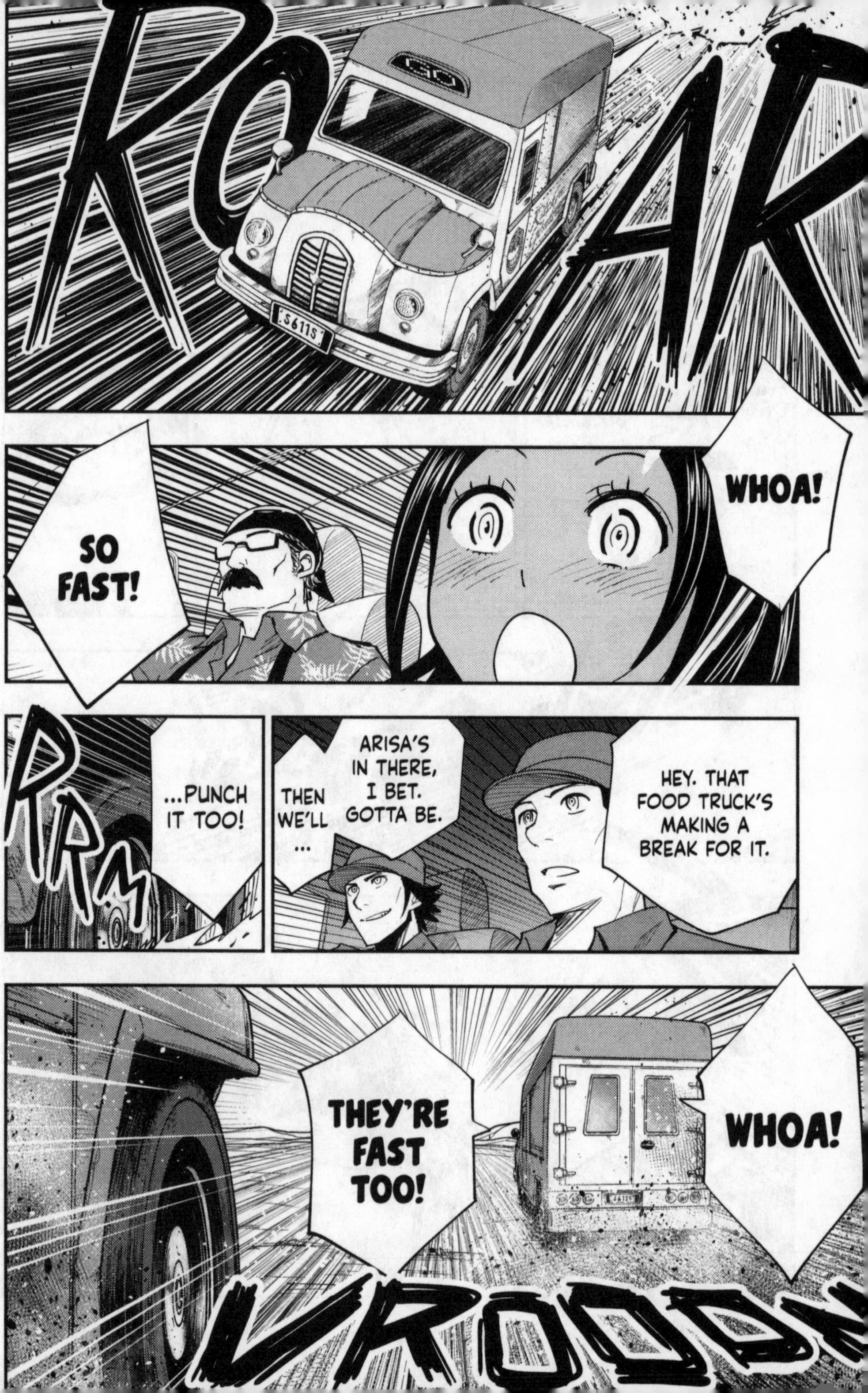
ROAR
WHOA!
SO FAST!
HEY. THAT FOOD TRUCK'S MAKING A BREAK FOR IT.
ARISA'S IN THERE, I BET. GOTTA BE.
THEN WE'LL ...
...PUNCH IT TOO!
RRRM
WHOA!
THEY'RE FAST TOO!
VROOO

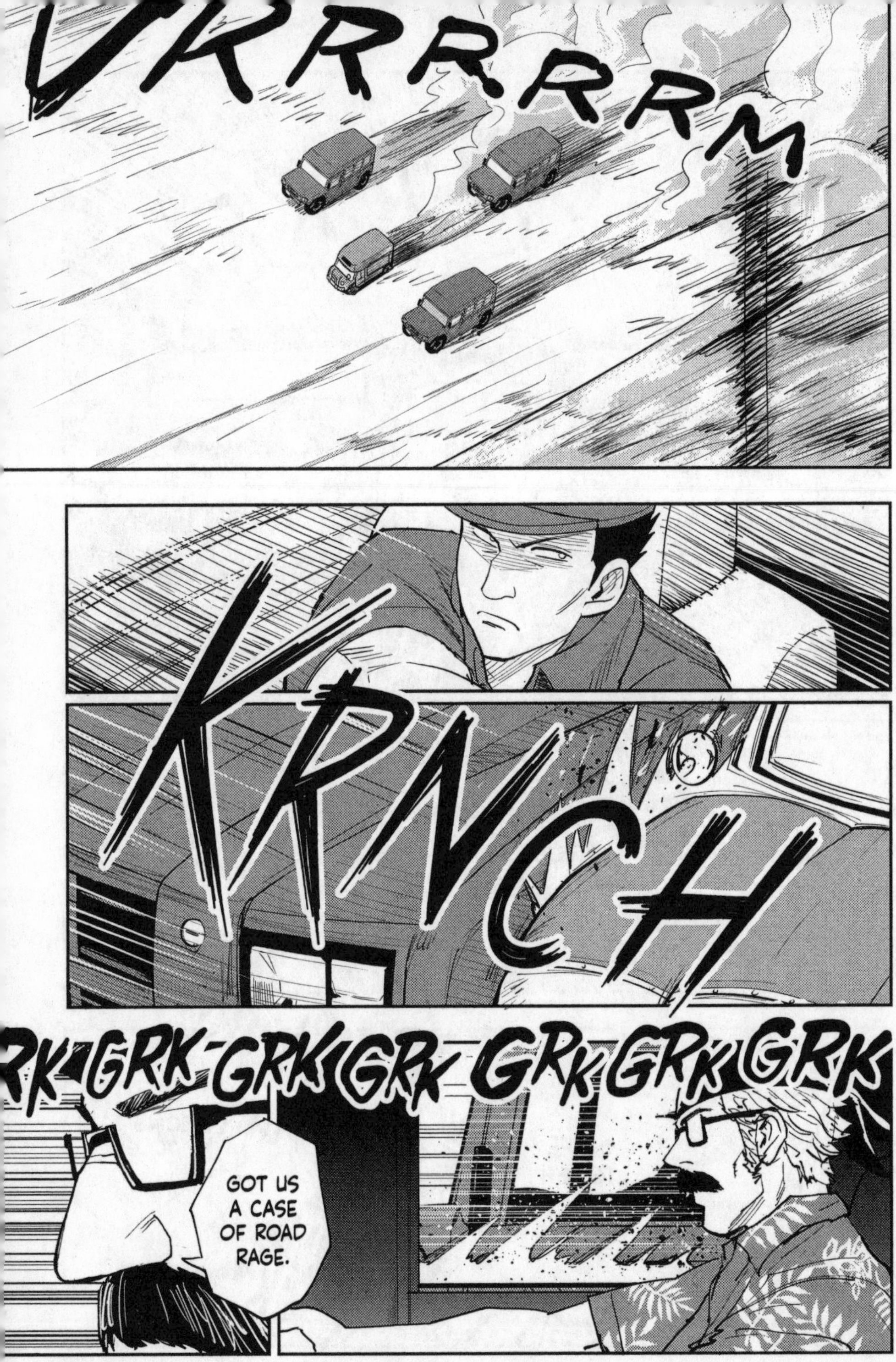
VRRRRRM
KRNCH
RK GRK GRK GRK GRK GRK GRK
GOT US A CASE OF ROAD RAGE.

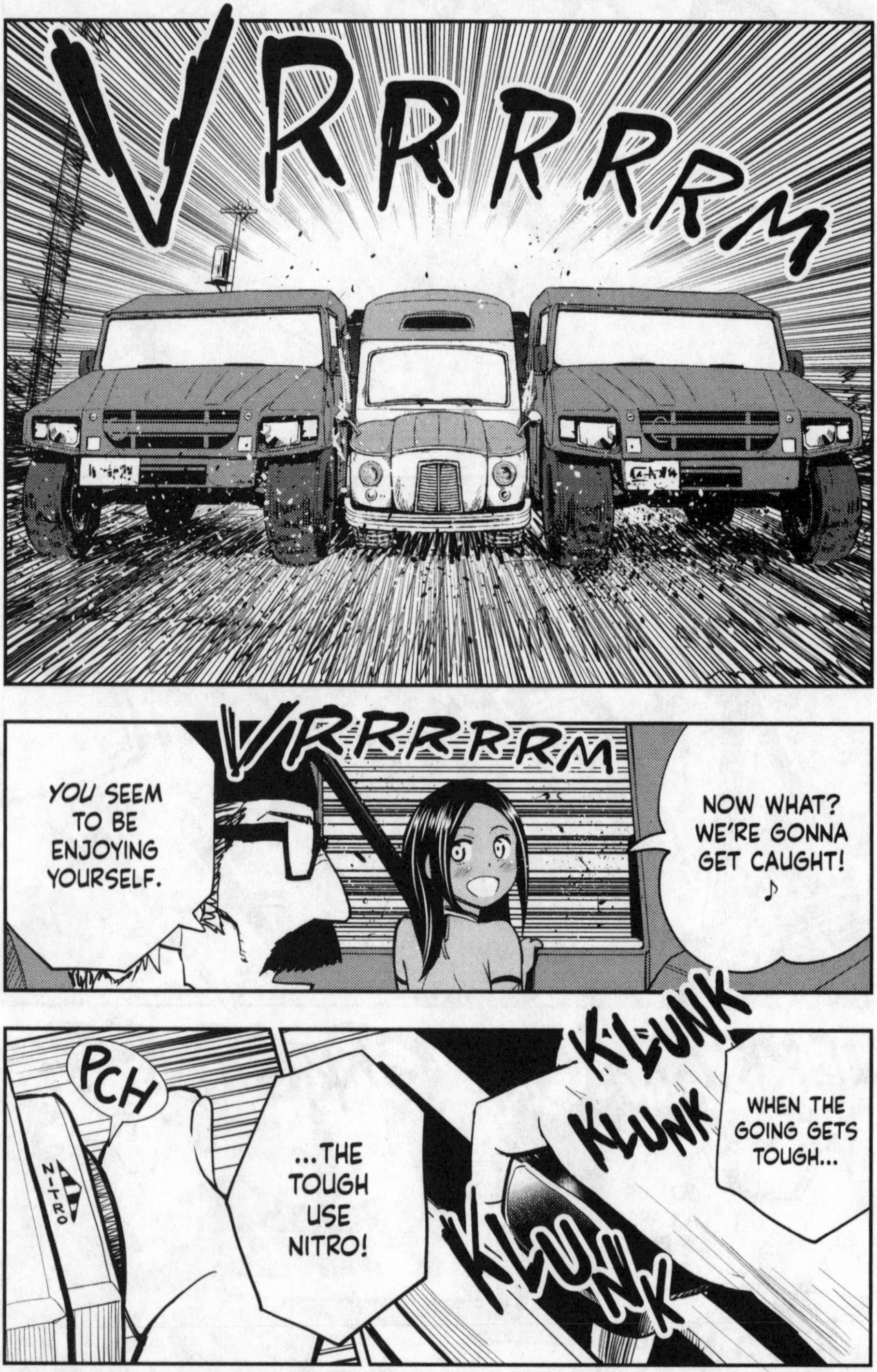
VRRRRRRM
NOW WHAT? WE'RE GONNA GET CAUGHT! ♪
VRRRRRRM
YOU SEEM TO BE ENJOYING YOURSELF.
WHEN THE GOING GETS TOUGH...
KLUNK
KLUNK
...THE TOUGH USE NITRO!
KLUNK
PCH
NITRO

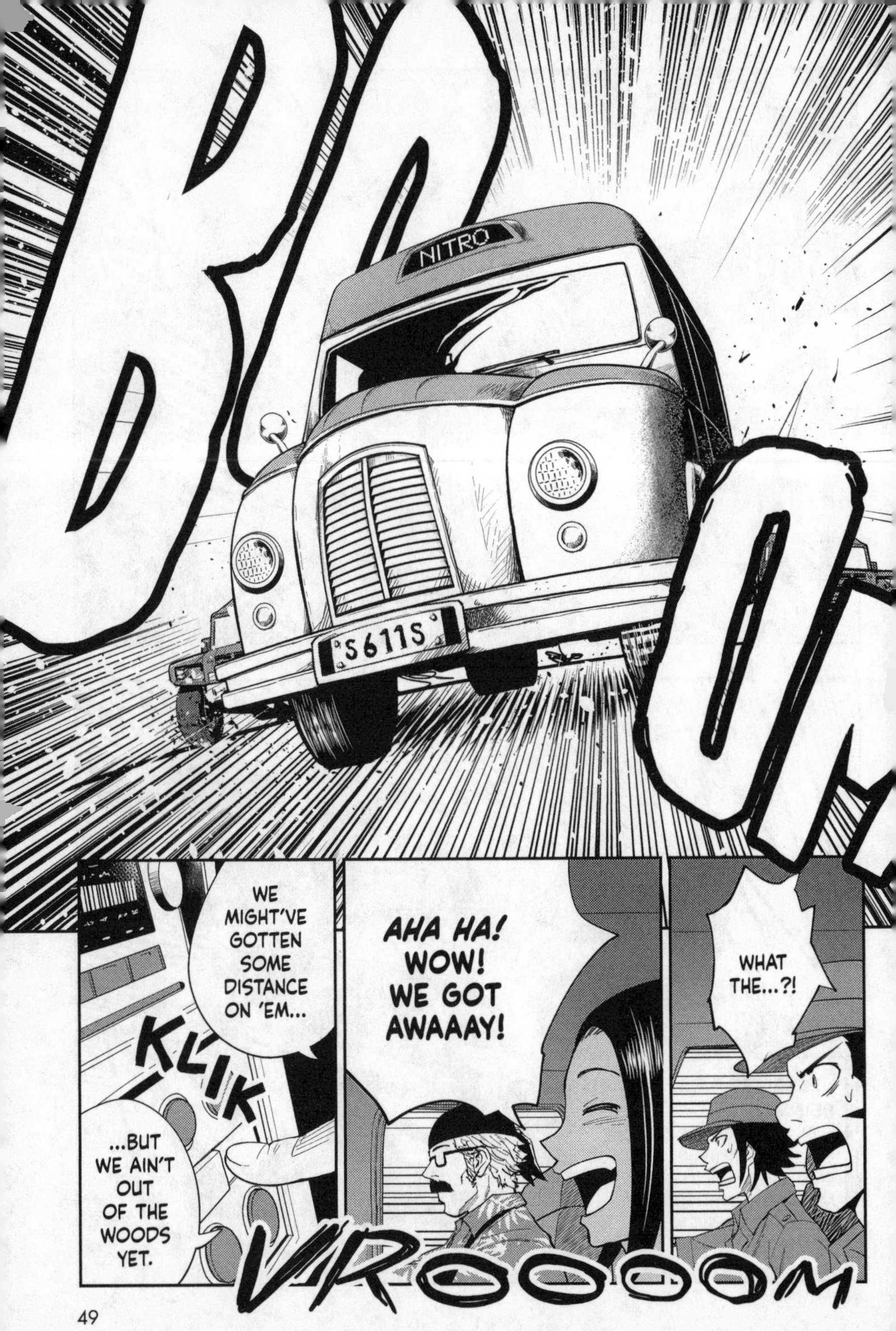
NITRO
S611S
WHAT THE...?!
AHA HA! WOW! WE GOT AWAAAY!
WE MIGHT'VE GOTTEN SOME DISTANCE ON 'EM...
KLIK
...BUT WE AIN'T OUT OF THE WOODS YET.
VROOOOOM

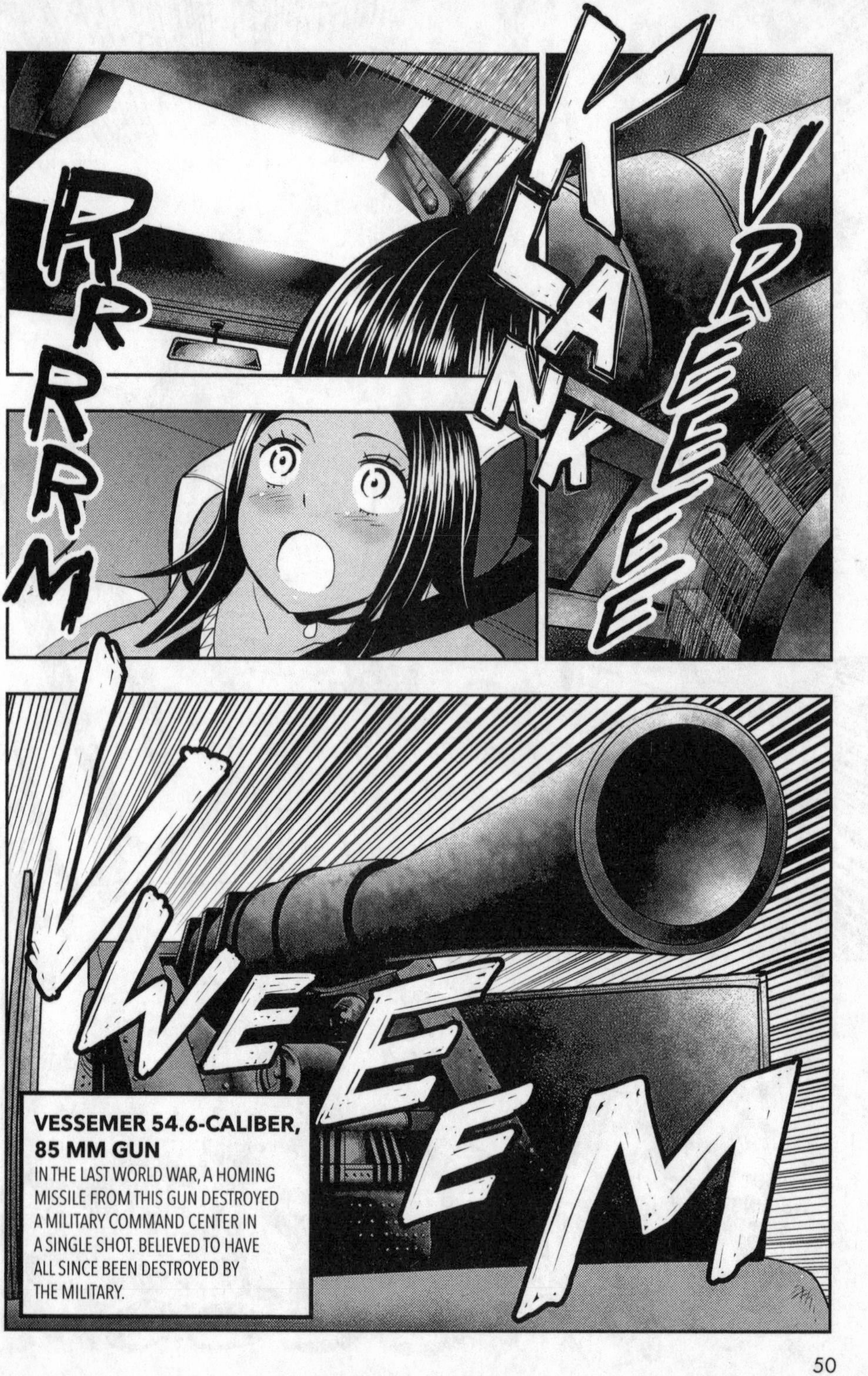
VREEEEE
KLANK
RRRRM
VWEEEM
VESSEMER 54.6-CALIBER, 85 MM GUN
IN THE LAST WORLD WAR, A HOMING MISSILE FROM THIS GUN DESTROYED A MILITARY COMMAND CENTER IN A SINGLE SHOT. BELIEVED TO HAVE ALL SINCE BEEN DESTROYED BY THE MILITARY.

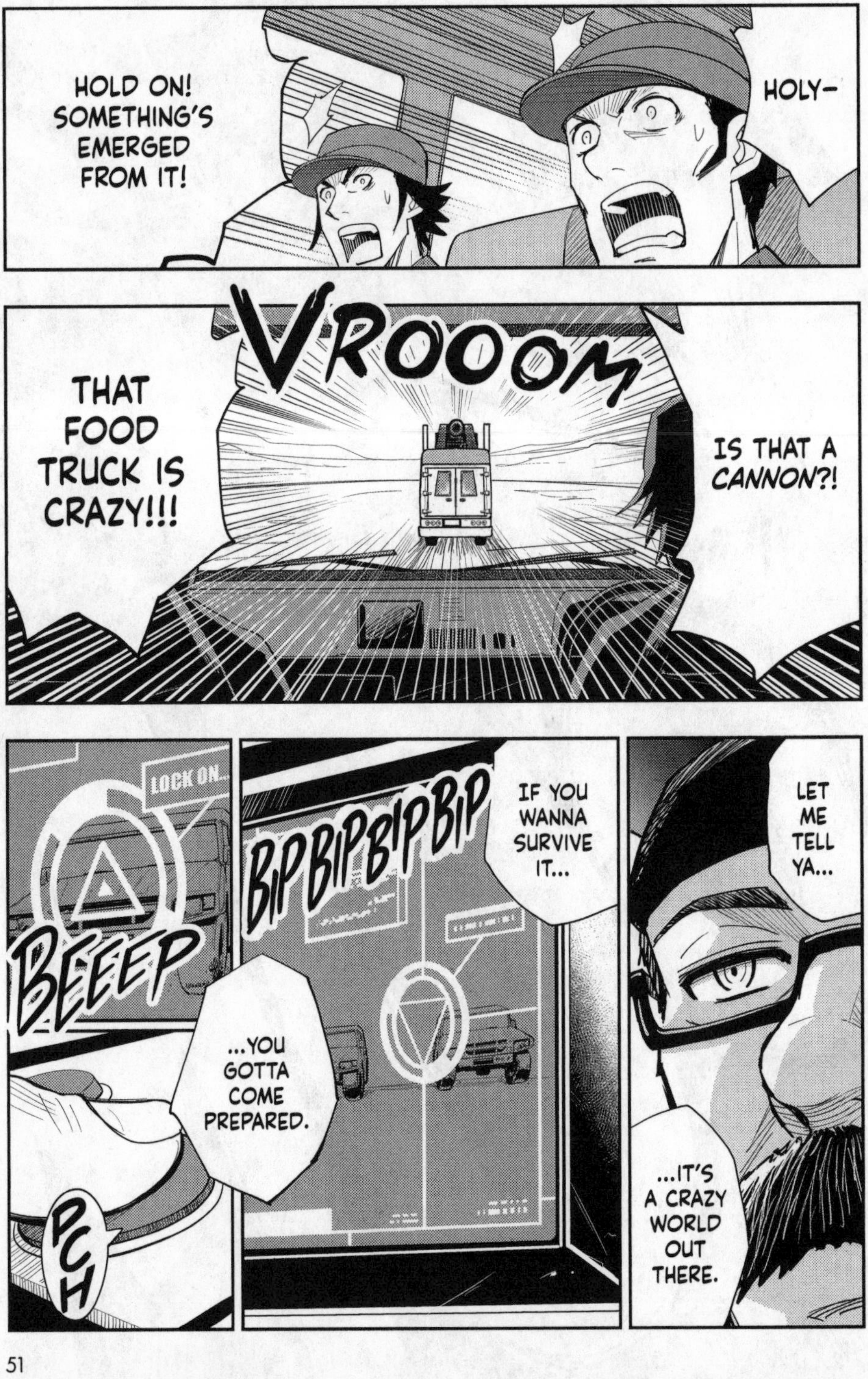
HOLY-
HOLD ON! SOMETHING'S EMERGED FROM IT!
VROOOM
IS THAT A CANNON?!
THAT FOOD TRUCK IS CRAZY!!!
LET ME TELL YA...
...IT'S A CRAZY WORLD OUT THERE.
IF YOU WANNA SURVIVE IT...
BIPBIPBIPBIP
...YOU GOTTA COME PREPARED.
LOCK ON...
BEEEP
PCH

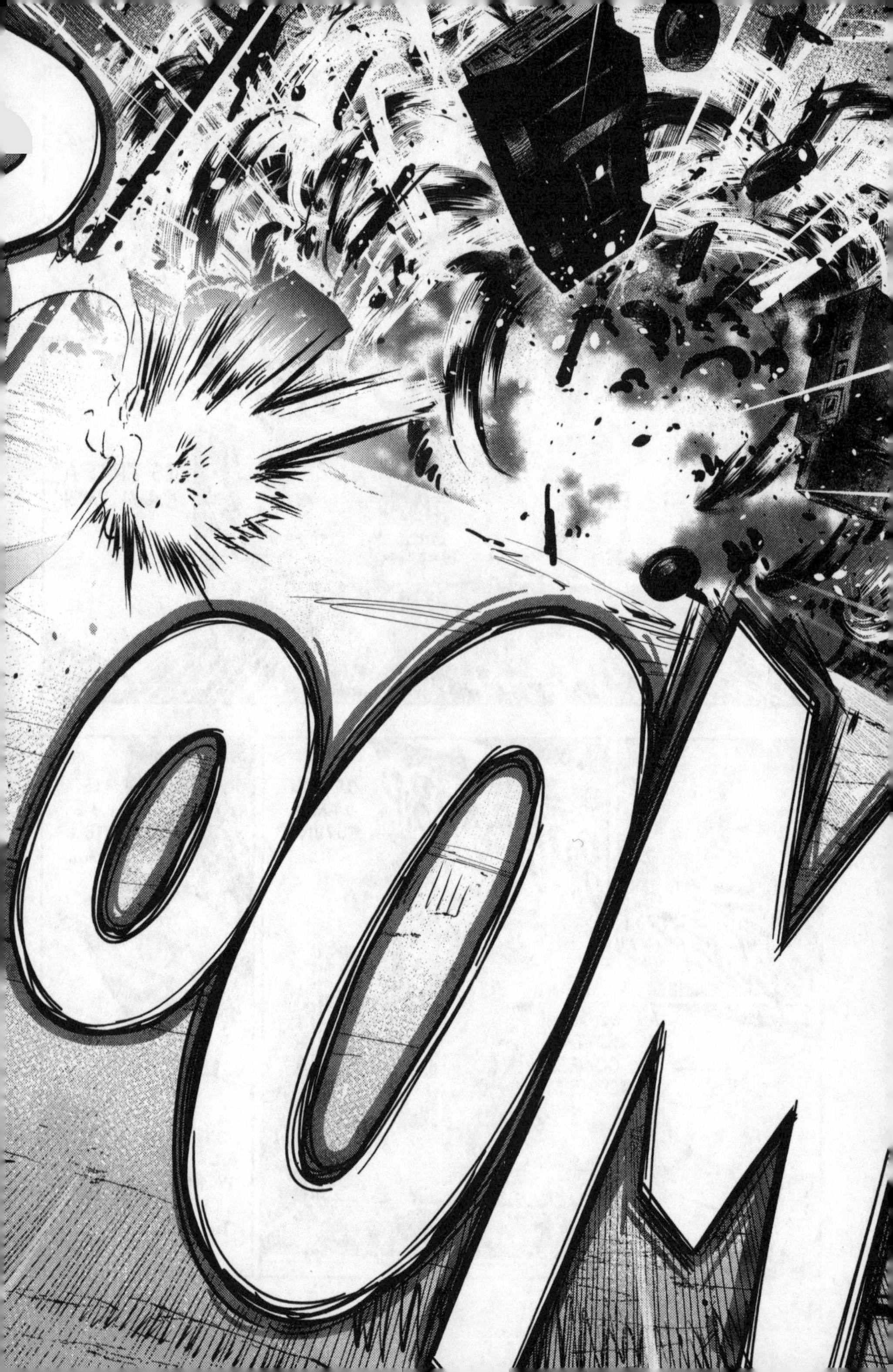

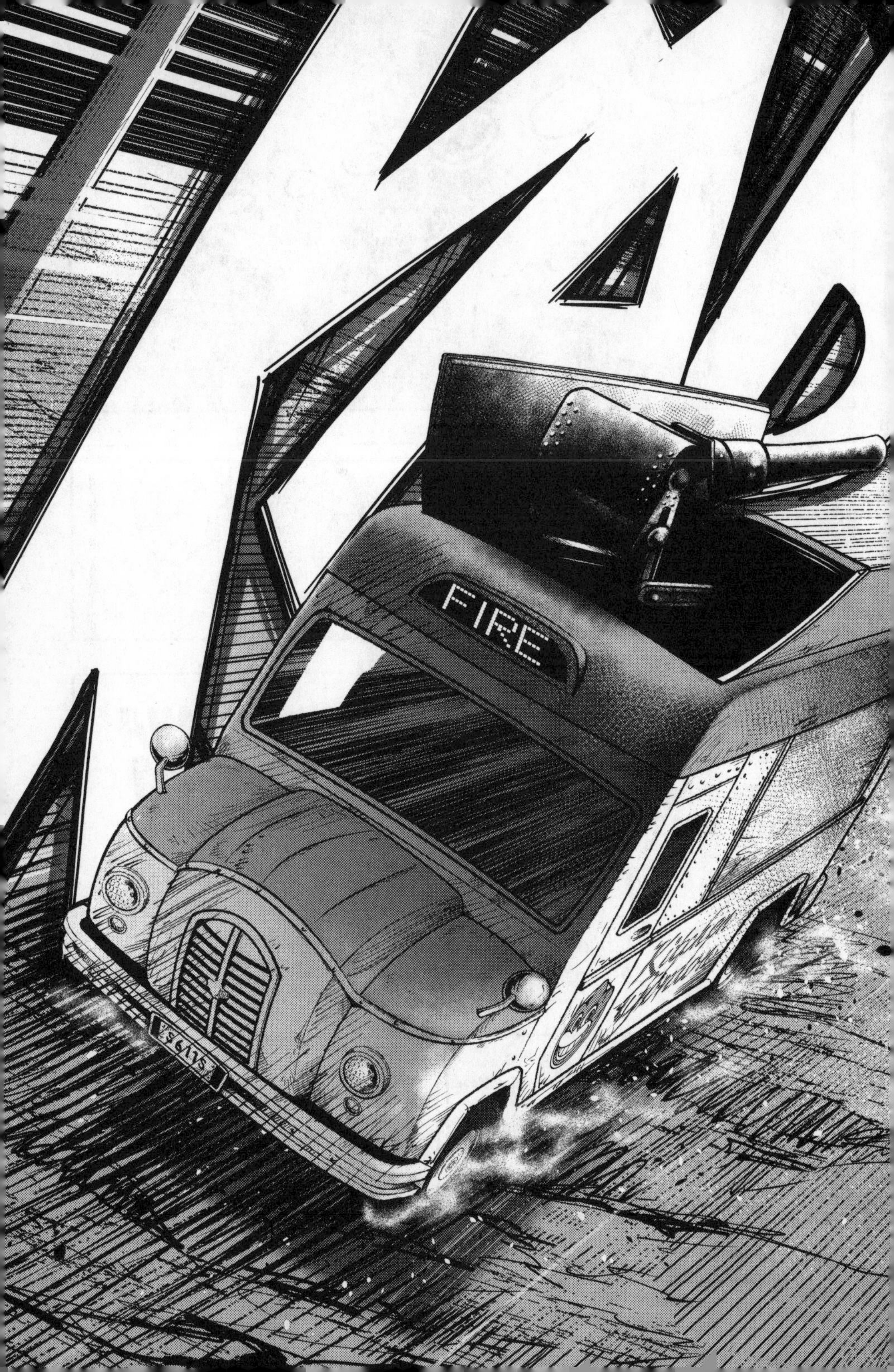
FIRE

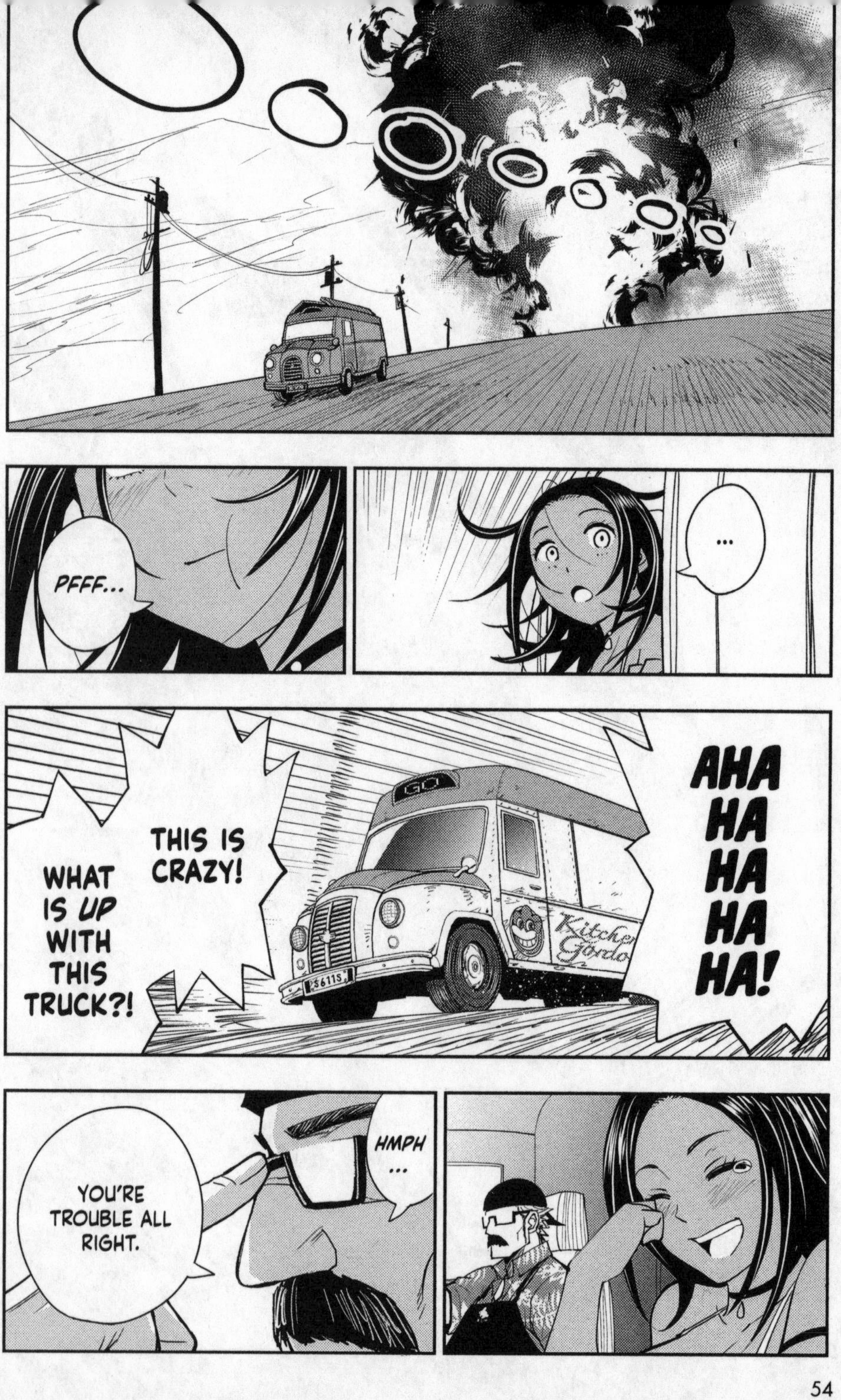
...
PFFF...
AHA HA HA HA HA HA!
THIS IS CRAZY!
WHAT IS *UP* WITH THIS TRUCK?!
HMPH...
YOU'RE TROUBLE ALL RIGHT.

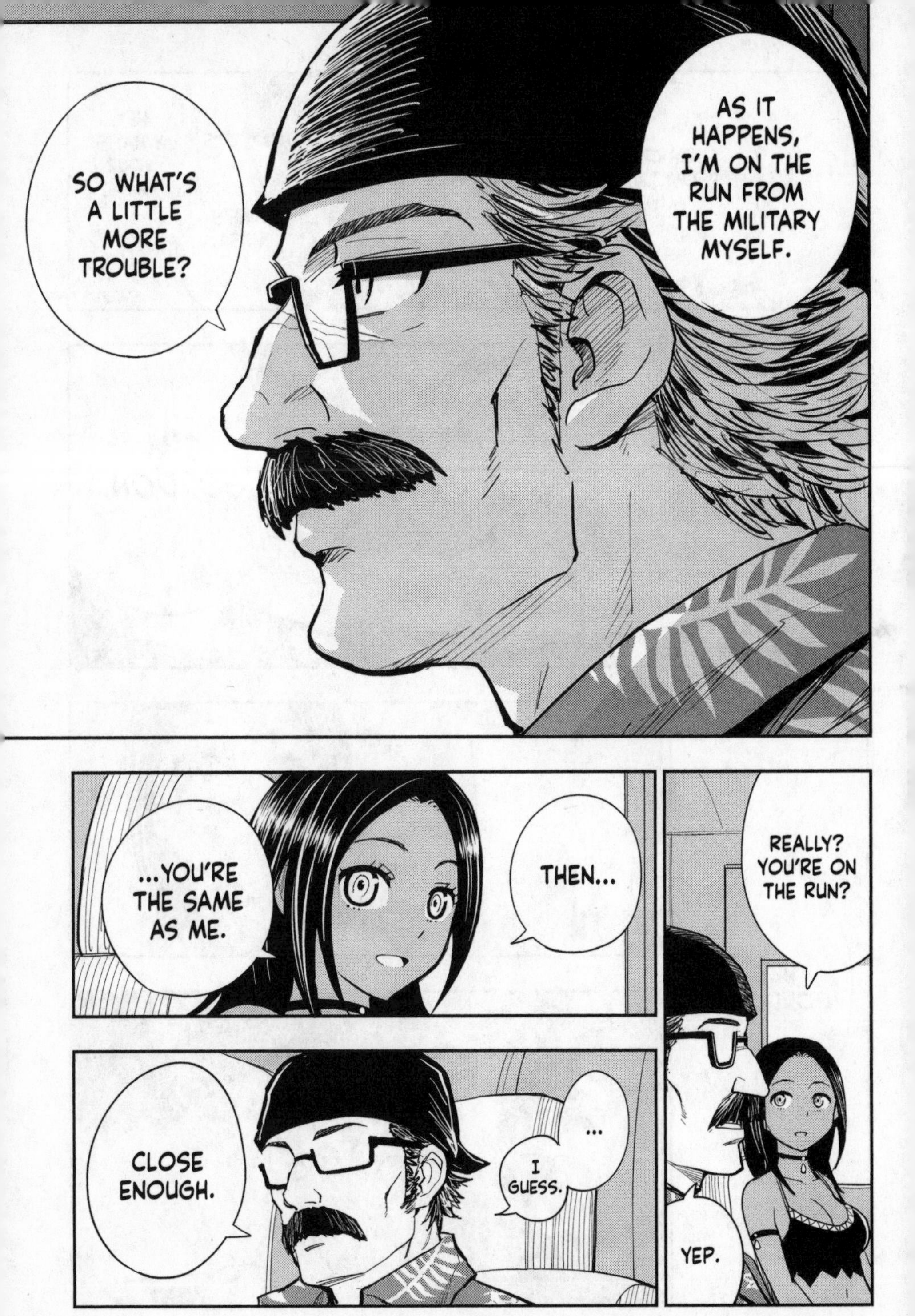
AS IT HAPPENS, I'M ON THE RUN FROM THE MILITARY MYSELF.
SO WHAT'S A LITTLE MORE TROUBLE?
REALLY? YOU'RE ON THE RUN?
YEP.
THEN...
...YOU'RE THE SAME AS ME.
... I GUESS.
CLOSE ENOUGH.

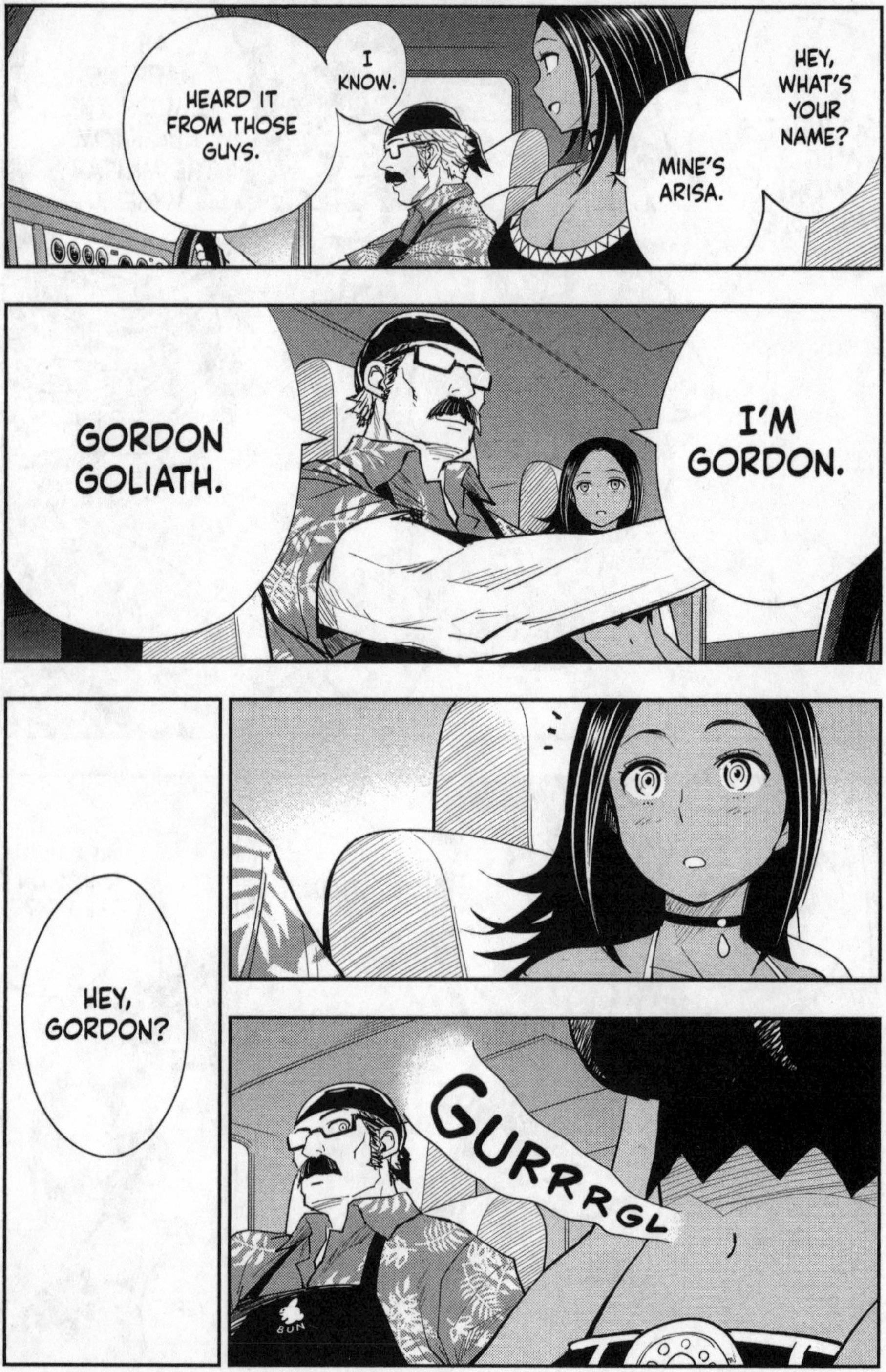
HEY, WHAT'S YOUR NAME?
MINE'S ARISA.
I KNOW.
HEARD IT FROM THOSE GUYS.
I'M GORDON.
GORDON GOLIATH.
GURRRGL
HEY, GORDON?

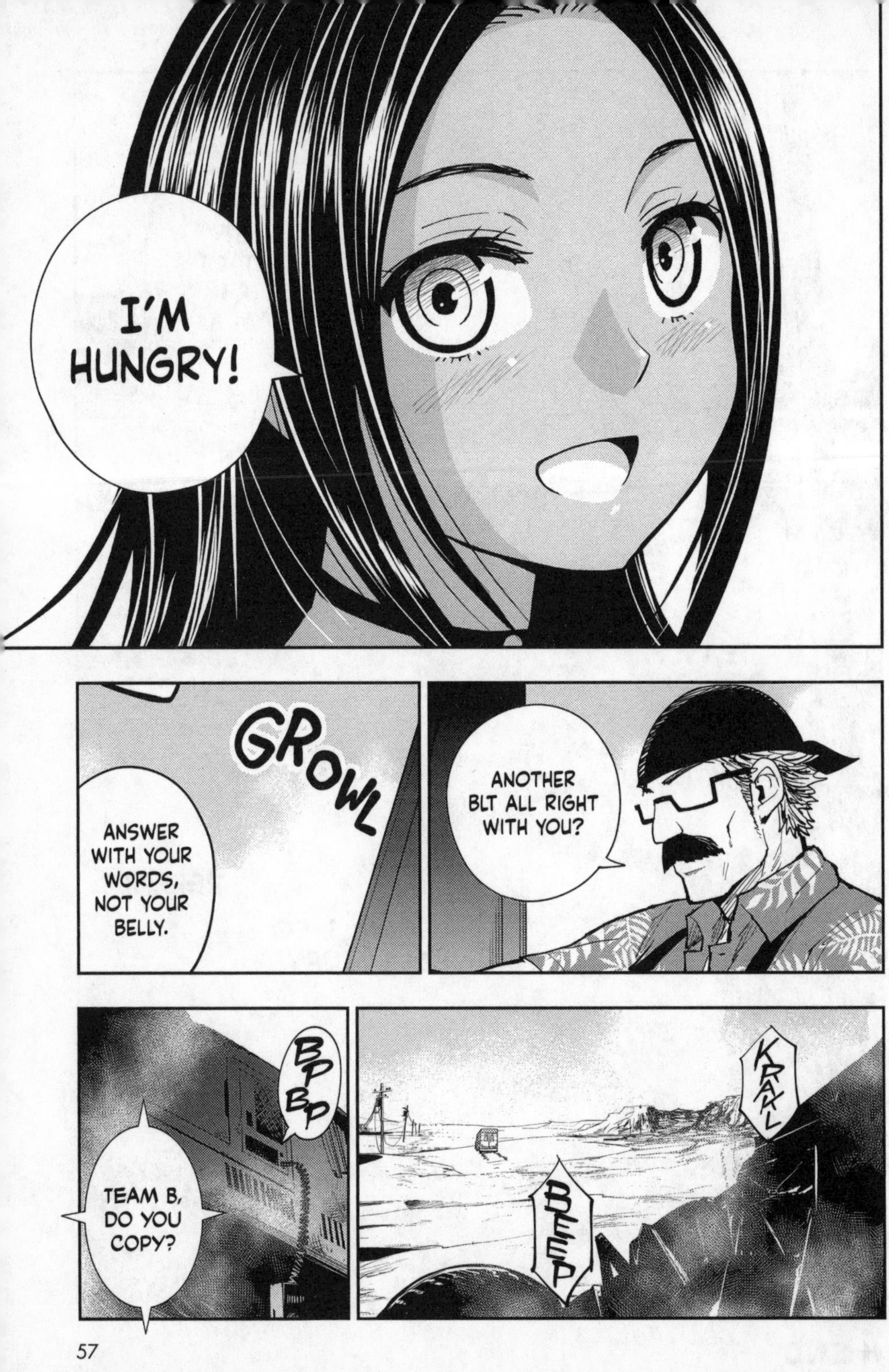
I'M HUNGRY!
ANOTHER BLT ALL RIGHT WITH YOU?
GROWL
ANSWER WITH YOUR WORDS, NOT YOUR BELLY.
KRAKL
BEEP
BPBP
TEAM B, DO YOU COPY?

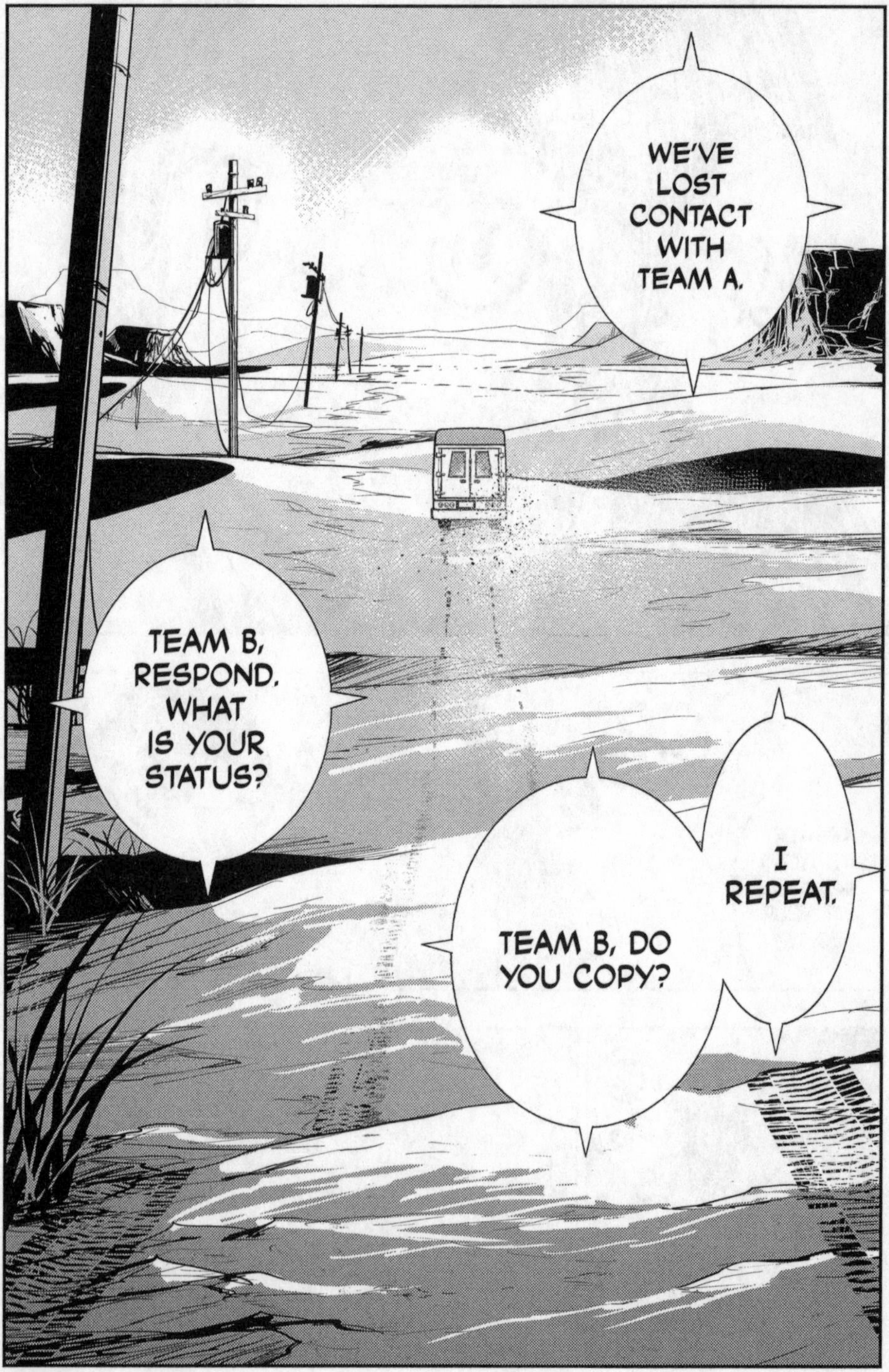
WE'VE LOST CONTACT WITH TEAM A.
TEAM B, RESPOND. WHAT IS YOUR STATUS?
I REPEAT.
TEAM B, DO YOU COPY?

#1 END

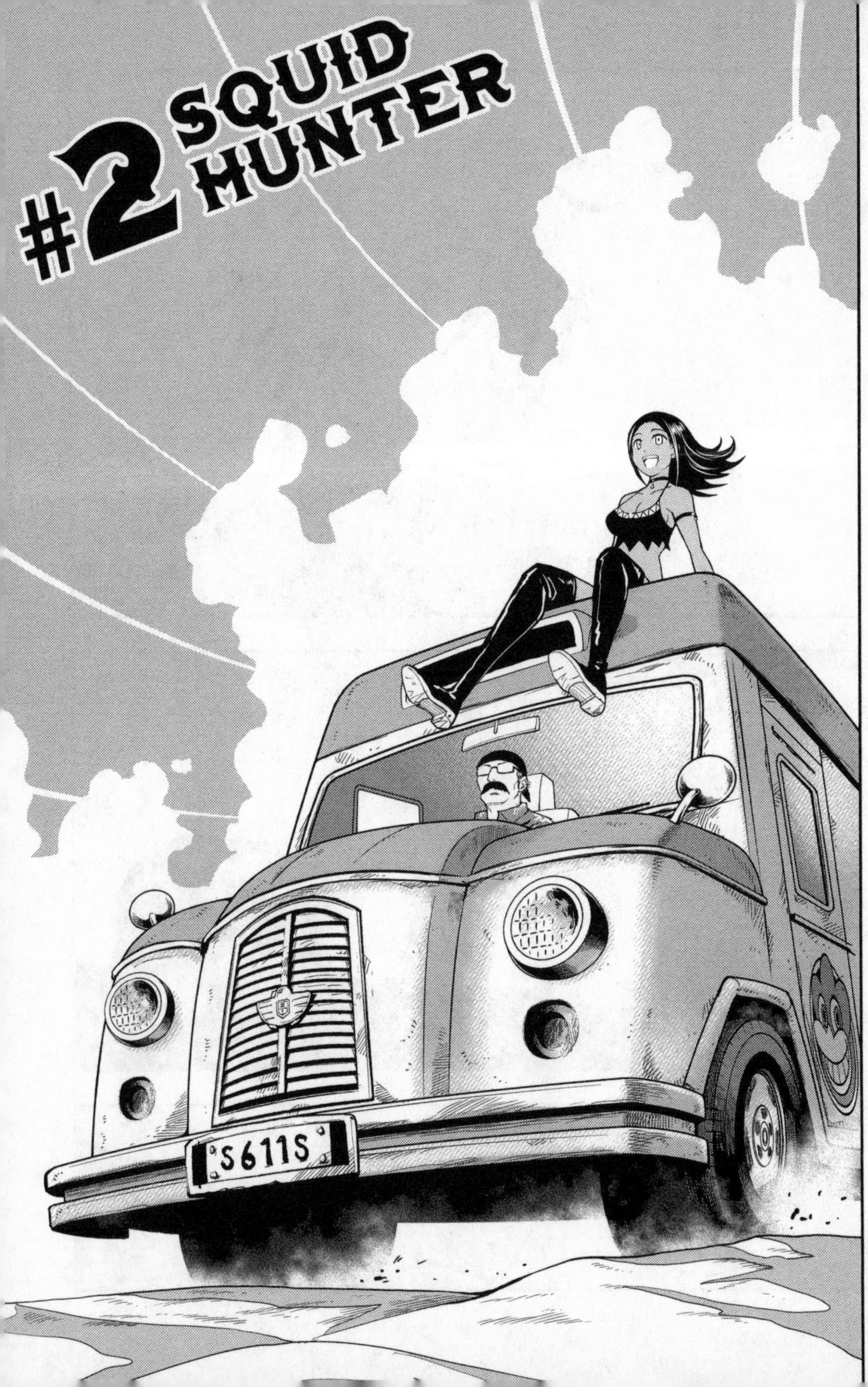
#2 SQUID HUNTER
S611S

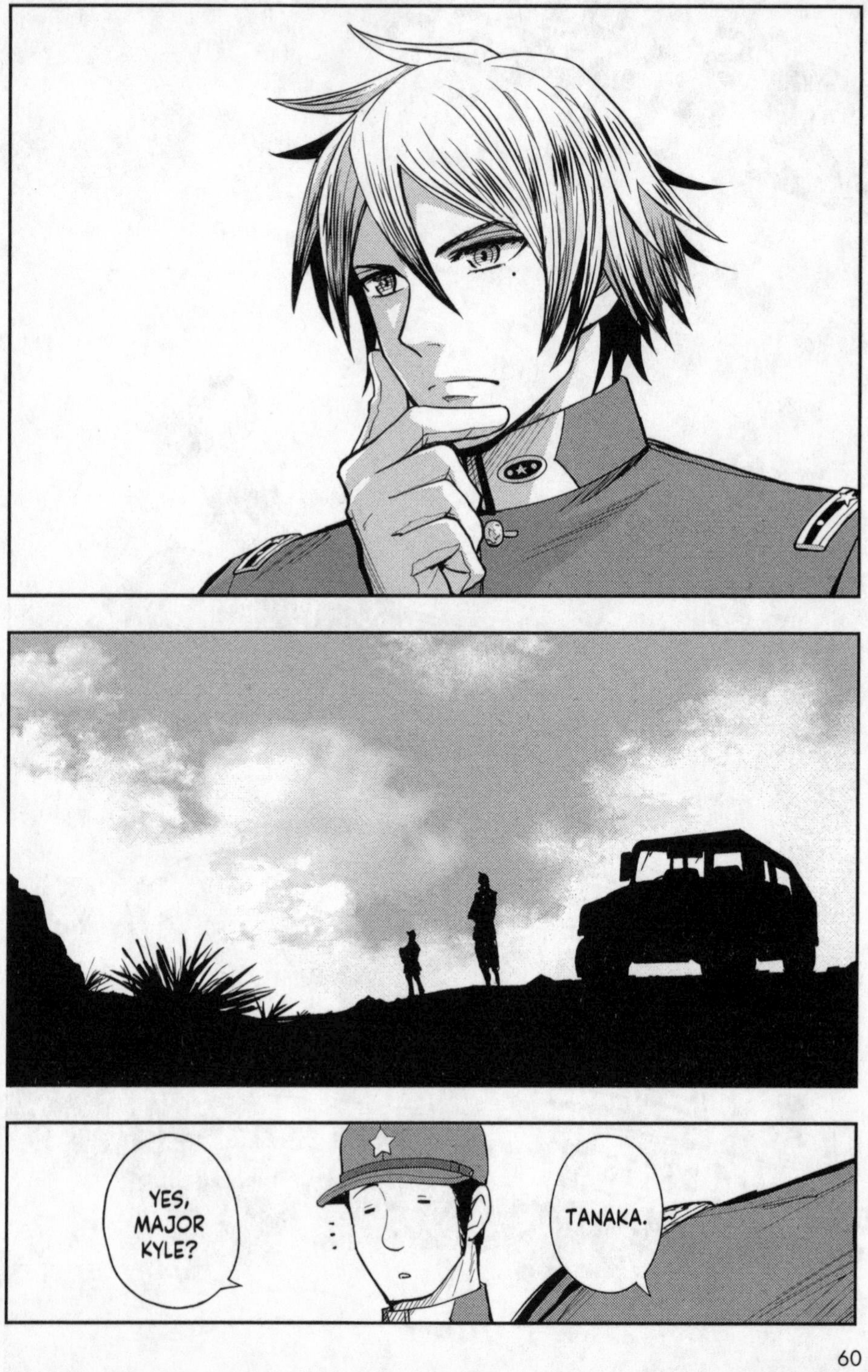
TANAKA.
YES, MAJOR KYLE?

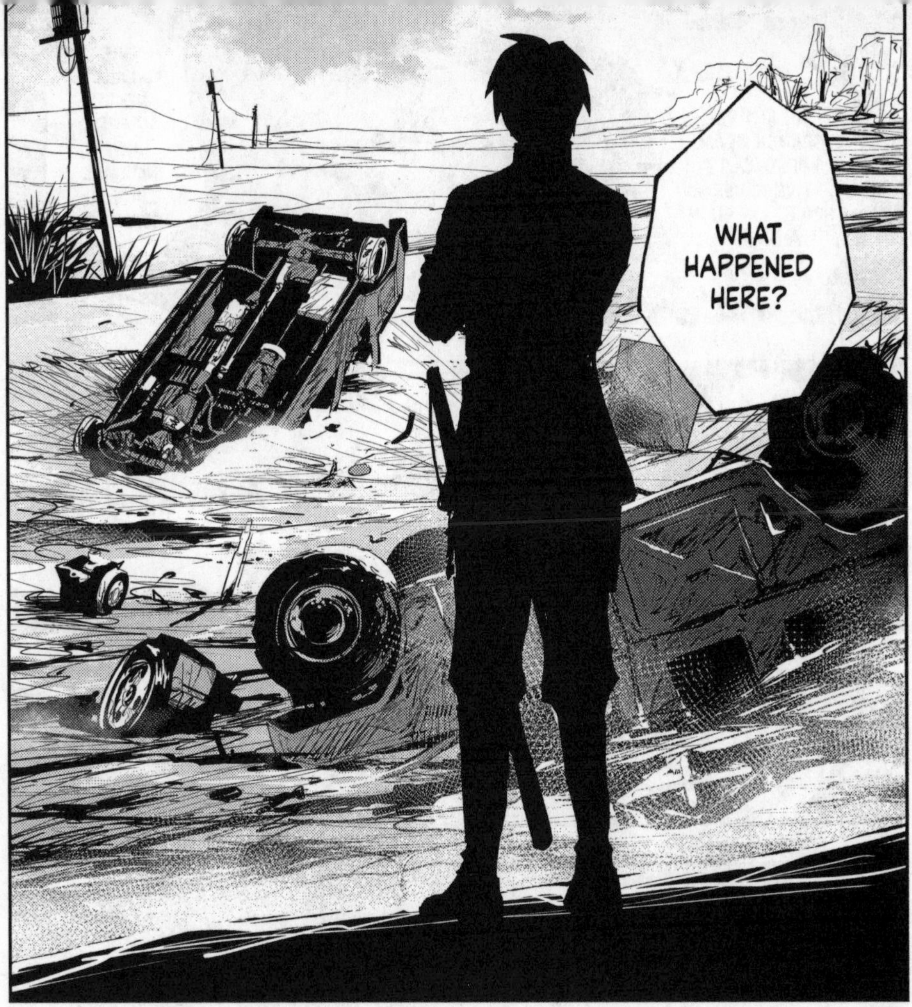
WHAT HAPPENED HERE?

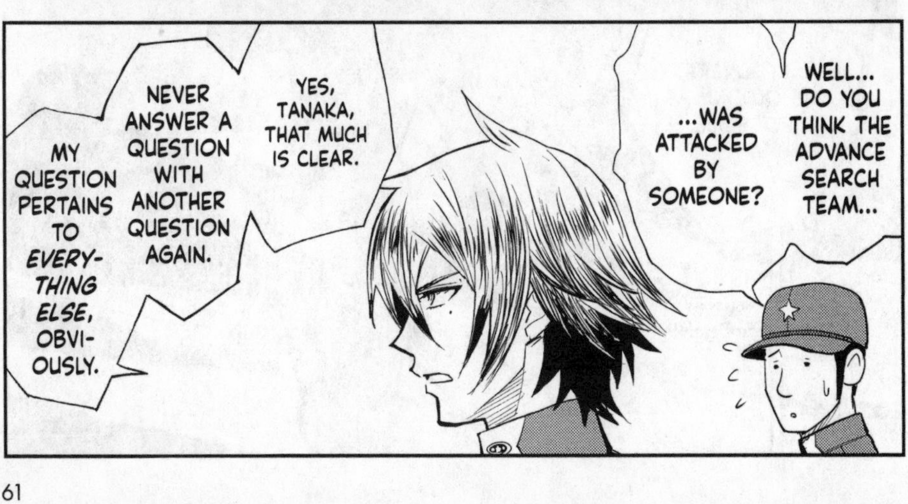
WELL... DO YOU THINK THE ADVANCE SEARCH TEAM...
...WAS ATTACKED BY SOMEONE?
YES, TANAKA, THAT MUCH IS CLEAR.
NEVER ANSWER A QUESTION WITH ANOTHER QUESTION AGAIN.
MY QUESTION PERTAINS TO *EVERYTHING ELSE*, OBVIOUSLY.

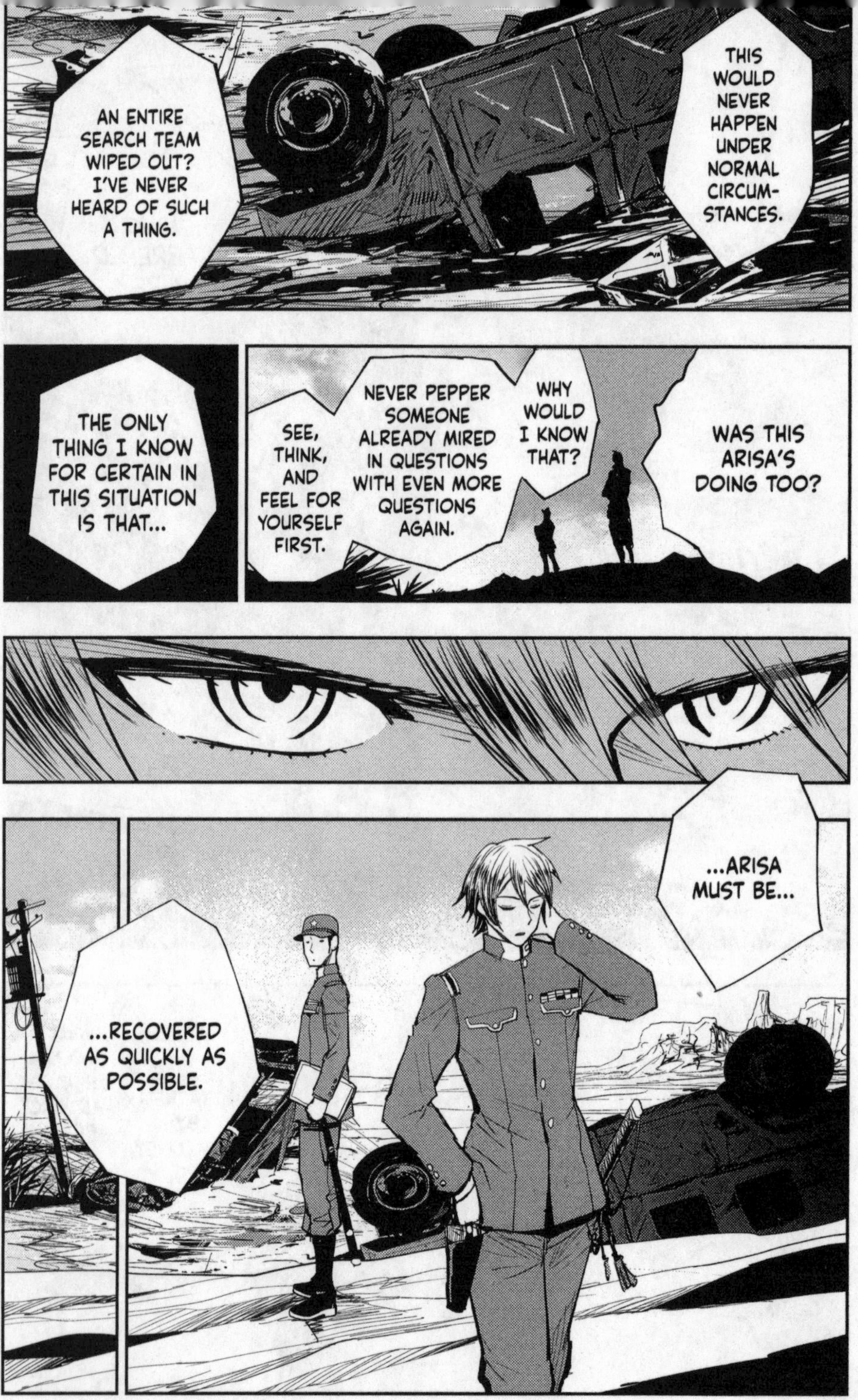
THIS WOULD NEVER HAPPEN UNDER NORMAL CIRCUM-STANCES.
AN ENTIRE SEARCH TEAM WIPED OUT? I'VE NEVER HEARD OF SUCH A THING.
WAS THIS ARISA'S DOING TOO?
WHY WOULD I KNOW THAT?
NEVER PEPPER SOMEONE ALREADY MIRED IN QUESTIONS WITH EVEN MORE QUESTIONS AGAIN.
SEE, THINK, AND FEEL FOR YOURSELF FIRST.
THE ONLY THING I KNOW FOR CERTAIN IN THIS SITUATION IS THAT...
...ARISA MUST BE...
...RECOVERED AS QUICKLY AS POSSIBLE.

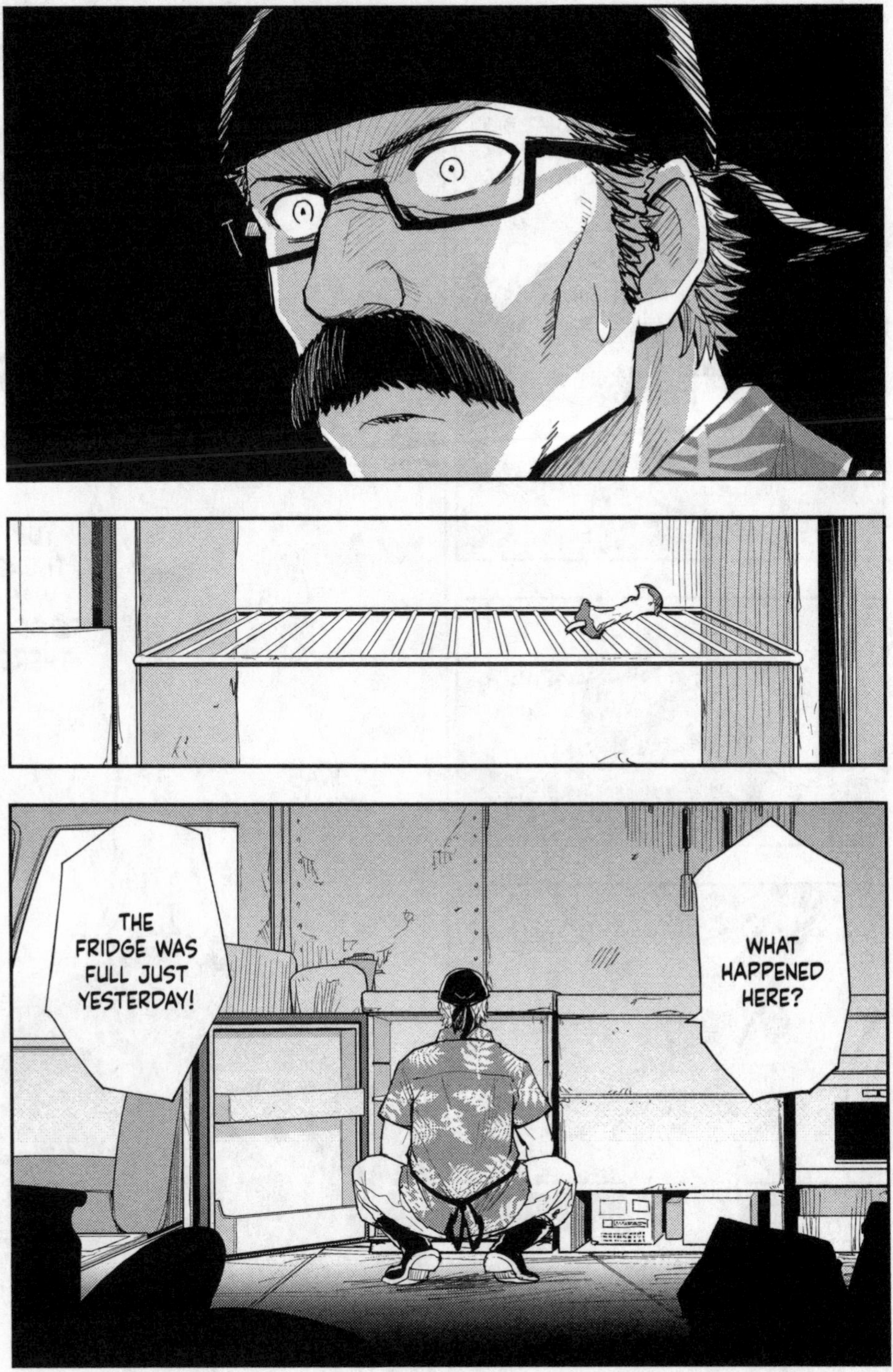
WHAT HAPPENED HERE?
THE FRIDGE WAS FULL JUST YESTERDAY!

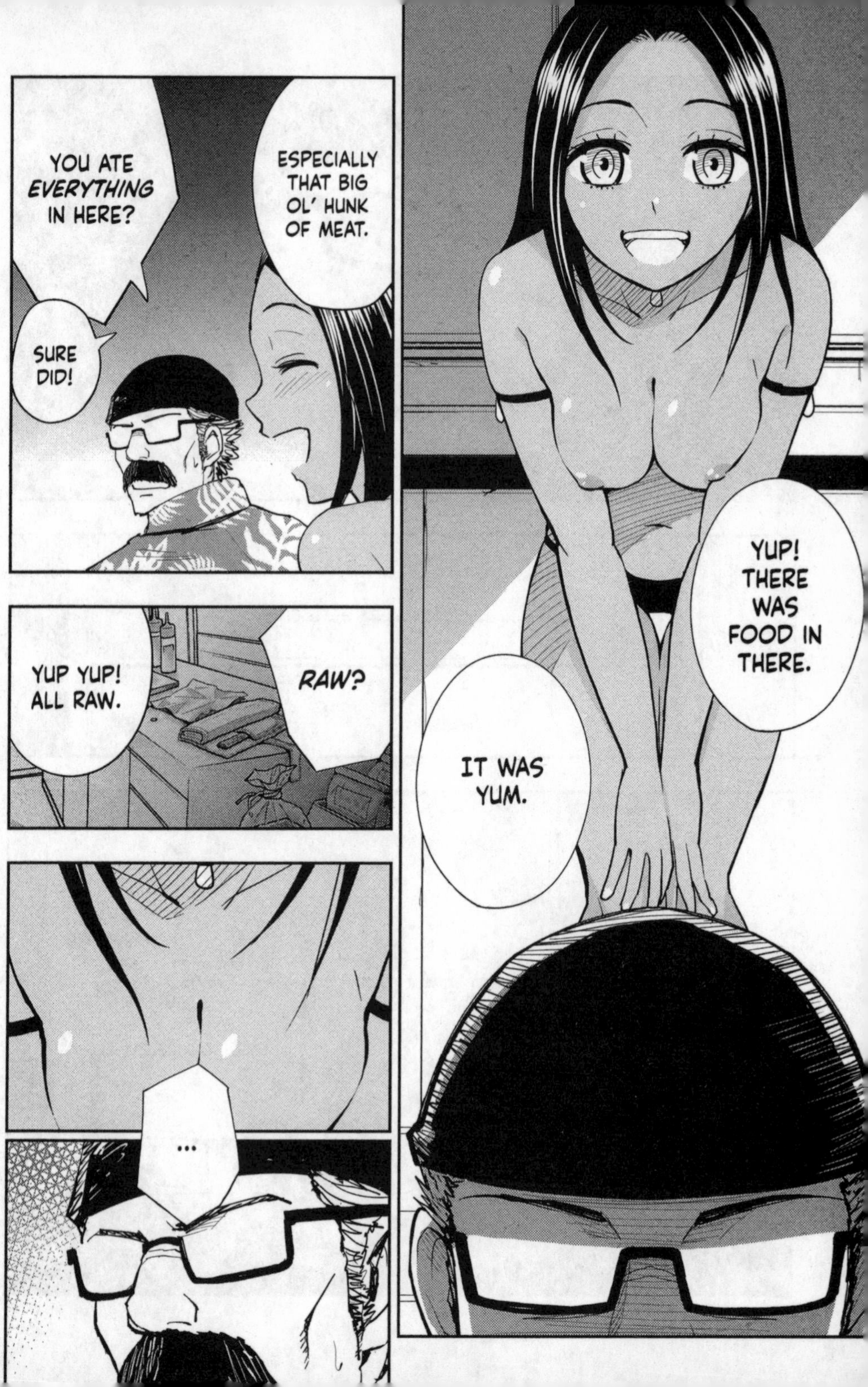
YUP! THERE WAS FOOD IN THERE.
IT WAS YUM.
ESPECIALLY THAT BIG OL' HUNK OF MEAT.
YOU ATE *EVERYTHING* IN HERE?
SURE DID!
RAW?
YUP YUP! ALL RAW.
...

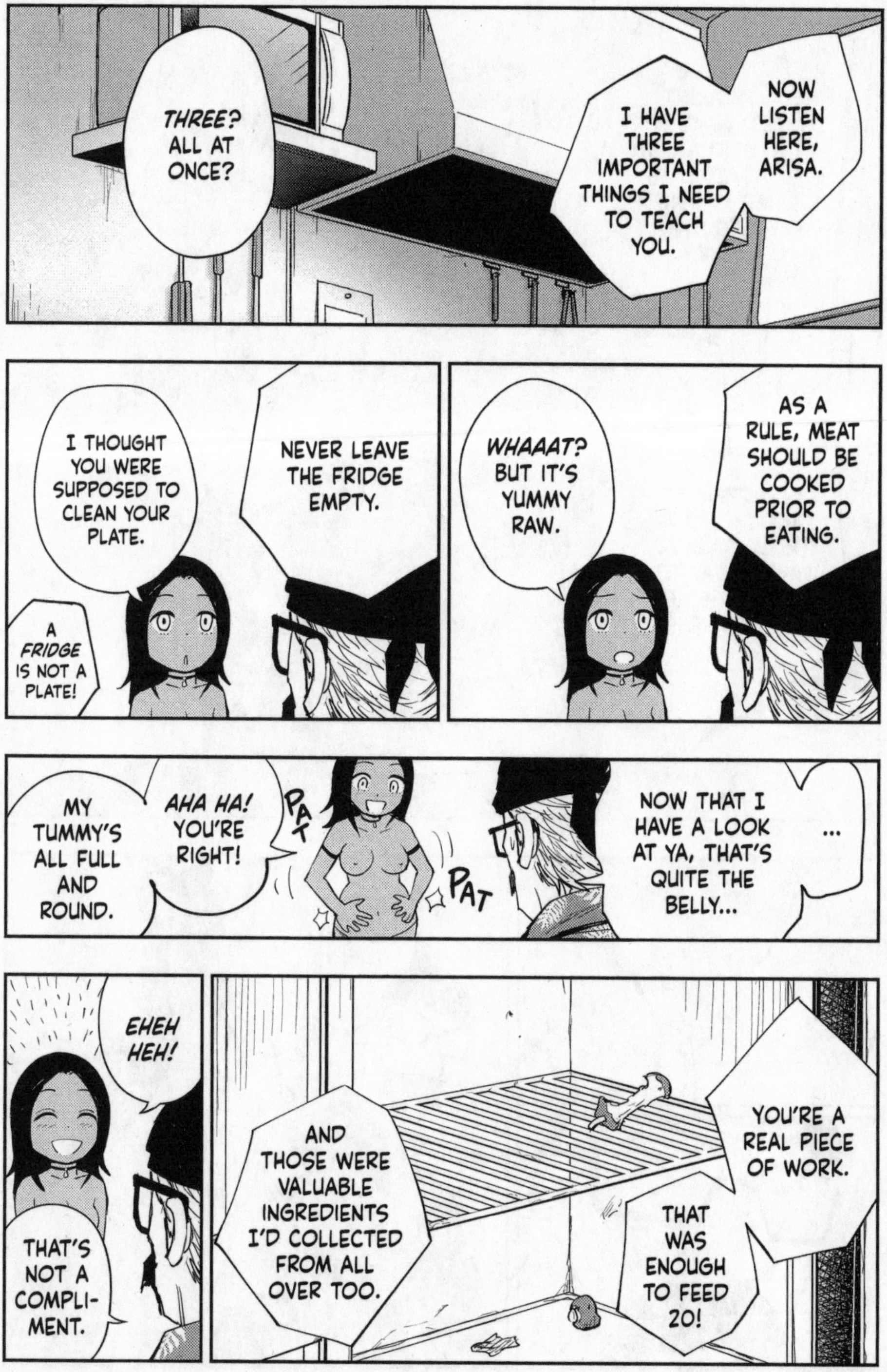
NOW LISTEN HERE, ARISA.
I HAVE THREE IMPORTANT THINGS I NEED TO TEACH YOU.
THREE? ALL AT ONCE?
AS A RULE, MEAT SHOULD BE COOKED PRIOR TO EATING.
WHAAAT? BUT IT'S YUMMY RAW.
NEVER LEAVE THE FRIDGE EMPTY.
I THOUGHT YOU WERE SUPPOSED TO CLEAN YOUR PLATE.
A FRIDGE IS NOT A PLATE!
...
NOW THAT I HAVE A LOOK AT YA, THAT'S QUITE THE BELLY...
PAT
PAT
AHA HA! YOU'RE RIGHT!
MY TUMMY'S ALL FULL AND ROUND.
YOU'RE A REAL PIECE OF WORK.
THAT WAS ENOUGH TO FEED 20!
AND THOSE WERE VALUABLE INGREDIENTS I'D COLLECTED FROM ALL OVER TOO.
EHEH HEH!
THAT'S NOT A COMPLIMENT.

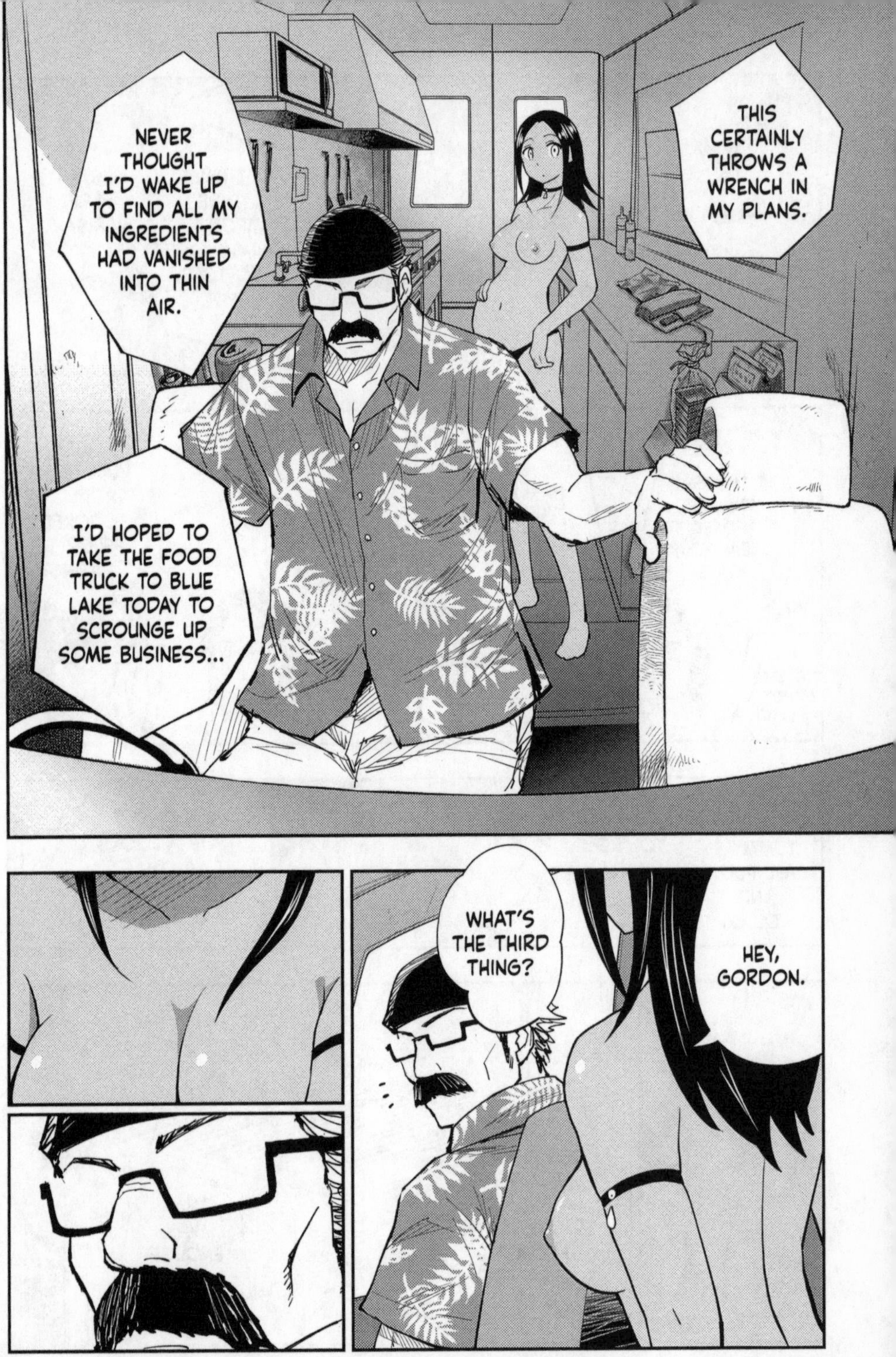
THIS CERTAINLY THROWS A WRENCH IN MY PLANS.
NEVER THOUGHT I'D WAKE UP TO FIND ALL MY INGREDIENTS HAD VANISHED INTO THIN AIR.
I'D HOPED TO TAKE THE FOOD TRUCK TO BLUE LAKE TODAY TO SCROUNGE UP SOME BUSINESS...
HEY, GORDON.
WHAT'S THE THIRD THING?

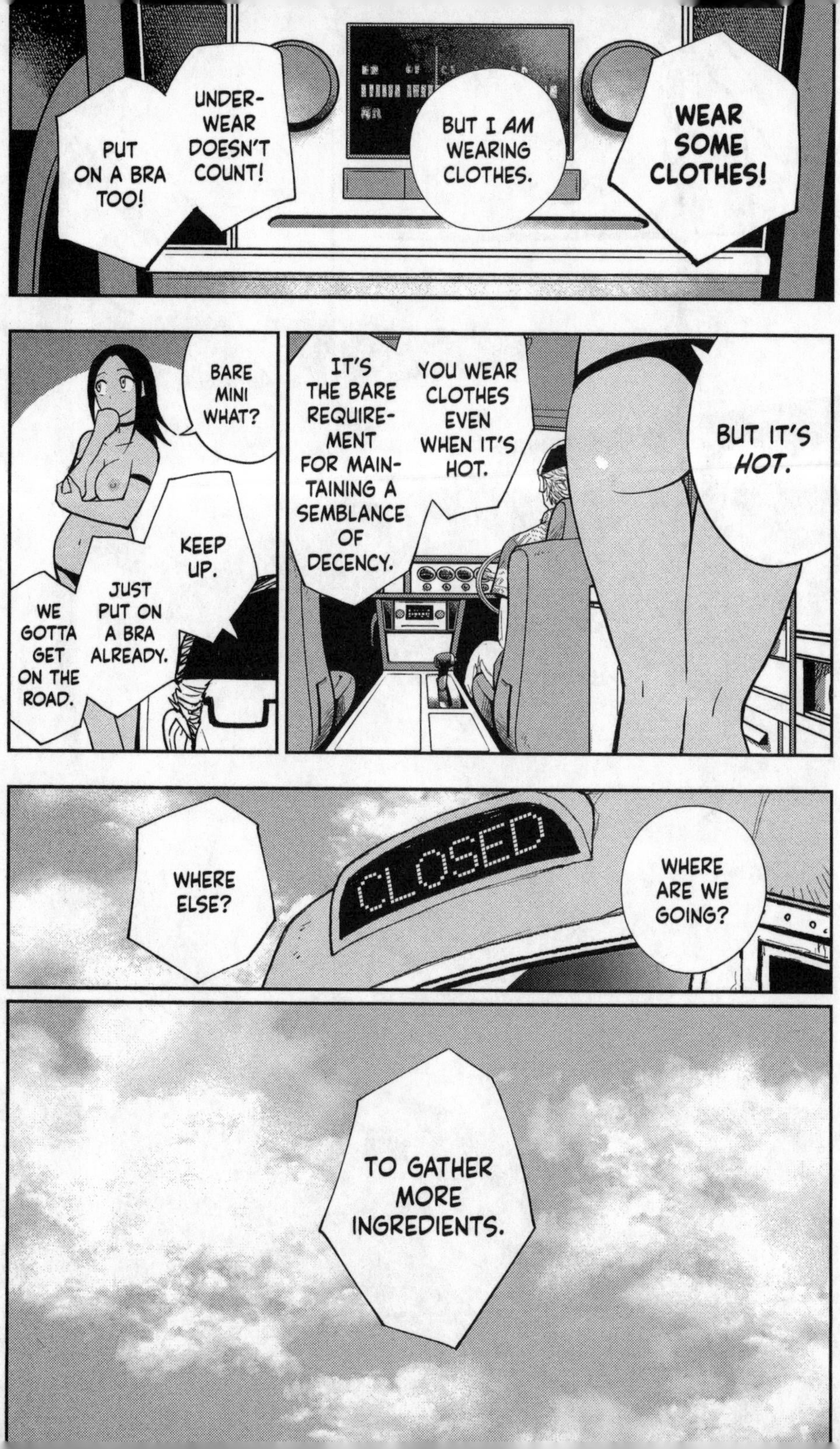
WEAR SOME CLOTHES!
BUT I *AM* WEARING CLOTHES.
UNDERWEAR DOESN'T COUNT!
PUT ON A BRA TOO!
BUT IT'S *HOT*.
YOU WEAR CLOTHES EVEN WHEN IT'S HOT.
IT'S THE BARE REQUIREMENT FOR MAINTAINING A SEMBLANCE OF DECENCY.
BARE MINI WHAT?
KEEP UP.
JUST PUT ON A BRA ALREADY.
WE GOTTA GET ON THE ROAD.
WHERE ARE WE GOING?
CLOSED
WHERE ELSE?
TO GATHER MORE INGREDIENTS.

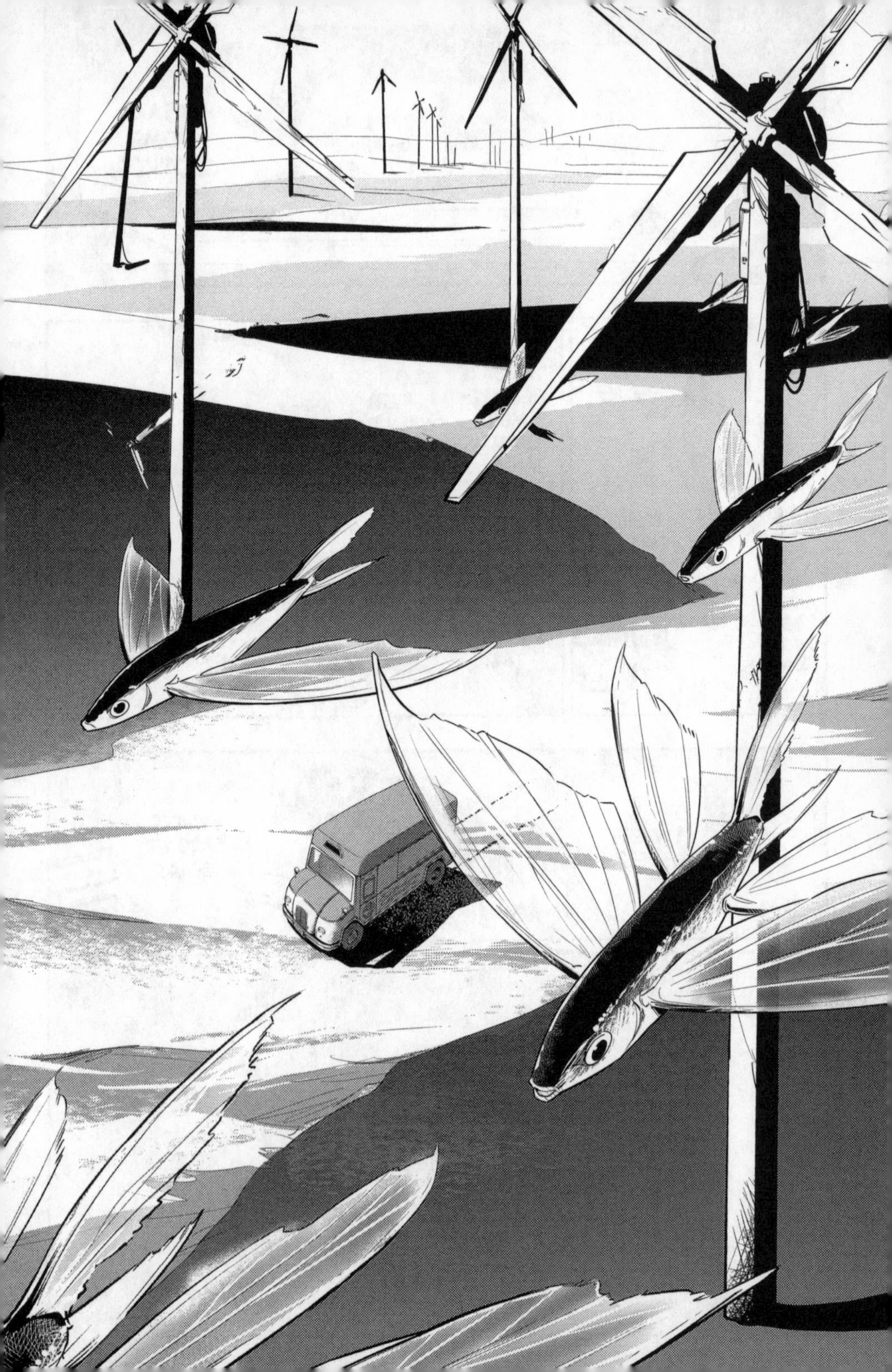

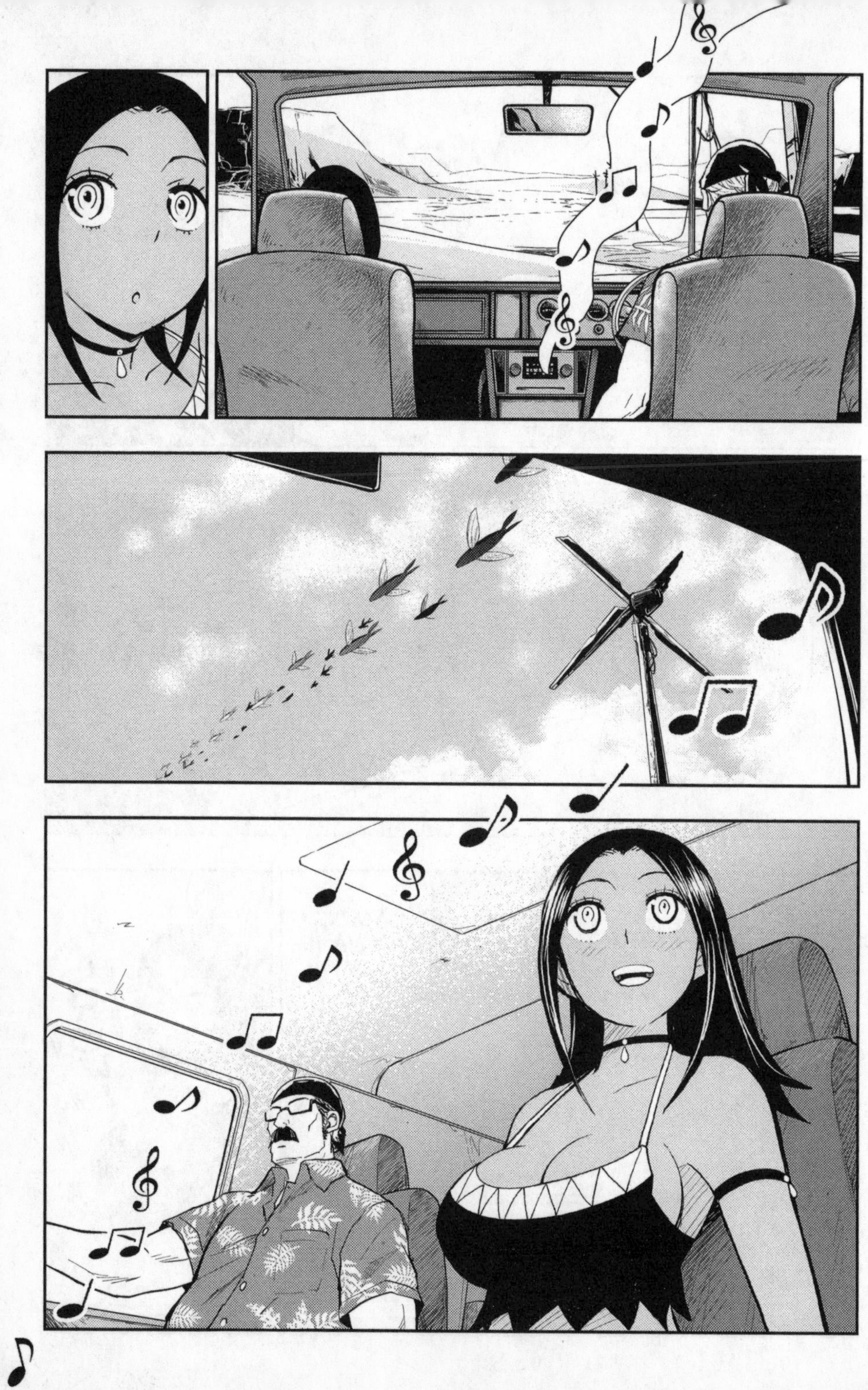

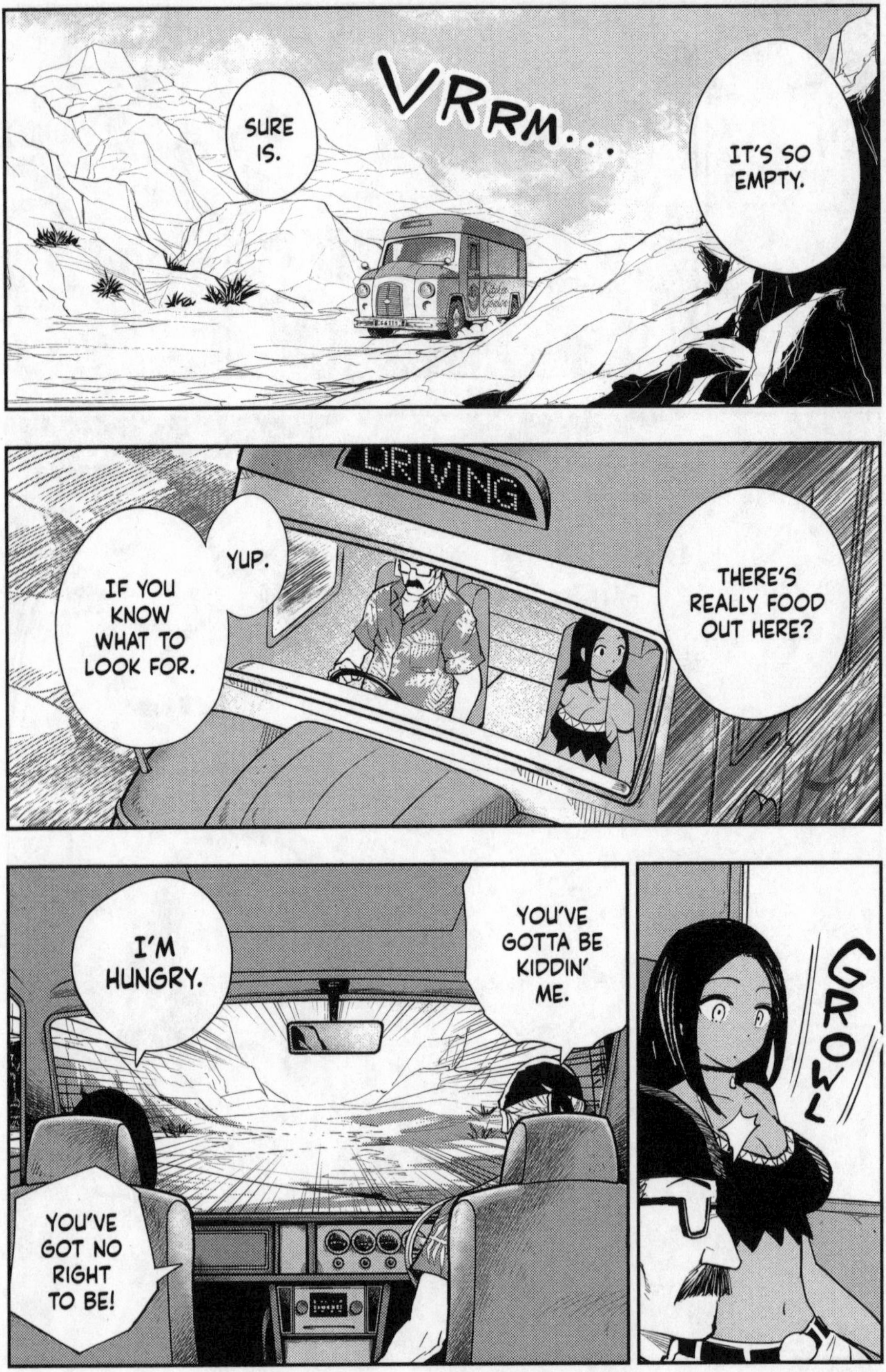
IT'S SO EMPTY.
VRRM...
SURE IS.
DRIVING
THERE'S REALLY FOOD OUT HERE?
YUP.
IF YOU KNOW WHAT TO LOOK FOR.
GROWL
I'M HUNGRY.
YOU'VE GOTTA BE KIDDIN' ME.
YOU'VE GOT NO RIGHT TO BE!

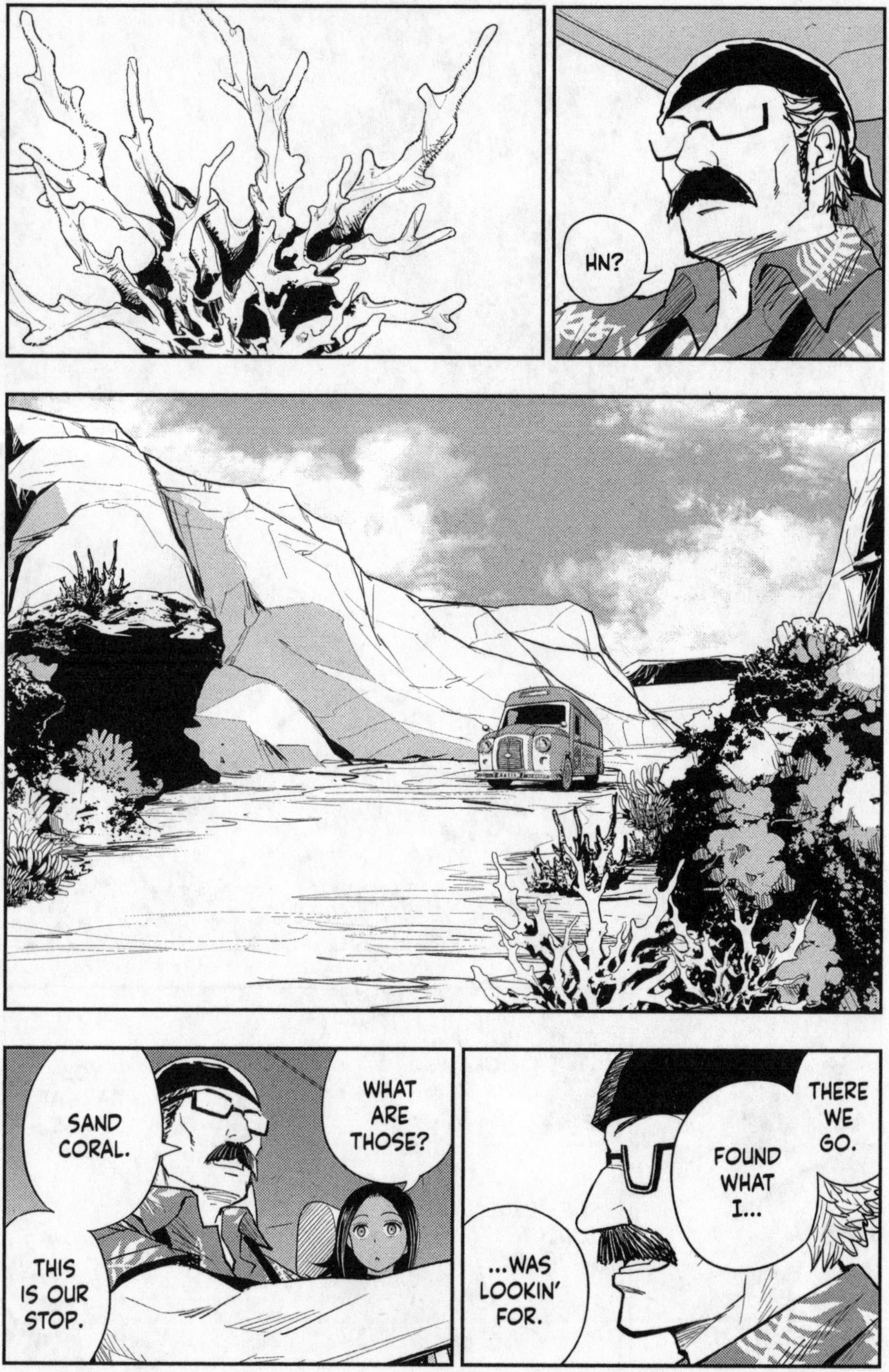
HN?
THERE WE GO.
FOUND WHAT I...
...WAS LOOKIN' FOR.
WHAT ARE THOSE?
SAND CORAL.
THIS IS OUR STOP.

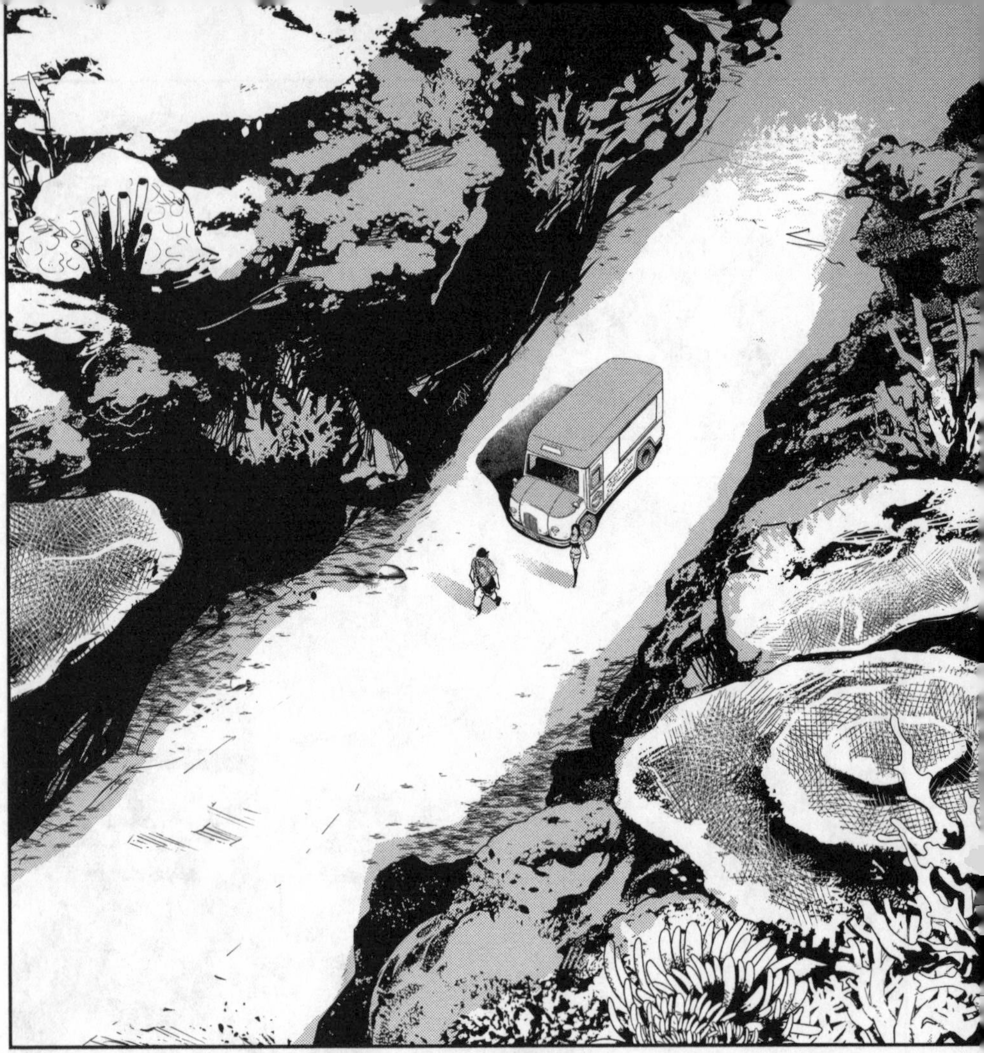
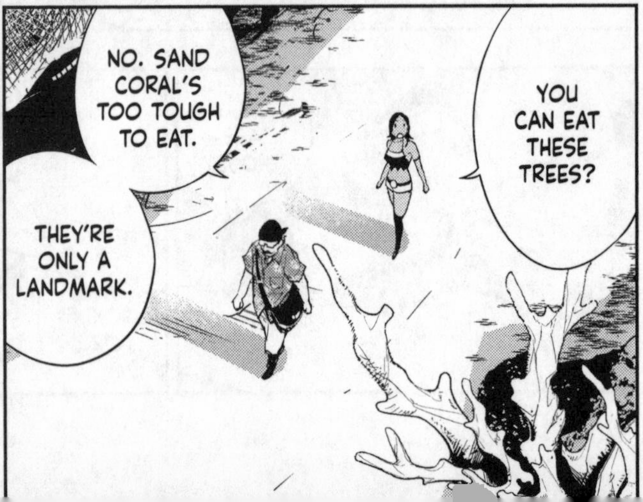
YOU CAN EAT THESE TREES?
NO. SAND CORAL'S TOO TOUGH TO EAT.
THEY'RE ONLY A LANDMARK.
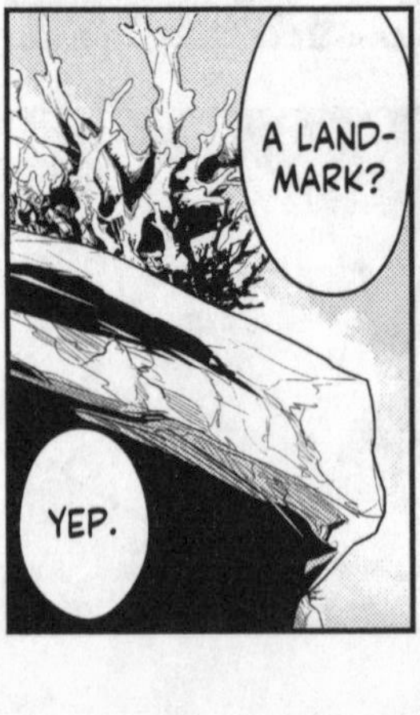
A LAND-MARK?
YEP.

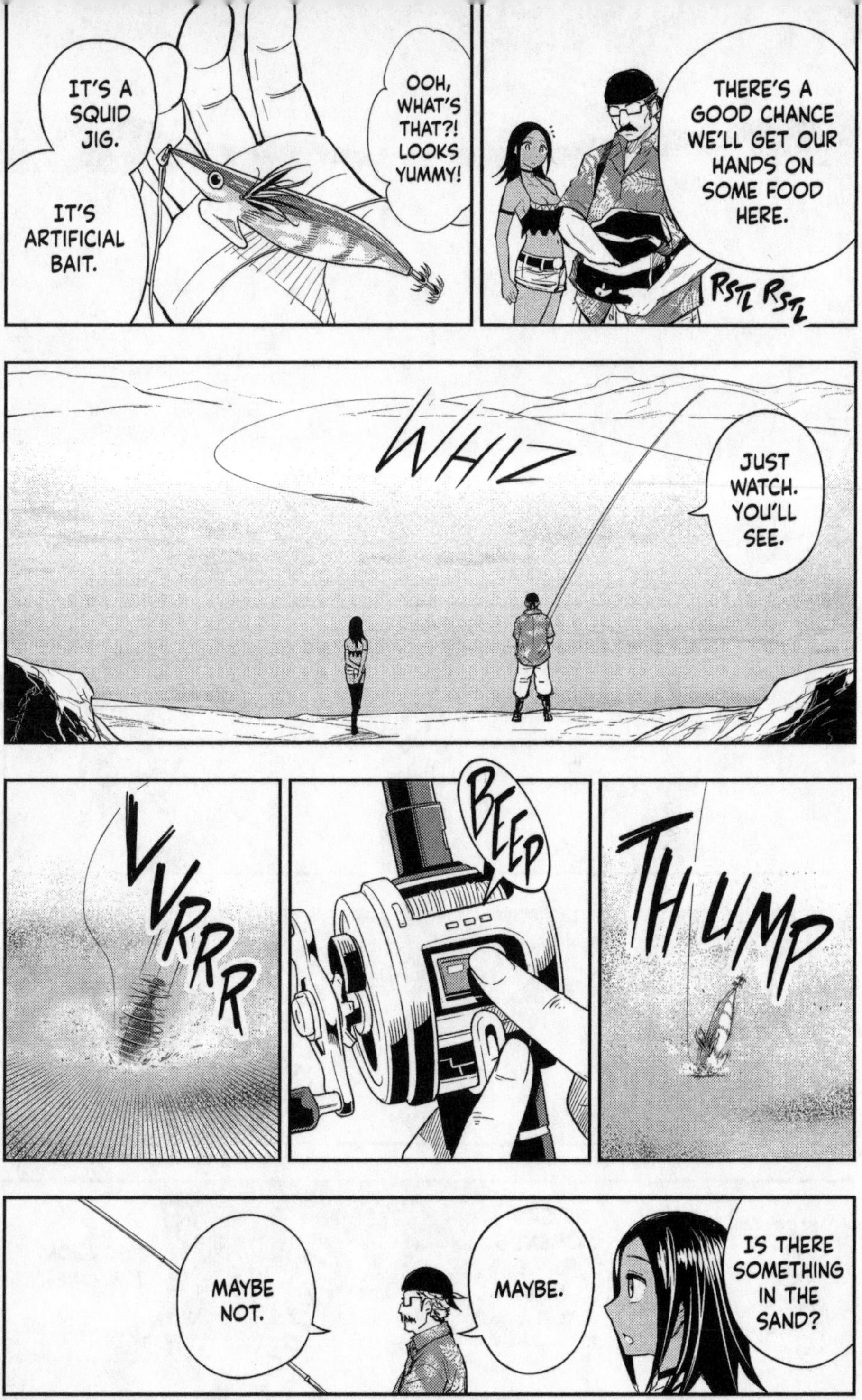
THERE'S A GOOD CHANCE WE'LL GET OUR HANDS ON SOME FOOD HERE.
RSTL RSTL
OOH, WHAT'S THAT?! LOOKS YUMMY!
IT'S A SQUID JIG.
IT'S ARTIFICIAL BAIT.
JUST WATCH. YOU'LL SEE.
WHIZ
THUMP
BEEP
VVRRRR
IS THERE SOMETHING IN THE SAND?
MAYBE.
MAYBE NOT.

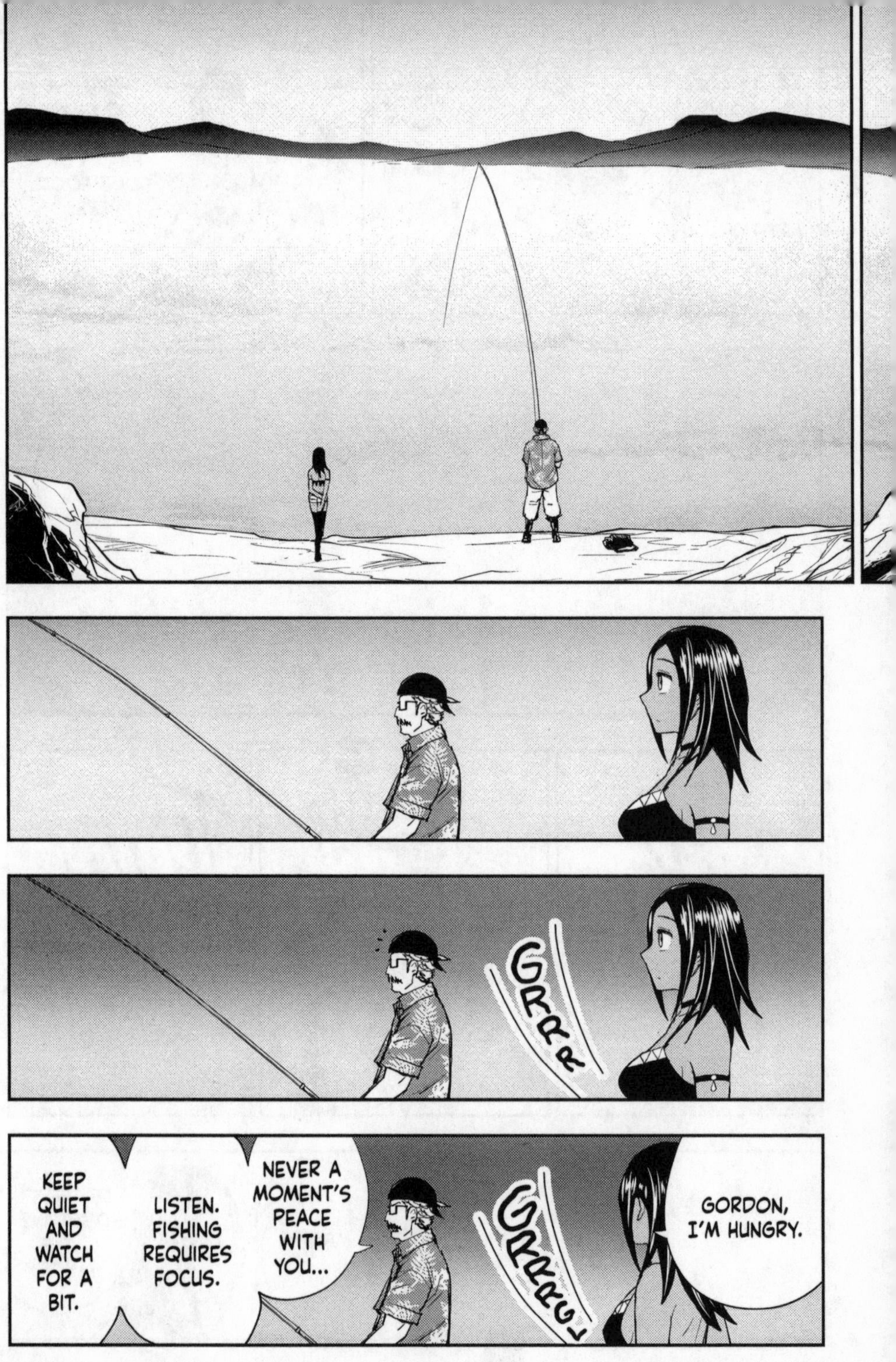
GRRR
GORDON, I'M HUNGRY.
GRRRGL
NEVER A MOMENT'S PEACE WITH YOU...
LISTEN. FISHING REQUIRES FOCUS.
KEEP QUIET AND WATCH FOR A BIT.

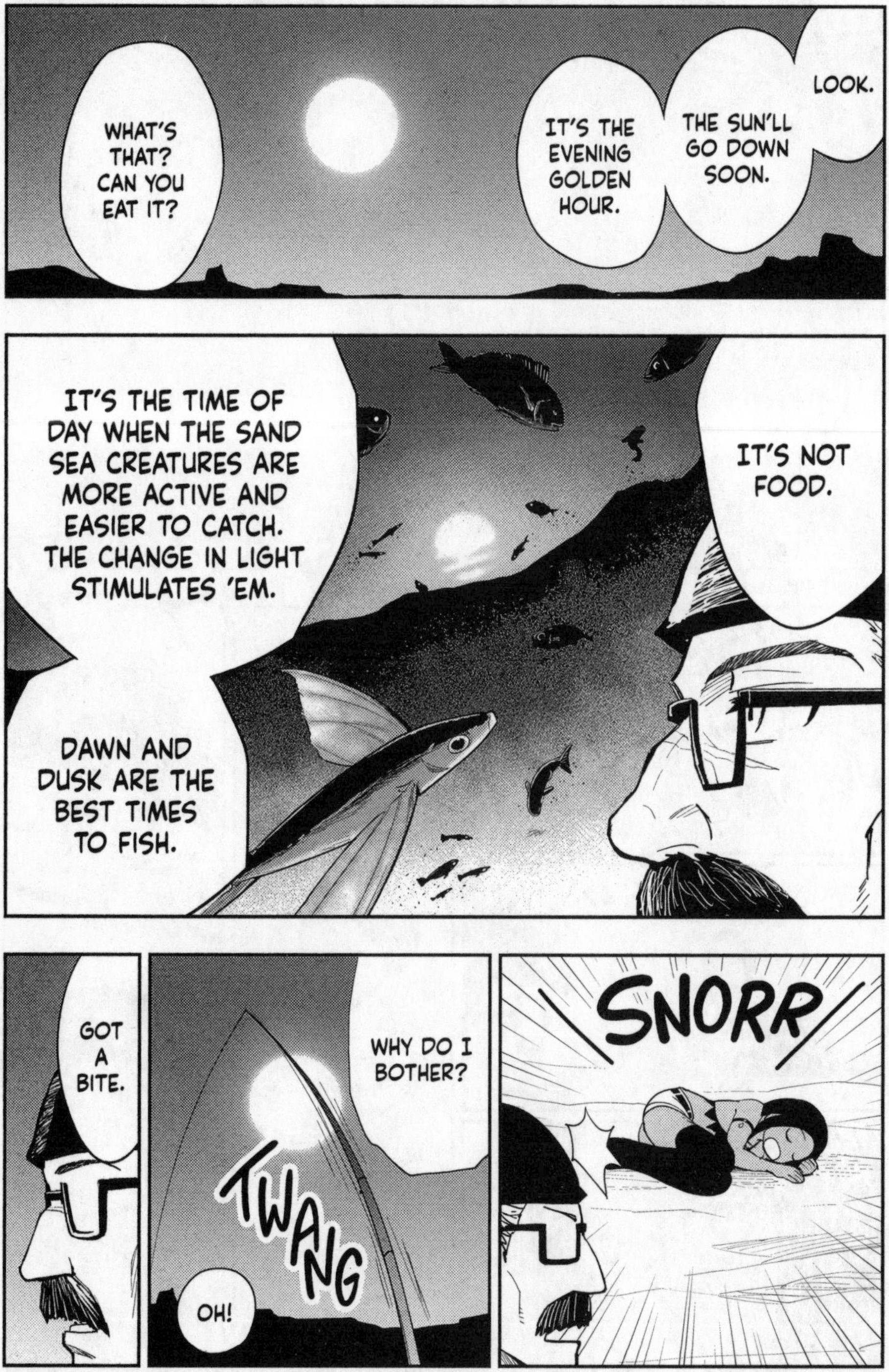
LOOK.
THE SUN'LL GO DOWN SOON.
IT'S THE EVENING GOLDEN HOUR.
WHAT'S THAT? CAN YOU EAT IT?
IT'S NOT FOOD.
IT'S THE TIME OF DAY WHEN THE SAND SEA CREATURES ARE MORE ACTIVE AND EASIER TO CATCH. THE CHANGE IN LIGHT STIMULATES 'EM.
DAWN AND DUSK ARE THE BEST TIMES TO FISH.
SNORR
WHY DO I BOTHER?
TWANG
OH!
GOT A BITE.

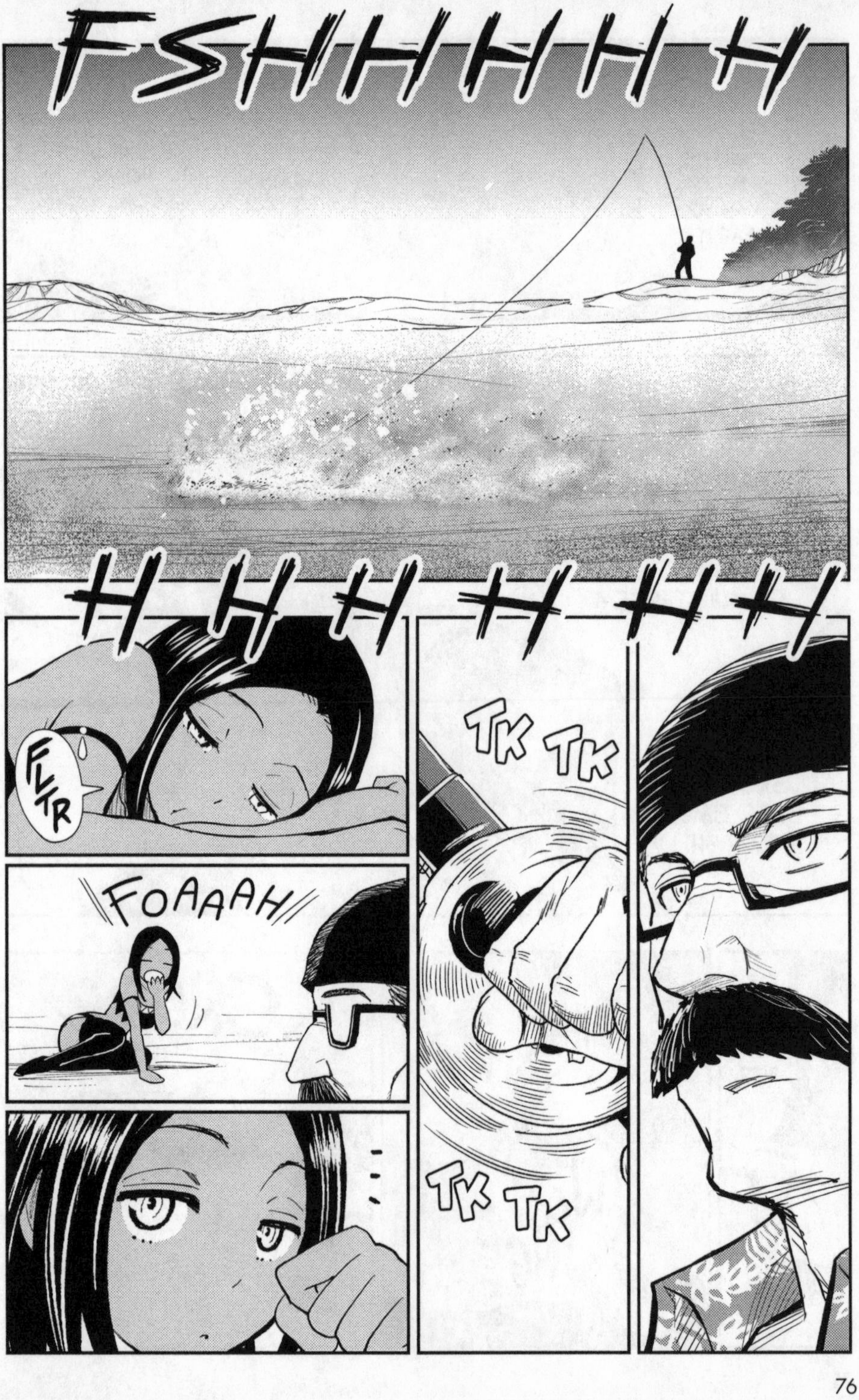
FSHHHHHHH
HHHHHHHH
TK TK
TK TK
FLTR
FOAAAH
...

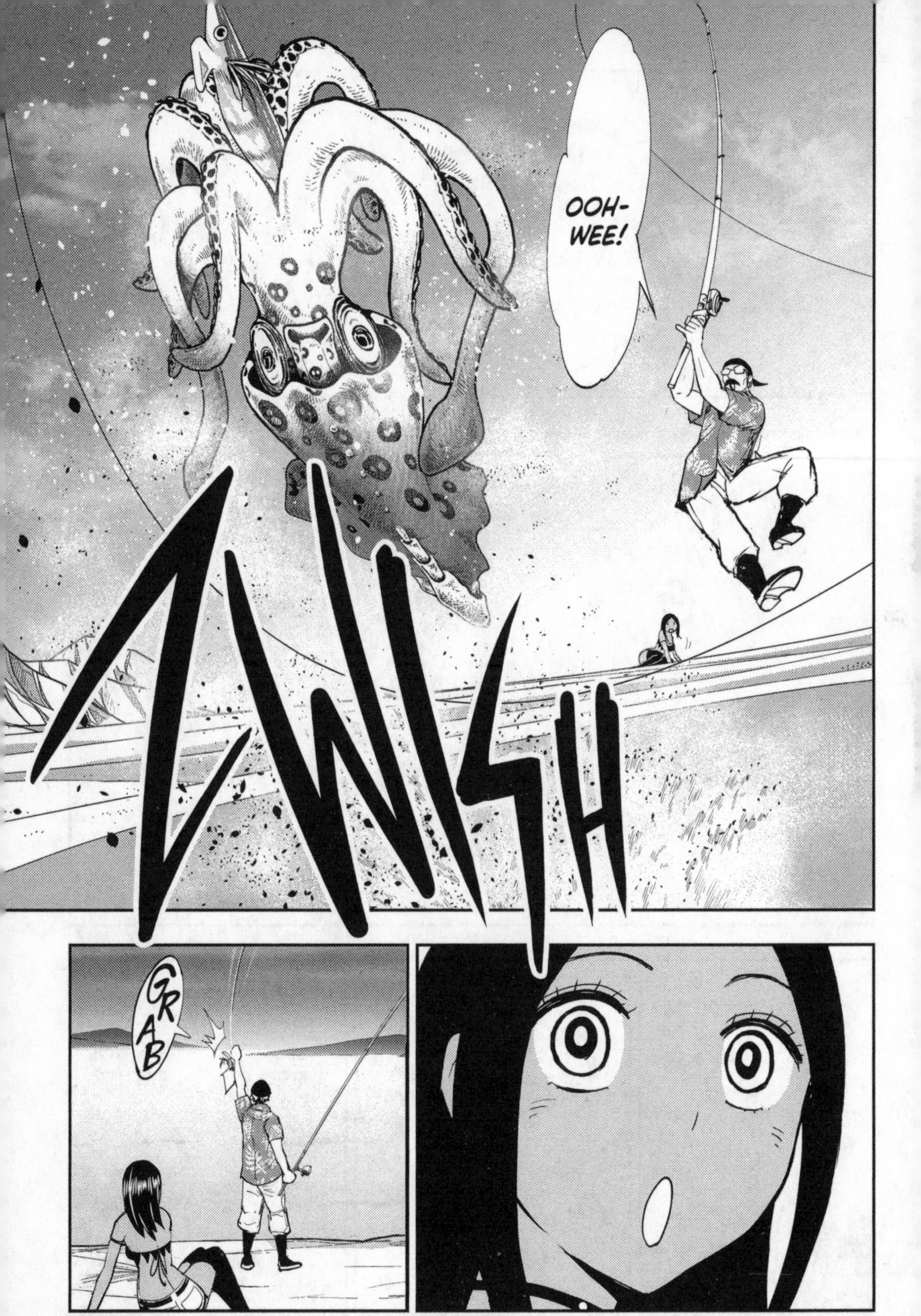
OOH-WEE!
ZWISH
GRAB

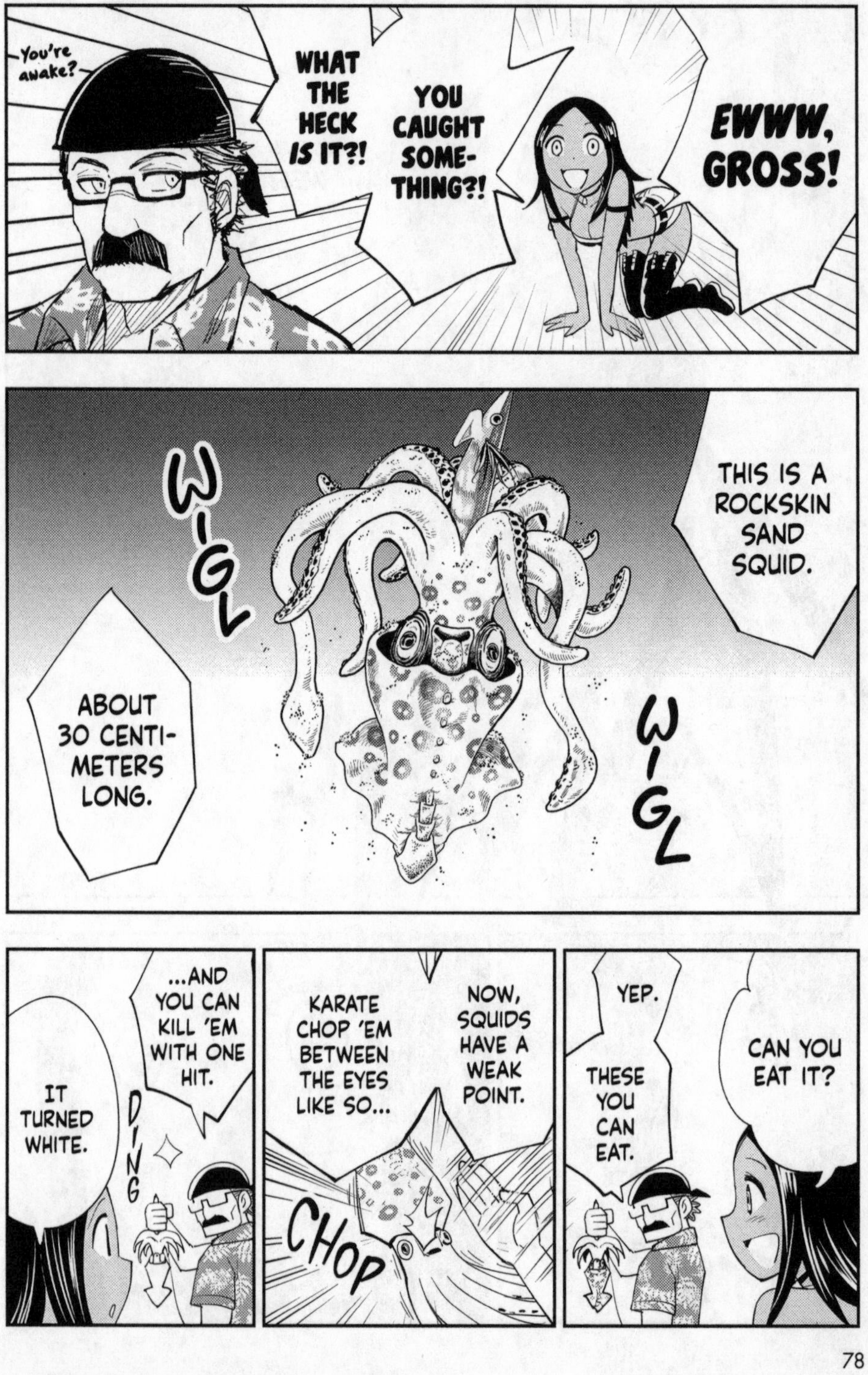
EWWW, GROSS!
YOU CAUGHT SOME-THING?!
WHAT THE HECK IS IT?!
You're awake?
THIS IS A ROCKSKIN SAND SQUID.
WIGL
WIGL
ABOUT 30 CENTI-METERS LONG.
CAN YOU EAT IT?
YEP.
THESE YOU CAN EAT.
NOW, SQUIDS HAVE A WEAK POINT.
KARATE CHOP 'EM BETWEEN THE EYES LIKE SO...
CHOP
...AND YOU CAN KILL 'EM WITH ONE HIT.
DING
IT TURNED WHITE.

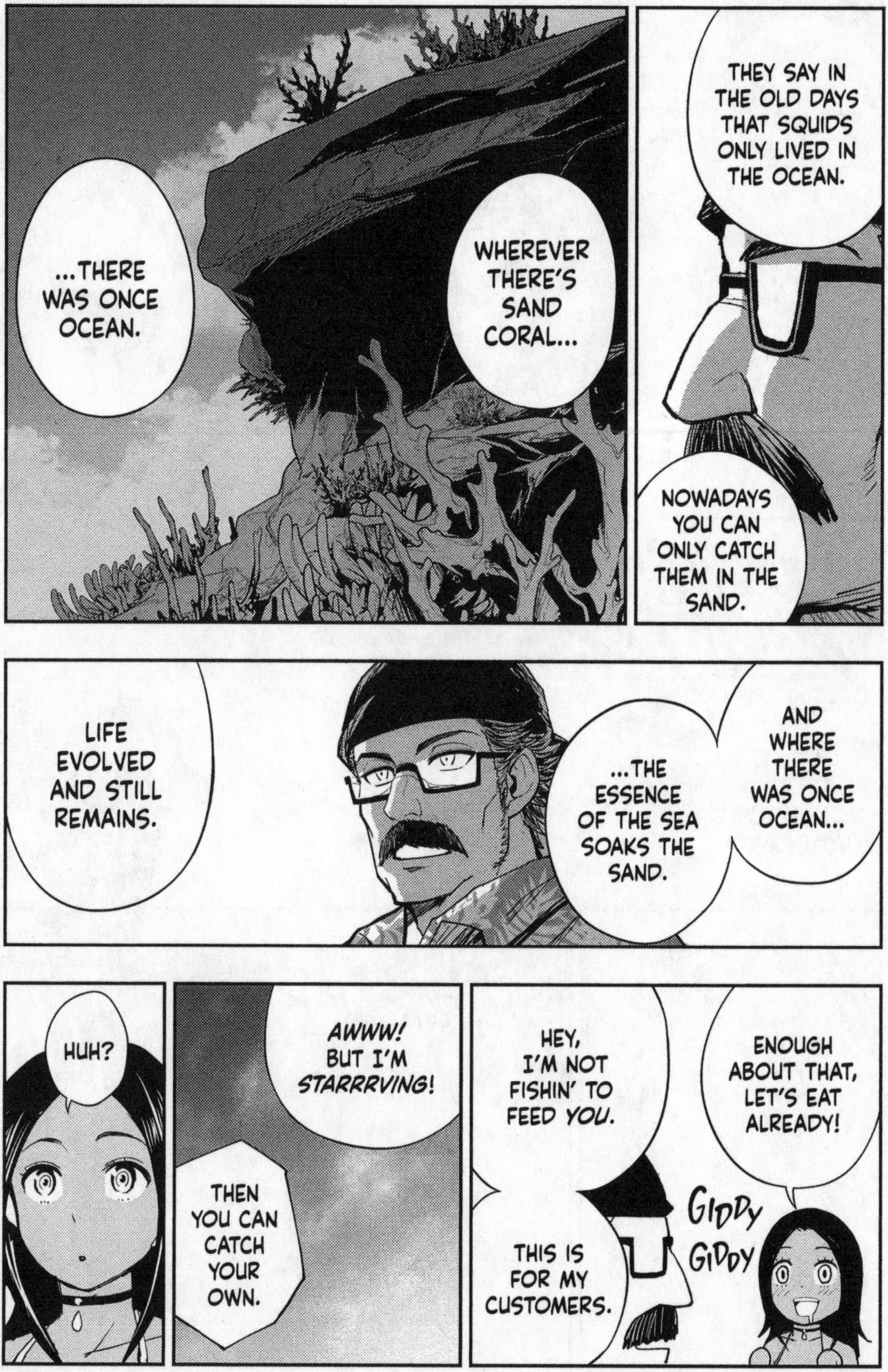
THEY SAY IN THE OLD DAYS THAT SQUIDS ONLY LIVED IN THE OCEAN.
NOWADAYS YOU CAN ONLY CATCH THEM IN THE SAND.
WHEREVER THERE'S SAND CORAL...
...THERE WAS ONCE OCEAN.
AND WHERE THERE WAS ONCE OCEAN...
...THE ESSENCE OF THE SEA SOAKS THE SAND.
LIFE EVOLVED AND STILL REMAINS.
ENOUGH ABOUT THAT, LET'S EAT ALREADY!
GIDDY GIDDY
HEY, I'M NOT FISHIN' TO FEED *YOU*.
THIS IS FOR MY CUSTOMERS.
AWWW! BUT I'M *STARRRVING!*
THEN YOU CAN CATCH YOUR OWN.
HUH?

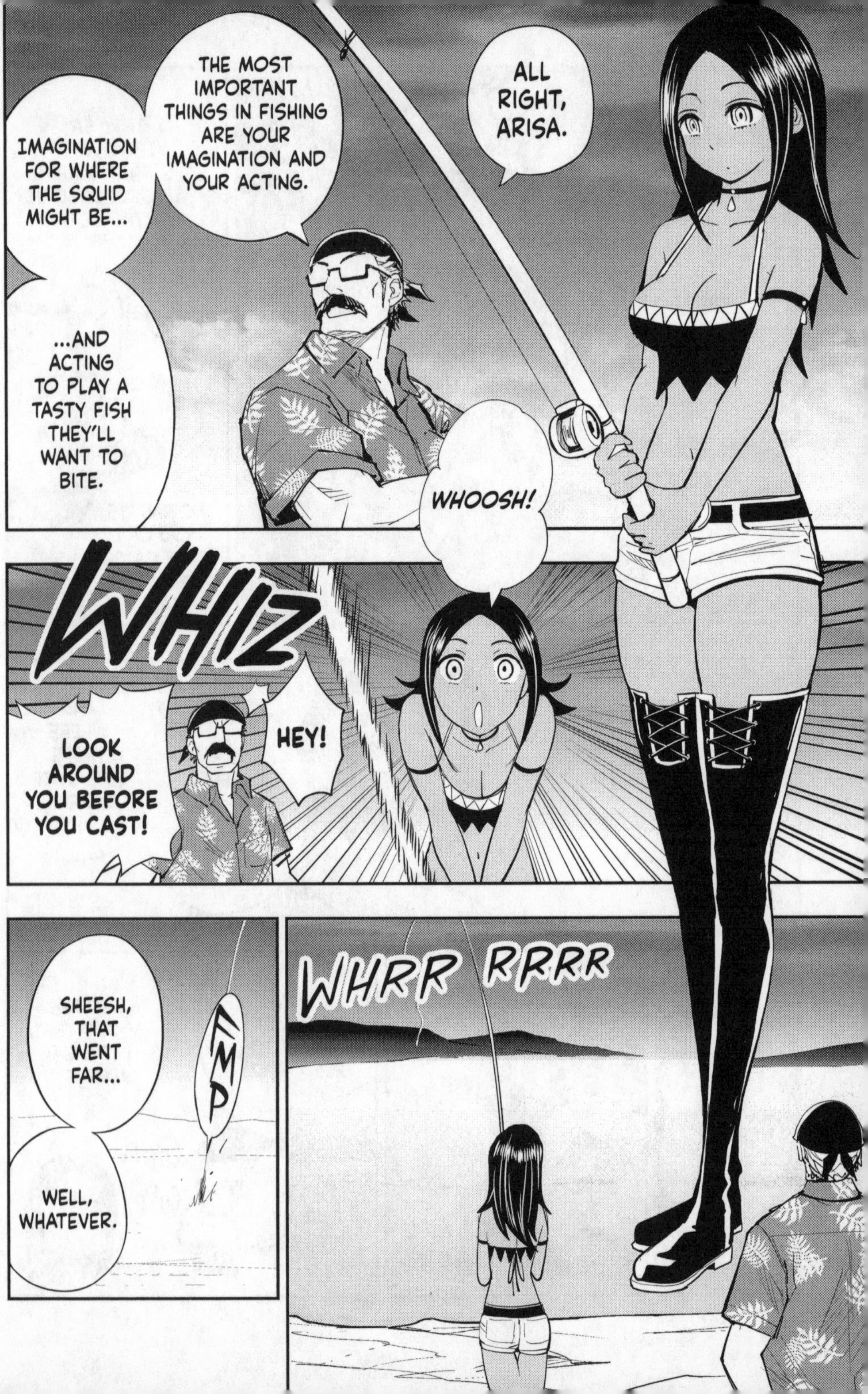
ALL RIGHT, ARISA.
THE MOST IMPORTANT THINGS IN FISHING ARE YOUR IMAGINATION AND YOUR ACTING.
IMAGINATION FOR WHERE THE SQUID MIGHT BE...
...AND ACTING TO PLAY A TASTY FISH THEY'LL WANT TO BITE.
WHOOSH!
WHIZ
HEY!
LOOK AROUND YOU BEFORE YOU CAST!
WHRR RRRR
FMP
SHEESH, THAT WENT FAR...
WELL, WHATEVER.

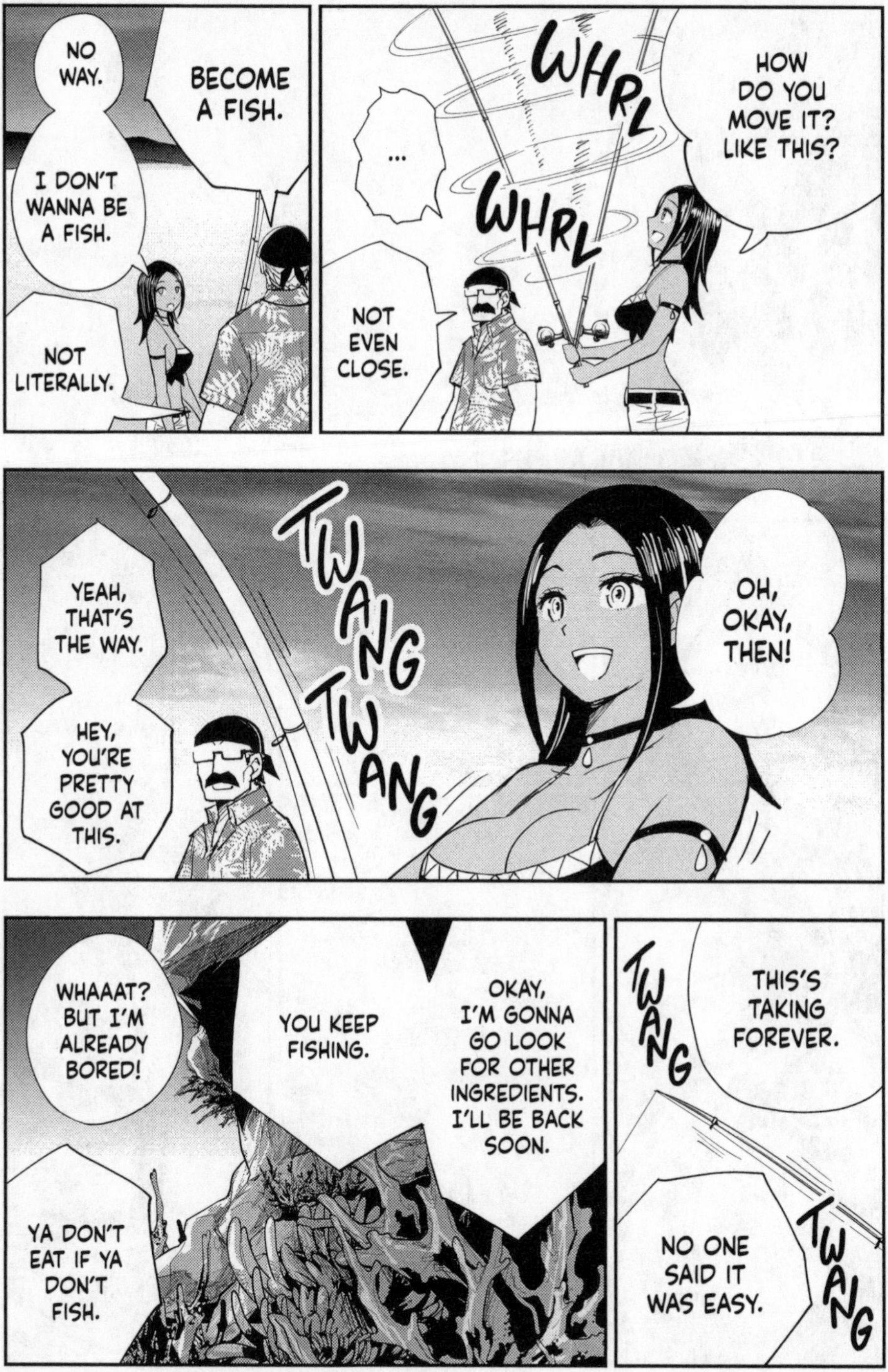
HOW DO YOU MOVE IT? LIKE THIS?
WHRL
WHRL
...
NOT EVEN CLOSE.
BECOME A FISH.
NO WAY.
I DON'T WANNA BE A FISH.
NOT LITERALLY.
OH, OKAY, THEN!
TWANG
TWANG
YEAH, THAT'S THE WAY.
HEY, YOU'RE PRETTY GOOD AT THIS.
THIS'S TAKING FOREVER.
TWANG
TWANG
NO ONE SAID IT WAS EASY.
OKAY, I'M GONNA GO LOOK FOR OTHER INGREDIENTS. I'LL BE BACK SOON.
YOU KEEP FISHING.
WHAAAT? BUT I'M ALREADY BORED!
YA DON'T EAT IF YA DON'T FISH.

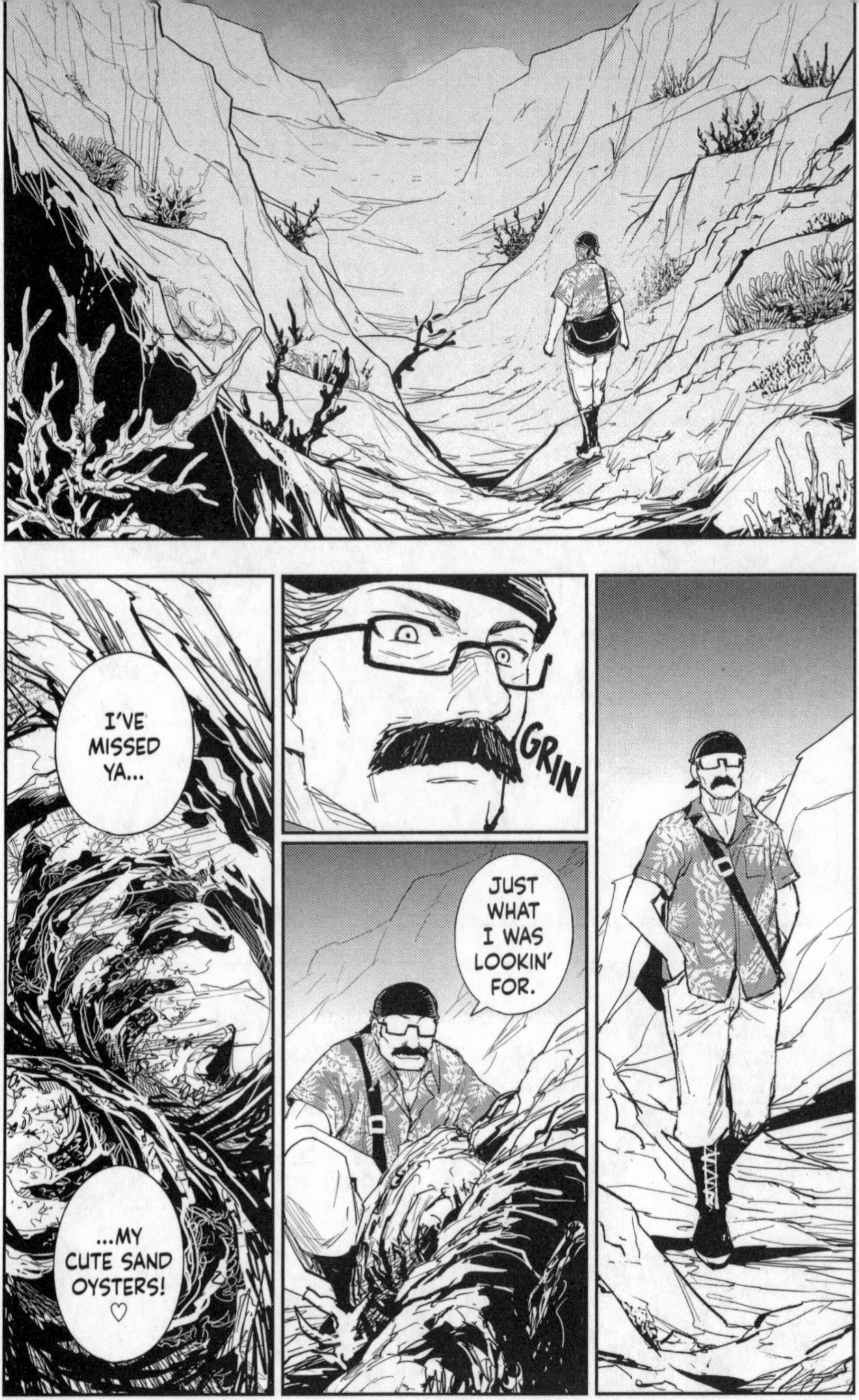
GRIN
JUST WHAT I WAS LOOKIN' FOR.
I'VE MISSED YA...
...MY CUTE SAND OYSTERS! ♡

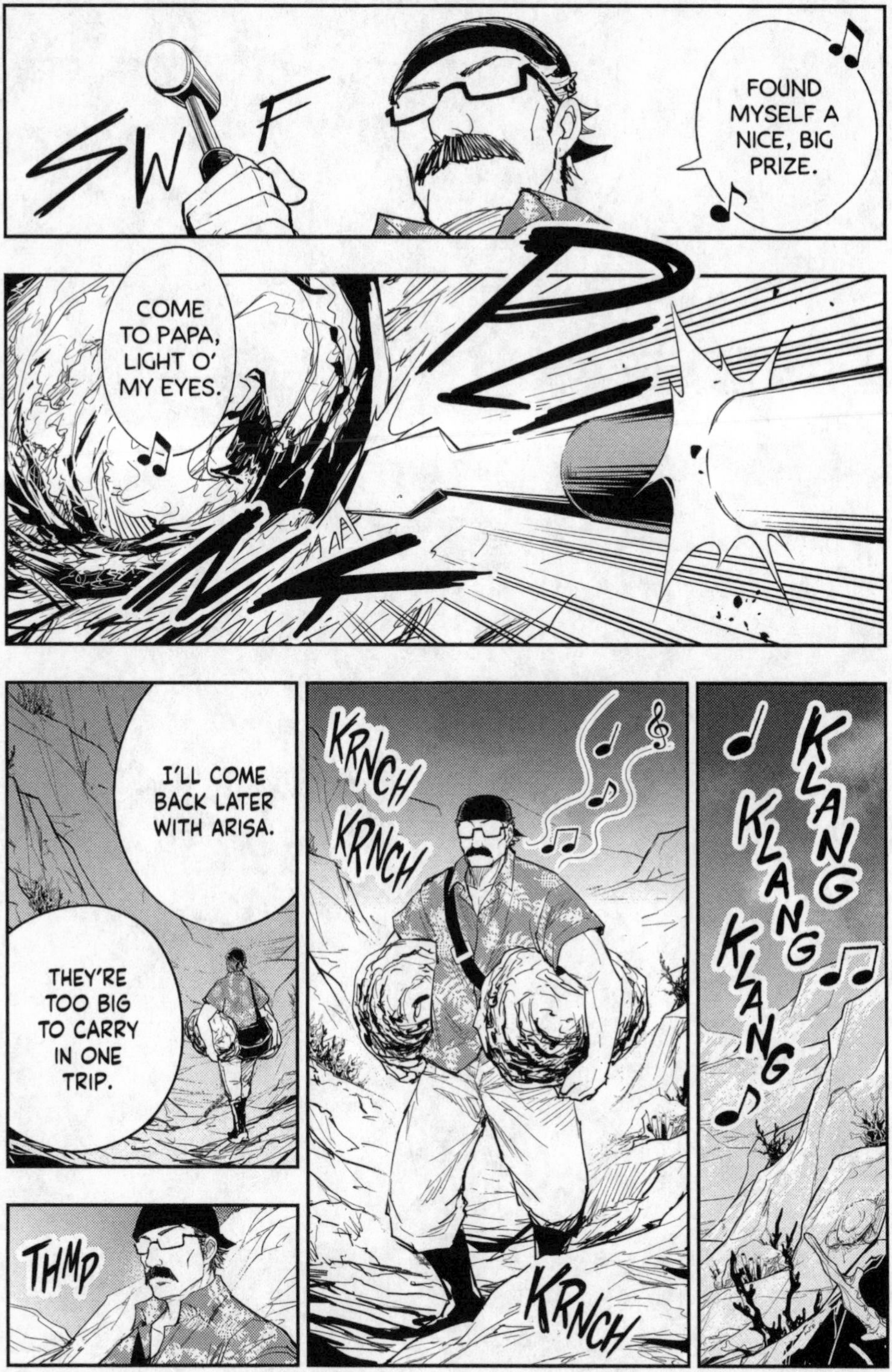
FOUND MYSELF A NICE, BIG PRIZE.
SWF
DINK
COME TO PAPA, LIGHT O' MY EYES.
KLANG
KLANG
KLANG
KRNCH
KRNCH
KRNCH
I'LL COME BACK LATER WITH ARISA.
THEY'RE TOO BIG TO CARRY IN ONE TRIP.
THMP

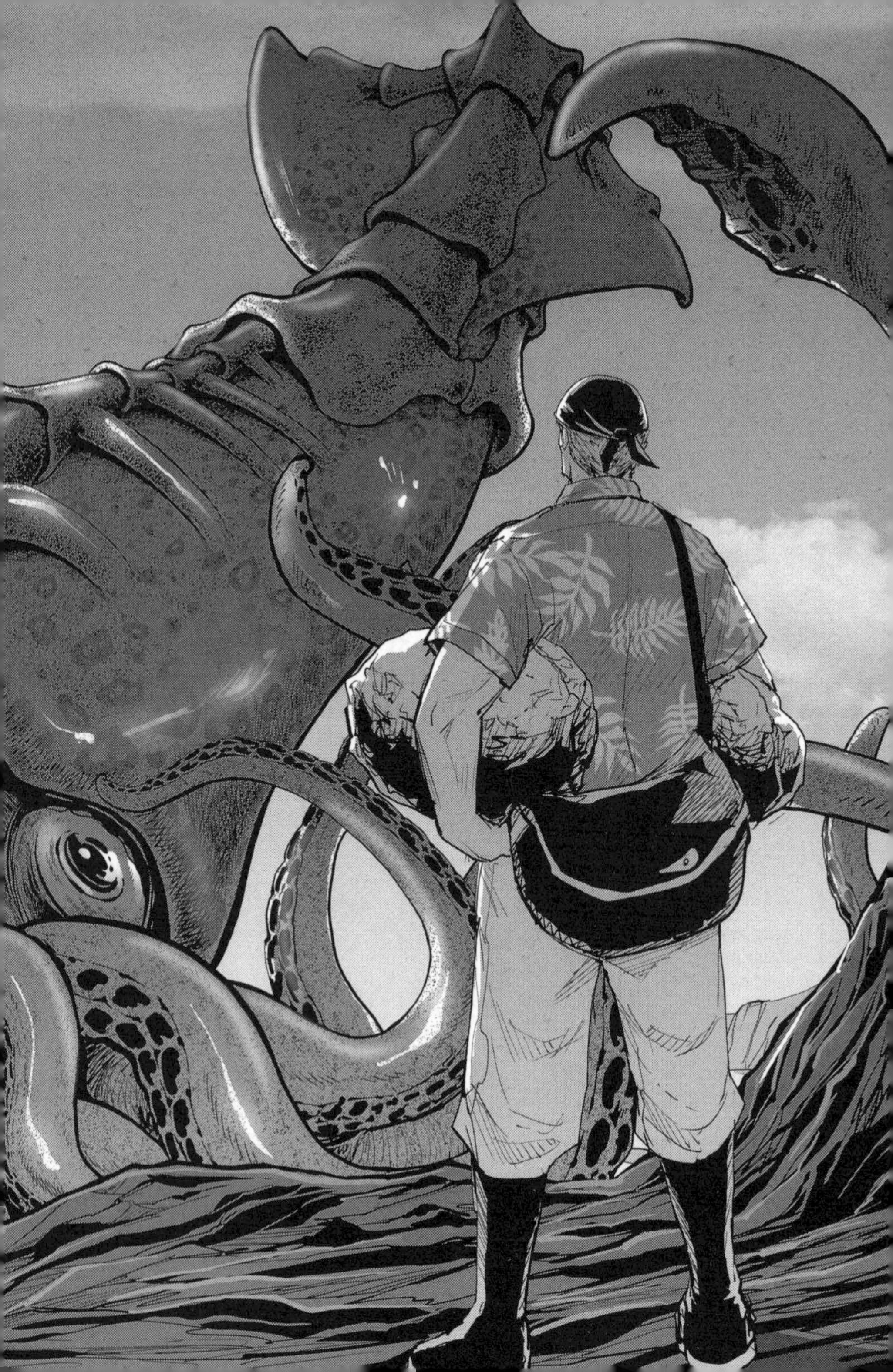

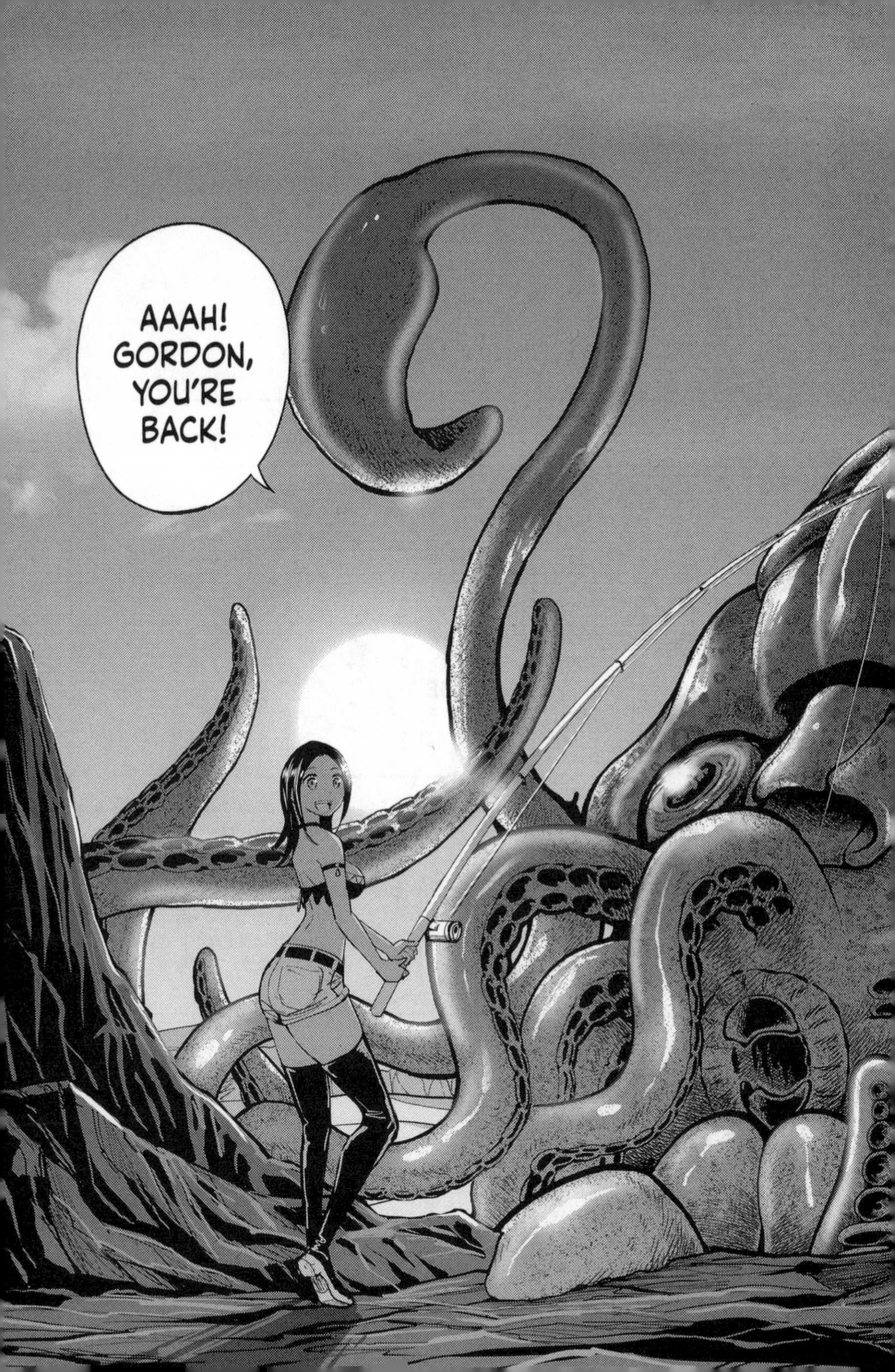
AAAH! GORDON, YOU'RE BACK!

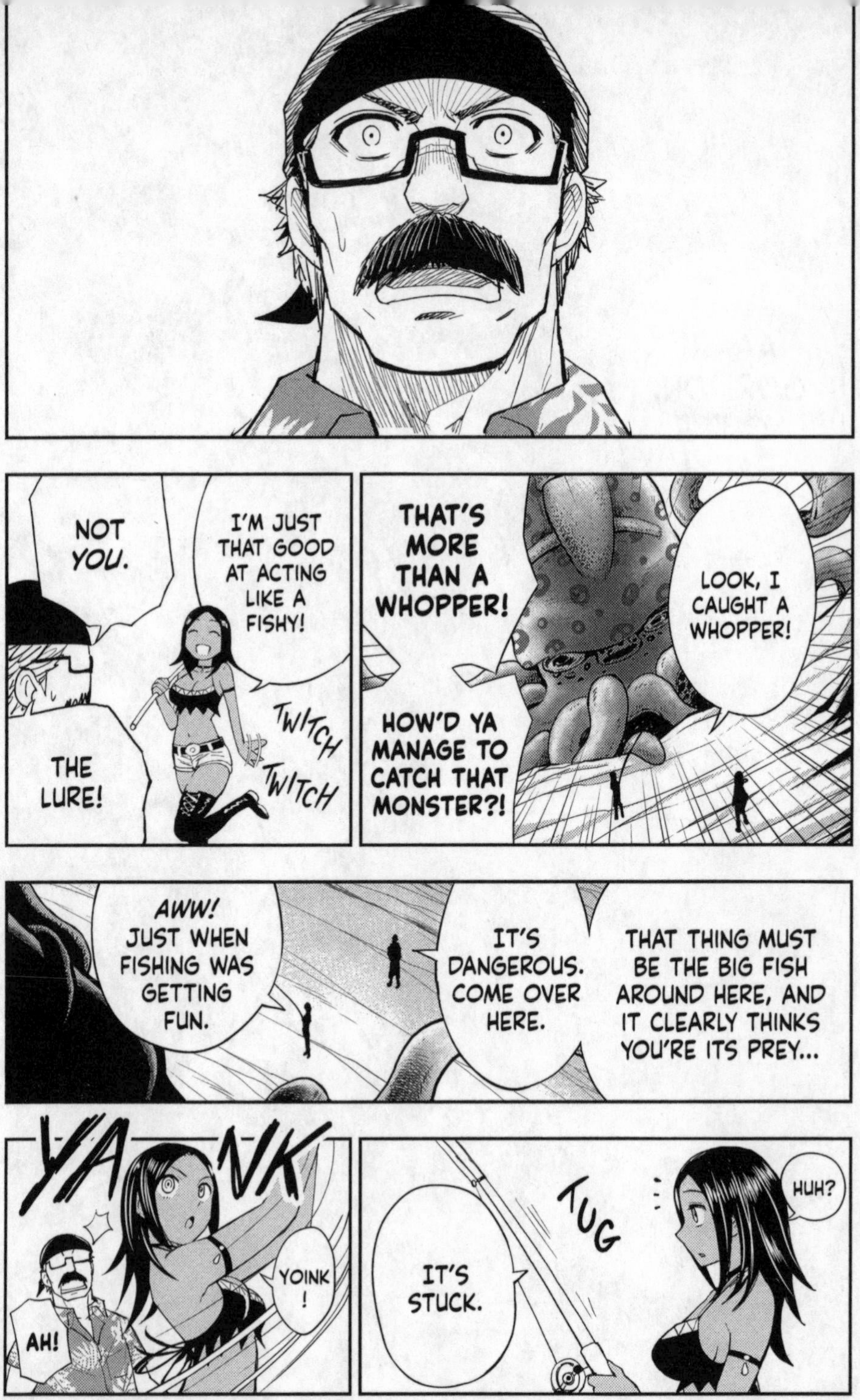
LOOK, I CAUGHT A WHOPPER!
THAT'S MORE THAN A WHOPPER!
HOW'D YA MANAGE TO CATCH THAT MONSTER?!
I'M JUST THAT GOOD AT ACTING LIKE A FISHY!
NOT YOU.
THE LURE!
TWITCH
TWITCH
THAT THING MUST BE THE BIG FISH AROUND HERE, AND IT CLEARLY THINKS YOU'RE ITS PREY...
IT'S DANGEROUS. COME OVER HERE.
AWW! JUST WHEN FISHING WAS GETTING FUN.
HUH?
TUG
IT'S STUCK.
YANK
YOINK!
AH!

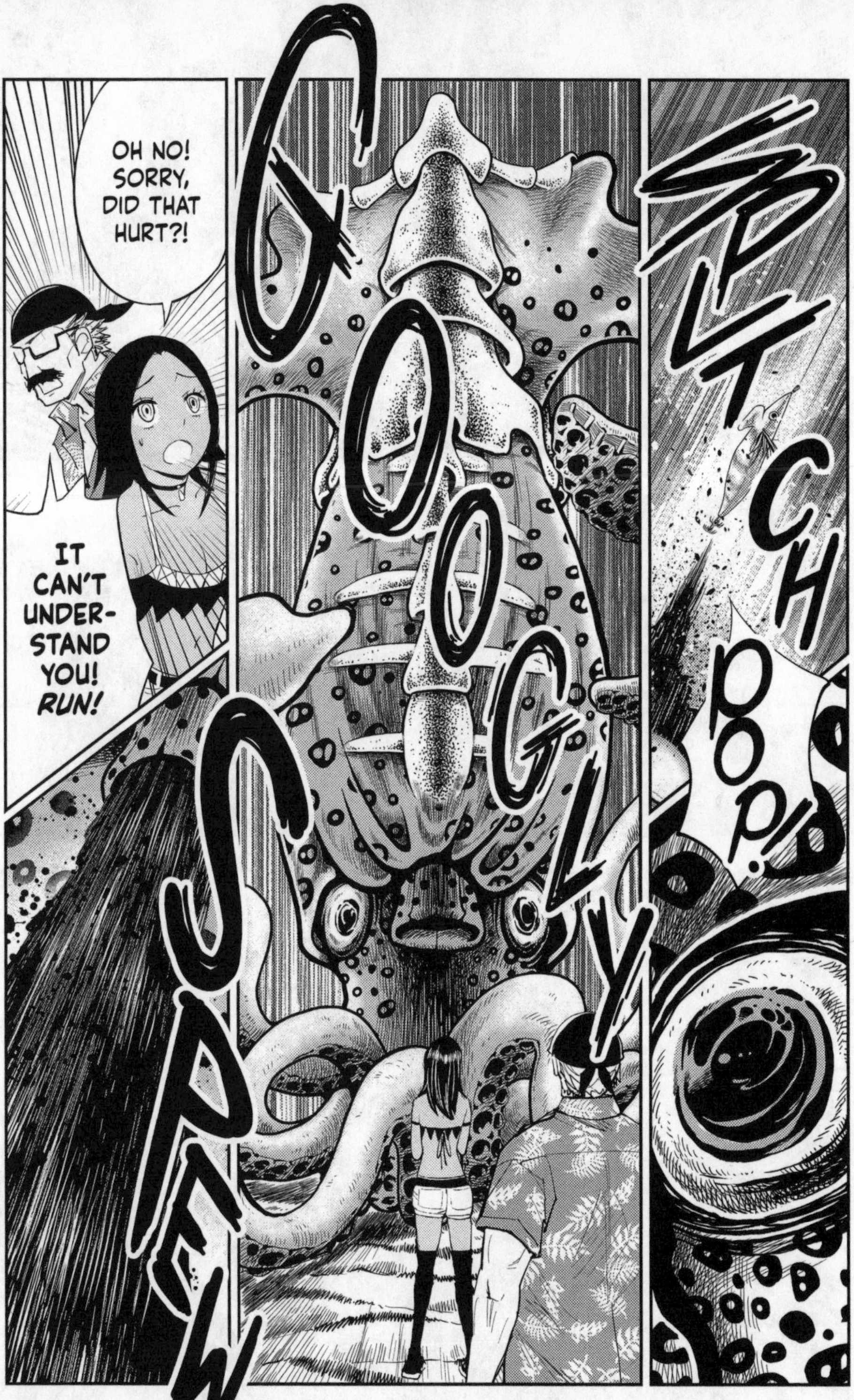
SPLTCH
POP!
GOOGLY
SPEW
OH NO! SORRY, DID THAT HURT?!
IT CAN'T UNDER-STAND YOU! *RUN!*

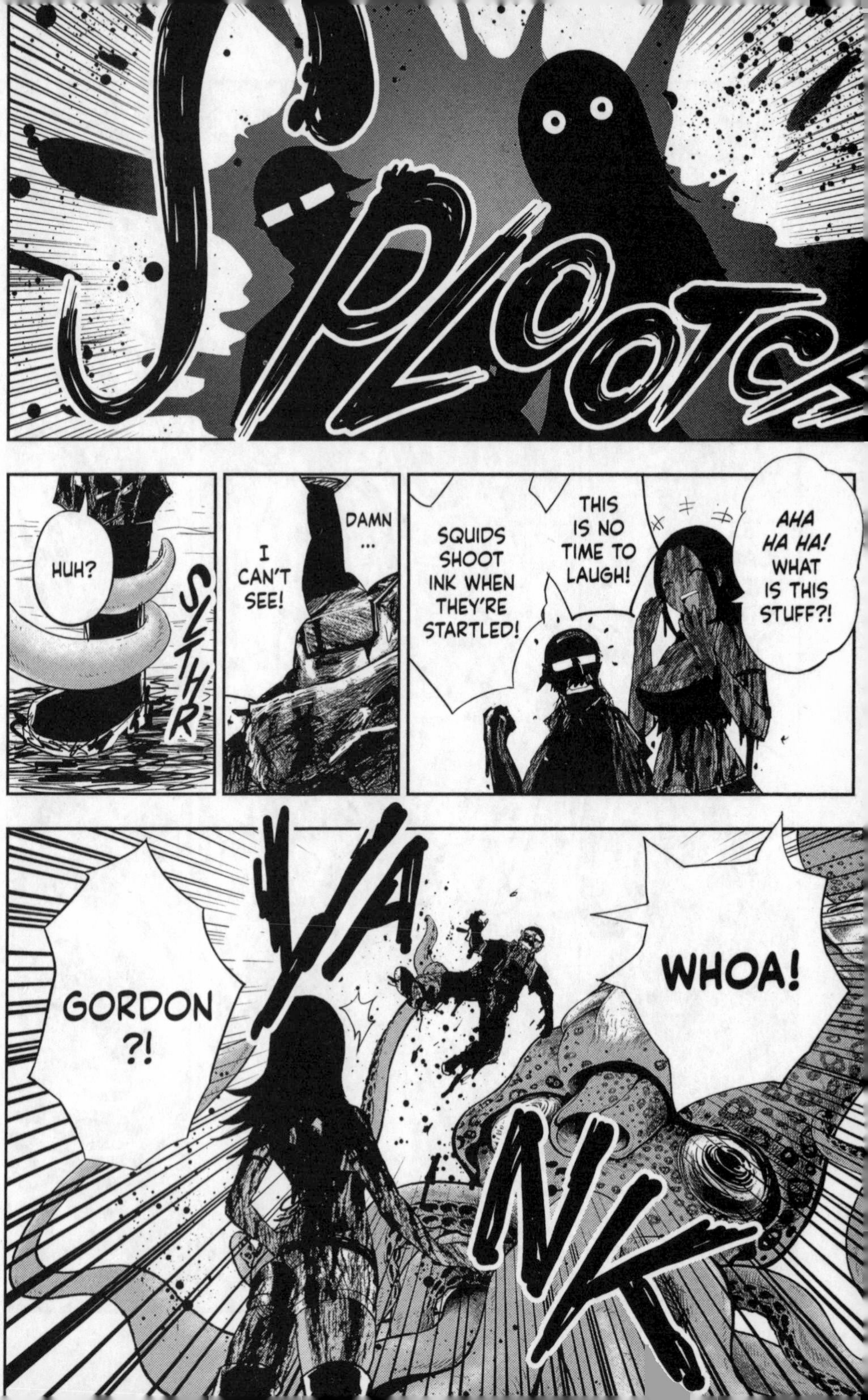
SPLOOTCH
AHA HA HA! WHAT IS THIS STUFF?!
THIS IS NO TIME TO LAUGH!
SQUIDS SHOOT INK WHEN THEY'RE STARTLED!
DAMN ...
I CAN'T SEE!
SLTHR
HUH?
WHOA!
YANK
GORDON ?!

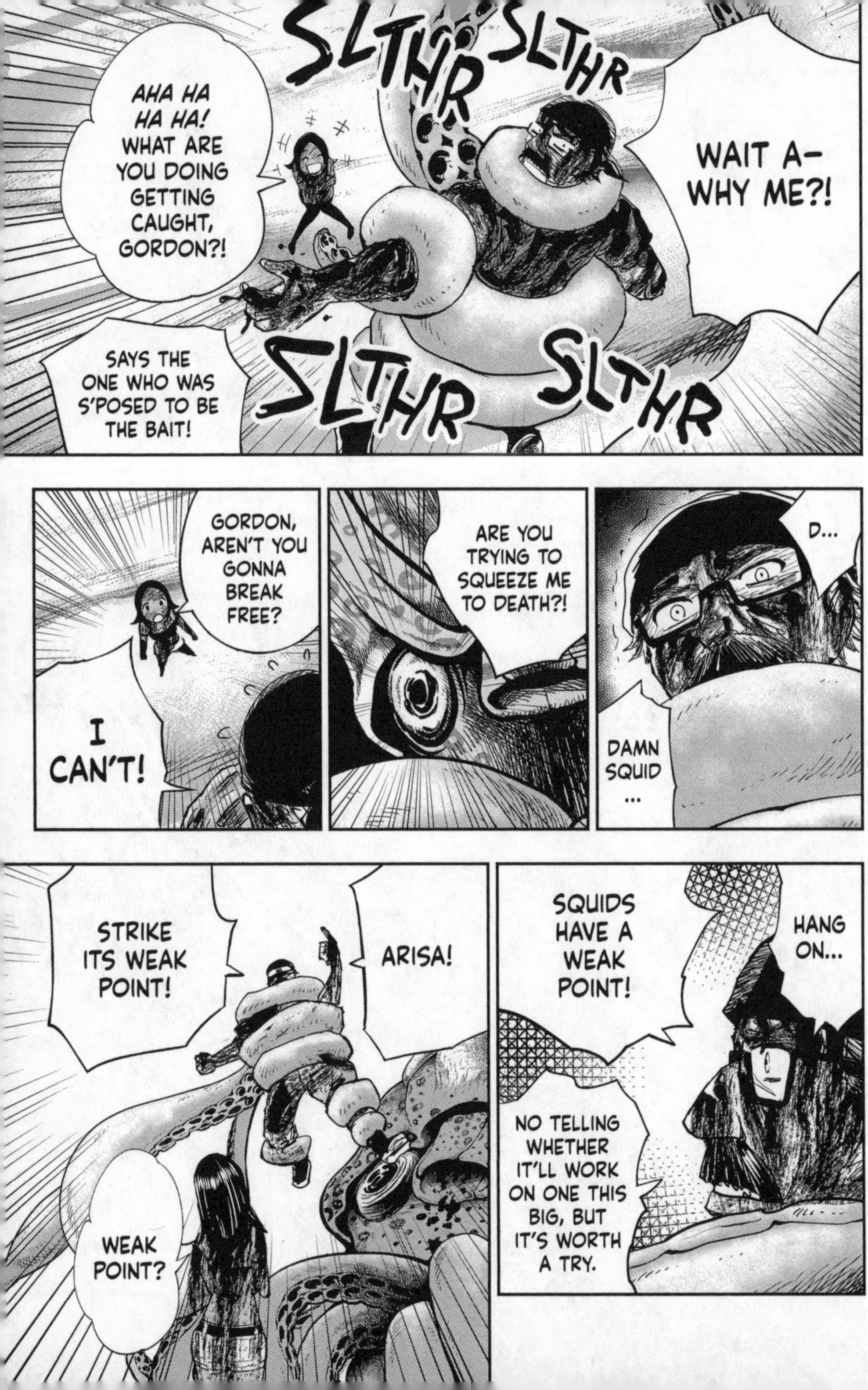
SLTHR SLTHR
WAIT A- WHY ME?!
AHA HA HA HA! WHAT ARE YOU DOING GETTING CAUGHT, GORDON?!
SLTHR SLTHR
SAYS THE ONE WHO WAS S'POSED TO BE THE BAIT!
D...
DAMN SQUID ...
ARE YOU TRYING TO SQUEEZE ME TO DEATH?!
GORDON, AREN'T YOU GONNA BREAK FREE?
I CAN'T!
HANG ON...
SQUIDS HAVE A WEAK POINT!
NO TELLING WHETHER IT'LL WORK ON ONE THIS BIG, BUT IT'S WORTH A TRY.
ARISA!
STRIKE ITS WEAK POINT!
WEAK POINT?

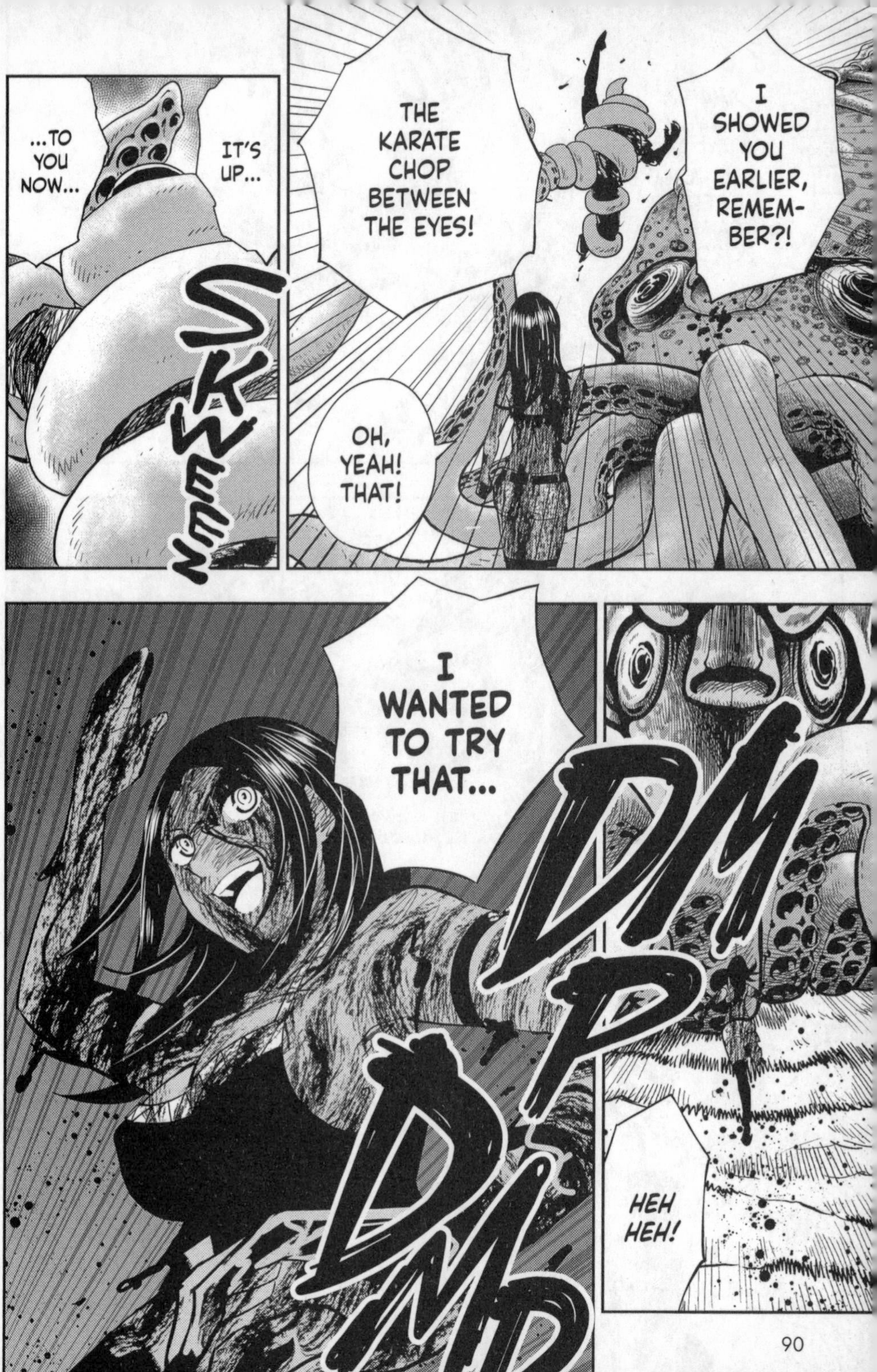
I SHOWED YOU EARLIER, REMEMBER?!
THE KARATE CHOP BETWEEN THE EYES!
OH, YEAH! THAT!
IT'S UP...
...TO YOU NOW...
SKWEEN
HEH HEH!
I WANTED TO TRY THAT...
DMP DMP

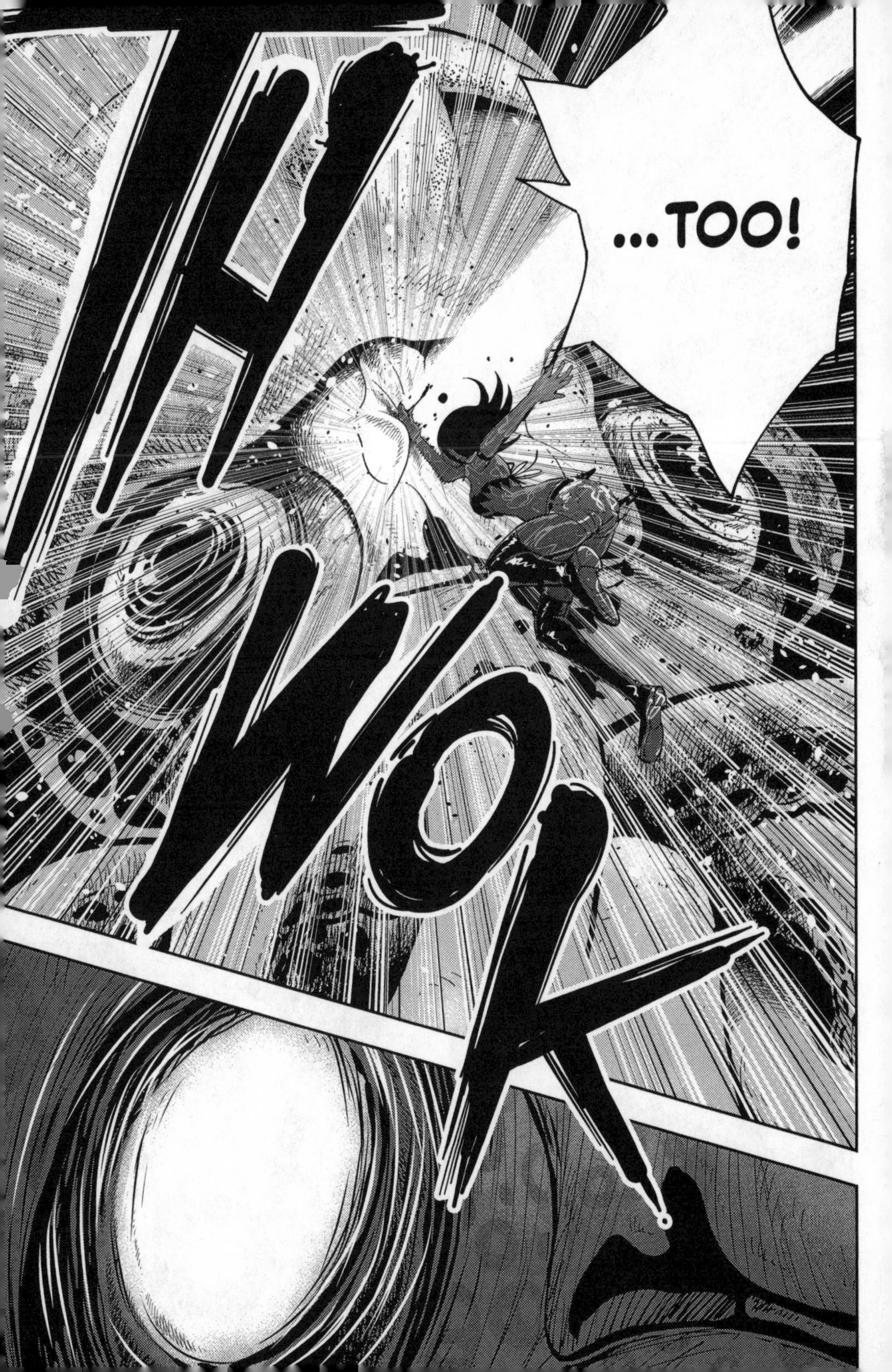
...TOO!
THWOK

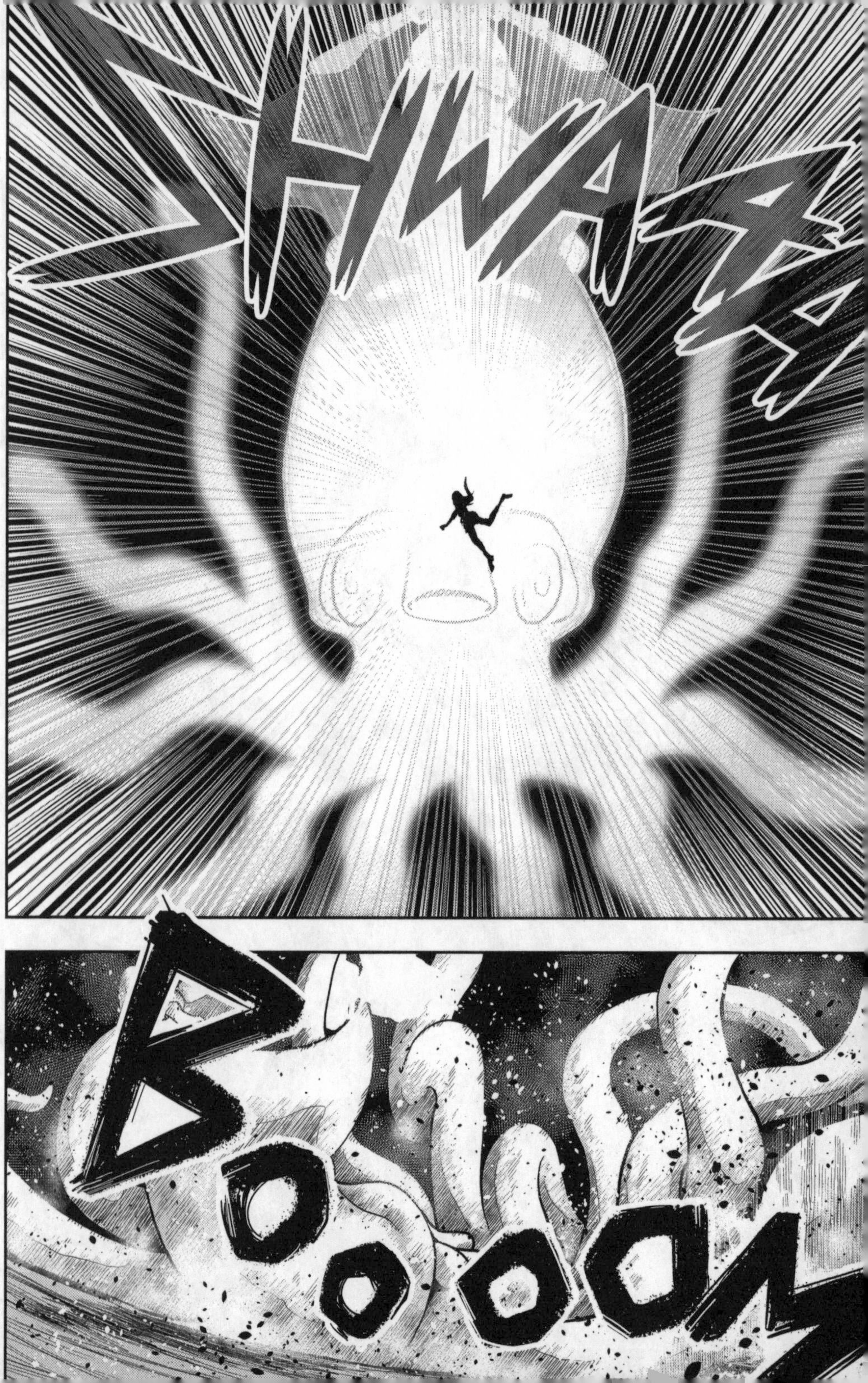
SHWAAA
BOOOOM

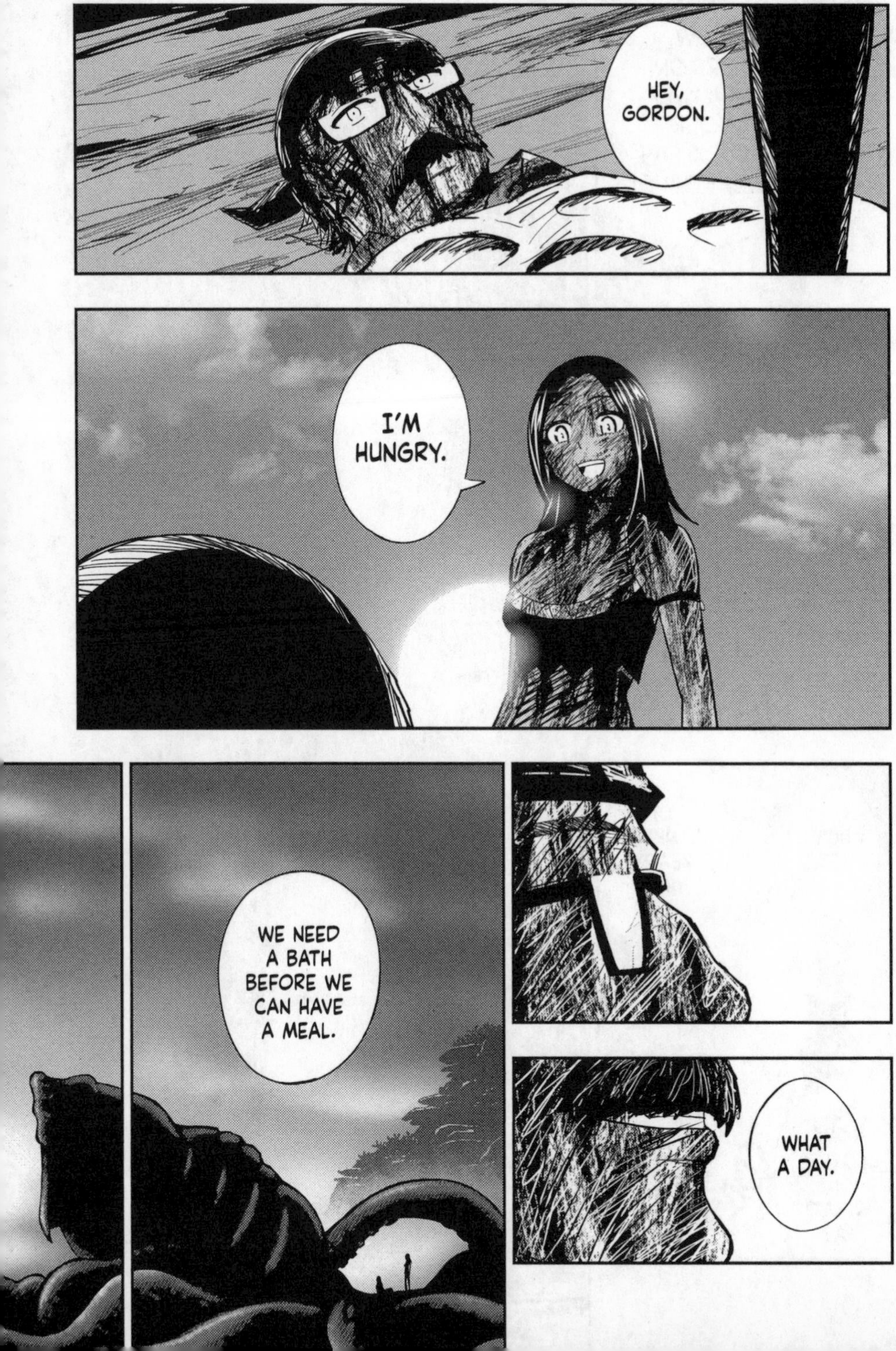
HEY, GORDON.
I'M HUNGRY.
WHAT A DAY.
WE NEED A BATH BEFORE WE CAN HAVE A MEAL.

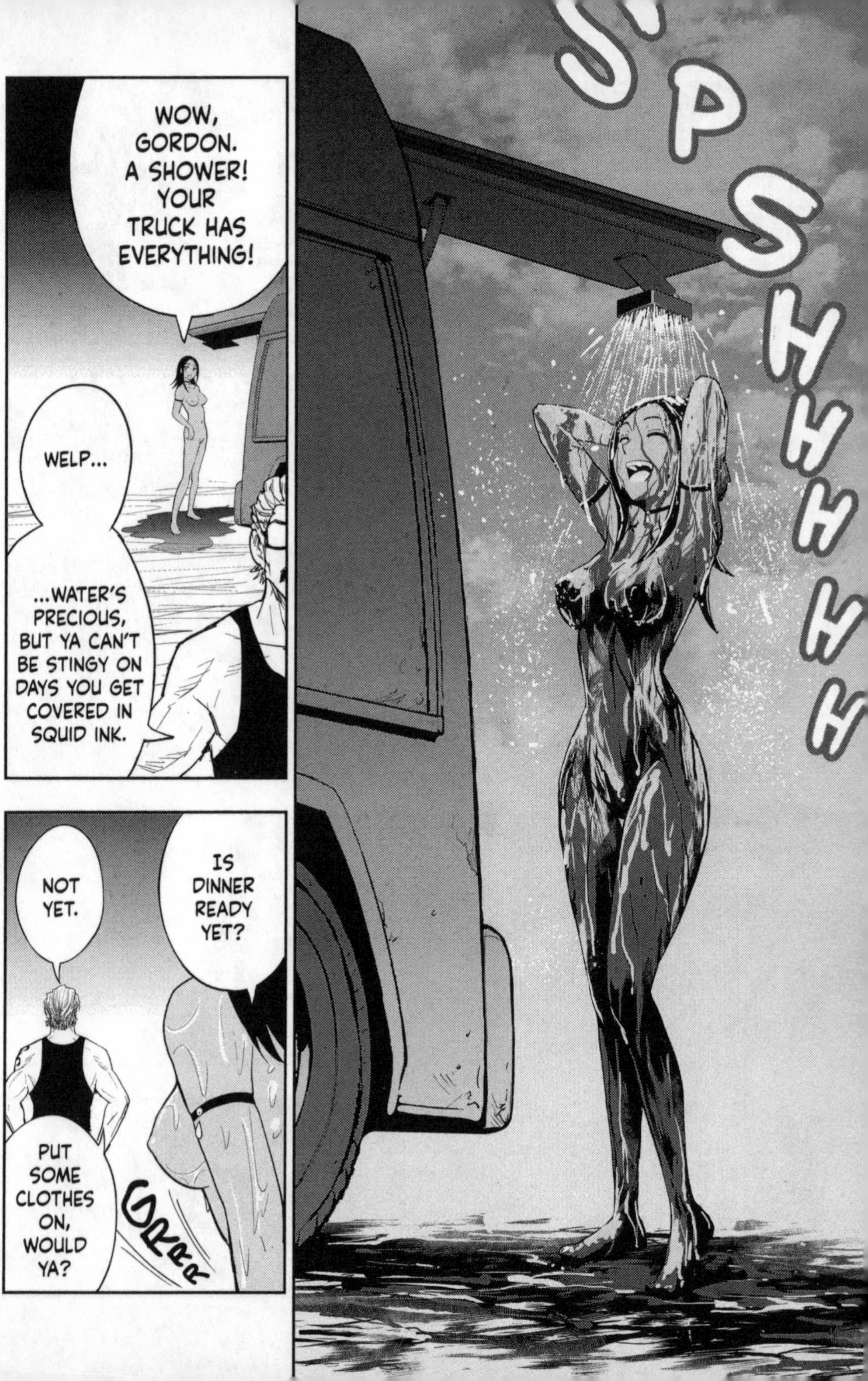
SPSHHHHH
WOW, GORDON. A SHOWER! YOUR TRUCK HAS EVERYTHING!
WELP...
...WATER'S PRECIOUS, BUT YA CAN'T BE STINGY ON DAYS YOU GET COVERED IN SQUID INK.
IS DINNER READY YET?
NOT YET.
GRRR
PUT SOME CLOTHES ON, WOULD YA?

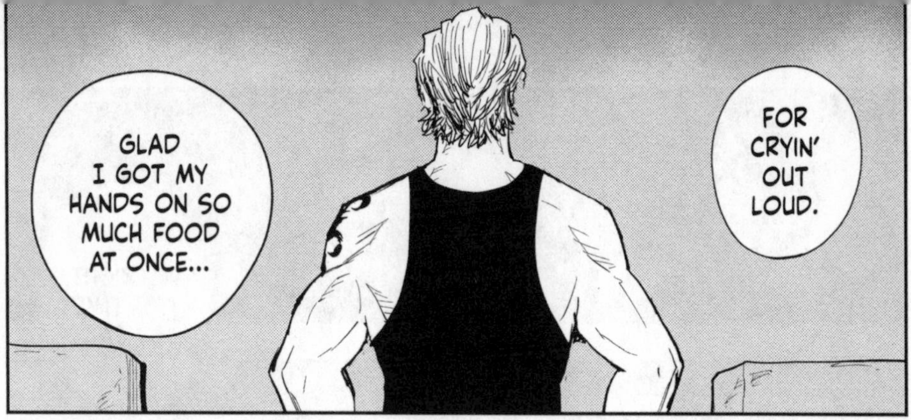
FOR CRYIN' OUT LOUD.
GLAD I GOT MY HANDS ON SO MUCH FOOD AT ONCE...

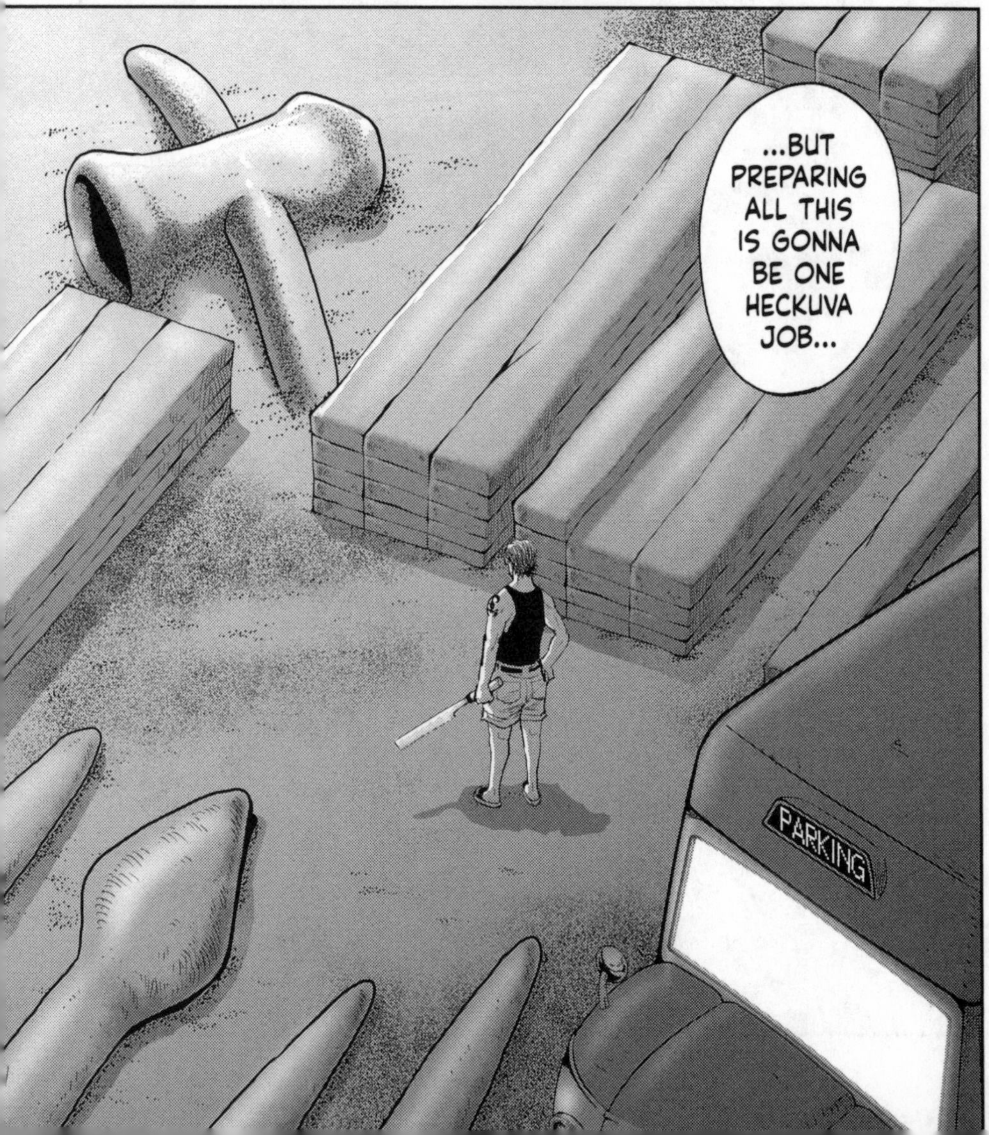
...BUT PREPARING ALL THIS IS GONNA BE ONE HECKUVA JOB...
PARKING

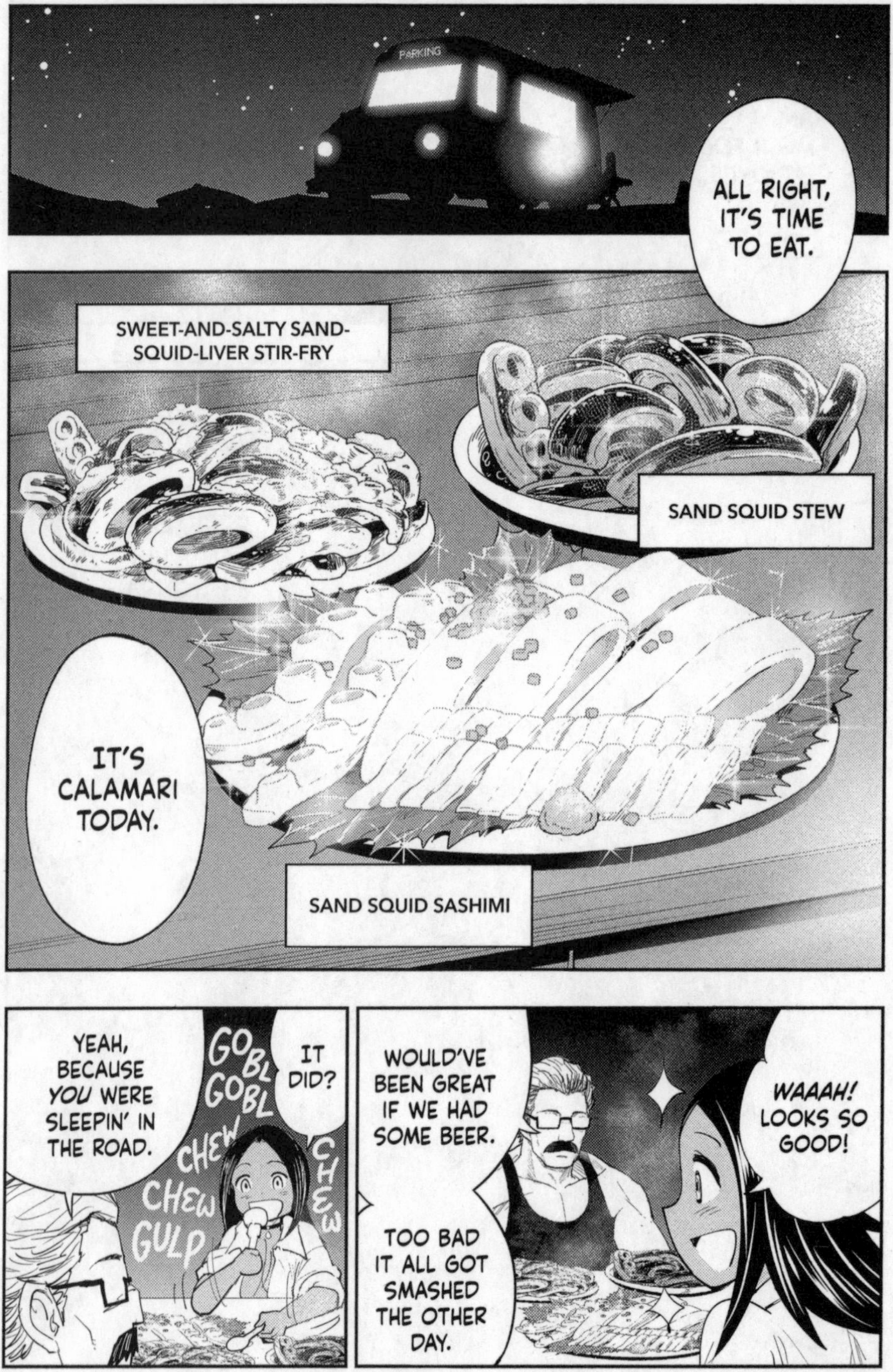
PARKING
ALL RIGHT, IT'S TIME TO EAT.
SWEET-AND-SALTY SAND-SQUID-LIVER STIR-FRY
SAND SQUID STEW
IT'S CALAMARI TODAY.
SAND SQUID SASHIMI
WAAAH! LOOKS SO GOOD!
WOULD'VE BEEN GREAT IF WE HAD SOME BEER.
TOO BAD IT ALL GOT SMASHED THE OTHER DAY.
IT DID?
CHEW
YEAH, BECAUSE *YOU* WERE SLEEPIN' IN THE ROAD.
GOBL GOBL
CHEW CHEW
GULP

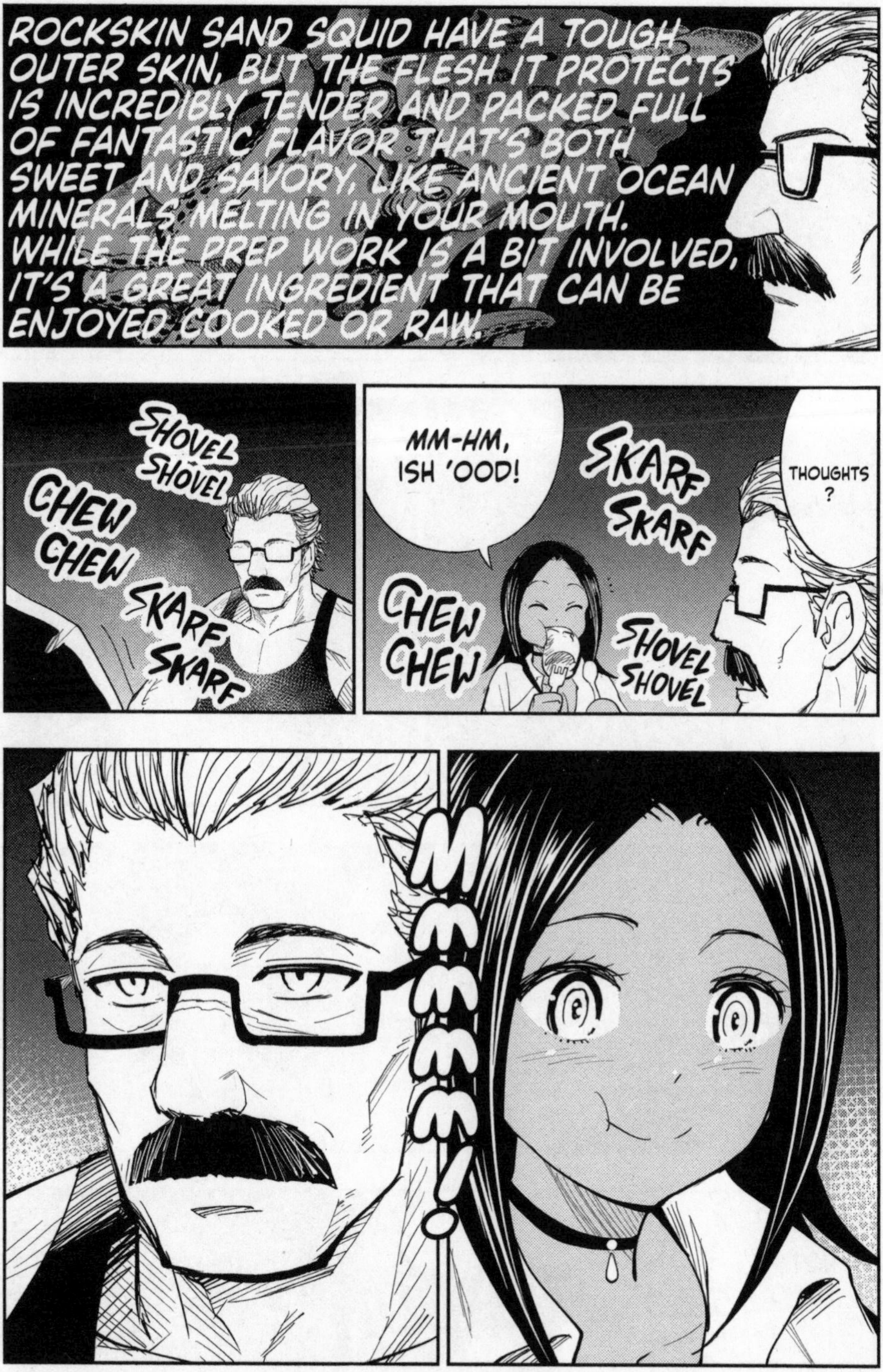
ROCKSKIN SAND SQUID HAVE A TOUGH OUTER SKIN, BUT THE FLESH IT PROTECTS IS INCREDIBLY TENDER AND PACKED FULL OF FANTASTIC FLAVOR THAT'S BOTH SWEET AND SAVORY, LIKE ANCIENT OCEAN MINERALS MELTING IN YOUR MOUTH. WHILE THE PREP WORK IS A BIT INVOLVED, IT'S A GREAT INGREDIENT THAT CAN BE ENJOYED COOKED OR RAW.
THOUGHTS?
SKARF SKARF
MM-HM, ISH 'OOD!
SHOVEL SHOVEL
CHEW CHEW
SHOVEL SHOVEL
CHEW CHEW
SKARF SKARF
MMMMM!

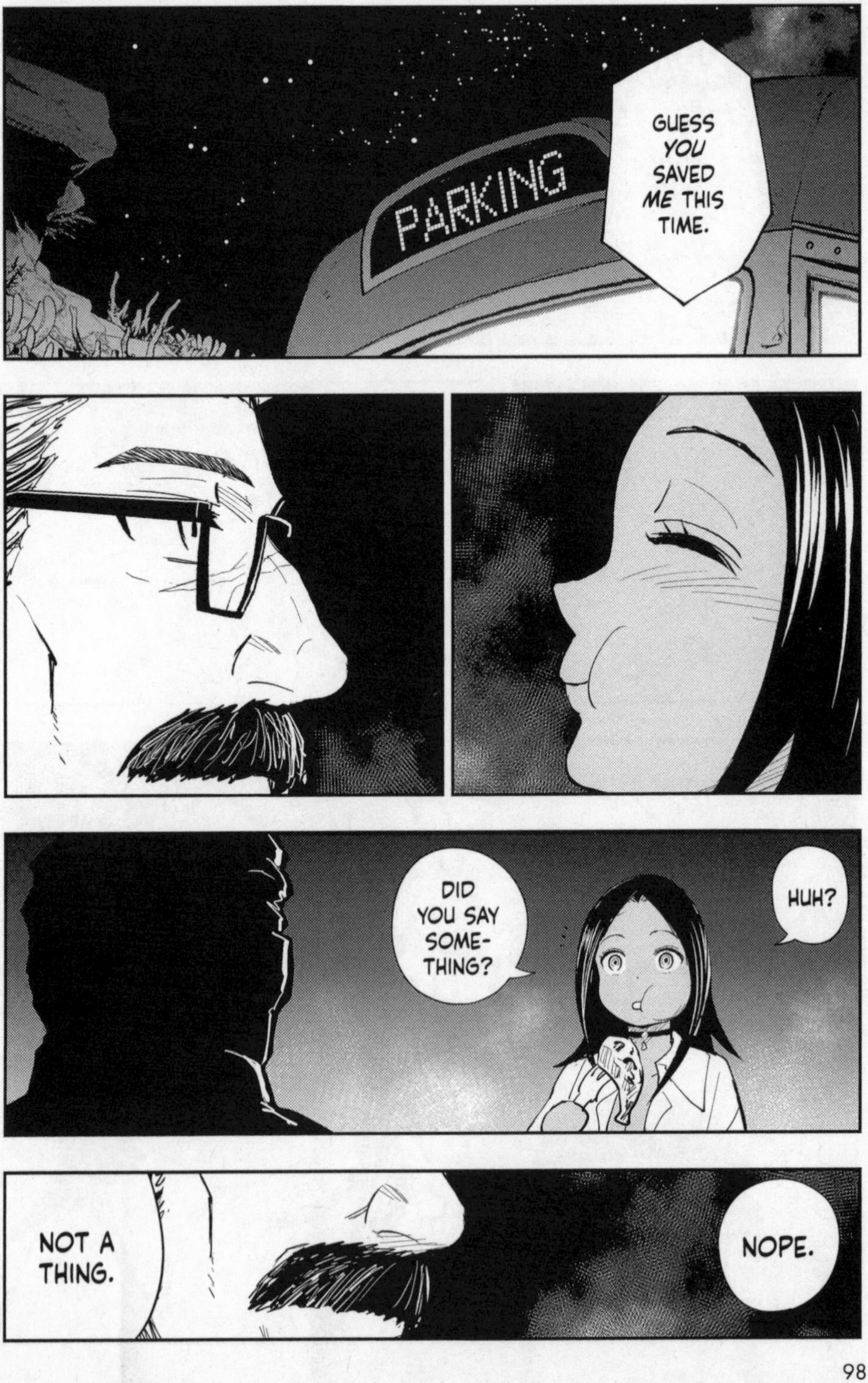
GUESS YOU SAVED ME THIS TIME.
PARKING
HUH?
DID YOU SAY SOME-THING?
NOPE.
NOT A THING.

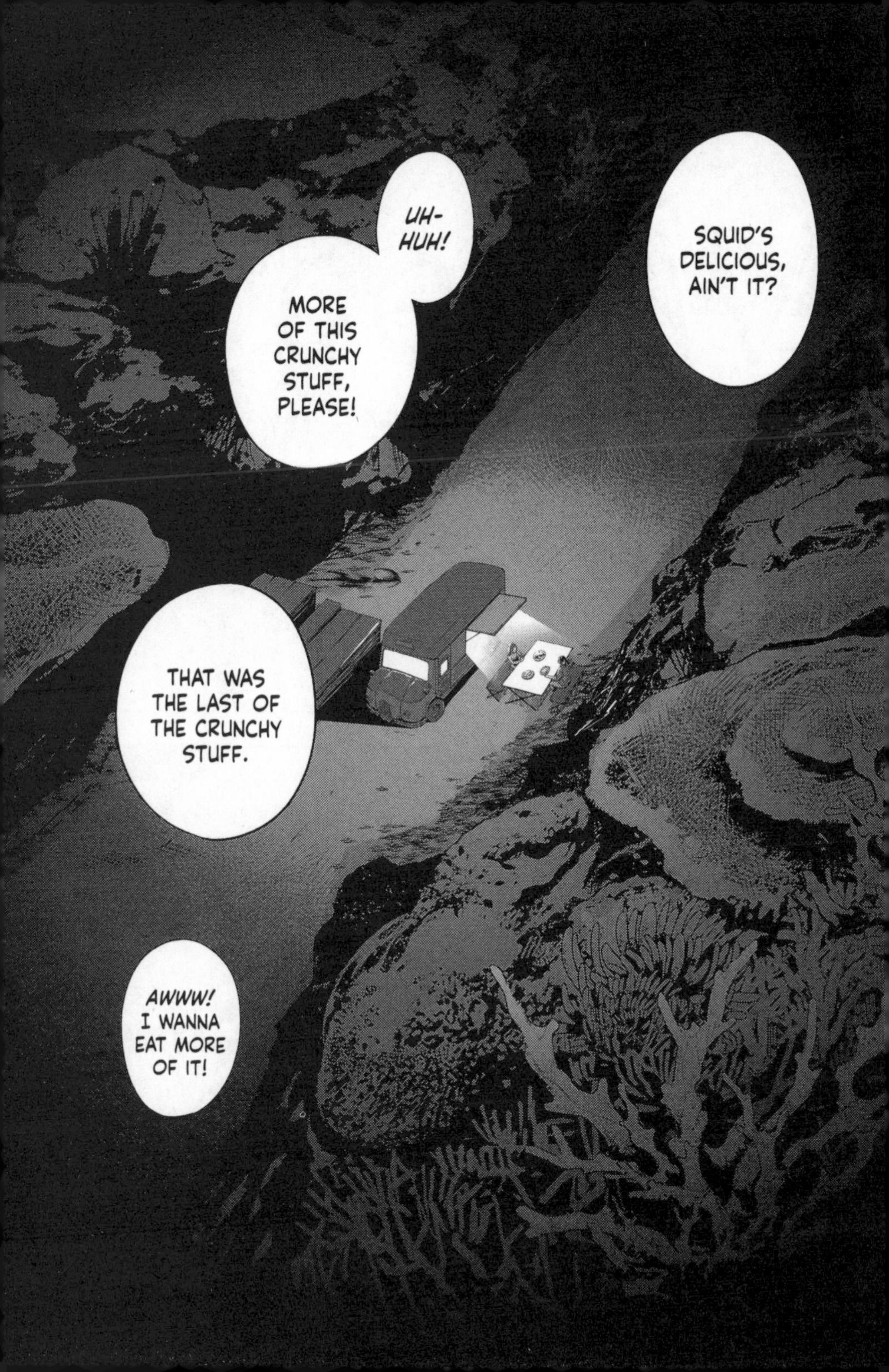
SQUID'S DELICIOUS, AIN'T IT?
UH-HUH!
MORE OF THIS CRUNCHY STUFF, PLEASE!
THAT WAS THE LAST OF THE CRUNCHY STUFF.
AWWW! I WANNA EAT MORE OF IT!

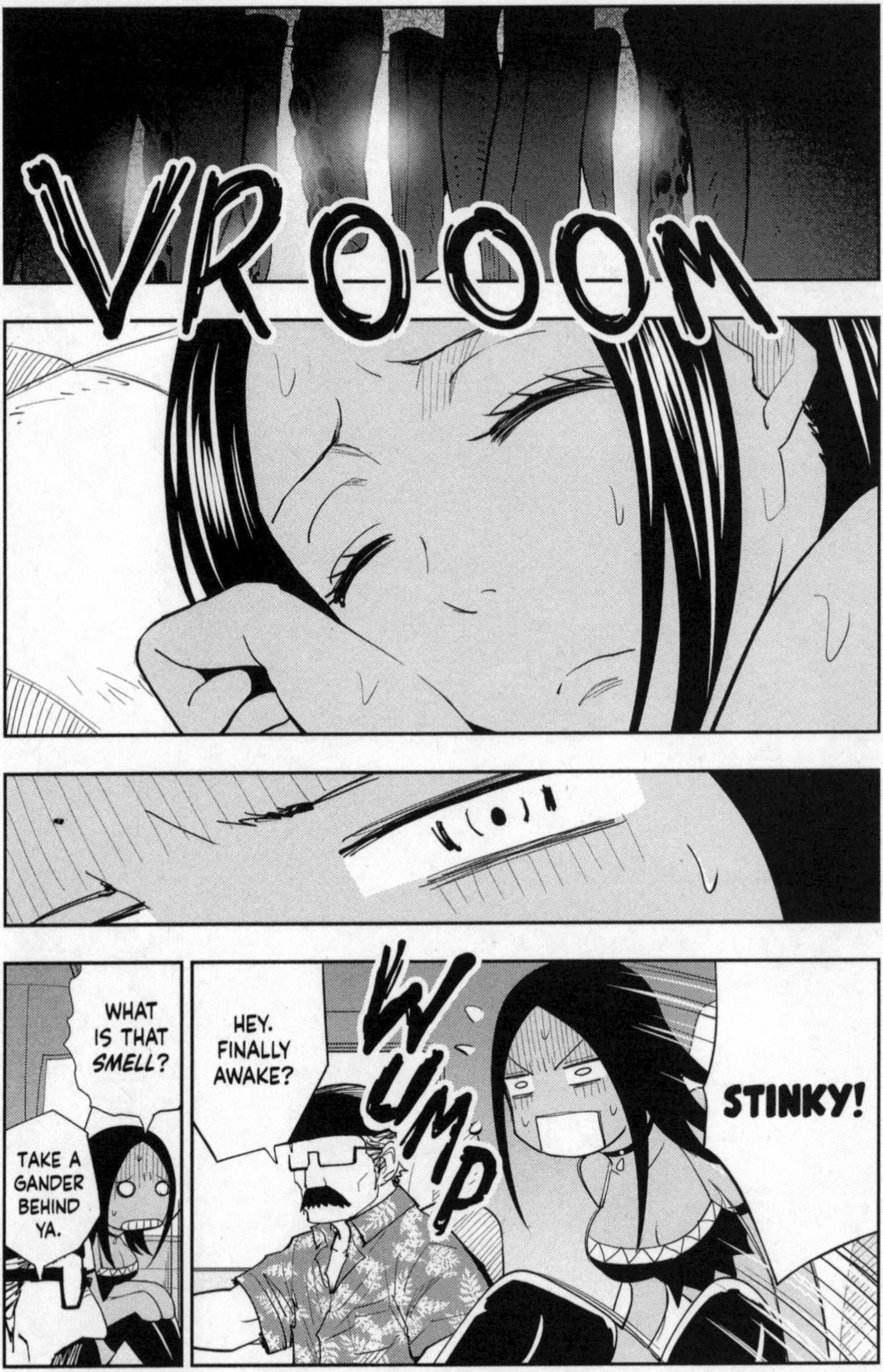
VROOOM
STINKY!
WUMP
HEY. FINALLY AWAKE?
WHAT IS THAT SMELL?
TAKE A GANDER BEHIND YA.

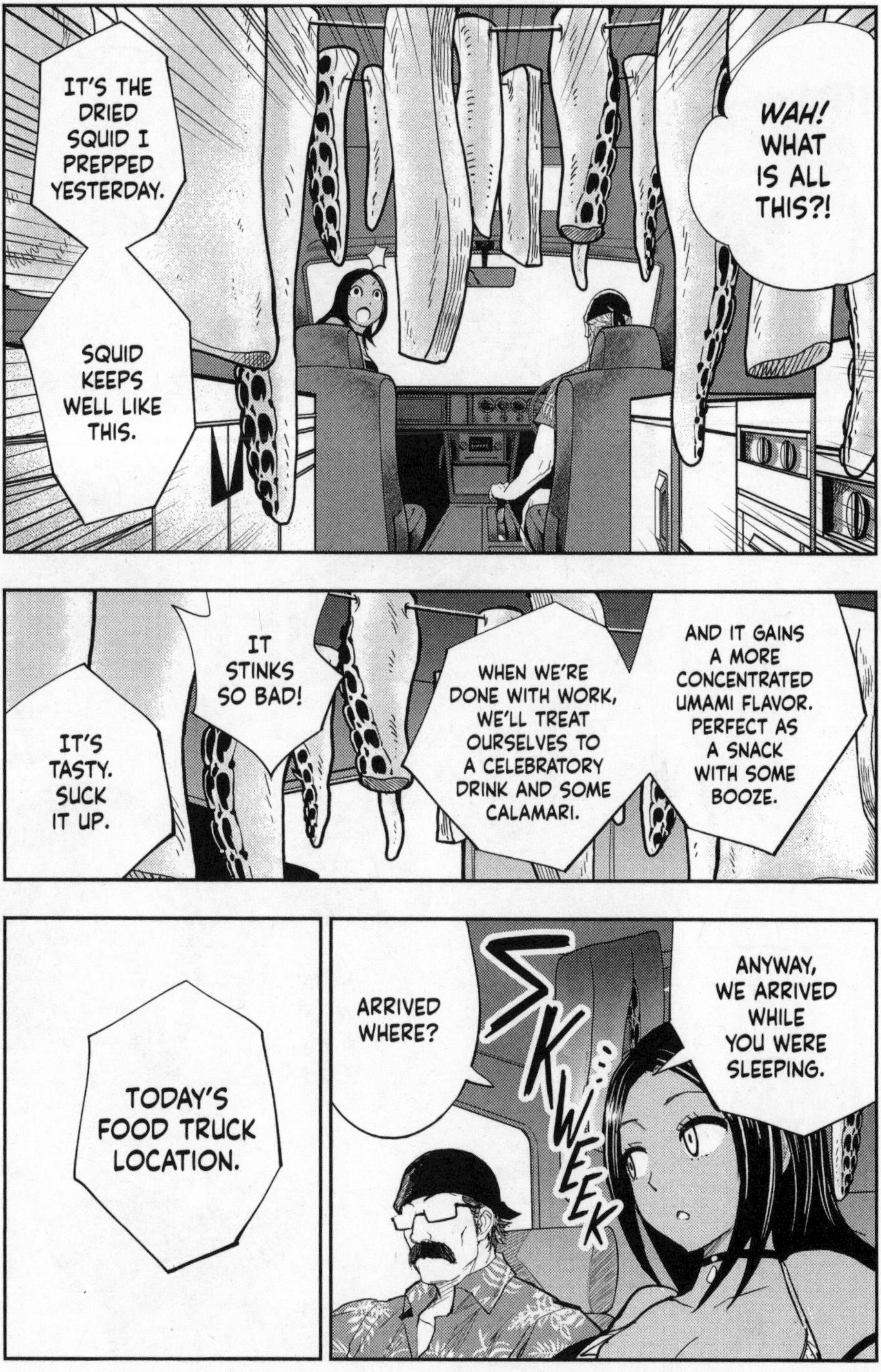
WAH! WHAT IS ALL THIS?!
IT'S THE DRIED SQUID I PREPPED YESTERDAY.
SQUID KEEPS WELL LIKE THIS.
AND IT GAINS A MORE CONCENTRATED UMAMI FLAVOR. PERFECT AS A SNACK WITH SOME BOOZE.
WHEN WE'RE DONE WITH WORK, WE'LL TREAT OURSELVES TO A CELEBRATORY DRINK AND SOME CALAMARI.
IT STINKS SO BAD!
IT'S TASTY. SUCK IT UP.
ANYWAY, WE ARRIVED WHILE YOU WERE SLEEPING.
SKWEEK
...
ARRIVED WHERE?
TODAY'S FOOD TRUCK LOCATION.

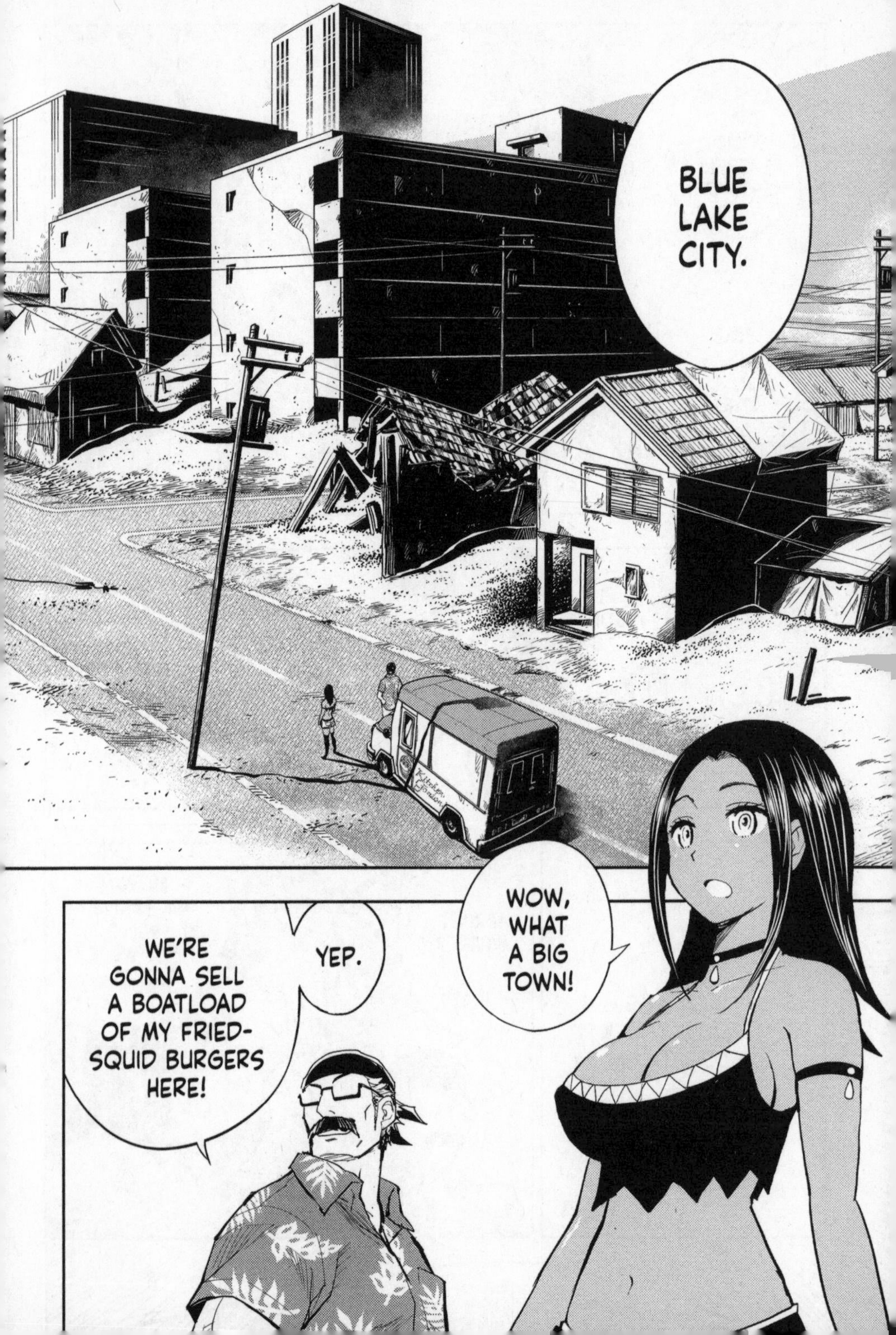
BLUE LAKE CITY.
WOW, WHAT A BIG TOWN!
YEP.
WE'RE GONNA SELL A BOATLOAD OF MY FRIED-SQUID BURGERS HERE!

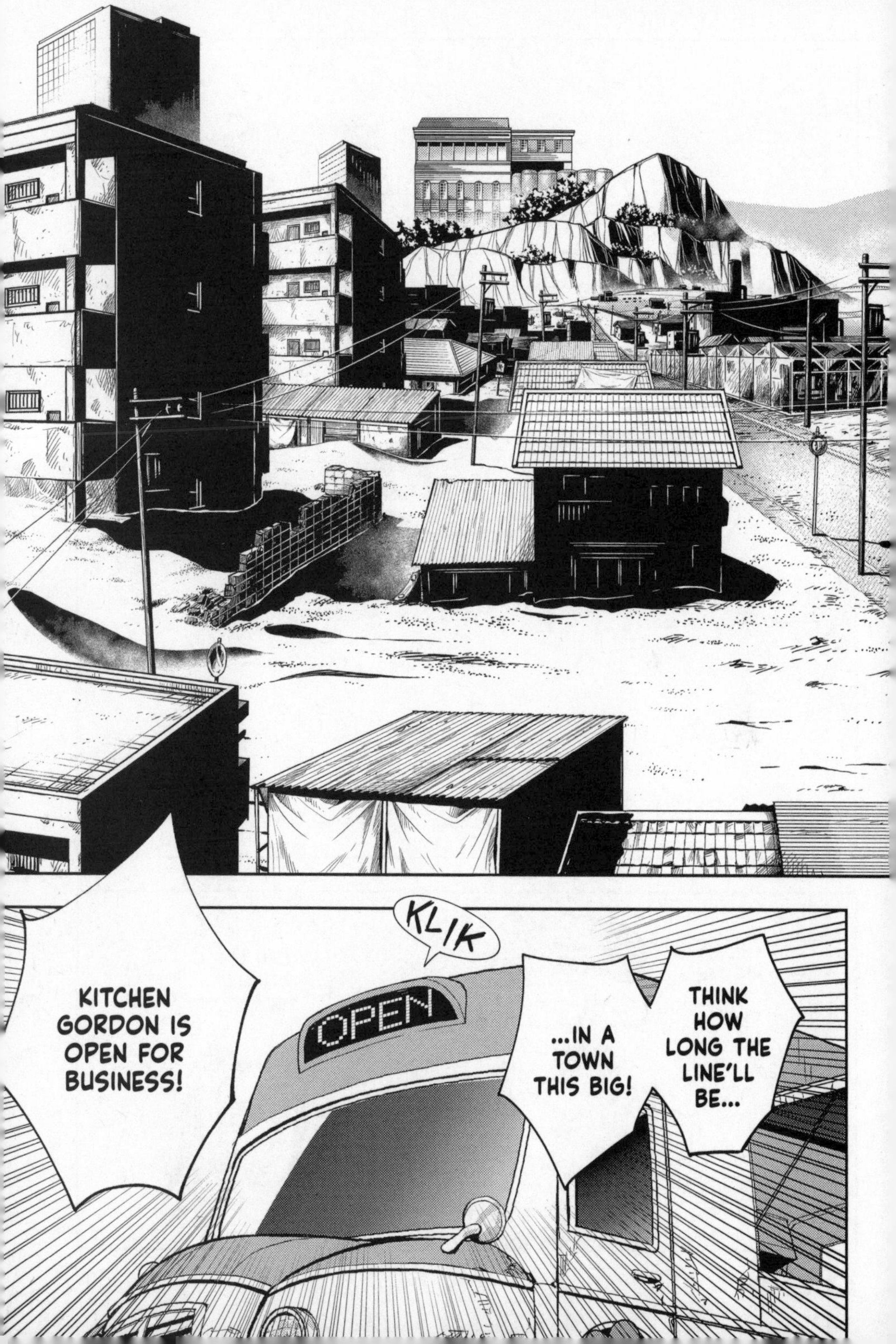
THINK HOW LONG THE LINE'LL BE...
...IN A TOWN THIS BIG!
KLIK
OPEN
KITCHEN GORDON IS OPEN FOR BUSINESS!

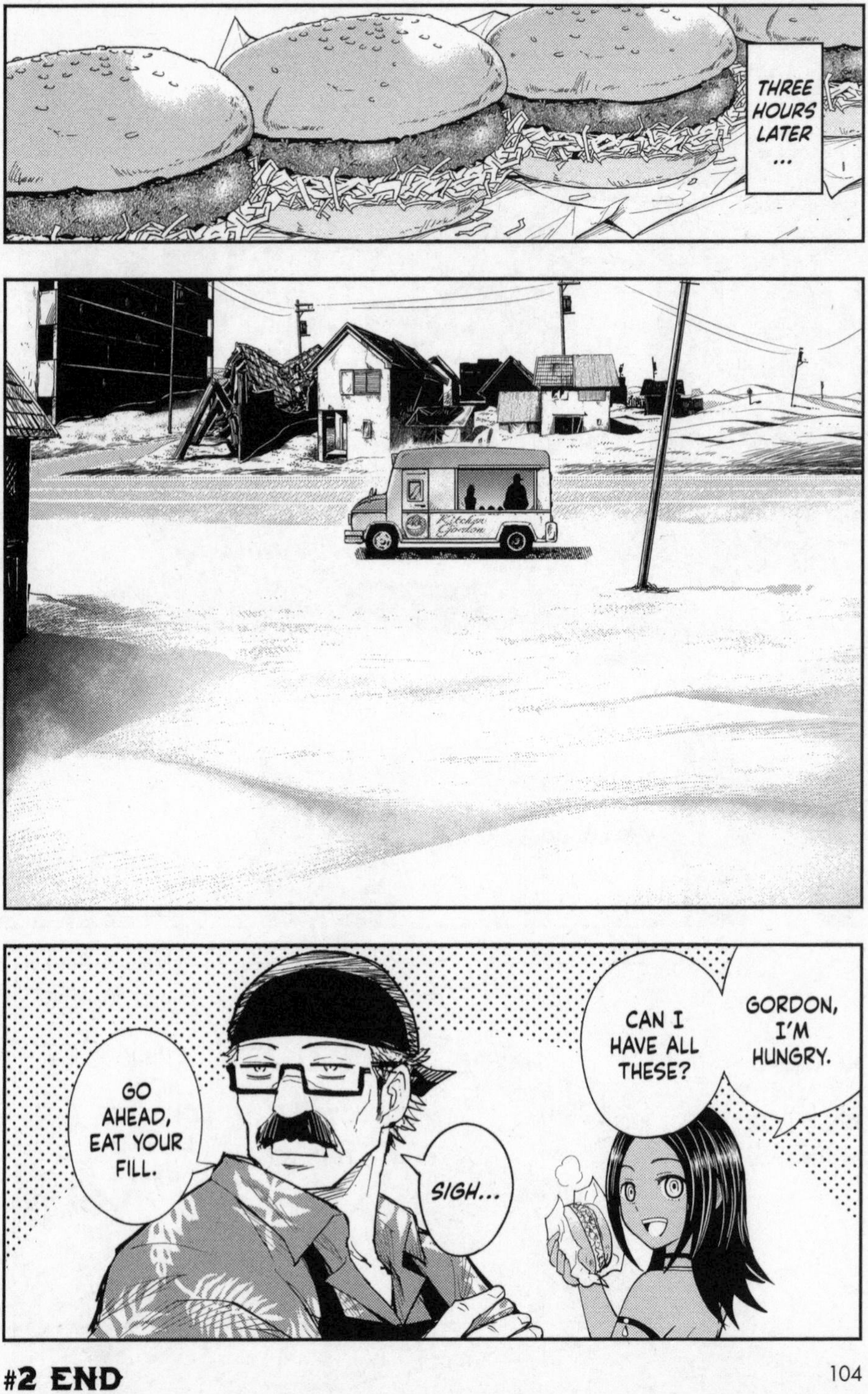
THREE HOURS LATER ...
Kitchen Gordon
GORDON, I'M HUNGRY.
CAN I HAVE ALL THESE?
SIGH...
GO AHEAD, EAT YOUR FILL.

#2 END

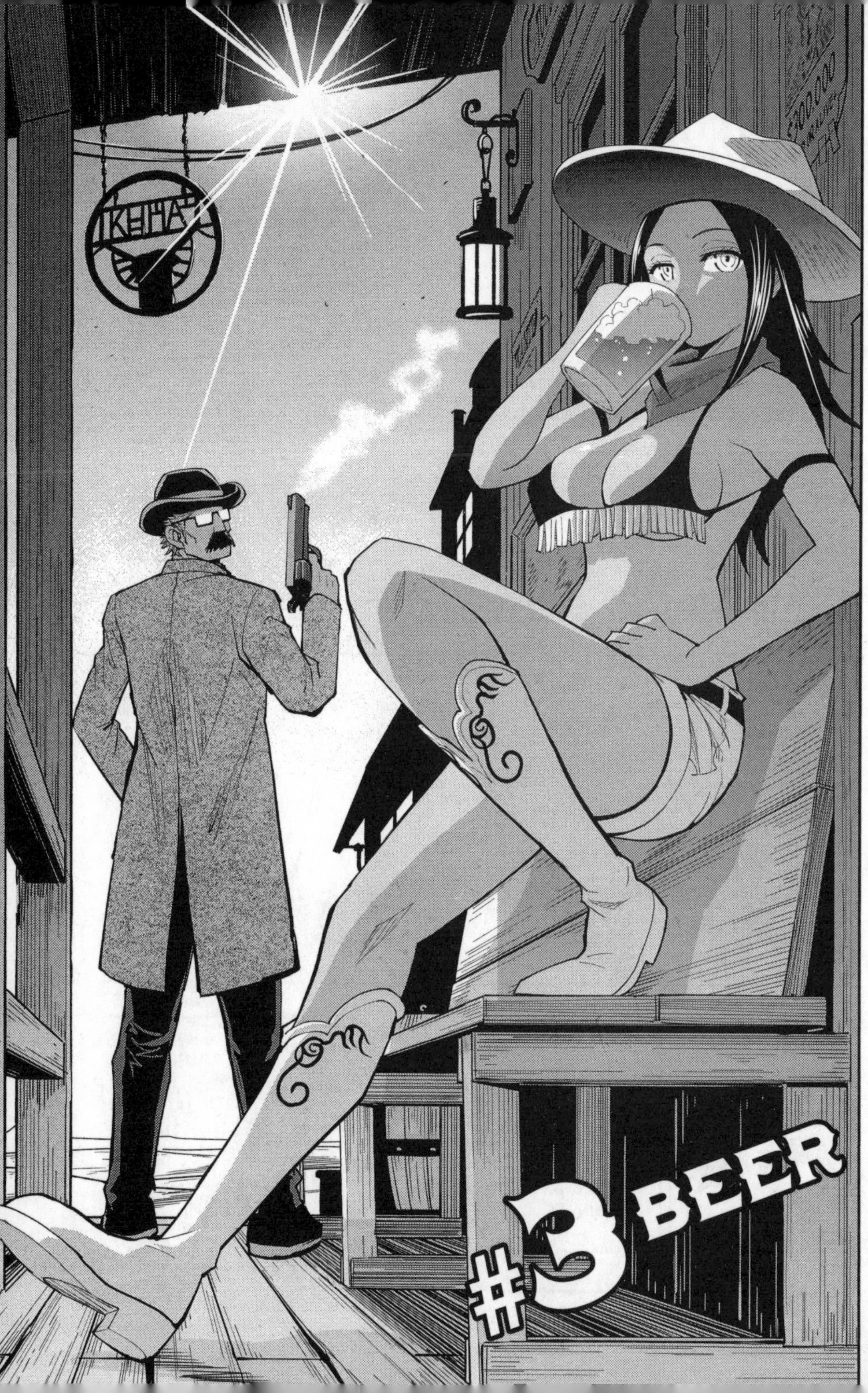
#3 BEER

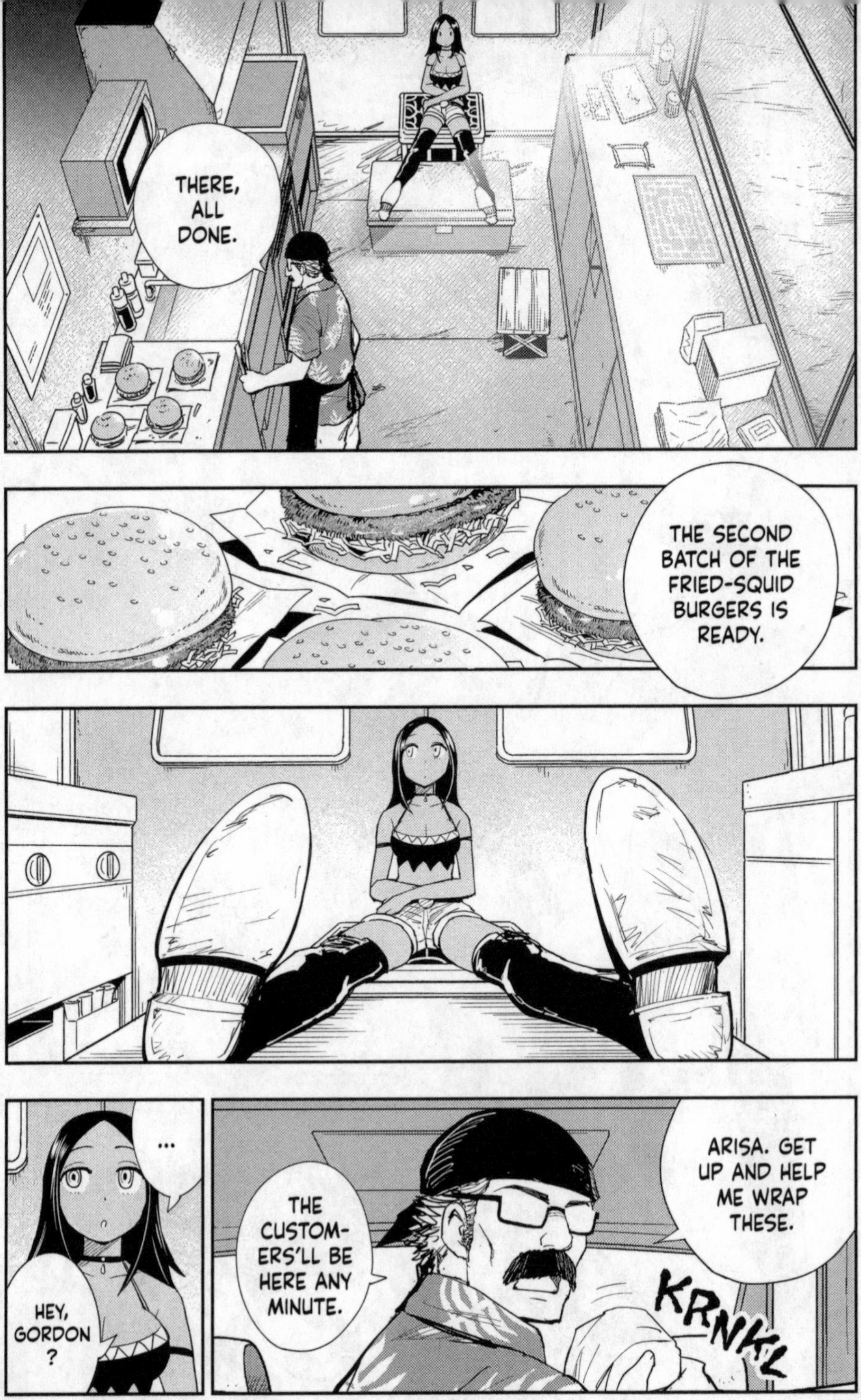
THERE, ALL DONE.
THE SECOND BATCH OF THE FRIED-SQUID BURGERS IS READY.
ARISA. GET UP AND HELP ME WRAP THESE.
KRNKL
THE CUSTOM-ERS'LL BE HERE ANY MINUTE.
...
HEY, GORDON?

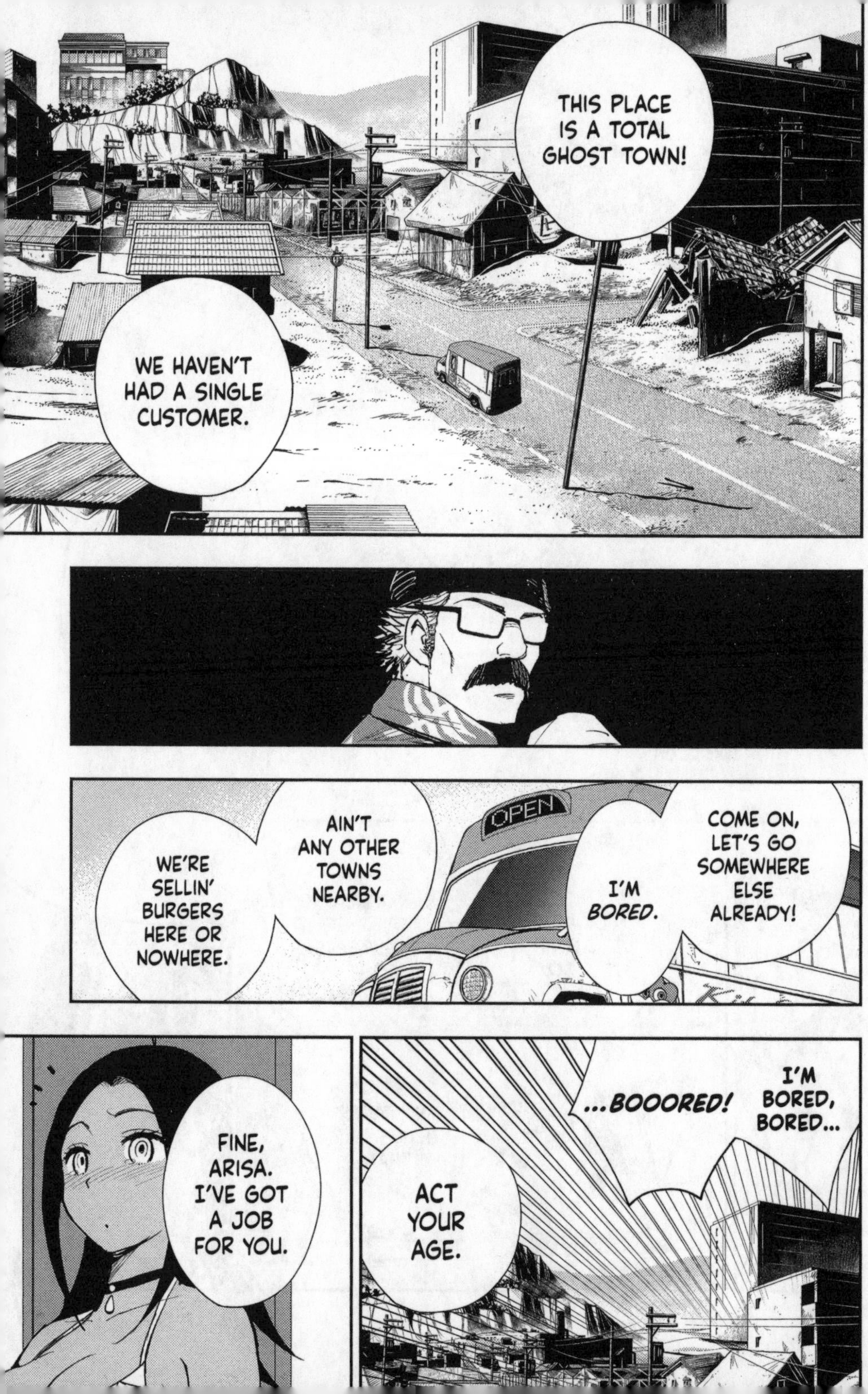
THIS PLACE IS A TOTAL GHOST TOWN!
WE HAVEN'T HAD A SINGLE CUSTOMER.
COME ON, LET'S GO SOMEWHERE ELSE ALREADY!
OPEN
I'M *BORED*.
AIN'T ANY OTHER TOWNS NEARBY.
WE'RE SELLIN' BURGERS HERE OR NOWHERE.
I'M BORED, BORED...
...BOOORED!
ACT YOUR AGE.
FINE, ARISA. I'VE GOT A JOB FOR YOU.

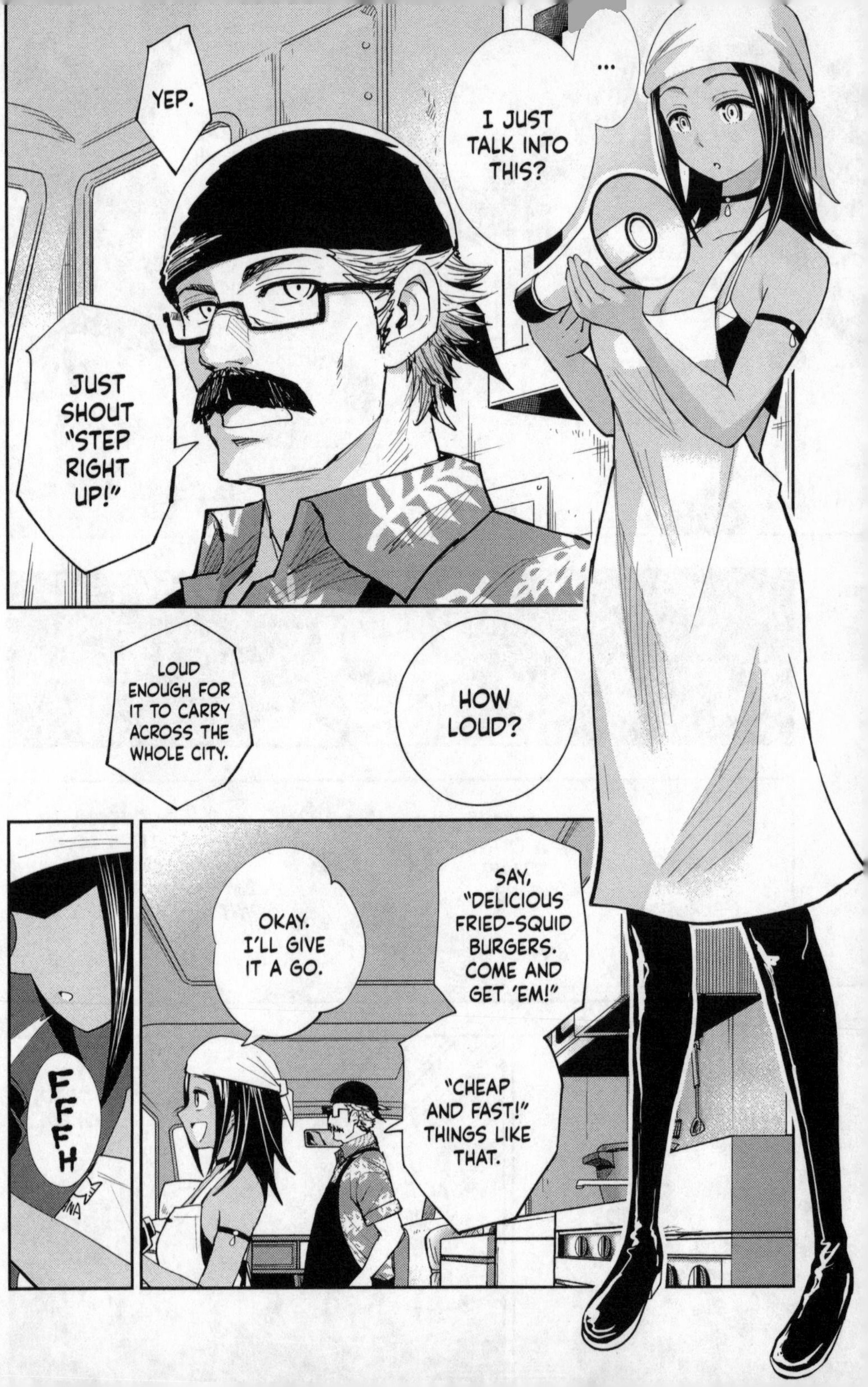
...
I JUST TALK INTO THIS?
YEP.
JUST SHOUT "STEP RIGHT UP!"
HOW LOUD?
LOUD ENOUGH FOR IT TO CARRY ACROSS THE WHOLE CITY.
SAY, "DELICIOUS FRIED-SQUID BURGERS. COME AND GET 'EM!"
"CHEAP AND FAST!" THINGS LIKE THAT.
OKAY. I'LL GIVE IT A GO.
FFFH

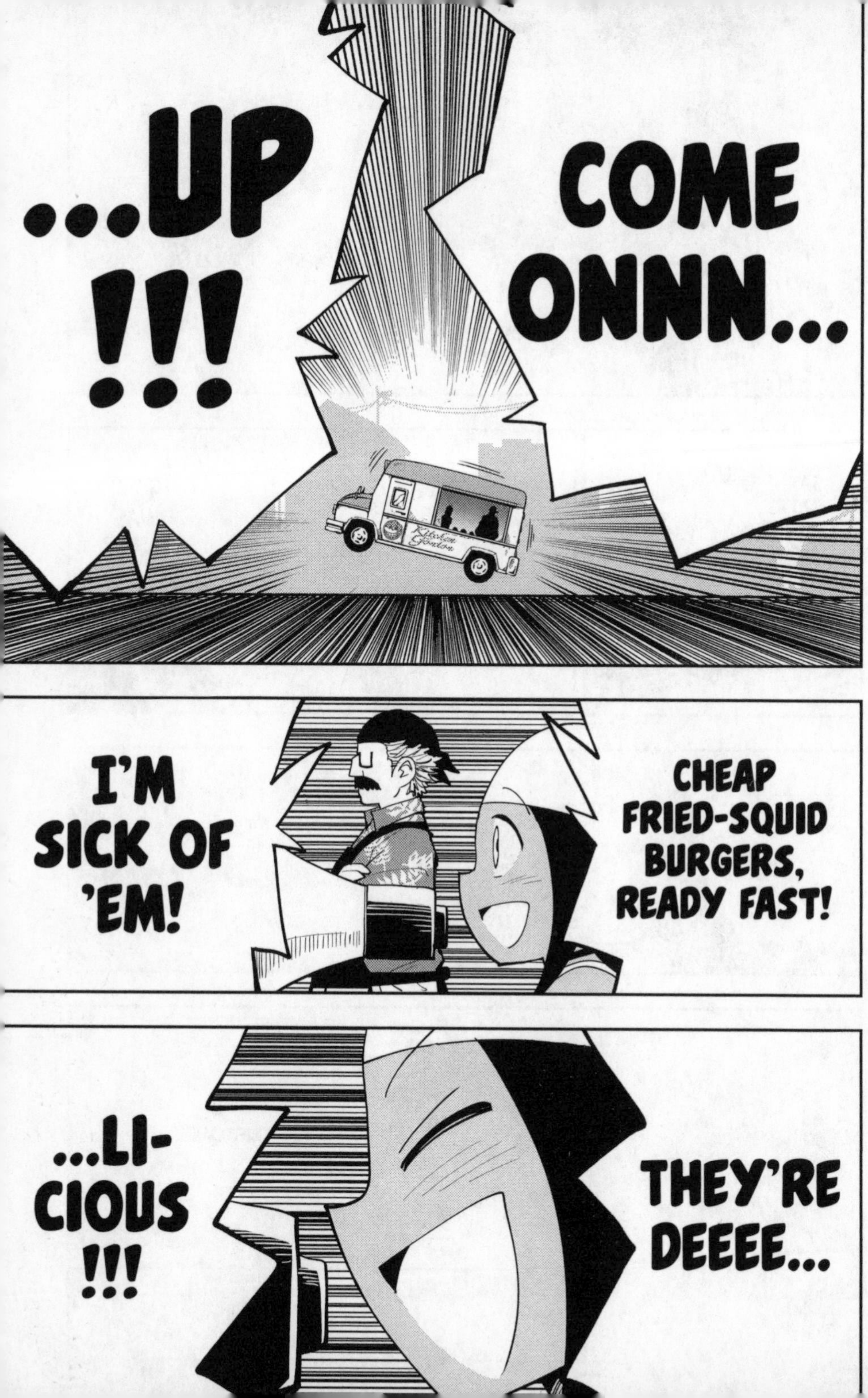
COME ONNN...
...UP !!!
CHEAP FRIED-SQUID BURGERS, READY FAST!
I'M SICK OF 'EM!
THEY'RE DEEEE...
...LI-CIOUS !!!

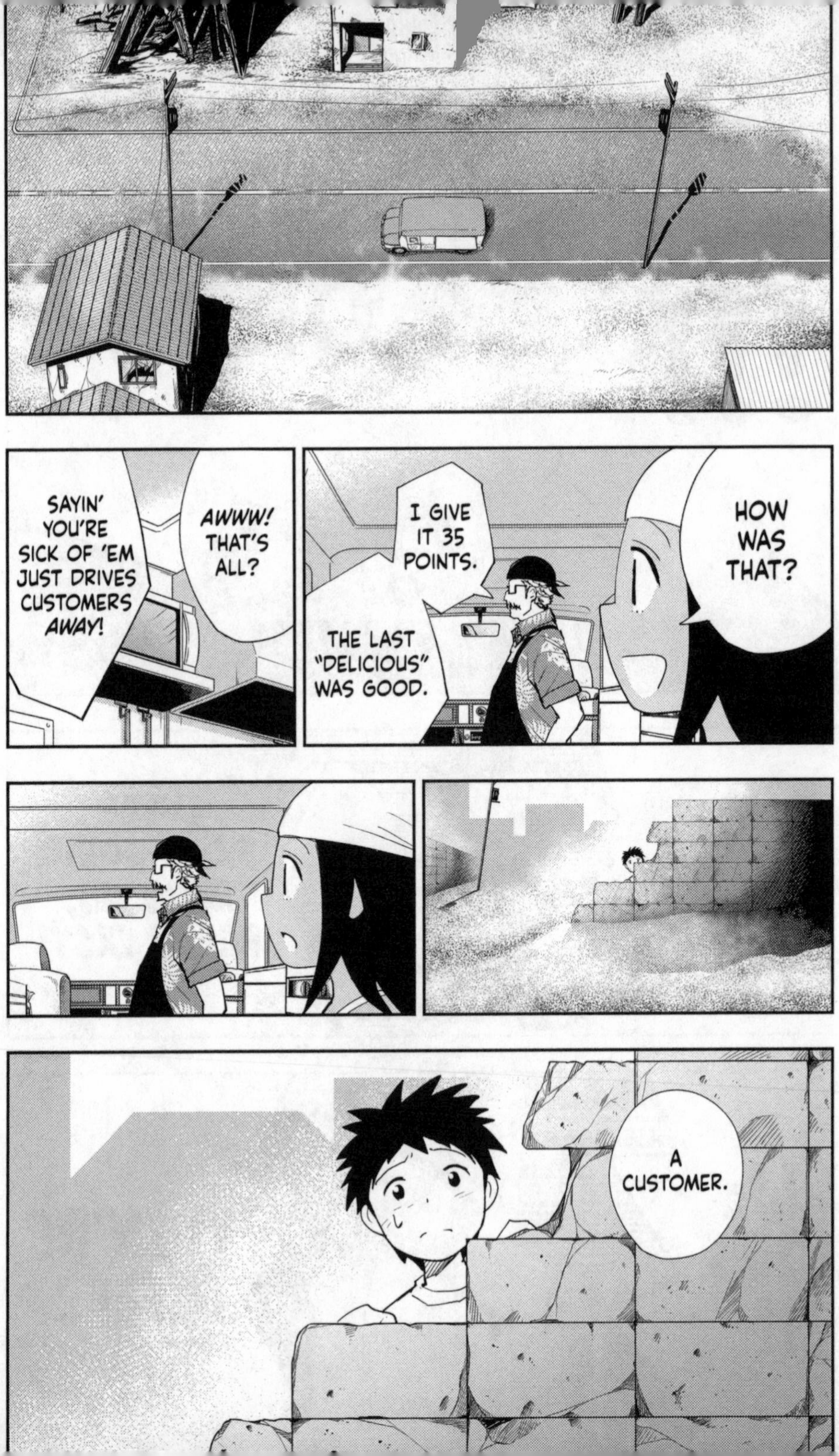
HOW WAS THAT?
I GIVE IT 35 POINTS.
THE LAST "DELICIOUS" WAS GOOD.
AWWW! THAT'S ALL?
SAYIN' YOU'RE SICK OF 'EM JUST DRIVES CUSTOMERS AWAY!
A CUSTOMER.

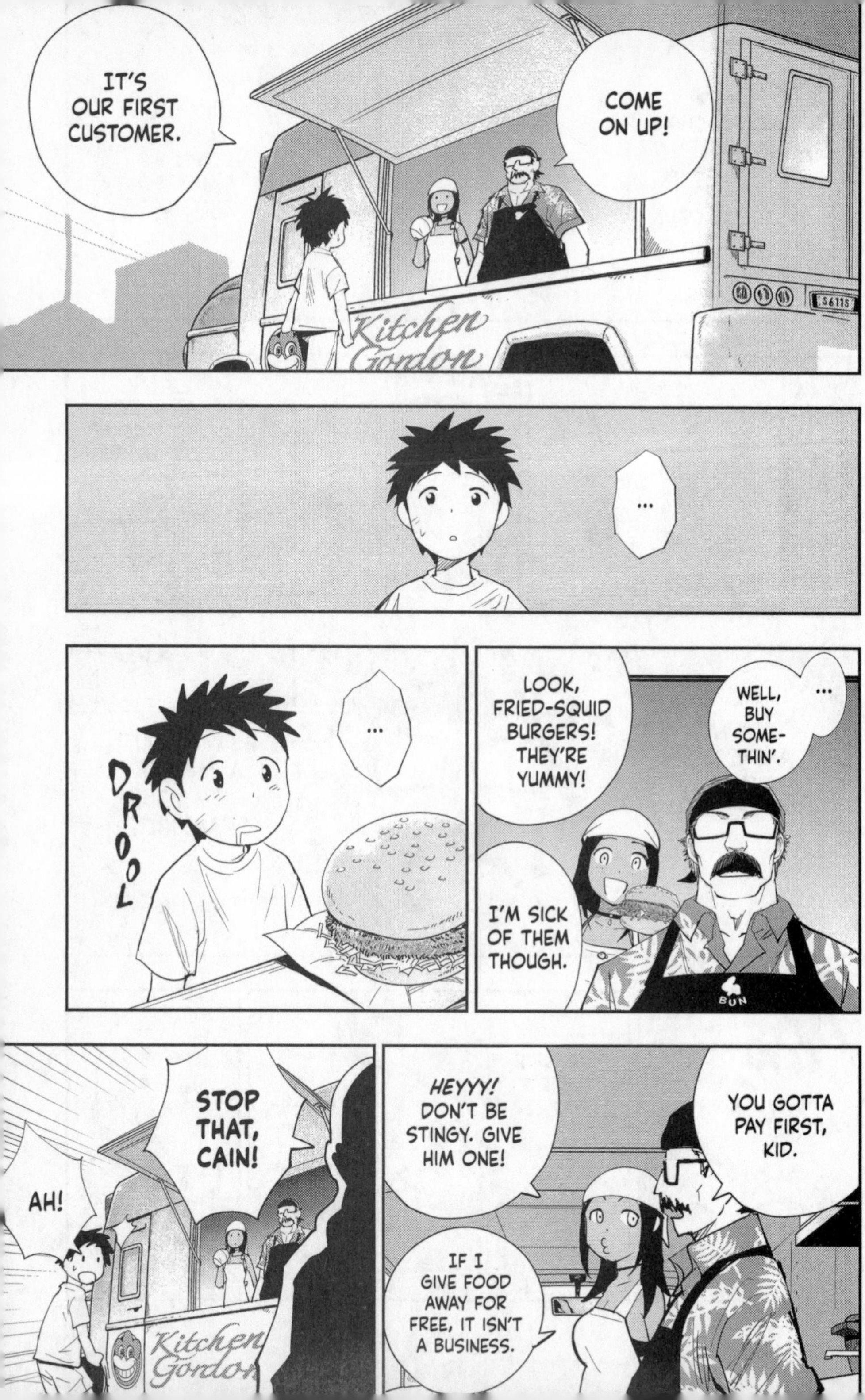
COME ON UP!
IT'S OUR FIRST CUSTOMER.
Kitchen Gordon
...
...
WELL, BUY SOME-THIN'.
LOOK, FRIED-SQUID BURGERS! THEY'RE YUMMY!
I'M SICK OF THEM THOUGH.
BUN
...
DROOL
YOU GOTTA PAY FIRST, KID.
HEYYY! DON'T BE STINGY. GIVE HIM ONE!
IF I GIVE FOOD AWAY FOR FREE, IT ISN'T A BUSINESS.
STOP THAT, CAIN!
AH!
Kitchen Gordon

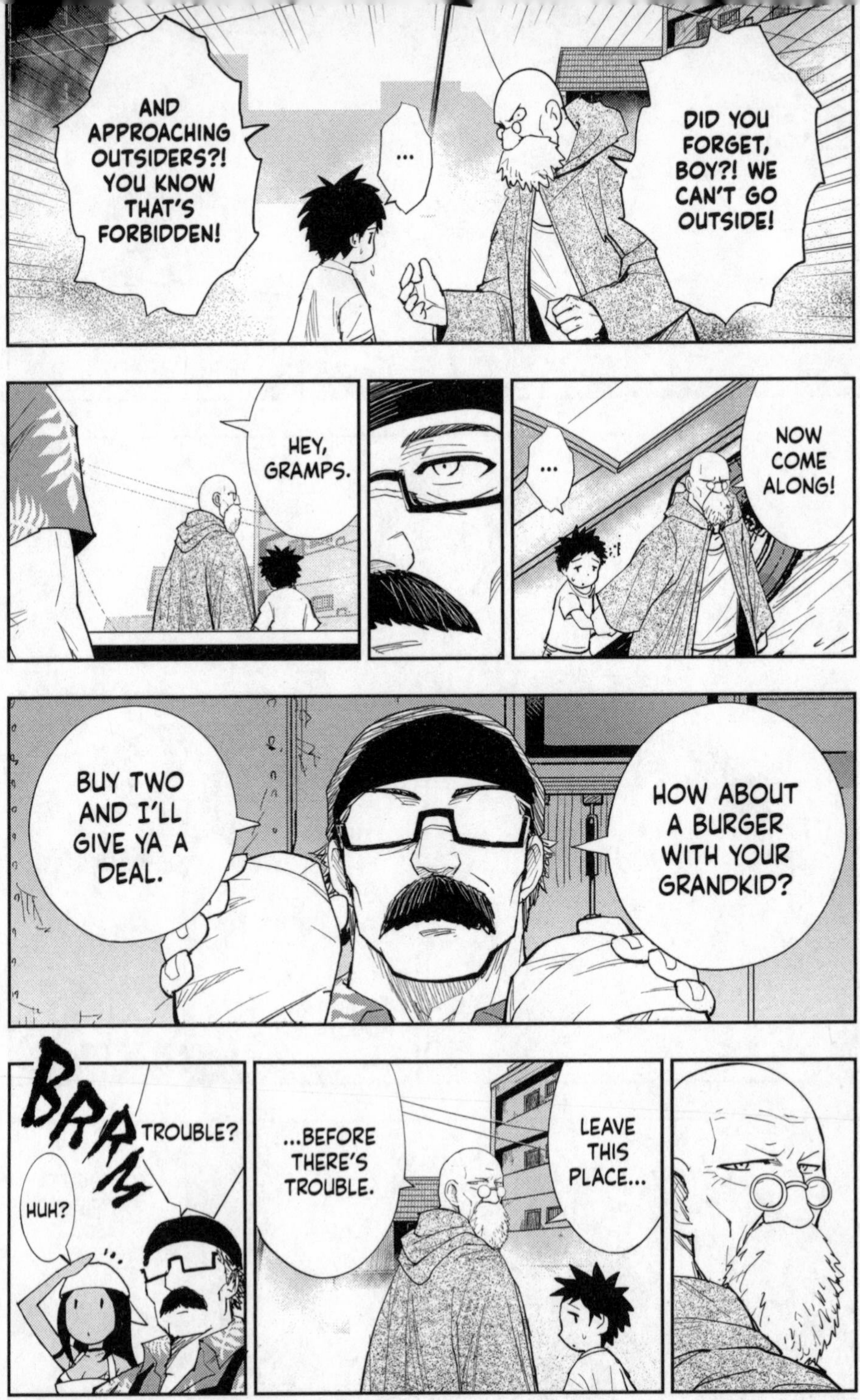
DID YOU FORGET, BOY?! WE CAN'T GO OUTSIDE!
...
AND APPROACHING OUTSIDERS?! YOU KNOW THAT'S FORBIDDEN!
NOW COME ALONG!
...
HEY, GRAMPS.
HOW ABOUT A BURGER WITH YOUR GRANDKID?
BUY TWO AND I'LL GIVE YA A DEAL.
LEAVE THIS PLACE...
...BEFORE THERE'S TROUBLE.
TROUBLE?
BRRM
HUH?

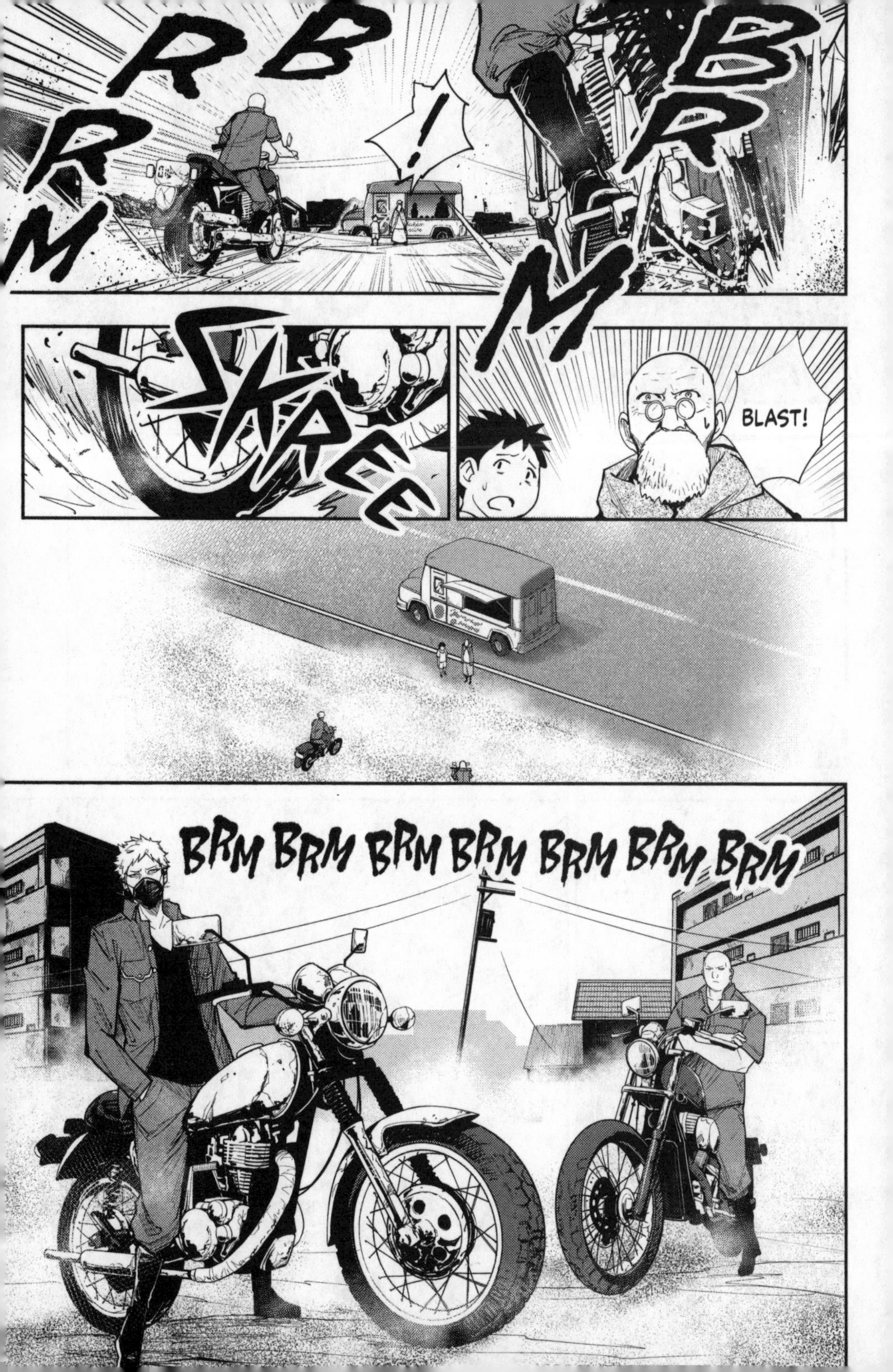
BRM
BRRM
!
BLAST!
SKREE
BRM BRM BRM BRM BRM BRM BRM

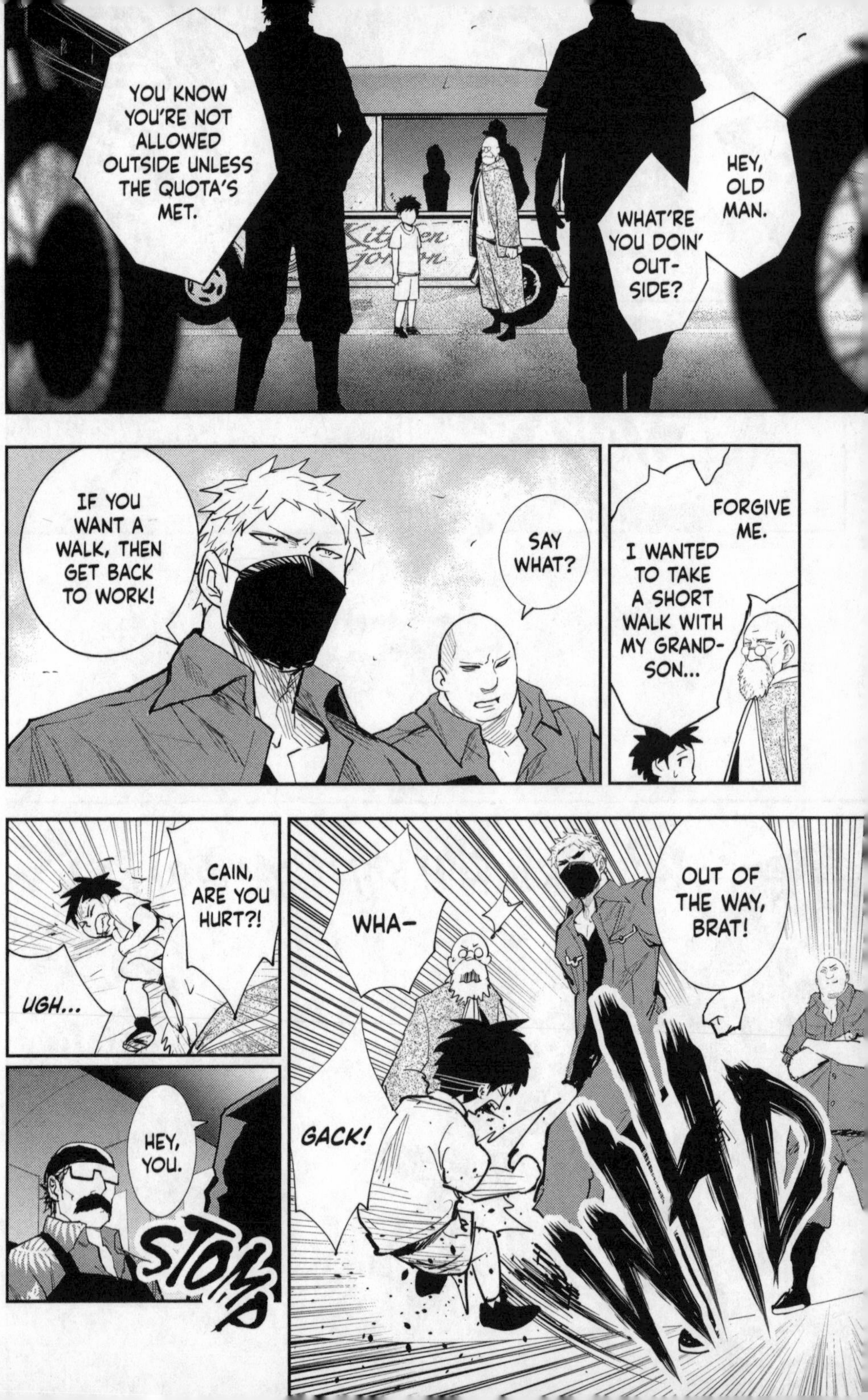
HEY, OLD MAN.
WHAT'RE YOU DOIN' OUT-SIDE?
YOU KNOW YOU'RE NOT ALLOWED OUTSIDE UNLESS THE QUOTA'S MET.
FORGIVE ME.
I WANTED TO TAKE A SHORT WALK WITH MY GRAND-SON...
SAY WHAT?
IF YOU WANT A WALK, THEN GET BACK TO WORK!
OUT OF THE WAY, BRAT!
WHA-
WHAP
GACK!
CAIN, ARE YOU HURT?!
UGH...
HEY, YOU.
STOMP

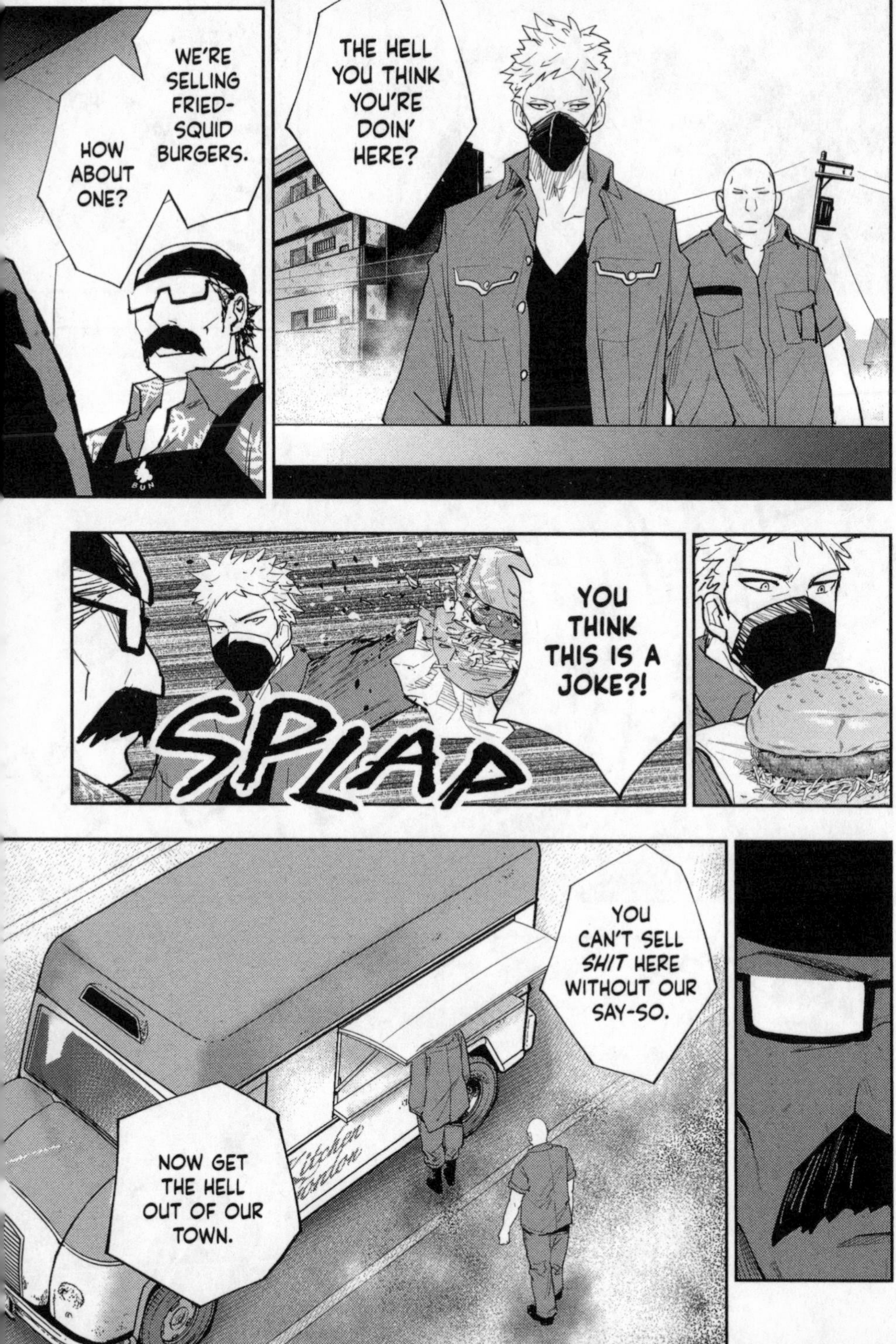
THE HELL YOU THINK YOU'RE DOIN' HERE?
WE'RE SELLING FRIED-SQUID BURGERS.
HOW ABOUT ONE?
YOU THINK THIS IS A JOKE?!
SPLAP
YOU CAN'T SELL *SHIT* HERE WITHOUT OUR SAY-SO.
NOW GET THE HELL OUT OF OUR TOWN.

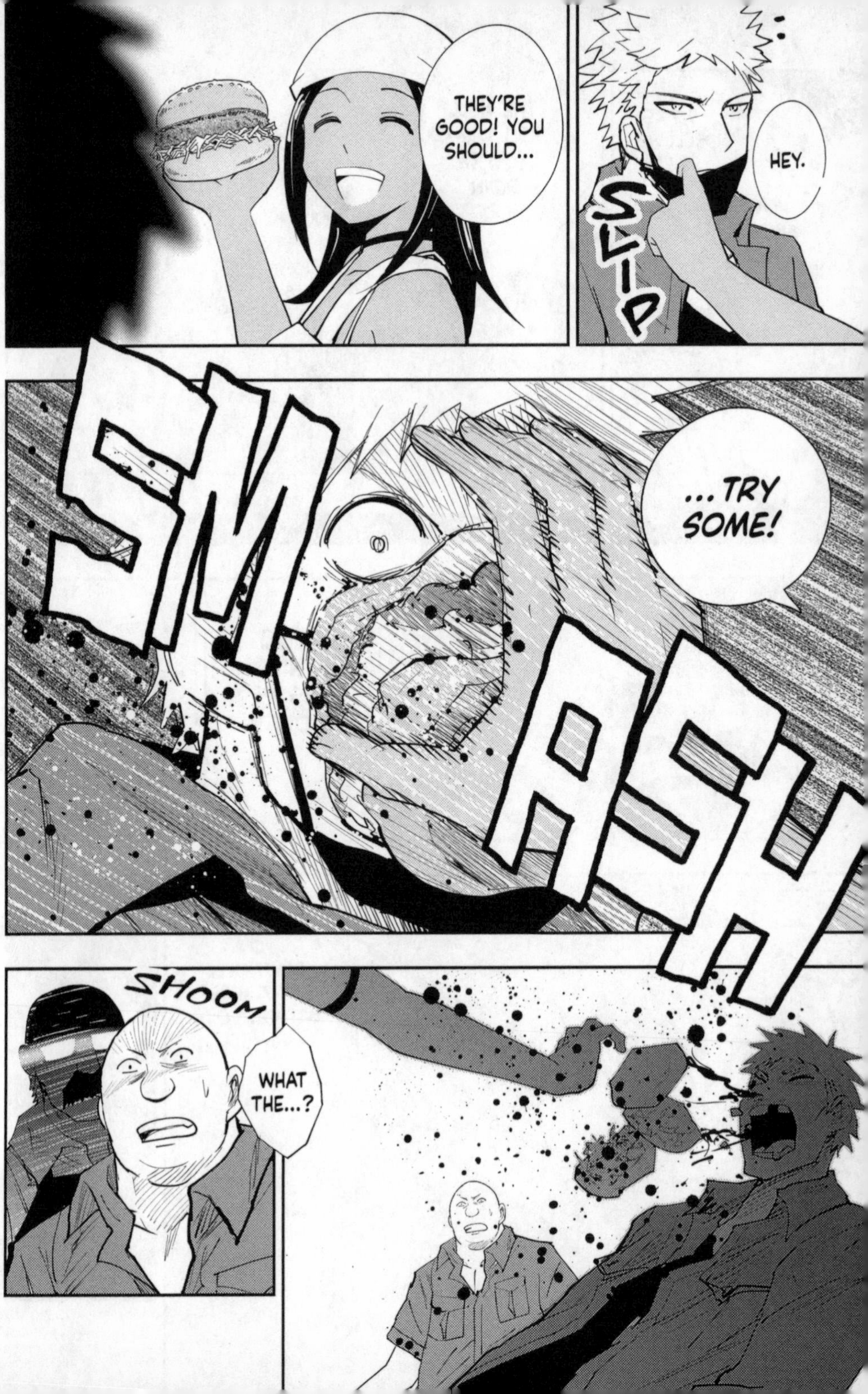
HEY.
SLIP
THEY'RE GOOD! YOU SHOULD...
...TRY SOME!
SMASH
SHOOM
WHAT THE...?

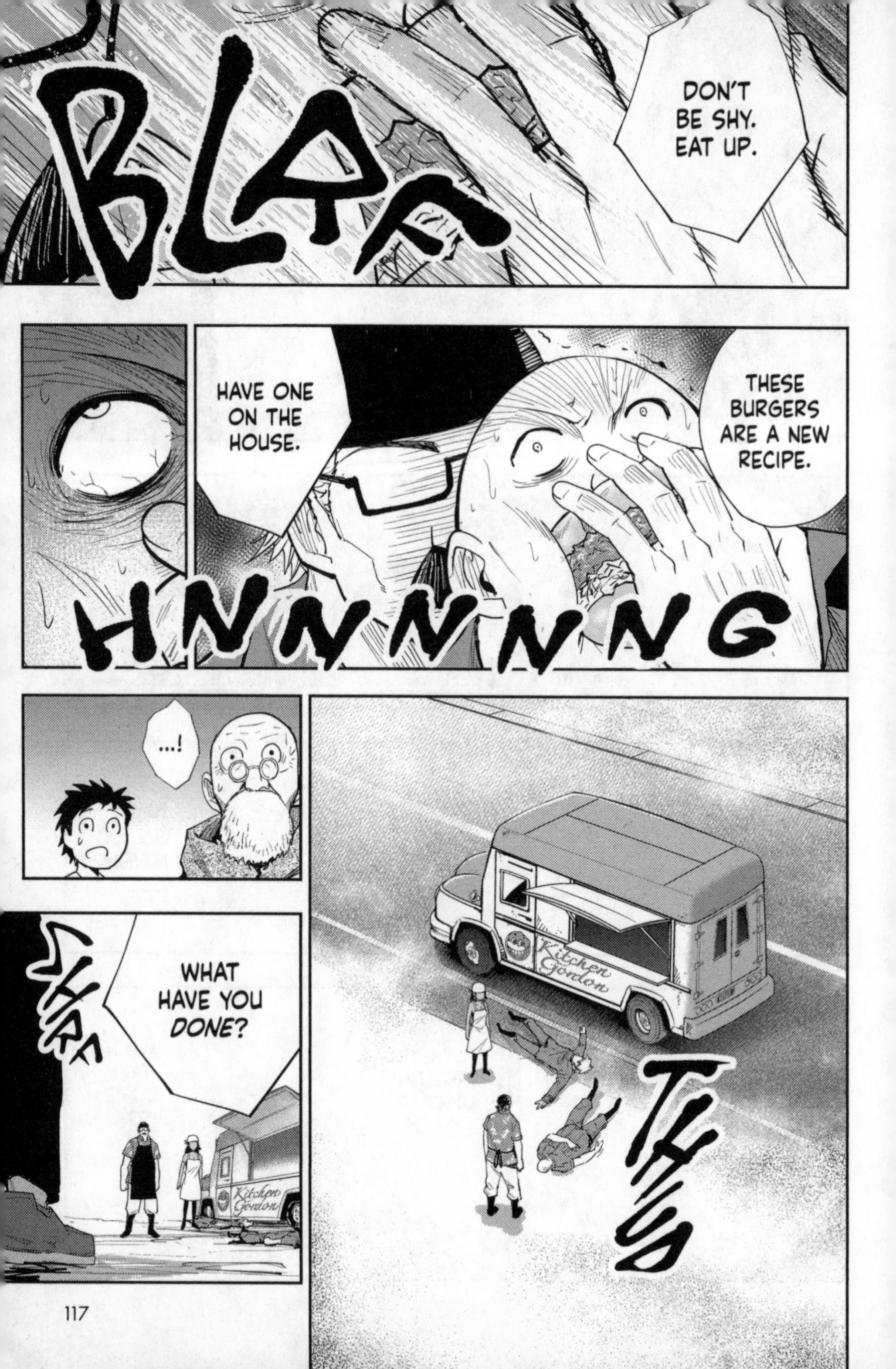
BLAM
DON'T BE SHY. EAT UP.
THESE BURGERS ARE A NEW RECIPE.
HAVE ONE ON THE HOUSE.
HNNNNNG
THUD
...!
WHAT HAVE YOU DONE?
SHRF

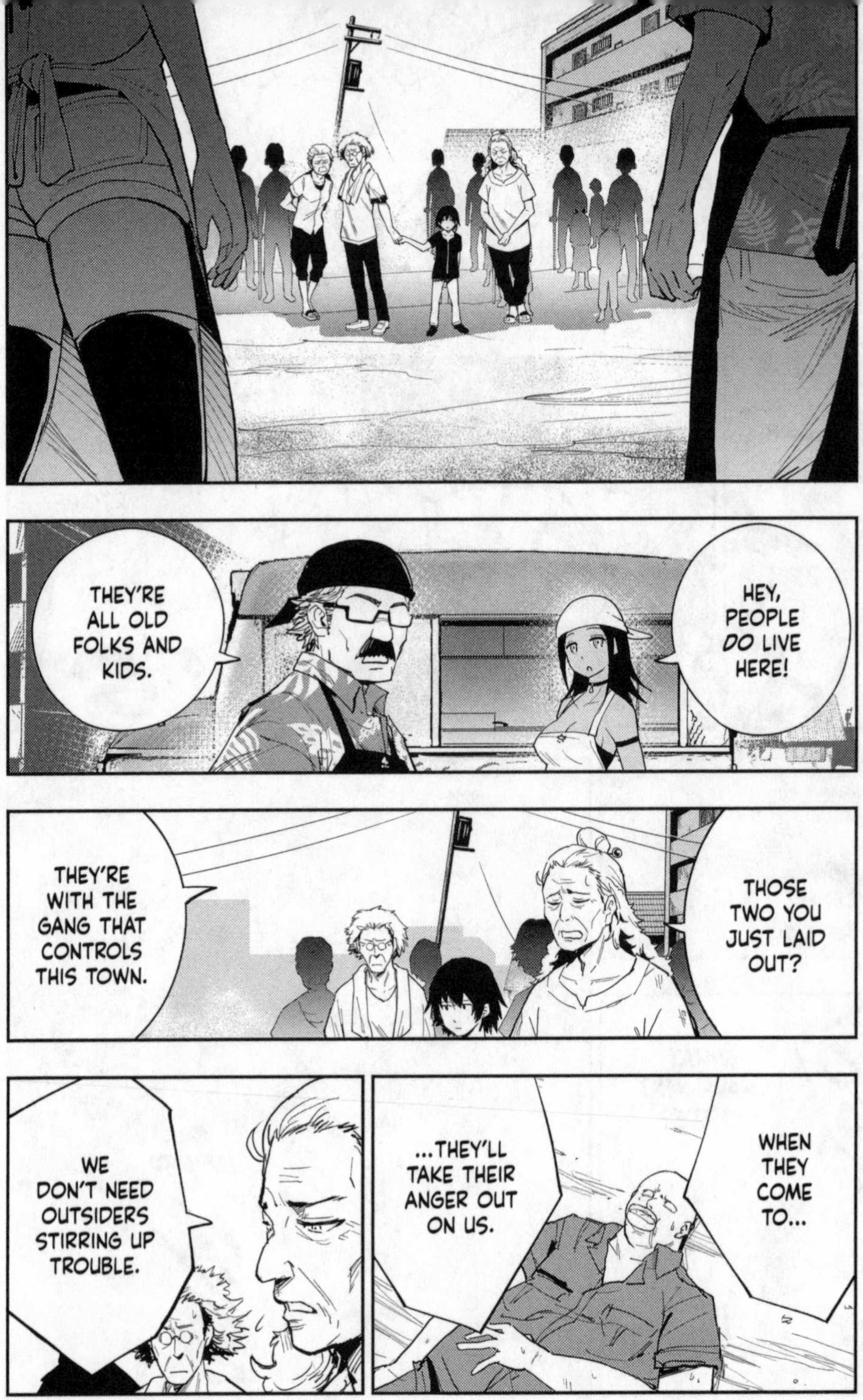
HEY, PEOPLE DO LIVE HERE!
THEY'RE ALL OLD FOLKS AND KIDS.
THOSE TWO YOU JUST LAID OUT?
THEY'RE WITH THE GANG THAT CONTROLS THIS TOWN.
WHEN THEY COME TO...
...THEY'LL TAKE THEIR ANGER OUT ON US.
WE DON'T NEED OUTSIDERS STIRRING UP TROUBLE.

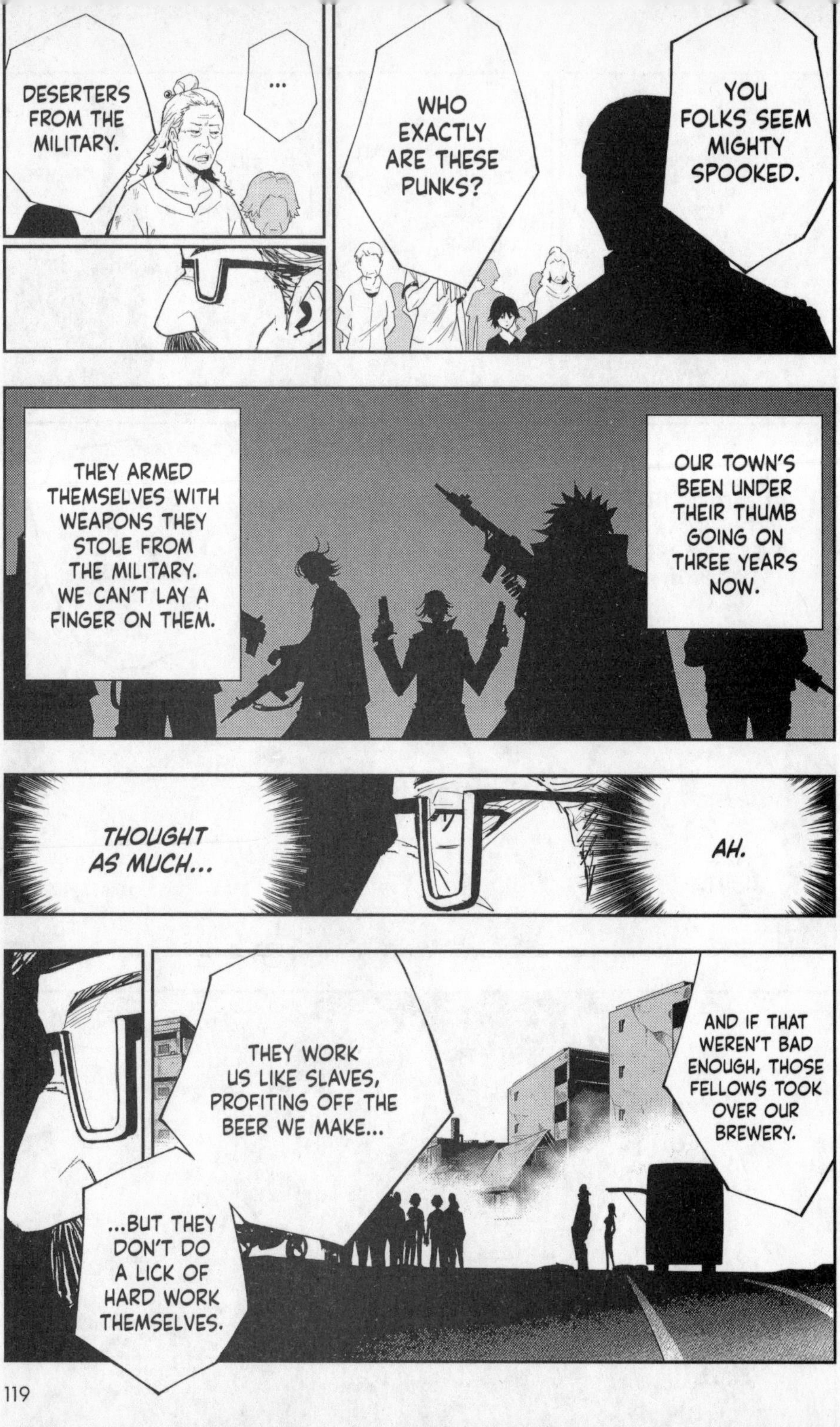
YOU FOLKS SEEM MIGHTY SPOOKED.
WHO EXACTLY ARE THESE PUNKS?
...
DESERTERS FROM THE MILITARY.
OUR TOWN'S BEEN UNDER THEIR THUMB GOING ON THREE YEARS NOW.
THEY ARMED THEMSELVES WITH WEAPONS THEY STOLE FROM THE MILITARY. WE CAN'T LAY A FINGER ON THEM.
AH.
THOUGHT AS MUCH...
AND IF THAT WEREN'T BAD ENOUGH, THOSE FELLOWS TOOK OVER OUR BREWERY.
THEY WORK US LIKE SLAVES, PROFITING OFF THE BEER WE MAKE...
...BUT THEY DON'T DO A LICK OF HARD WORK THEMSELVES.

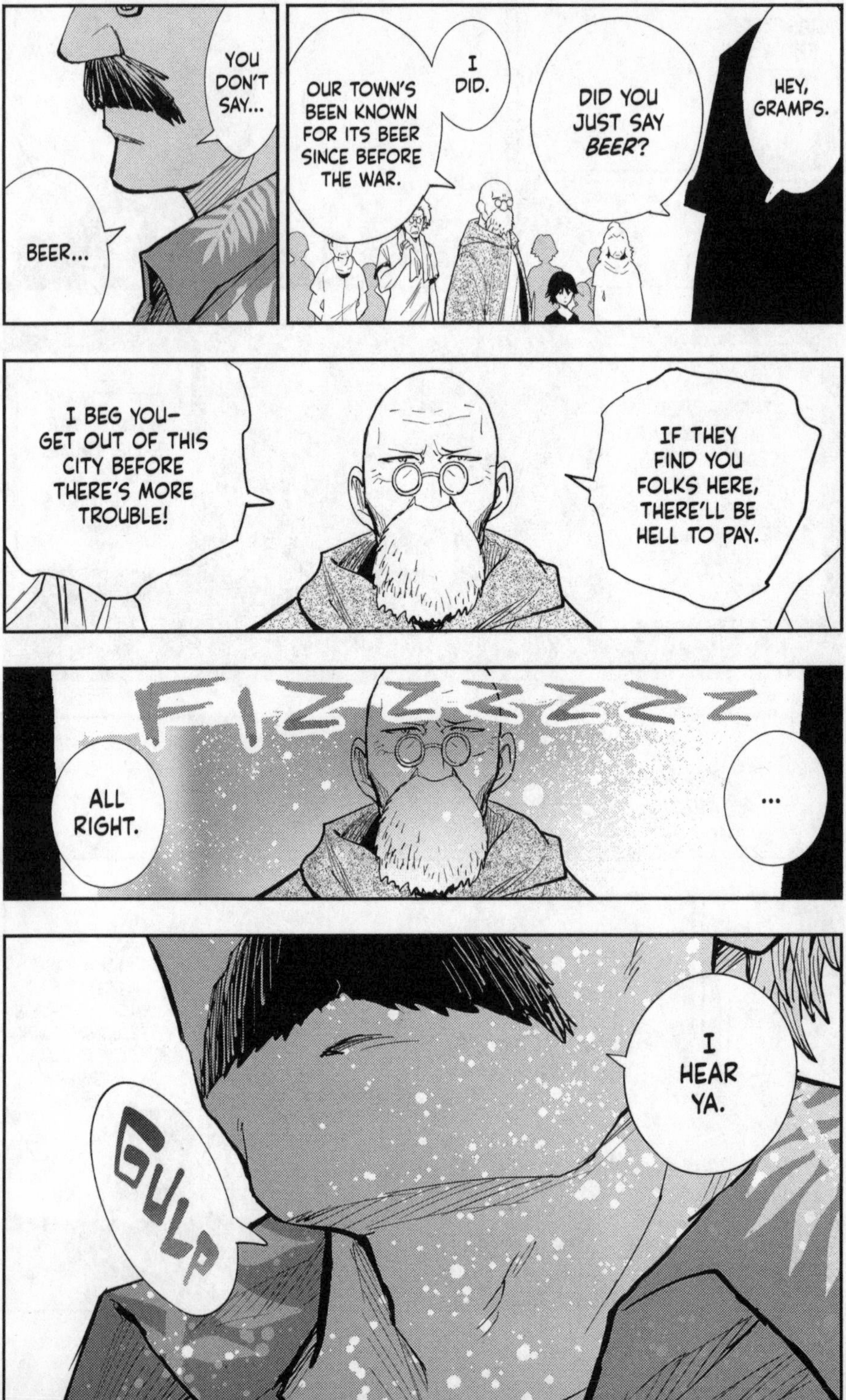
HEY, GRAMPS.
DID YOU JUST SAY *BEER*?
I DID.
OUR TOWN'S BEEN KNOWN FOR ITS BEER SINCE BEFORE THE WAR.
YOU DON'T SAY...
BEER...
IF THEY FIND YOU FOLKS HERE, THERE'LL BE HELL TO PAY.
I BEG YOU— GET OUT OF THIS CITY BEFORE THERE'S MORE TROUBLE!
FIZZZZZZ
...
ALL RIGHT.
I HEAR YA.
GULP

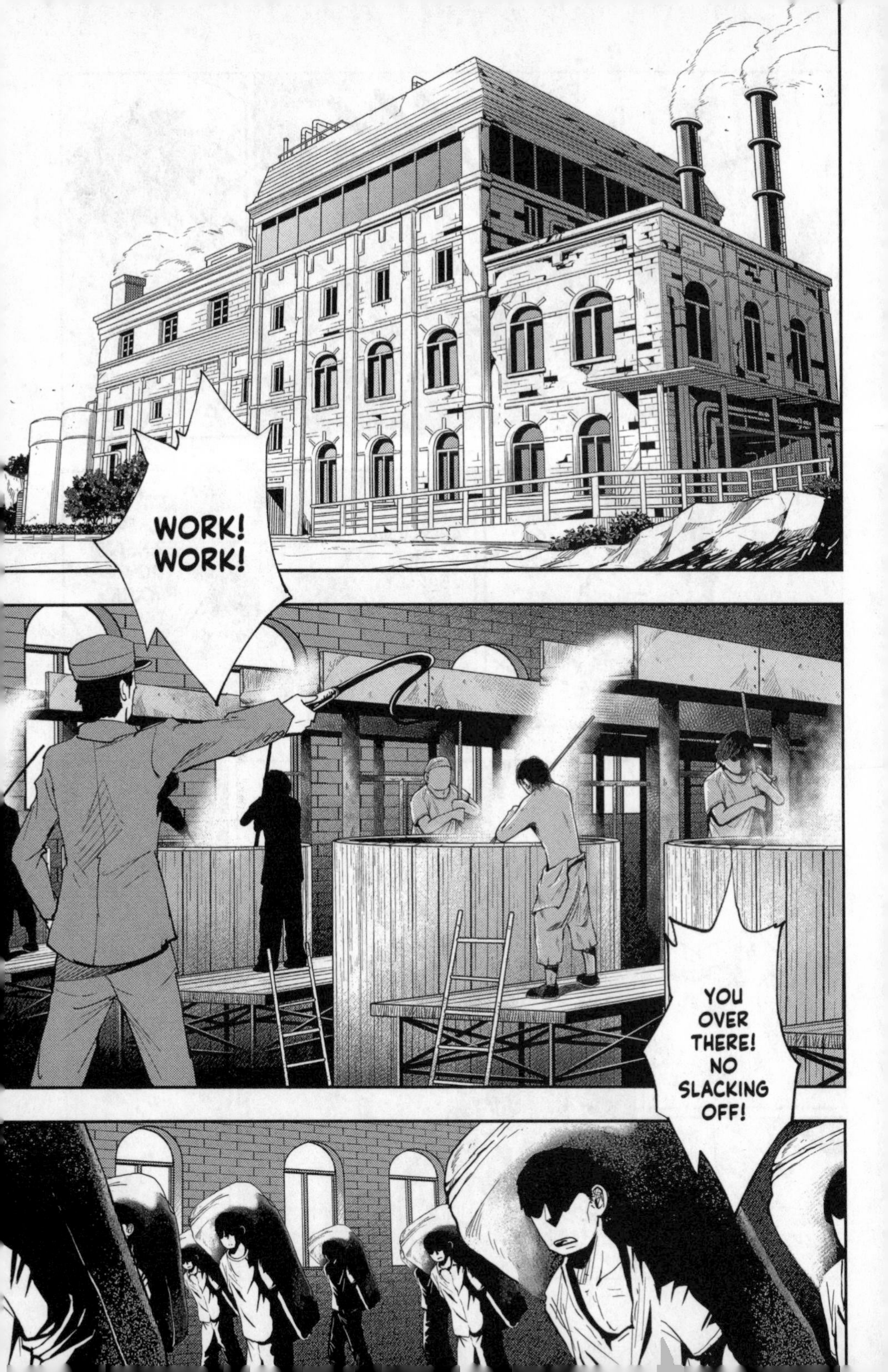
WORK! WORK!
YOU OVER THERE! NO SLACKING OFF!

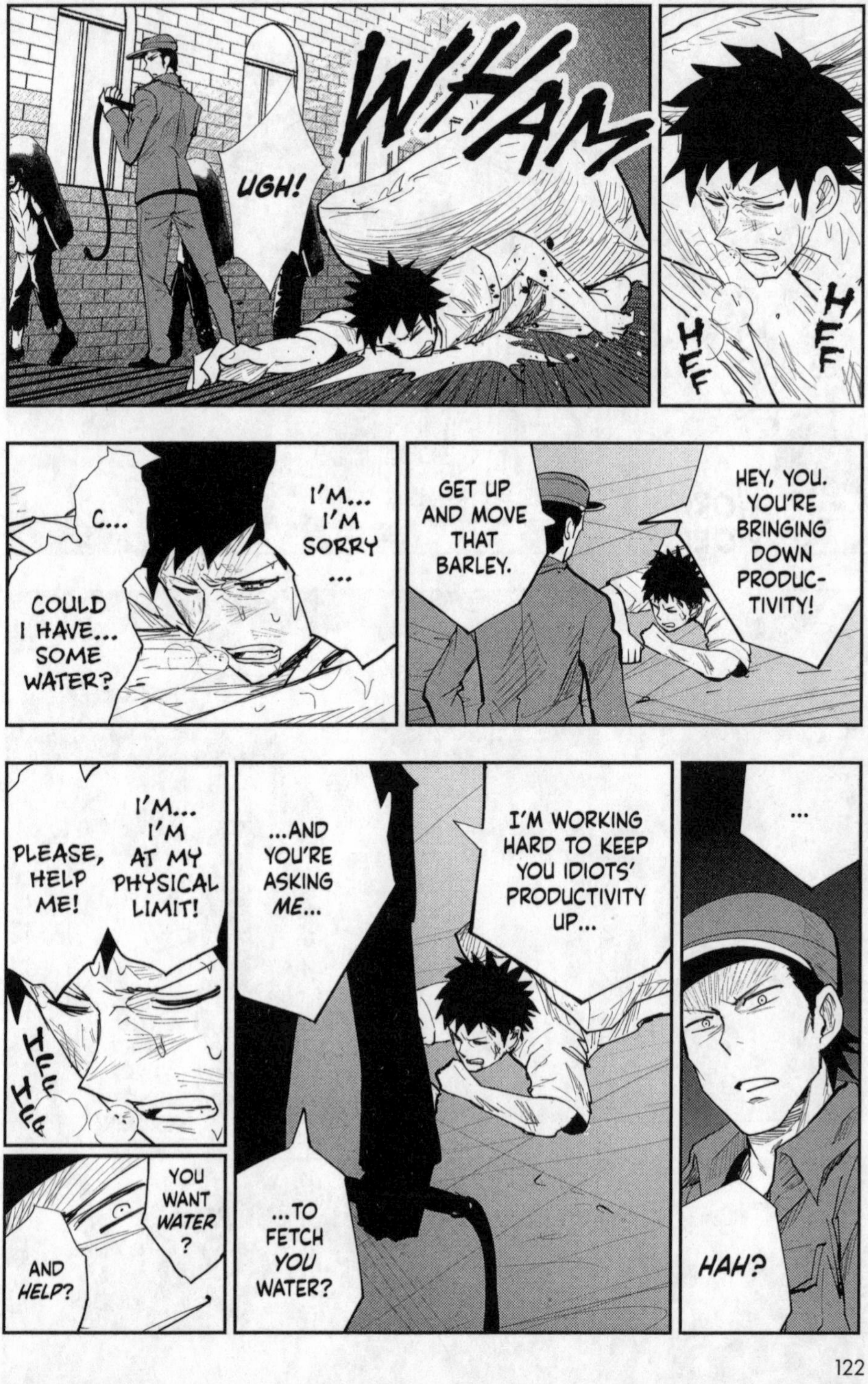
HEFF
HEFF
WHAM
UGH!
HEY, YOU. YOU'RE BRINGING DOWN PRODUC- TIVITY!
GET UP AND MOVE THAT BARLEY.
I'M... I'M SORRY ...
C...
COULD I HAVE... SOME WATER?
...
HAH?
I'M WORKING HARD TO KEEP YOU IDIOTS' PRODUCTIVITY UP...
...AND YOU'RE ASKING *ME*...
...TO FETCH *YOU* WATER?
I'M... I'M AT MY PHYSICAL LIMIT!
PLEASE, HELP ME!
HEFF
HEFF
YOU WANT *WATER* ?
AND *HELP*?

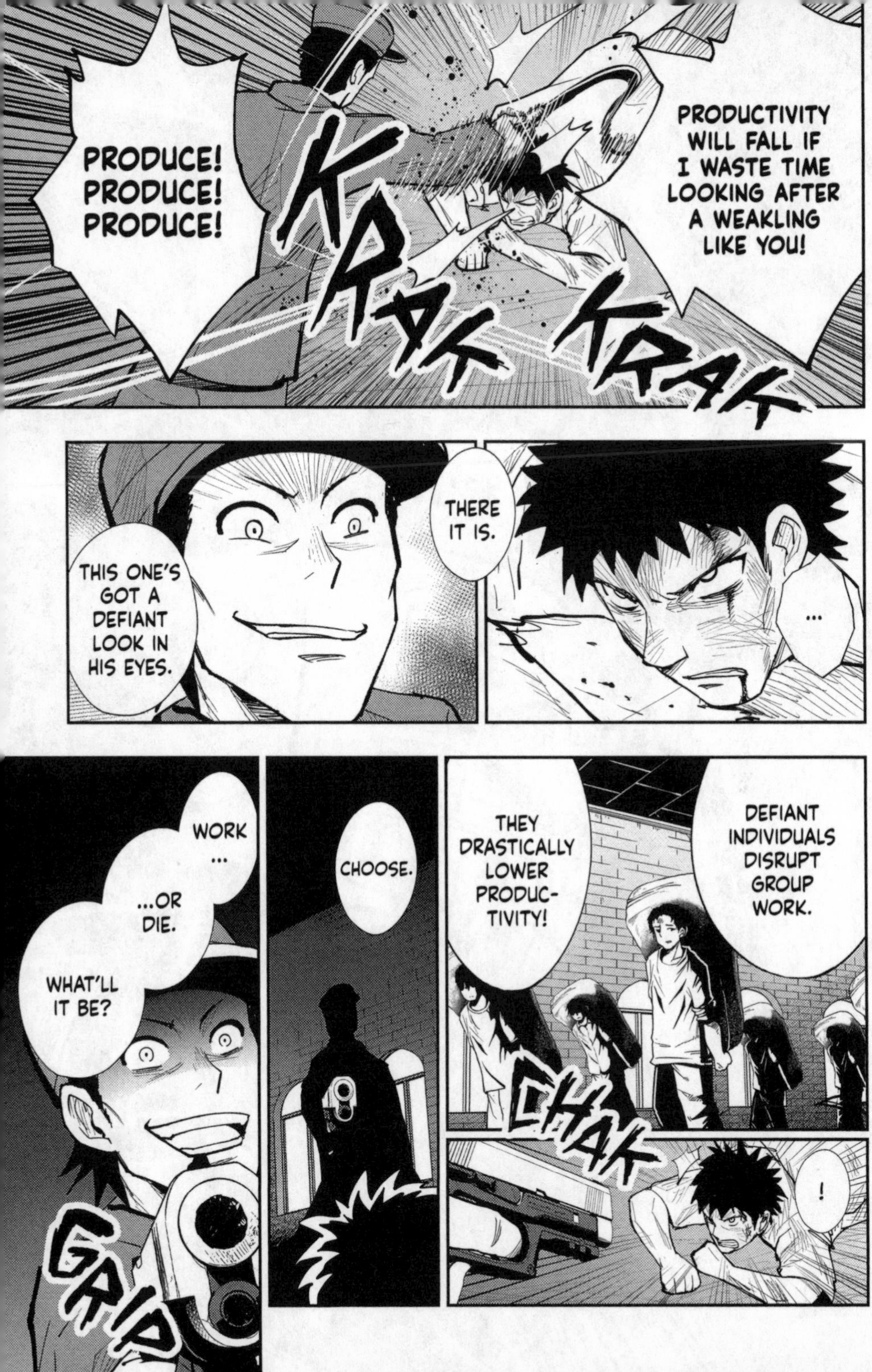
PRODUCTIVITY WILL FALL IF I WASTE TIME LOOKING AFTER A WEAKLING LIKE YOU!
PRODUCE! PRODUCE! PRODUCE!
KRAK KRAK
THERE IT IS.
...
THIS ONE'S GOT A DEFIANT LOOK IN HIS EYES.
DEFIANT INDIVIDUALS DISRUPT GROUP WORK.
THEY DRASTICALLY LOWER PRODUC-TIVITY!
CHAK
!
CHOOSE.
WORK ...
...OR DIE.
WHAT'LL IT BE?
GRIP

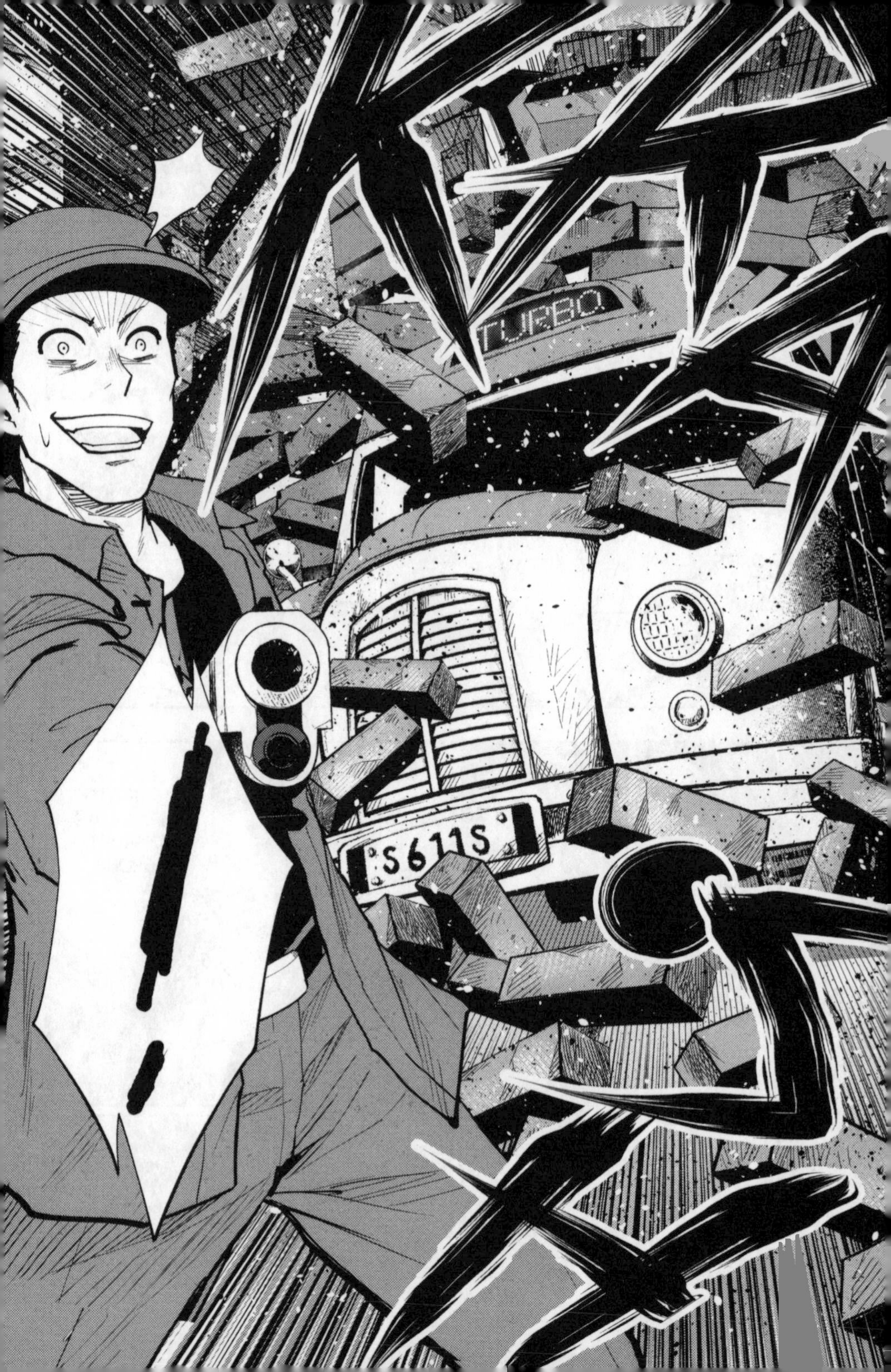
TURBO
S611S

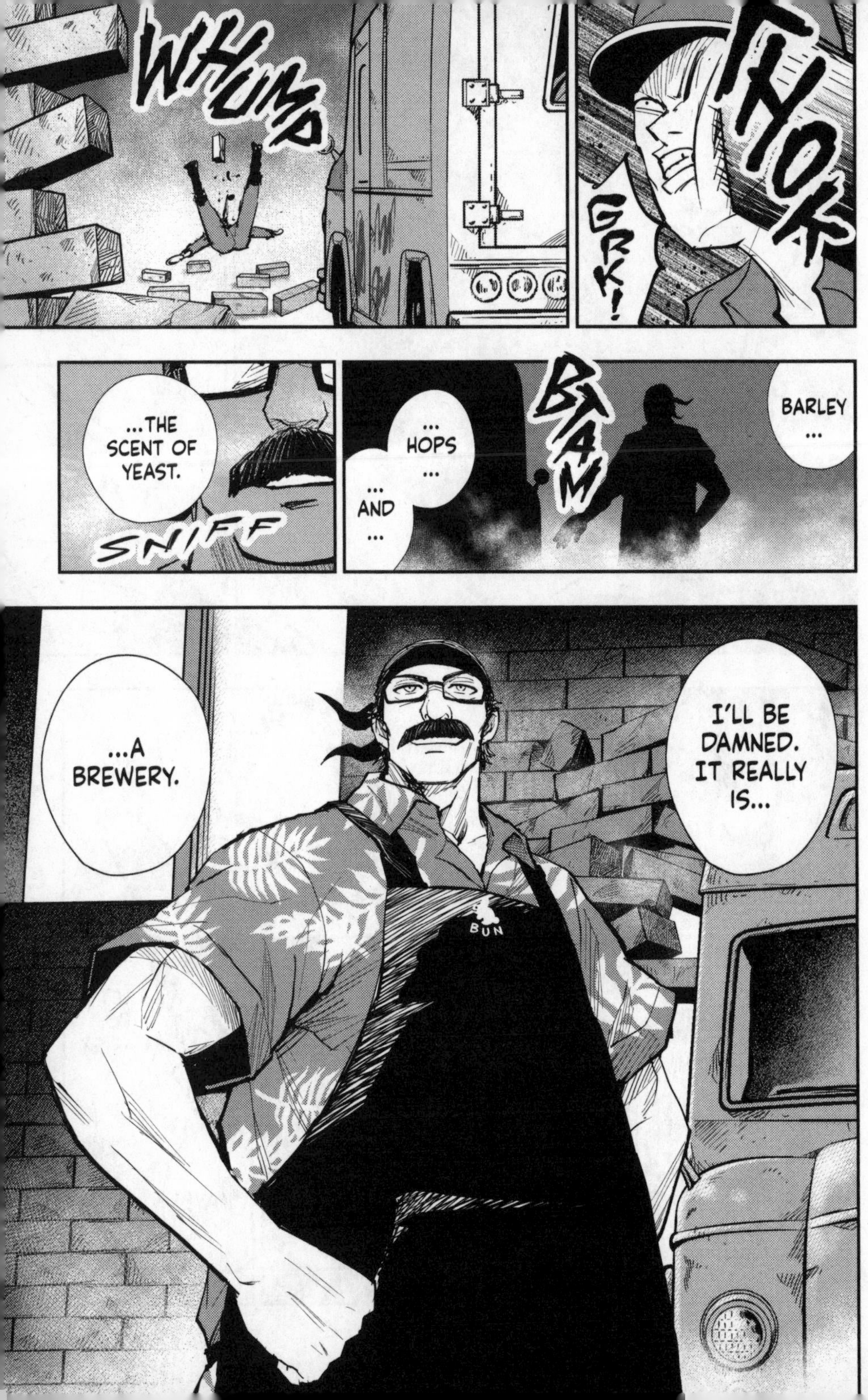
THOK
GRK!
WHUMP
BARLEY ...
BLAM
... HOPS ...
... AND ...
...THE SCENT OF YEAST.
SNIFF
I'LL BE DAMNED. IT REALLY IS...
...A BREWERY.
BUN

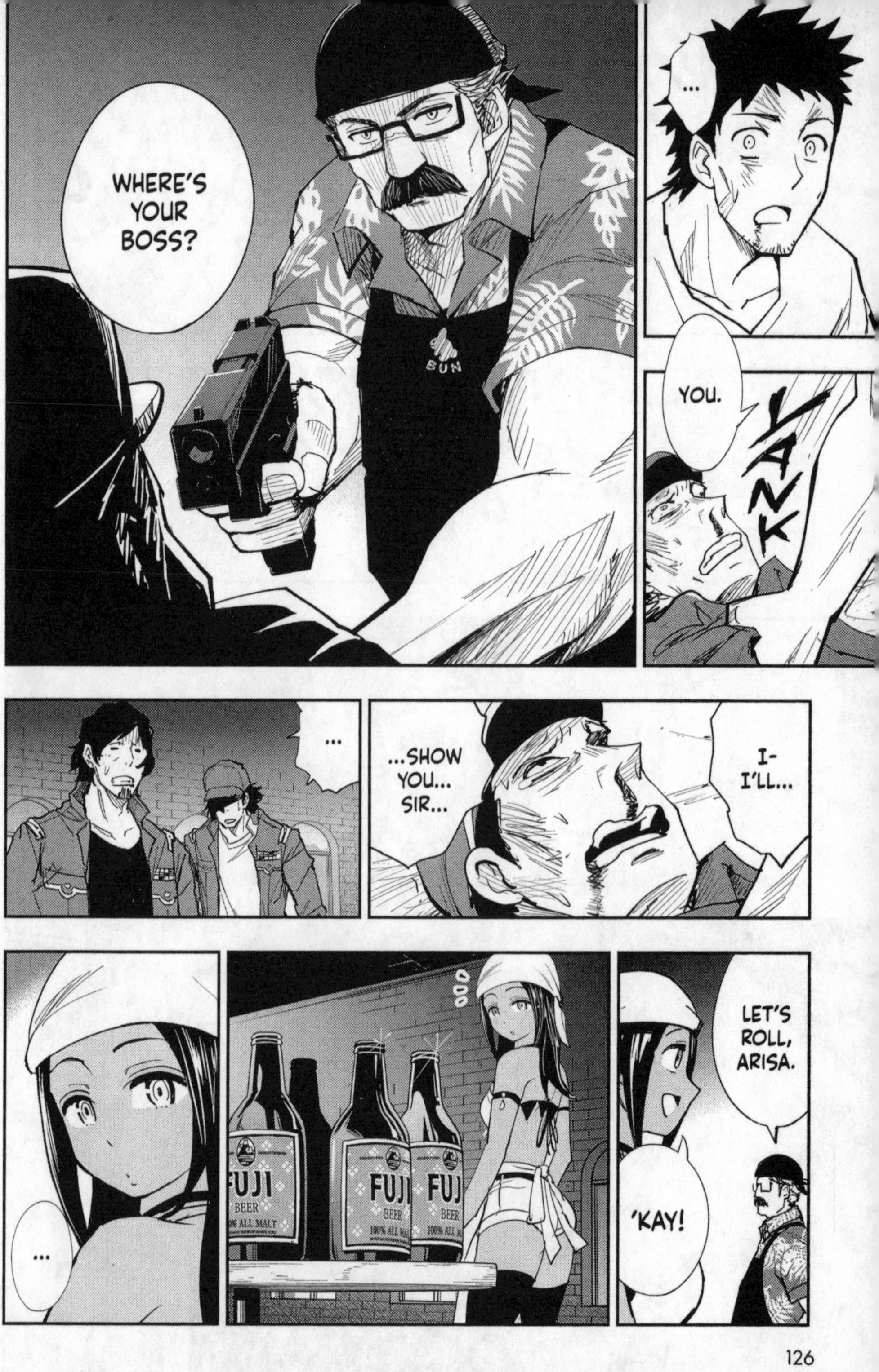
...
YOU.
YANK
WHERE'S YOUR BOSS?
BUN
I- I'LL...
...SHOW YOU... SIR...
...
LET'S ROLL, ARISA.
'KAY!
FUJI BEER 100% ALL MALT
FUJI BEER 100% ALL MALT
...

KNOCK KNOCK

ENTER.

GCHAK

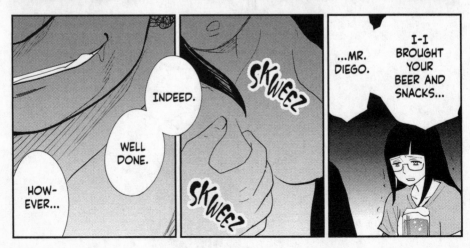

INDEED.

WELL DONE.

HOW- EVER...

SKWEEZ

SKWEEZ

...MR. DIEGO.

I-I BROUGHT YOUR BEER AND SNACKS...

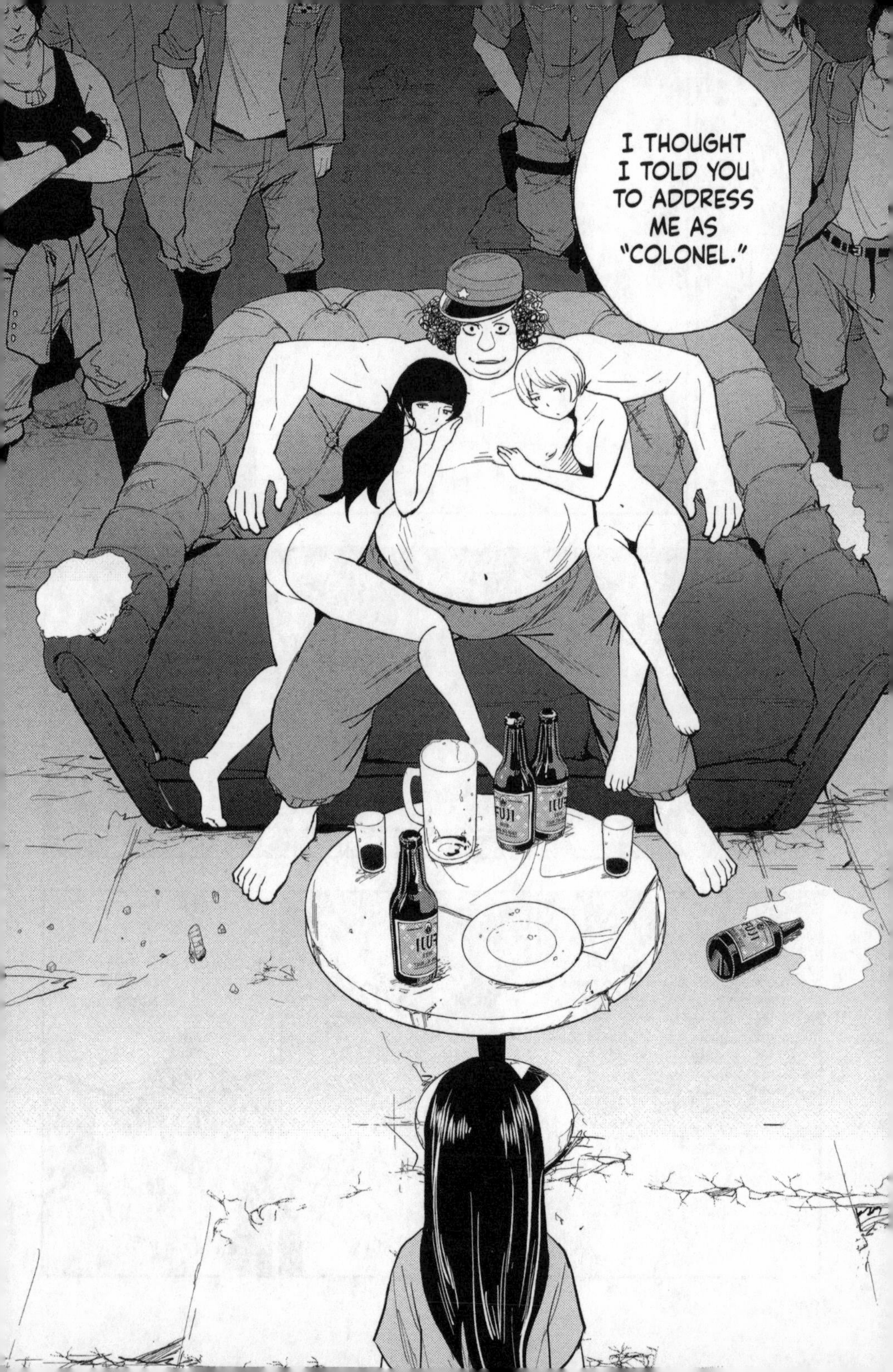
I THOUGHT I TOLD YOU TO ADDRESS ME AS "COLONEL."

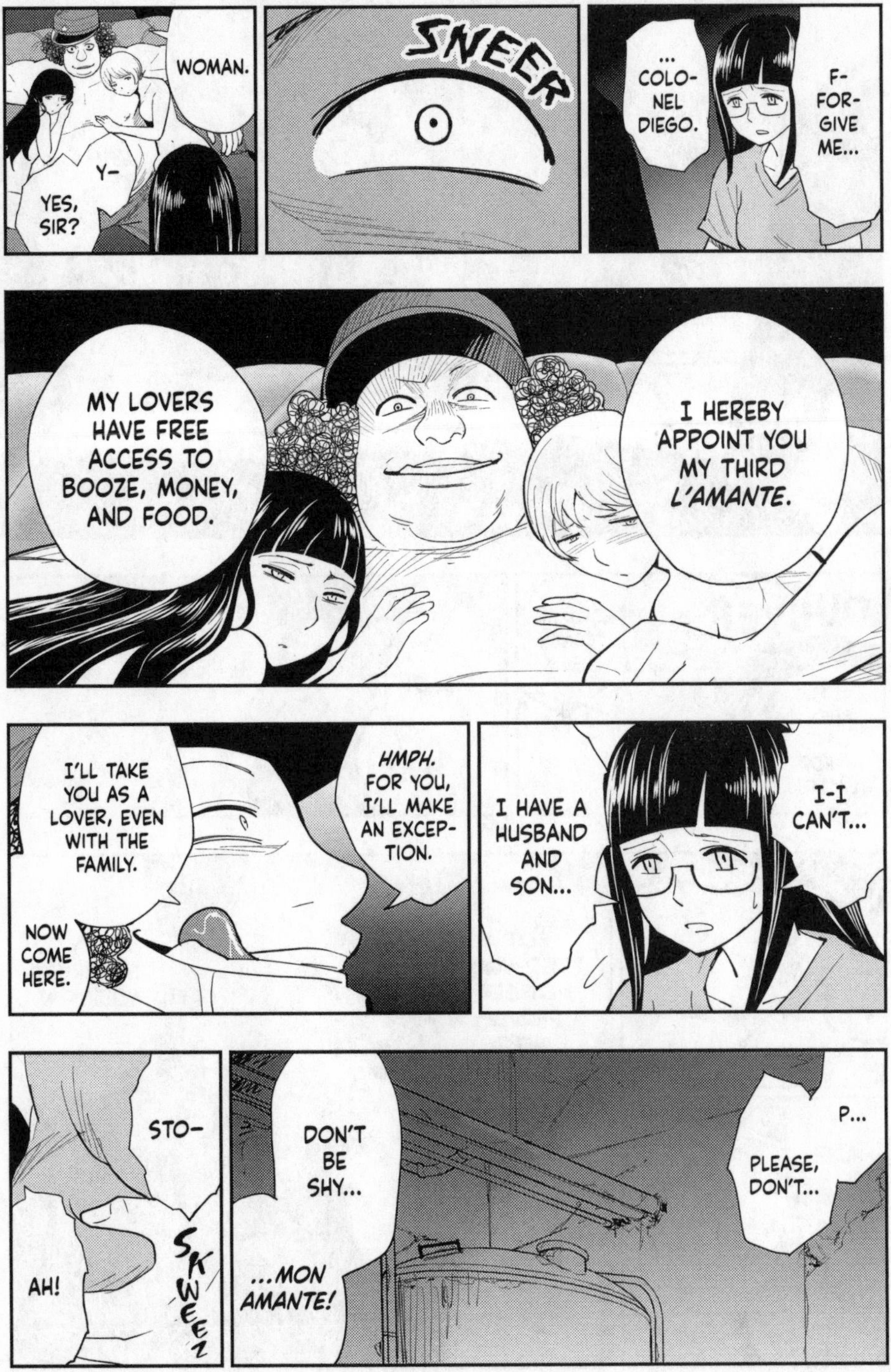
F-FORGIVE ME...
...COLONEL DIEGO.
SNEER
WOMAN.
Y-
YES, SIR?
I HEREBY APPOINT YOU MY THIRD *L'AMANTE.*
MY LOVERS HAVE FREE ACCESS TO BOOZE, MONEY, AND FOOD.
I-I CAN'T...
I HAVE A HUSBAND AND SON...
HMPH. FOR YOU, I'LL MAKE AN EXCEPTION.
I'LL TAKE YOU AS A LOVER, EVEN WITH THE FAMILY.
NOW COME HERE.
P...
PLEASE, DON'T...
DON'T BE SHY...
...MON AMANTE!
STO-
SKWEEZ
AH!

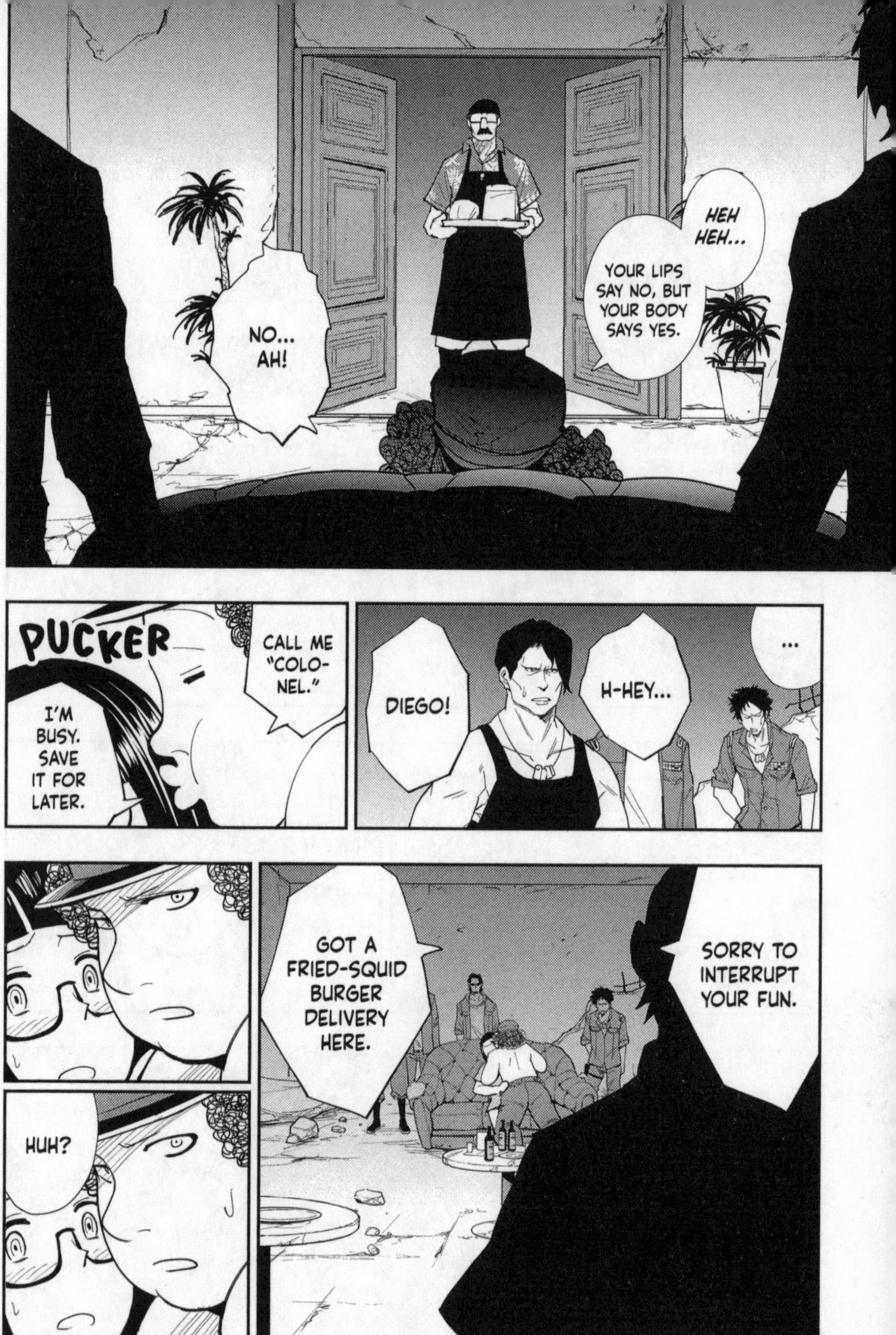
HEH HEH...
YOUR LIPS SAY NO, BUT YOUR BODY SAYS YES.
NO... AH!
...
H-HEY...
DIEGO!
CALL ME "COLO-NEL."
PUCKER
I'M BUSY. SAVE IT FOR LATER.
SORRY TO INTERRUPT YOUR FUN.
GOT A FRIED-SQUID BURGER DELIVERY HERE.
HUH?

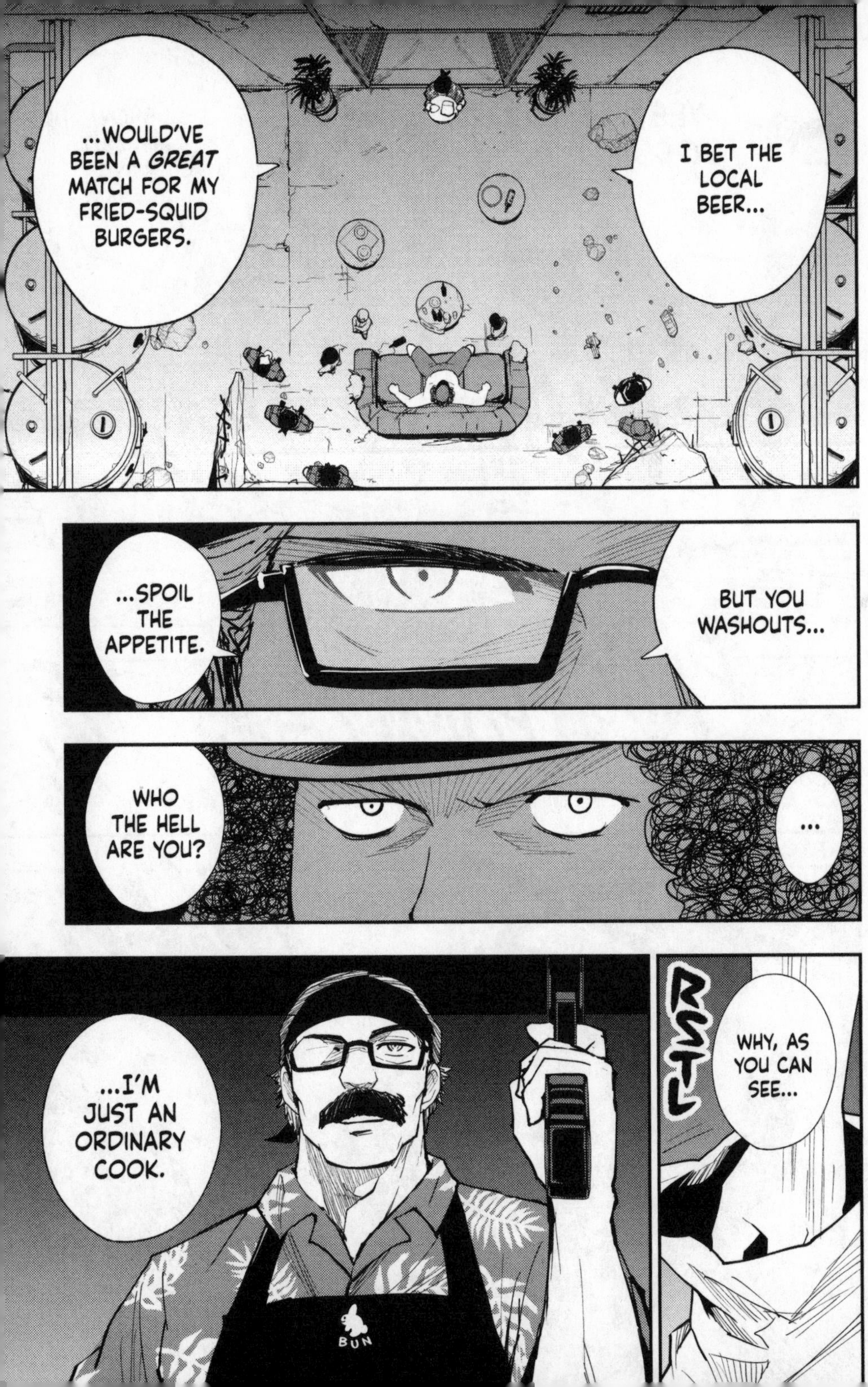
I BET THE LOCAL BEER...
...WOULD'VE BEEN A *GREAT* MATCH FOR MY FRIED-SQUID BURGERS.
BUT YOU WASHOUTS...
...SPOIL THE APPETITE.
...
WHO THE HELL ARE YOU?
RSTL
WHY, AS YOU CAN SEE...
...I'M JUST AN ORDINARY COOK.
BUN

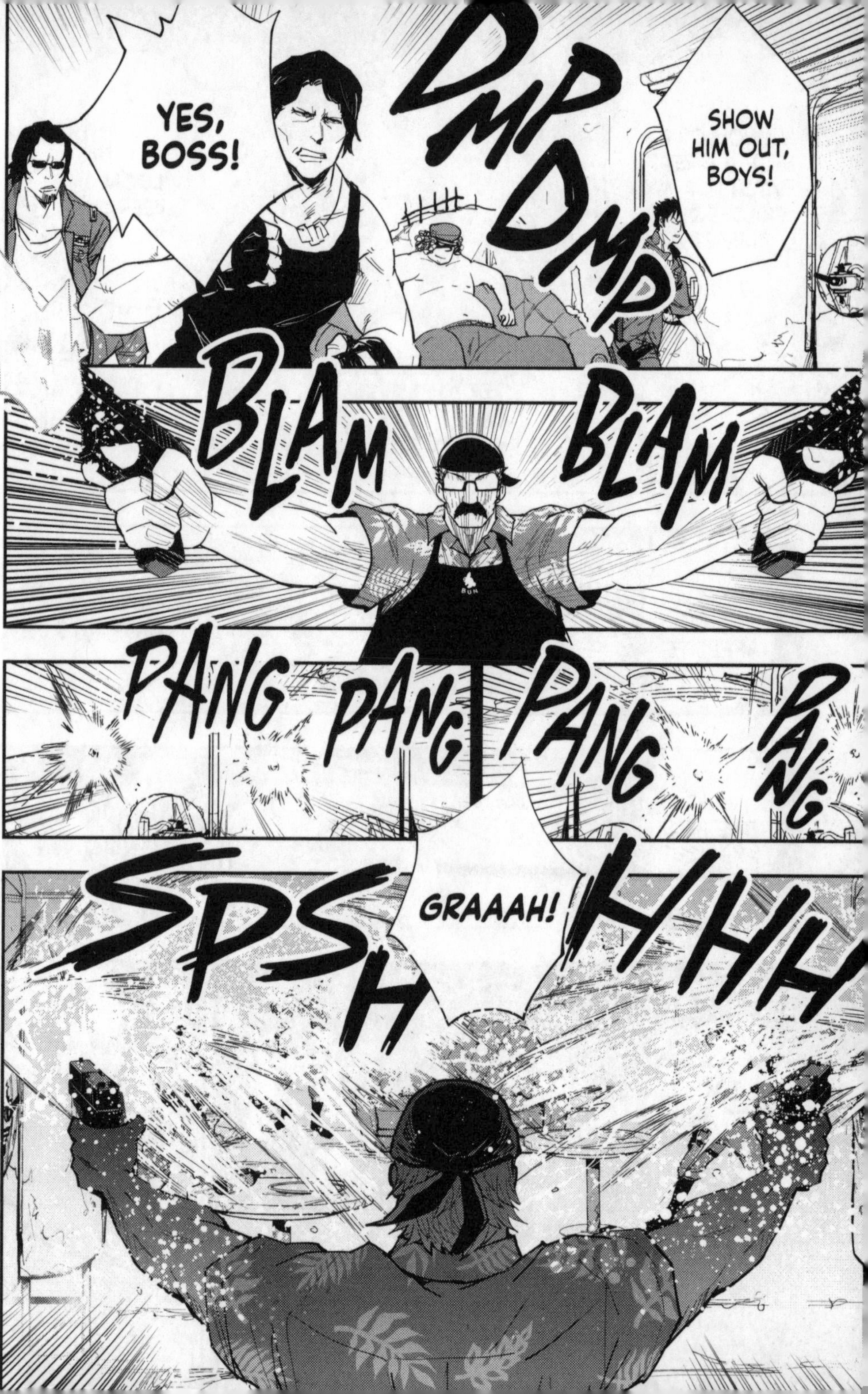
SHOW HIM OUT, BOYS!
DMP DMP DMP
YES, BOSS!
BLAM BLAM
BLAM
PANG
PANG
PANG
PANG
SPSHHHH
GRAAAH!

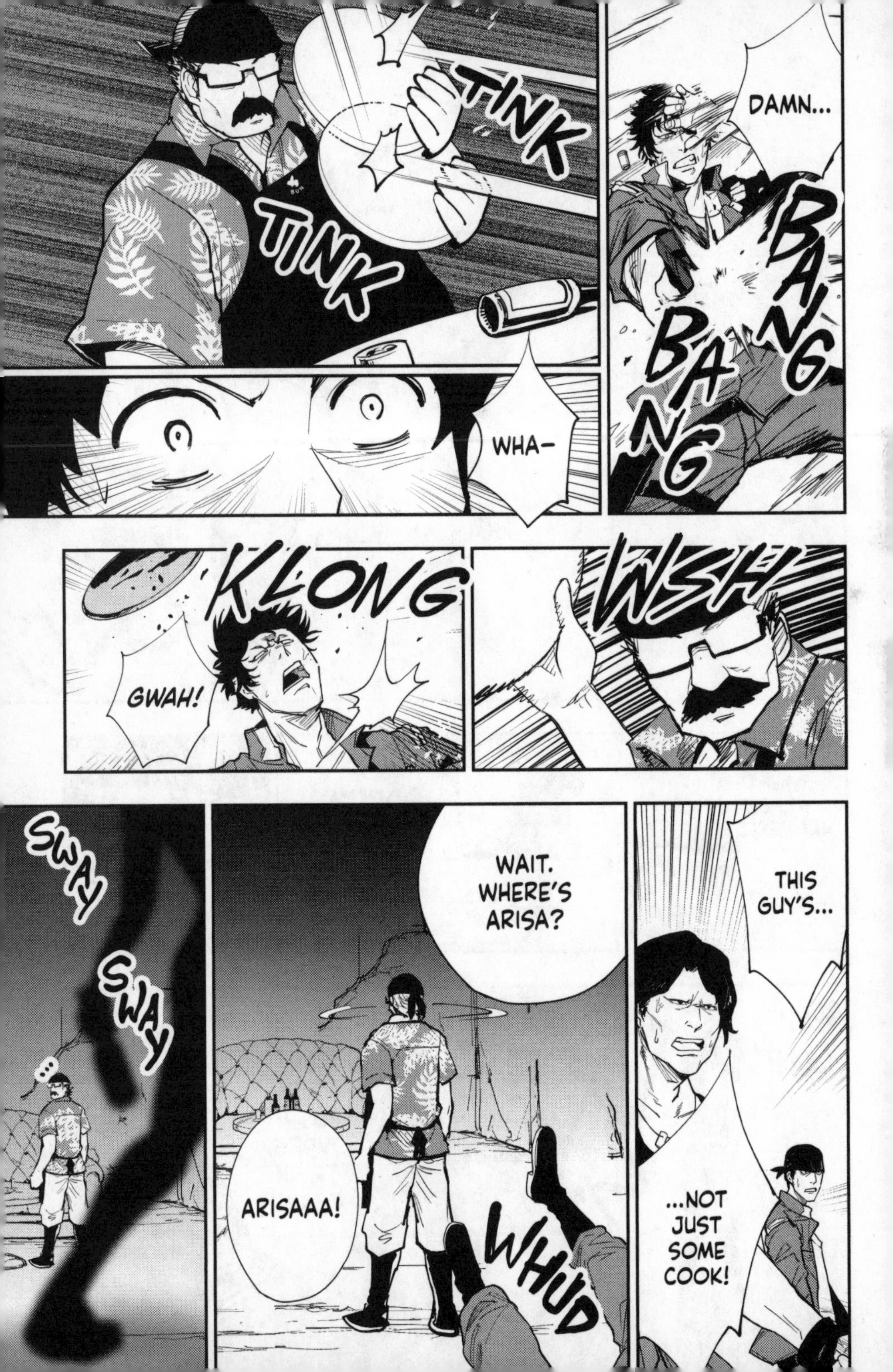
DAMN...
BANG
BANG
TINK
TINK
WHA-
WSH
KLONG
GWAH!
THIS GUY'S...
...NOT JUST SOME COOK!
WAIT. WHERE'S ARISA?
ARISAAA!
WHUD
SWAY
SWAY
...

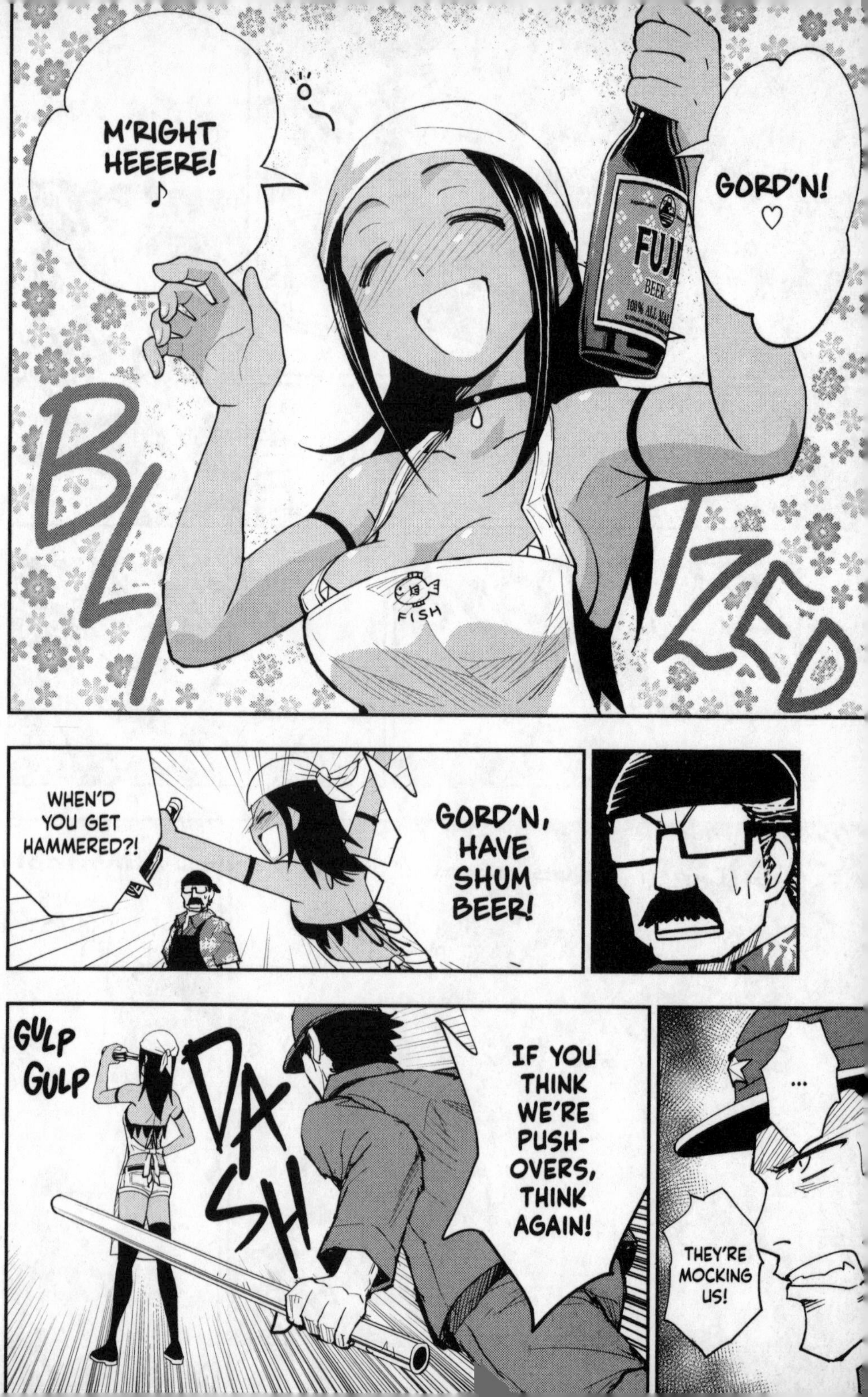
GORD'N! ♡
M'RIGHT HEEERE! ♪
BLI
TZED
GORD'N, HAVE SHUM BEER!
WHEN'D YOU GET HAMMERED?!
...
THEY'RE MOCKING US!
IF YOU THINK WE'RE PUSH-OVERS, THINK AGAIN!
DA
SH
GULP GULP

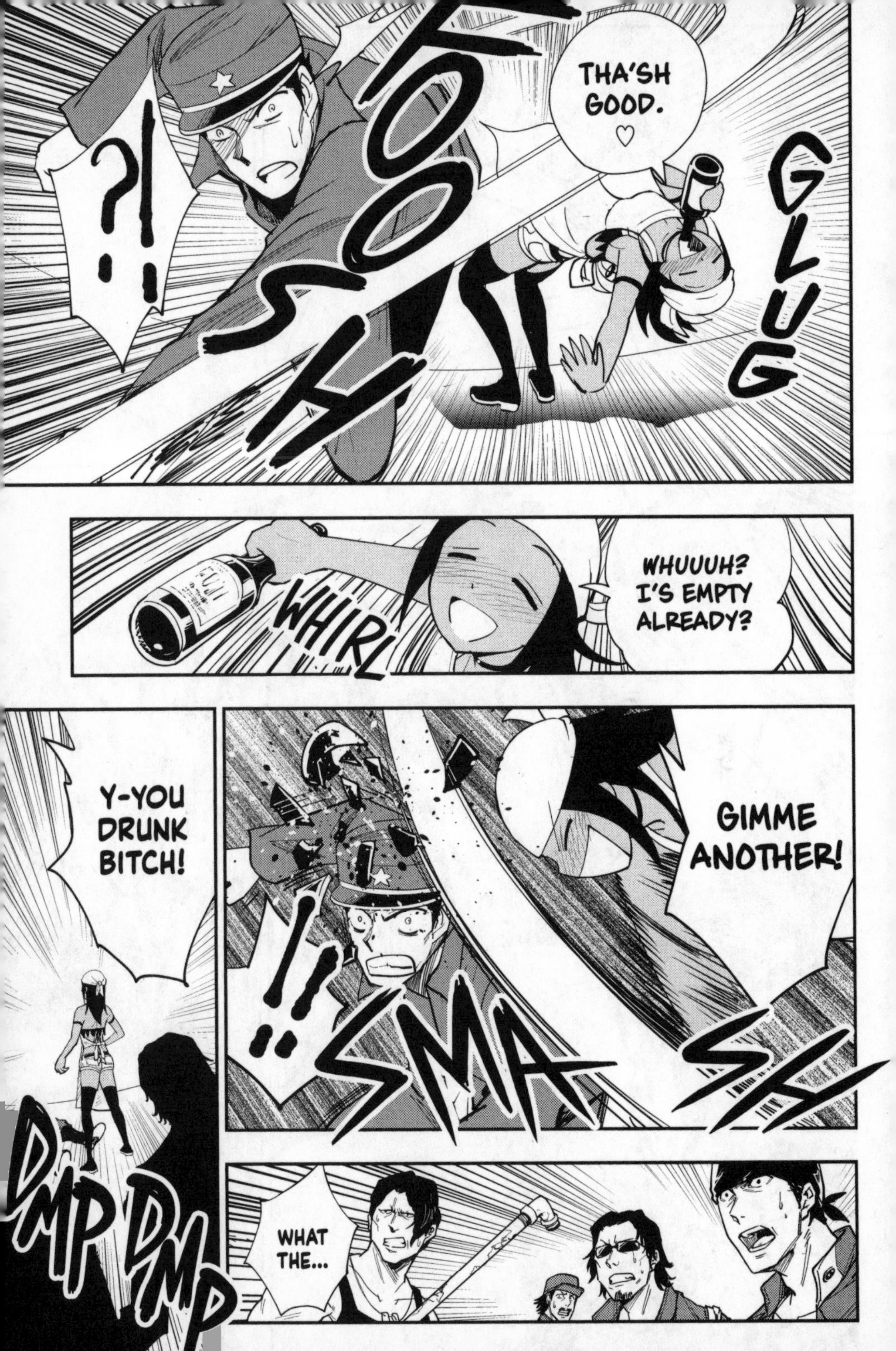

THA'SH GOOD. ♡
GLUG
FOOSH
?!
WHUUUH? I'S EMPTY ALREADY?
WHIRL
GIMME ANOTHER!
!!
SMASH
Y-YOU DRUNK BITCH!
DMP DMP
WHAT THE...

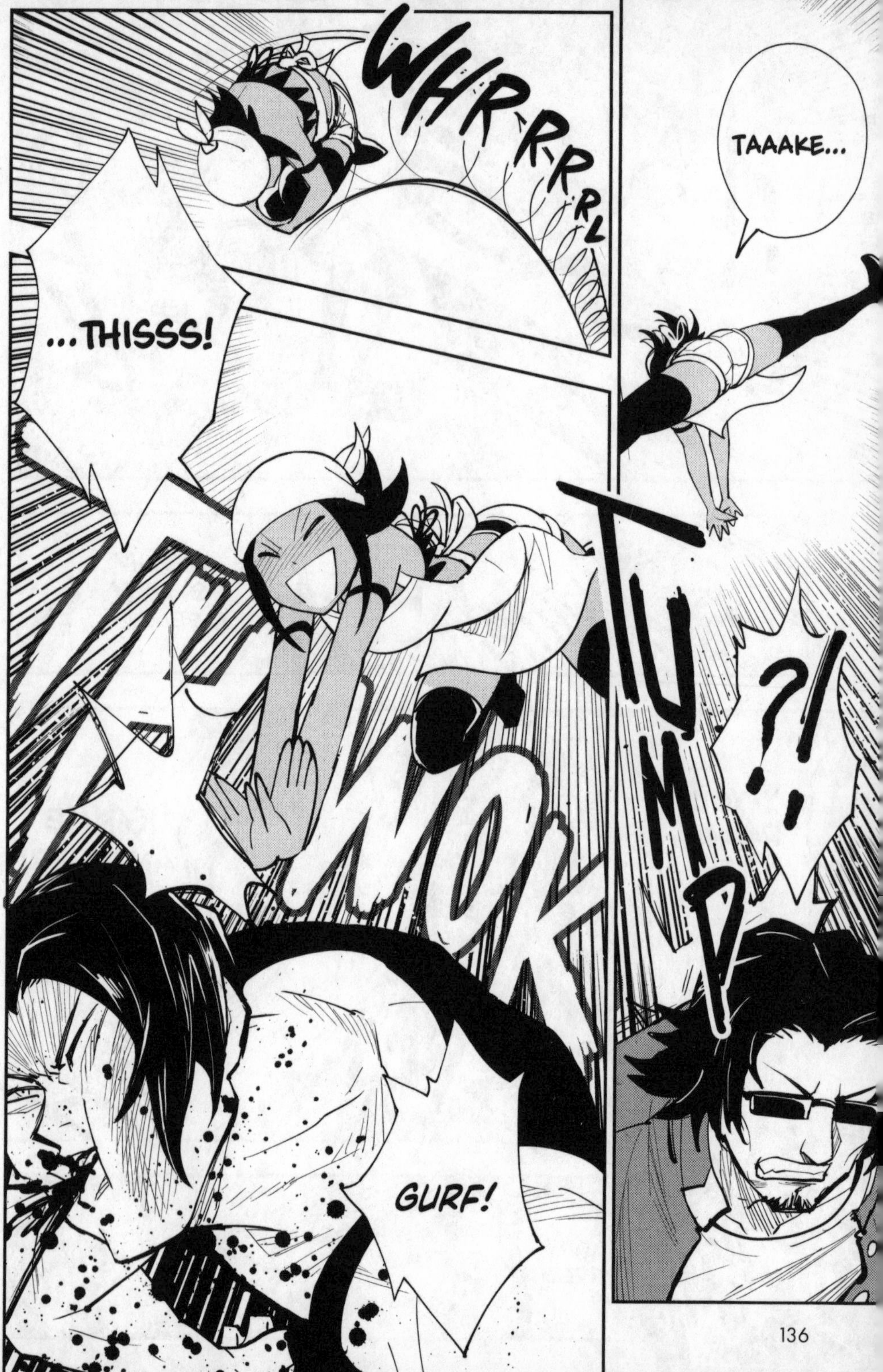
TAAAKE...
WHR-R-R-RRL
...THISSS!
THUMP
?!
WOK
GURF!

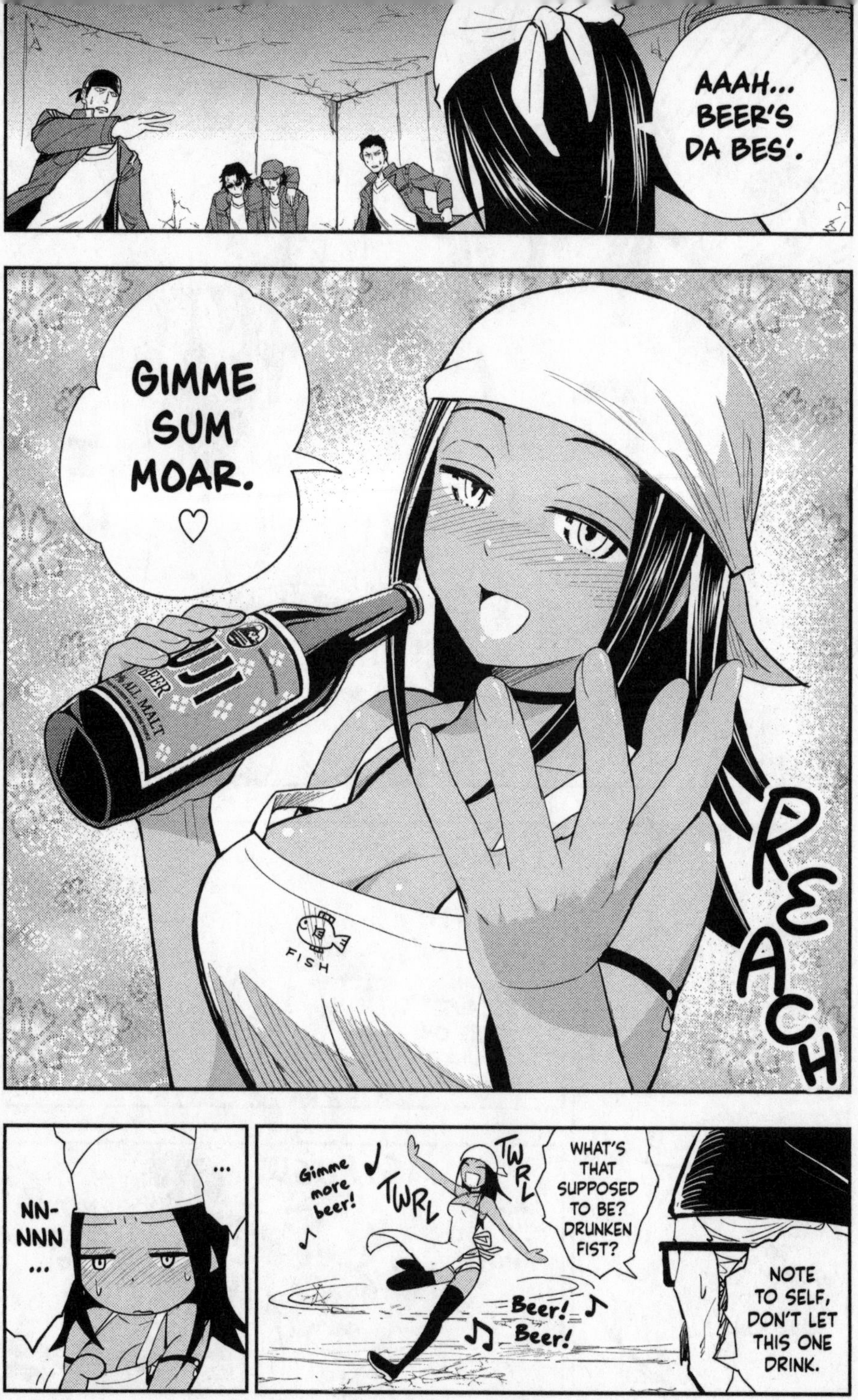
AAAH... BEER'S DA BES'.
GIMME SUM MOAR. ♡
REACH
WHAT'S THAT SUPPOSED TO BE? DRUNKEN FIST?
TWRL
Gimme more beer!
TWRL
NOTE TO SELF, DON'T LET THIS ONE DRINK.
Beer! Beer!
...
NN-NNN ...

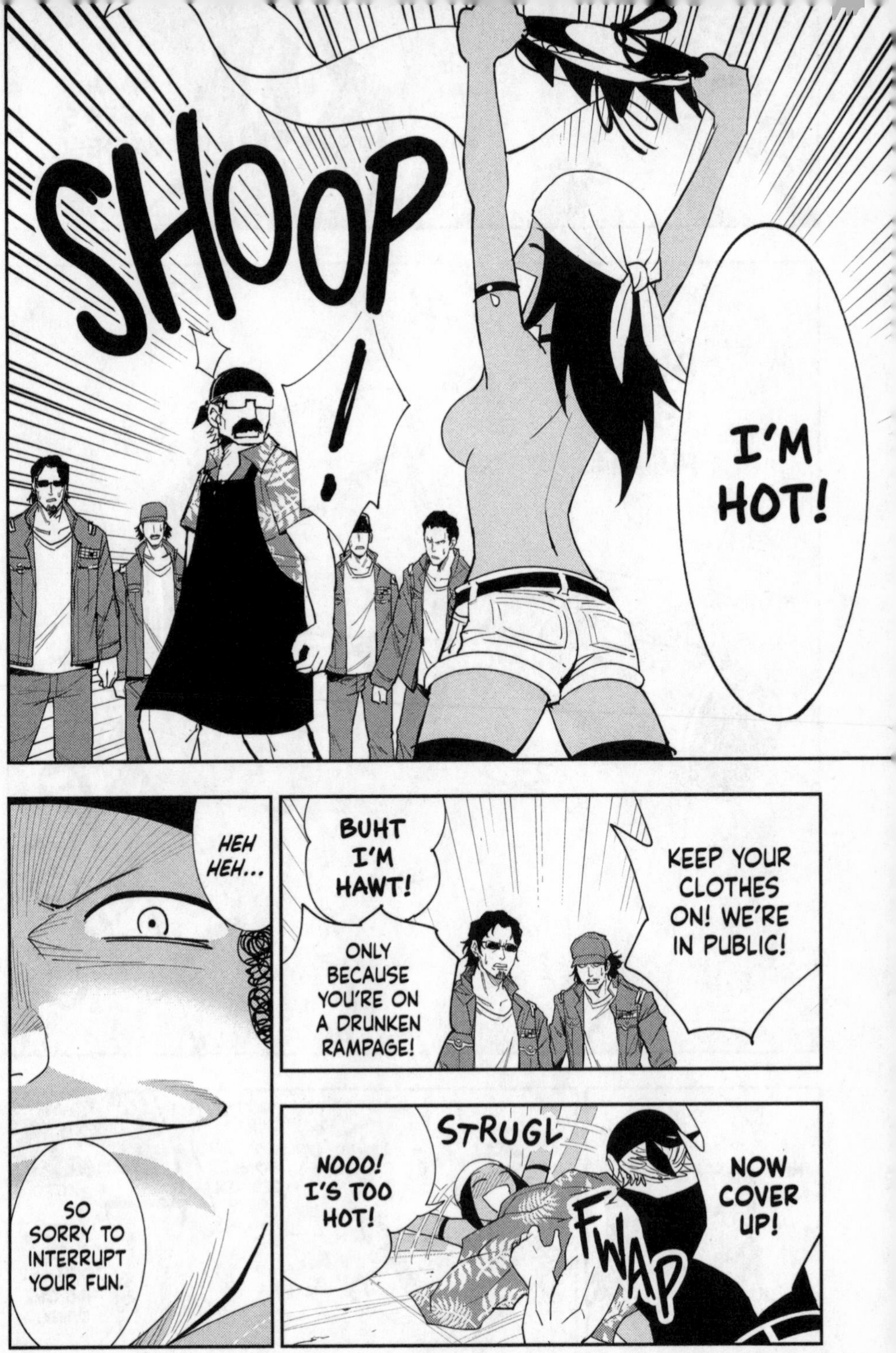
SHOOP
I'M HOT!
!
KEEP YOUR CLOTHES ON! WE'RE IN PUBLIC!
BUHT I'M HAWT!
ONLY BECAUSE YOU'RE ON A DRUNKEN RAMPAGE!
NOW COVER UP!
FWAP
STRUGL
NOOO! I'S TOO HOT!
HEH HEH...
SO SORRY TO INTERRUPT YOUR FUN.

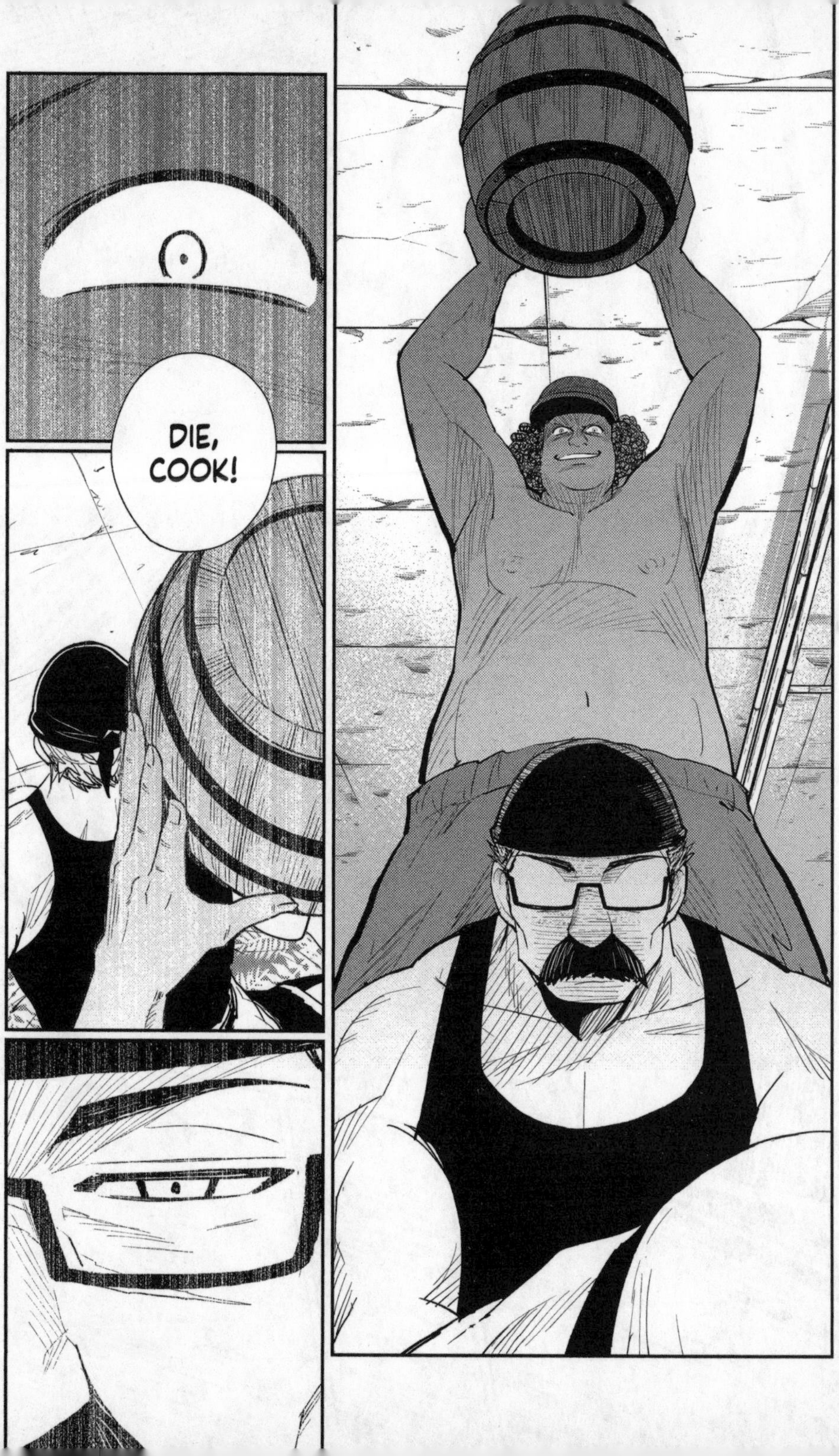
DIE, COOK!

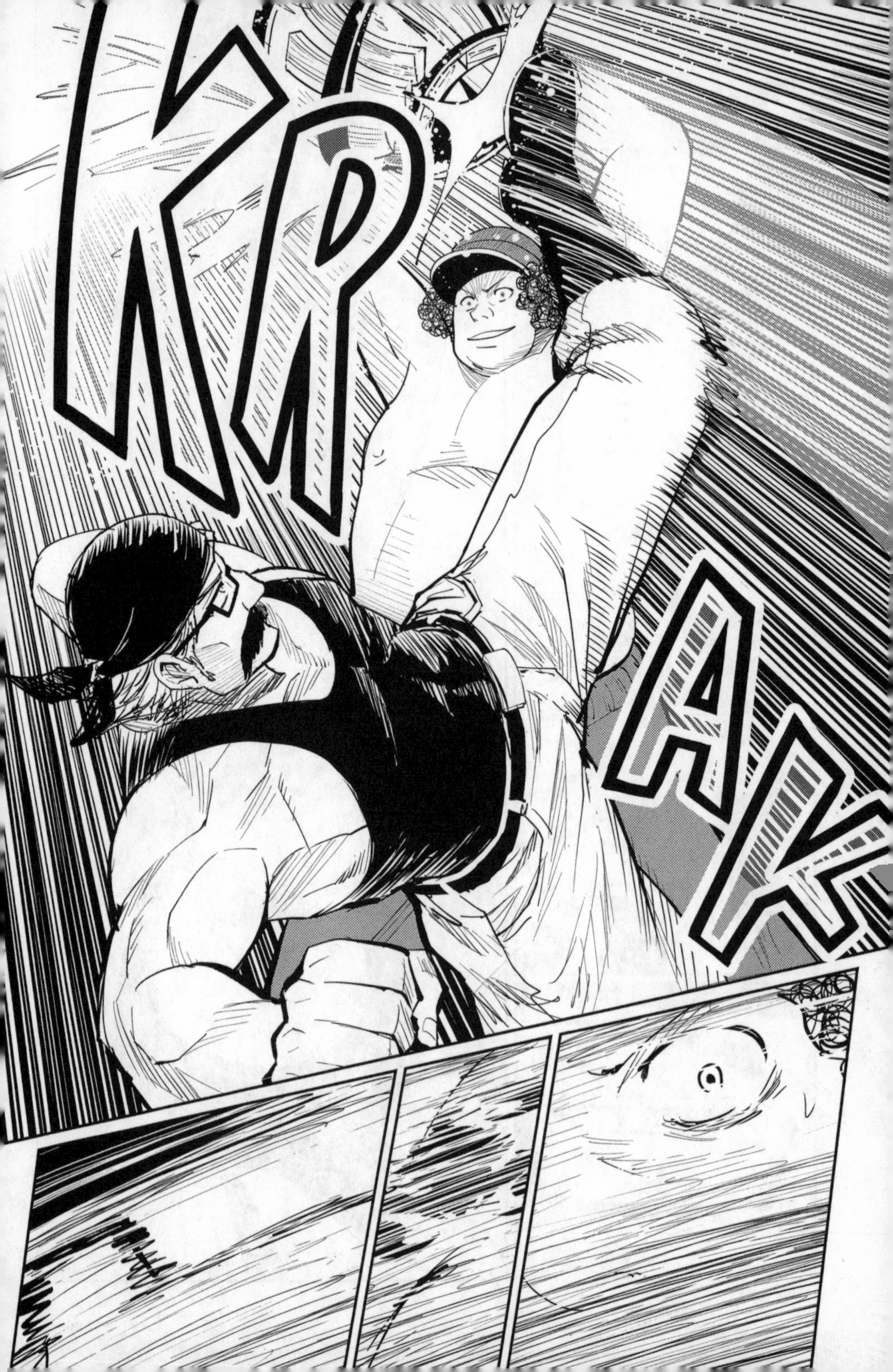
KRAK

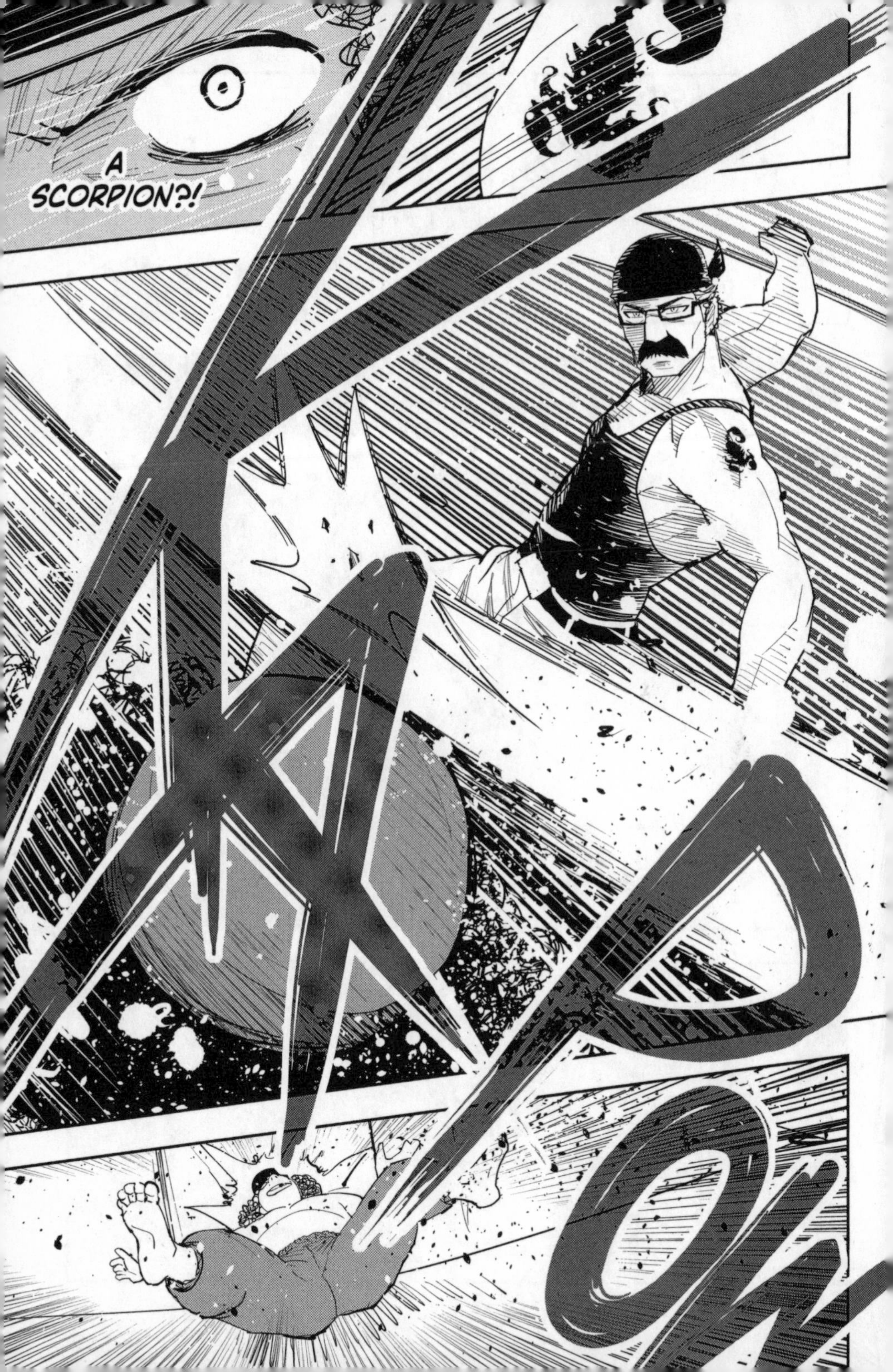
A SCORPION?!

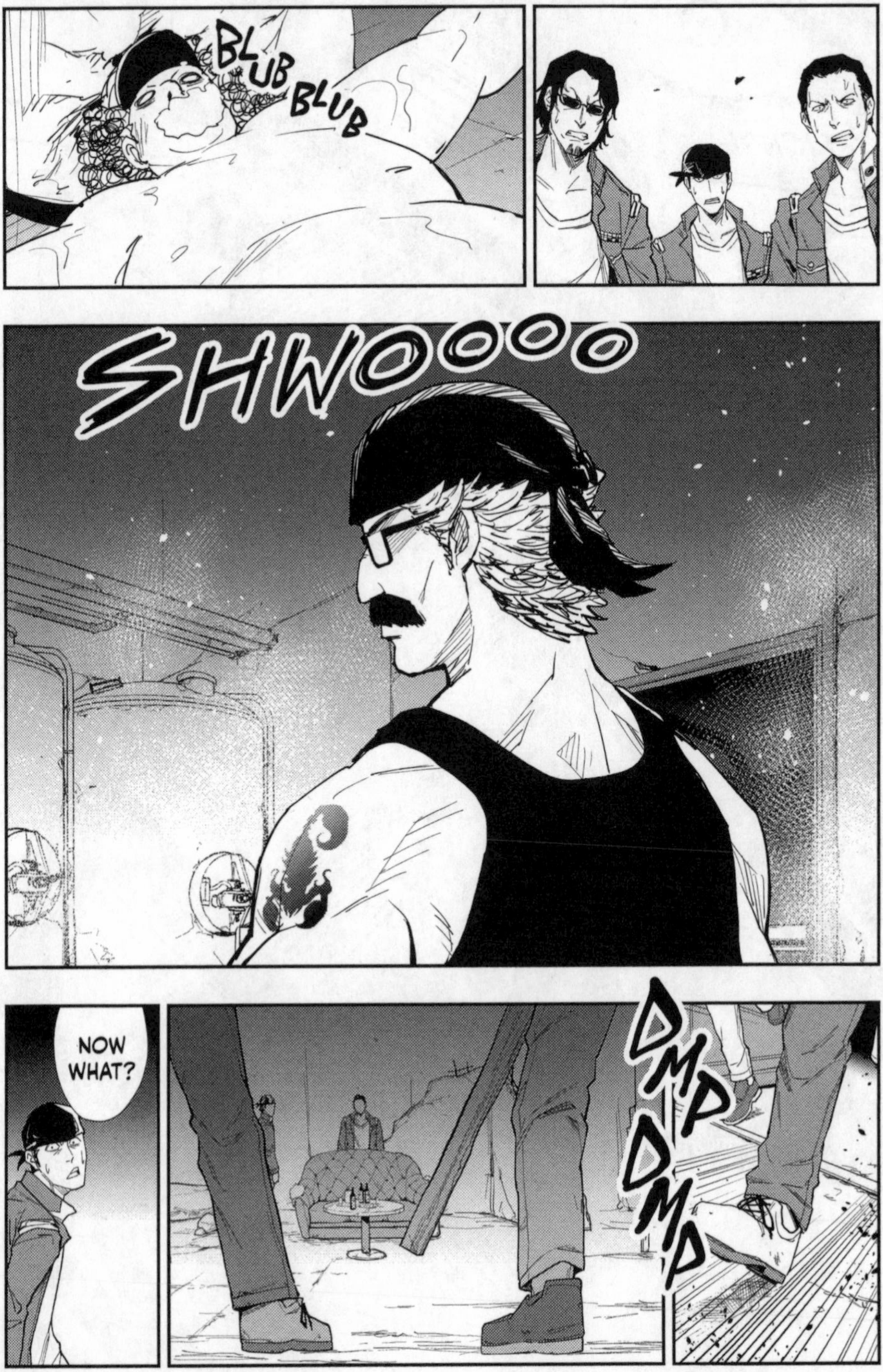
BLUB BLUB
SHWOOOO
DMP DMP DMP
NOW WHAT?

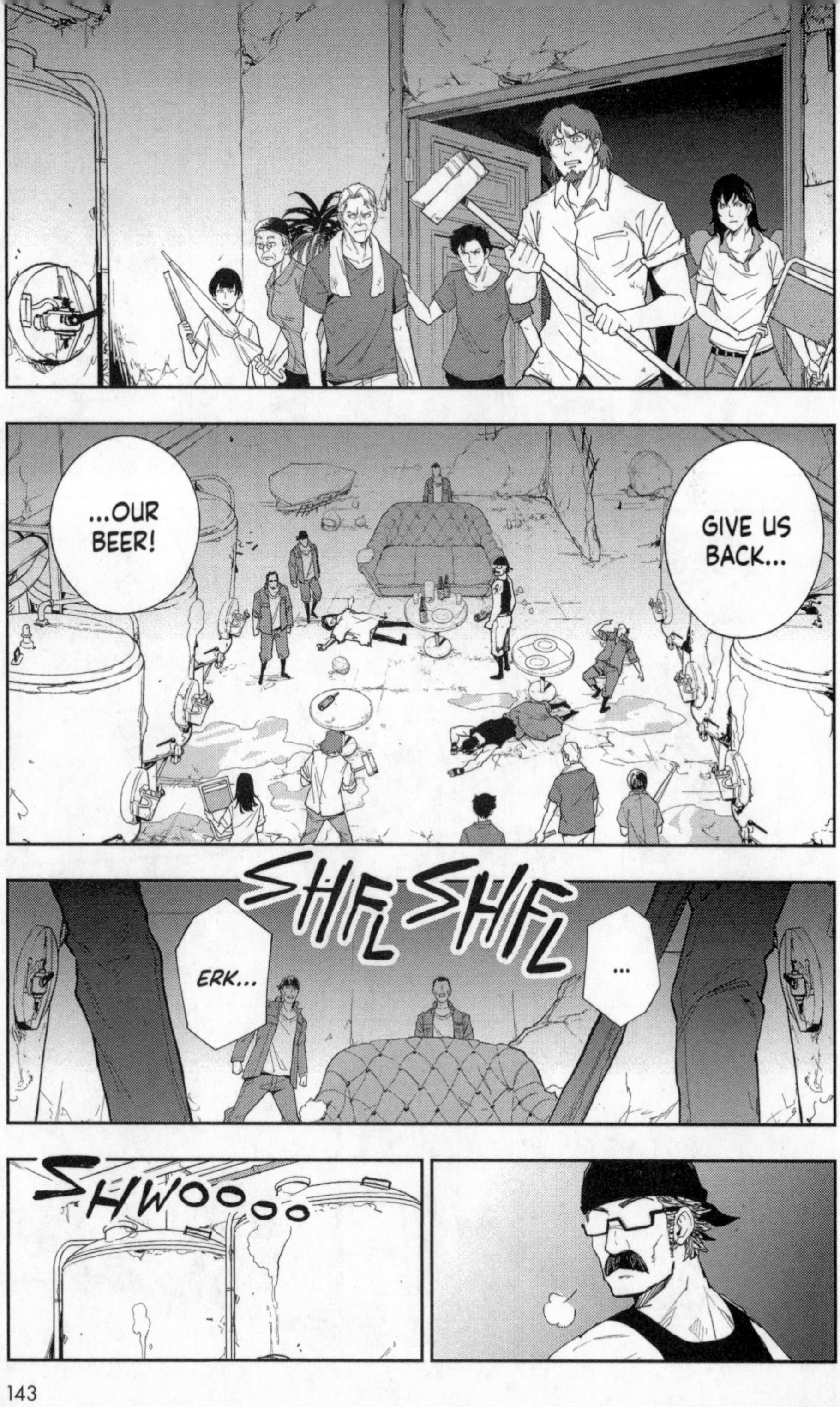
GIVE US BACK...
...OUR BEER!
SHFL SHFL
...
ERK...
SHWOOOO

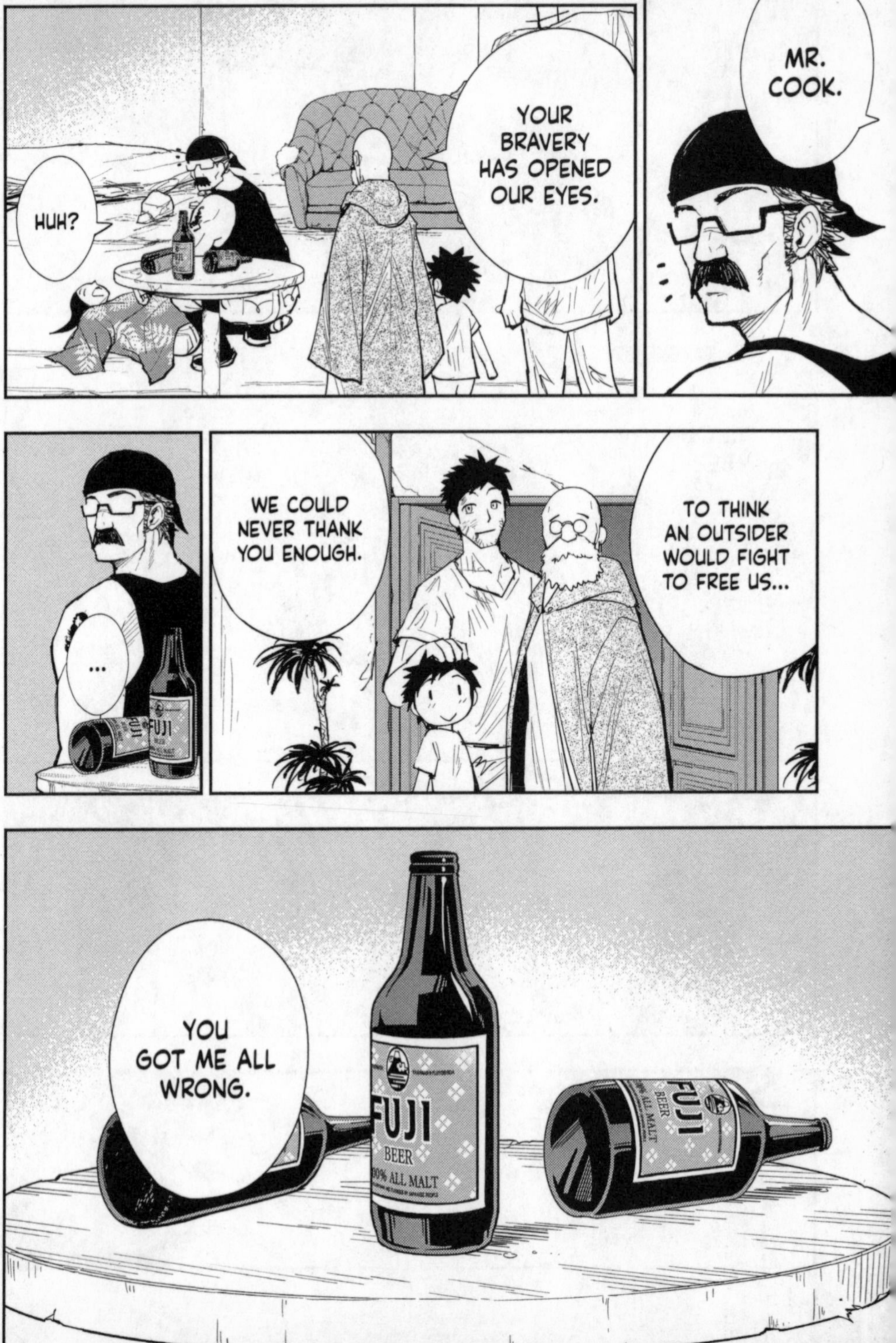
MR. COOK.
YOUR BRAVERY HAS OPENED OUR EYES.
HUH?
TO THINK AN OUTSIDER WOULD FIGHT TO FREE US...
WE COULD NEVER THANK YOU ENOUGH.
...
YOU GOT ME ALL WRONG.
FUJI
BEER

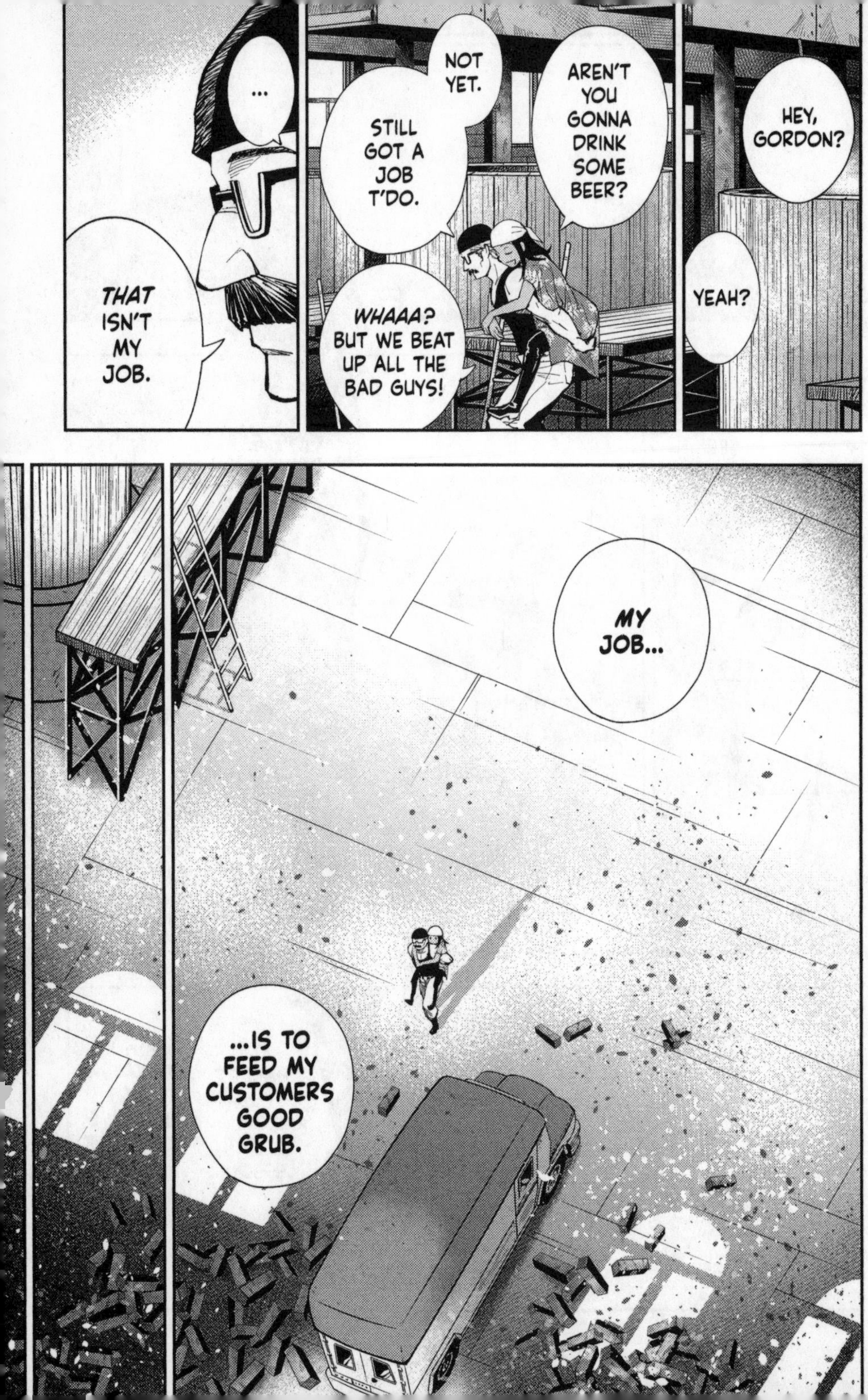
HEY, GORDON?
YEAH?
AREN'T YOU GONNA DRINK SOME BEER?
NOT YET.
STILL GOT A JOB T'DO.
WHAAA? BUT WE BEAT UP ALL THE BAD GUYS!
...
THAT ISN'T MY JOB.
MY JOB...
...IS TO FEED MY CUSTOMERS GOOD GRUB.

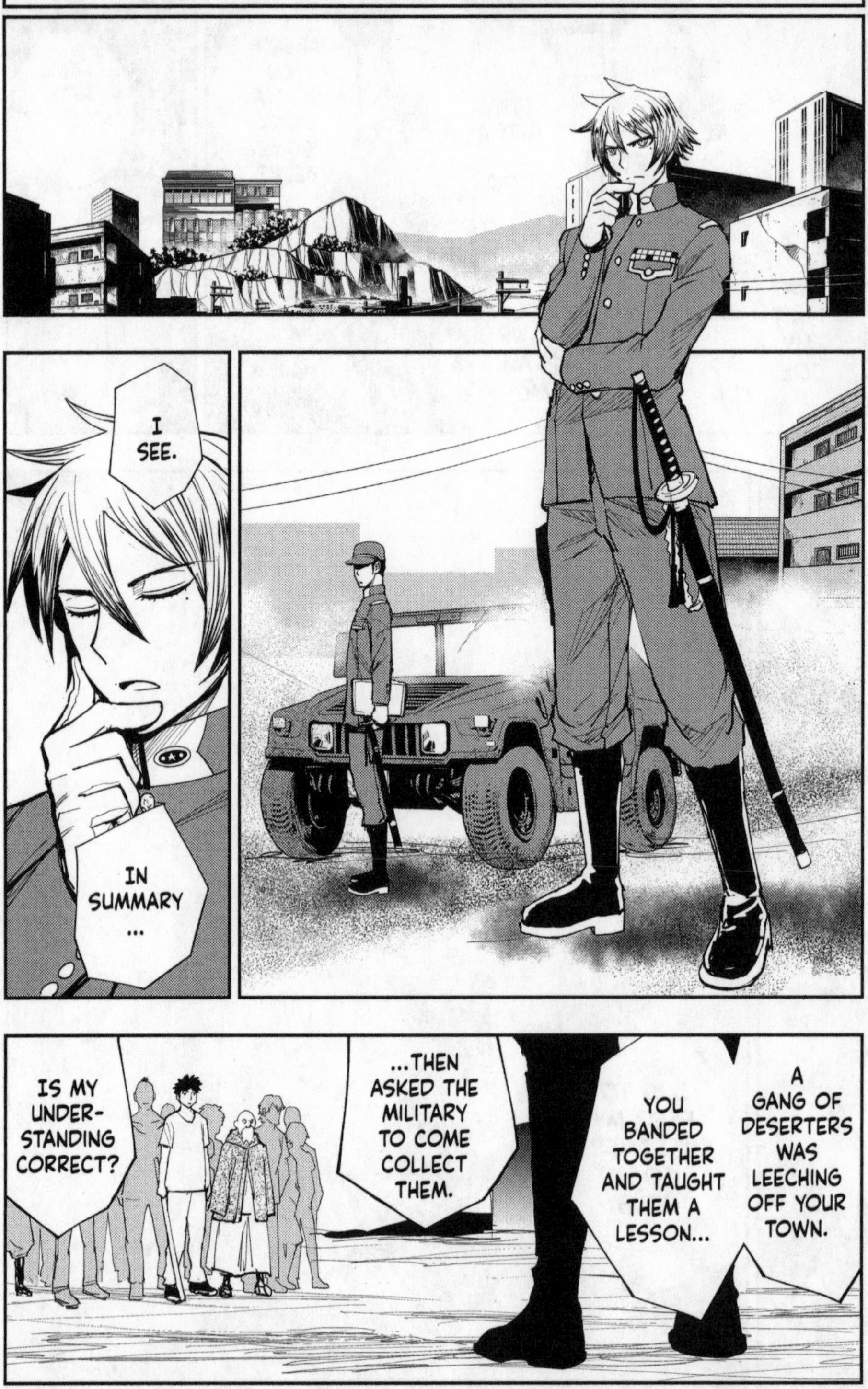
I SEE.
IN SUMMARY ...
A GANG OF DESERTERS WAS LEECHING OFF YOUR TOWN.
YOU BANDED TOGETHER AND TAUGHT THEM A LESSON...
...THEN ASKED THE MILITARY TO COME COLLECT THEM.
IS MY UNDER-STANDING CORRECT?

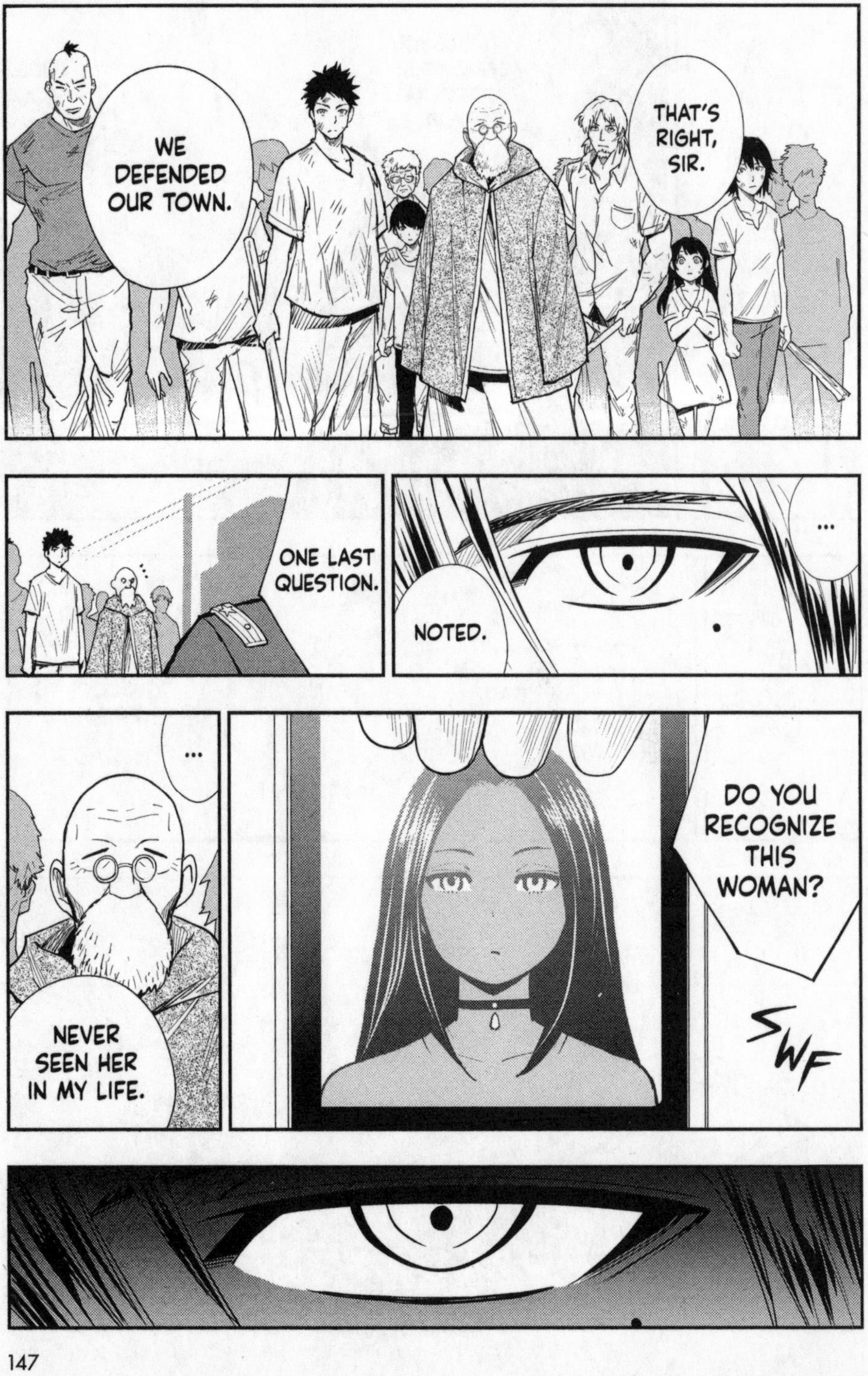
THAT'S RIGHT, SIR.
WE DEFENDED OUR TOWN.
...
NOTED.
ONE LAST QUESTION.
DO YOU RECOGNIZE THIS WOMAN?
SWF
...
NEVER SEEN HER IN MY LIFE.

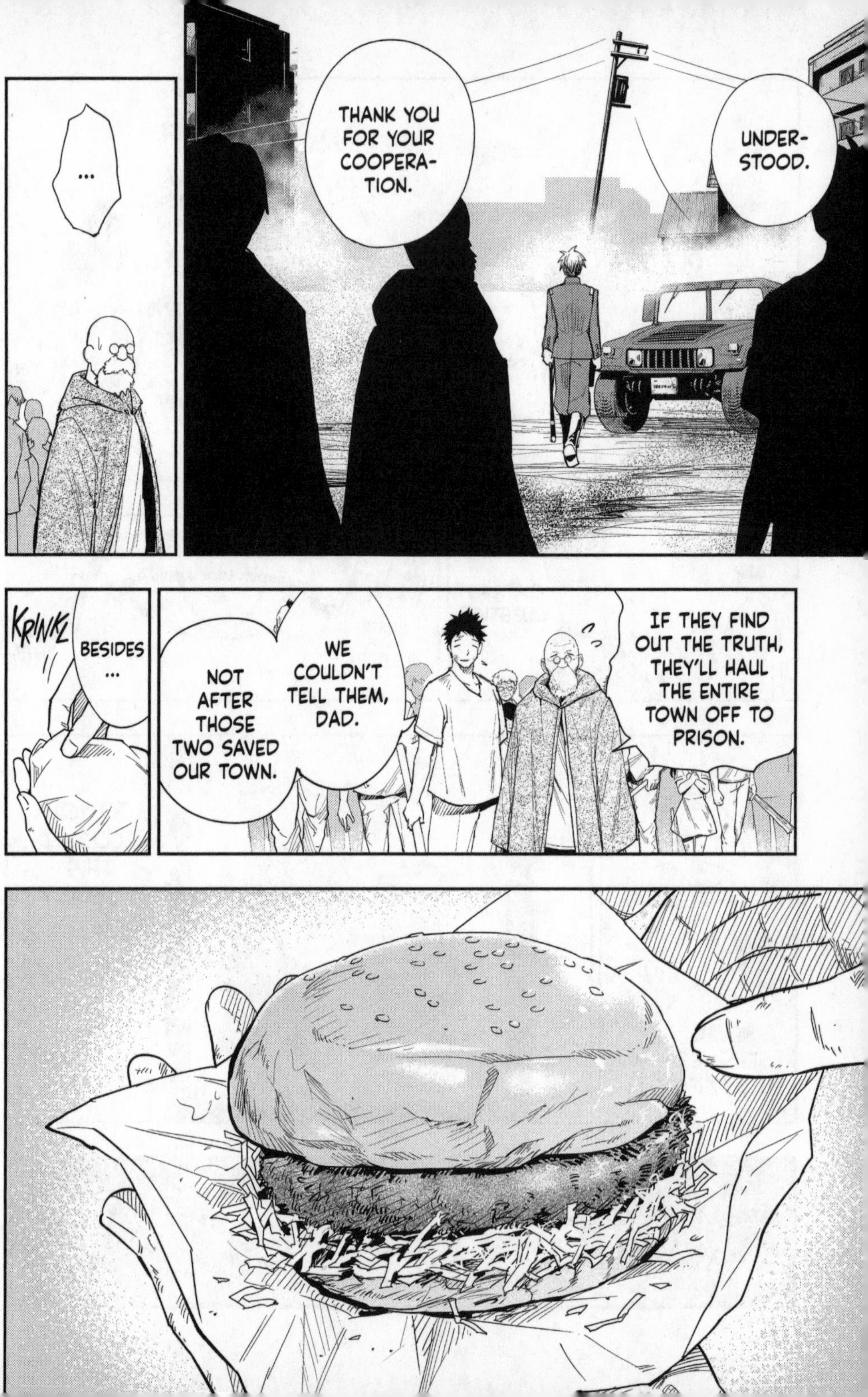
UNDER-
STOOD.
THANK YOU
FOR YOUR
COOPERA-
TION.
...
IF THEY FIND
OUT THE TRUTH,
THEY'LL HAUL
THE ENTIRE
TOWN OFF TO
PRISON.
WE
COULDN'T
TELL THEM,
DAD.
NOT
AFTER
THOSE
TWO SAVED
OUR TOWN.
KRINKL
BESIDES
...

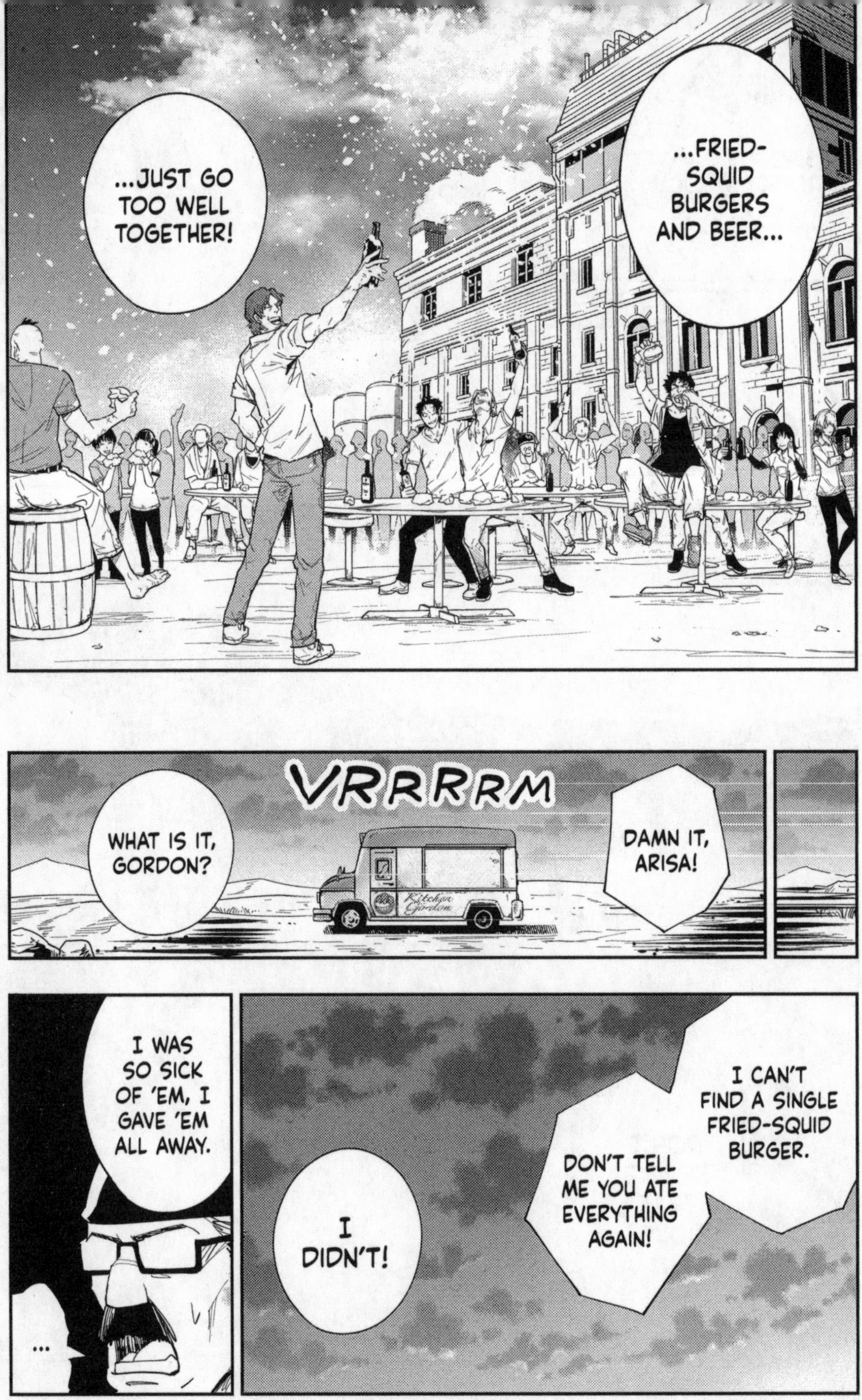
...FRIED-SQUID BURGERS AND BEER...
...JUST GO TOO WELL TOGETHER!
VRRRRM
DAMN IT, ARISA!
WHAT IS IT, GORDON?
Kitchen Gordon
I CAN'T FIND A SINGLE FRIED-SQUID BURGER.
DON'T TELL ME YOU ATE EVERYTHING AGAIN!
I DIDN'T!
I WAS SO SICK OF 'EM, I GAVE 'EM ALL AWAY.
...

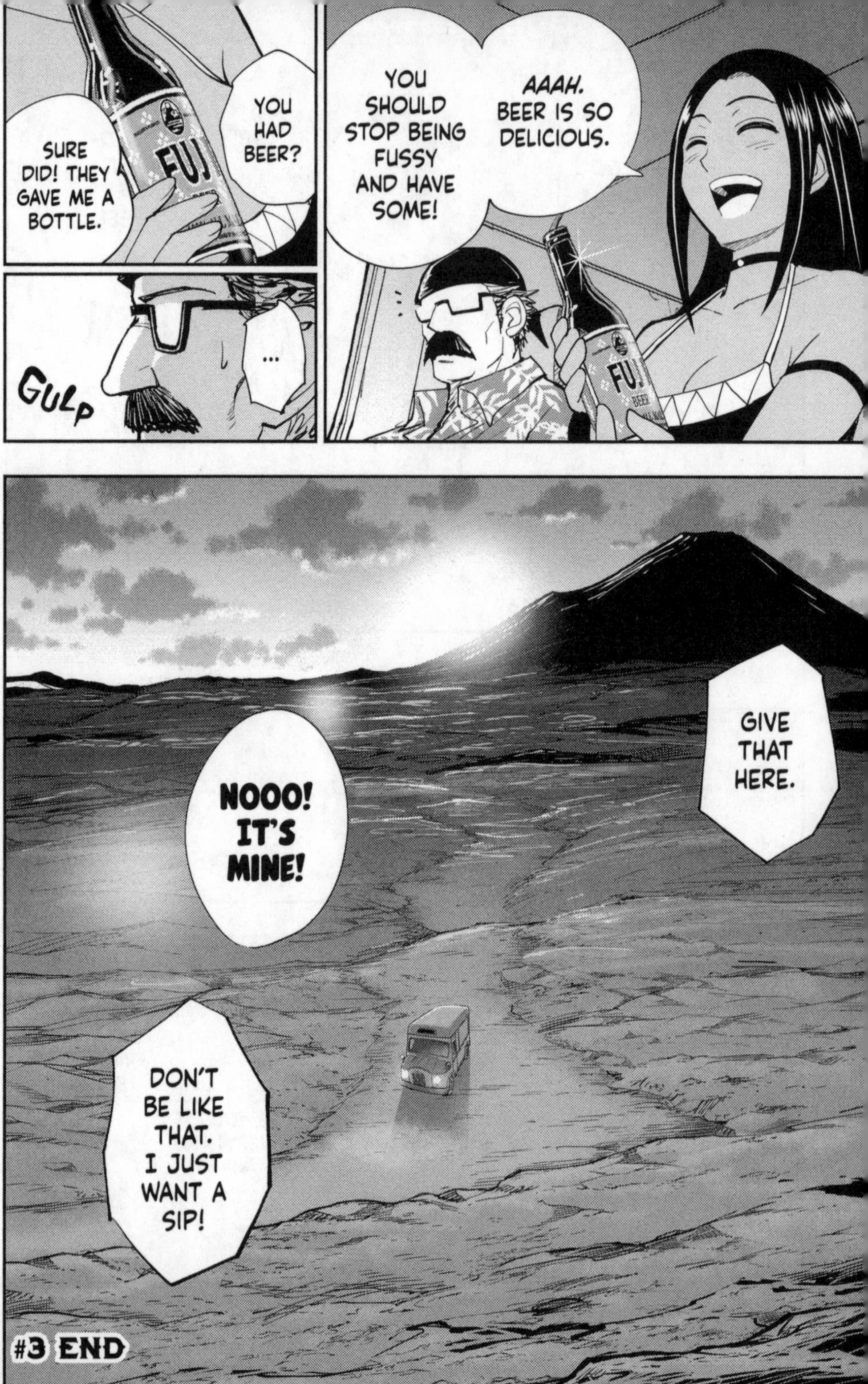
AAAH. BEER IS SO DELICIOUS.
YOU SHOULD STOP BEING FUSSY AND HAVE SOME!
YOU HAD BEER?
SURE DID! THEY GAVE ME A BOTTLE.
...
GULP
GIVE THAT HERE.
NOOO! IT'S MINE!
DON'T BE LIKE THAT. I JUST WANT A SIP!
#3 END

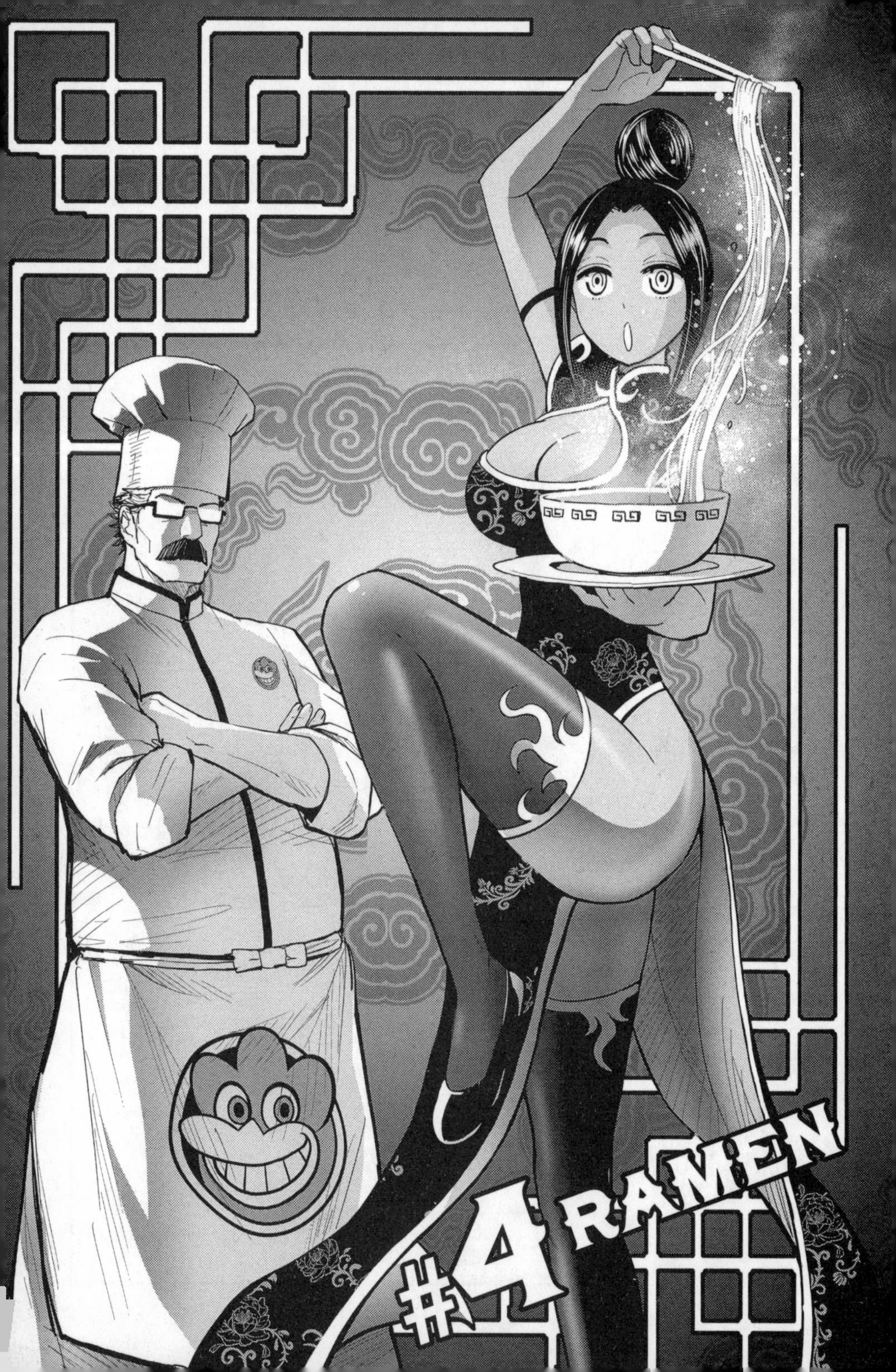
#4 RAMEN

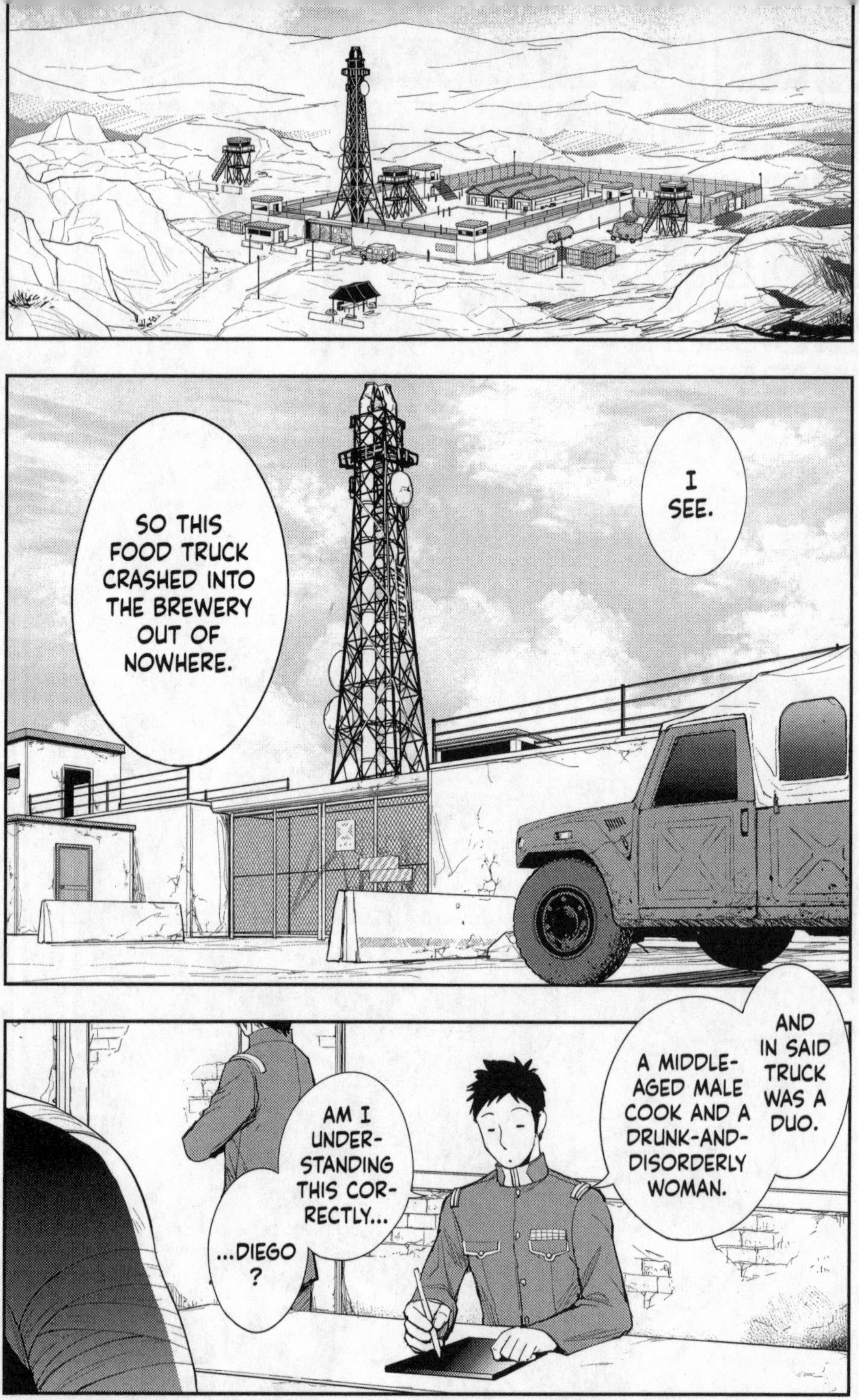
SO THIS FOOD TRUCK CRASHED INTO THE BREWERY OUT OF NOWHERE.
I SEE.
AND IN SAID TRUCK WAS A DUO.
A MIDDLE-AGED MALE COOK AND A DRUNK-AND-DISORDERLY WOMAN.
AM I UNDERSTANDING THIS CORRECTLY...
...DIEGO?

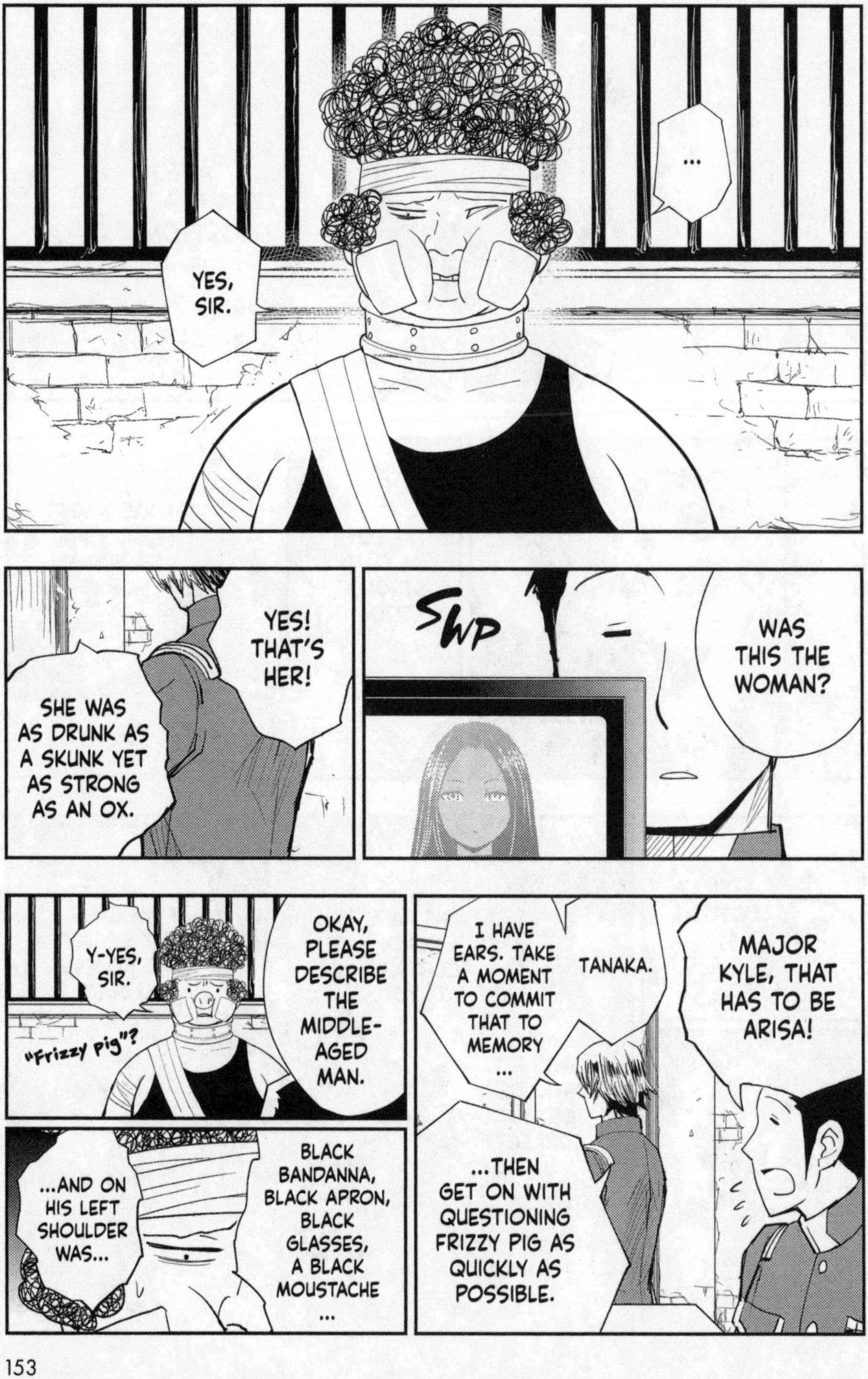
...
YES, SIR.
WAS THIS THE WOMAN?
SWP
YES! THAT'S HER!
SHE WAS AS DRUNK AS A SKUNK YET AS STRONG AS AN OX.
MAJOR KYLE, THAT HAS TO BE ARISA!
TANAKA.
I HAVE EARS. TAKE A MOMENT TO COMMIT THAT TO MEMORY ...
...THEN GET ON WITH QUESTIONING FRIZZY PIG AS QUICKLY AS POSSIBLE.
OKAY, PLEASE DESCRIBE THE MIDDLE-AGED MAN.
Y-YES, SIR.
"Frizzy pig"?
BLACK BANDANNA, BLACK APRON, BLACK GLASSES, A BLACK MOUSTACHE ...
...AND ON HIS LEFT SHOULDER WAS...

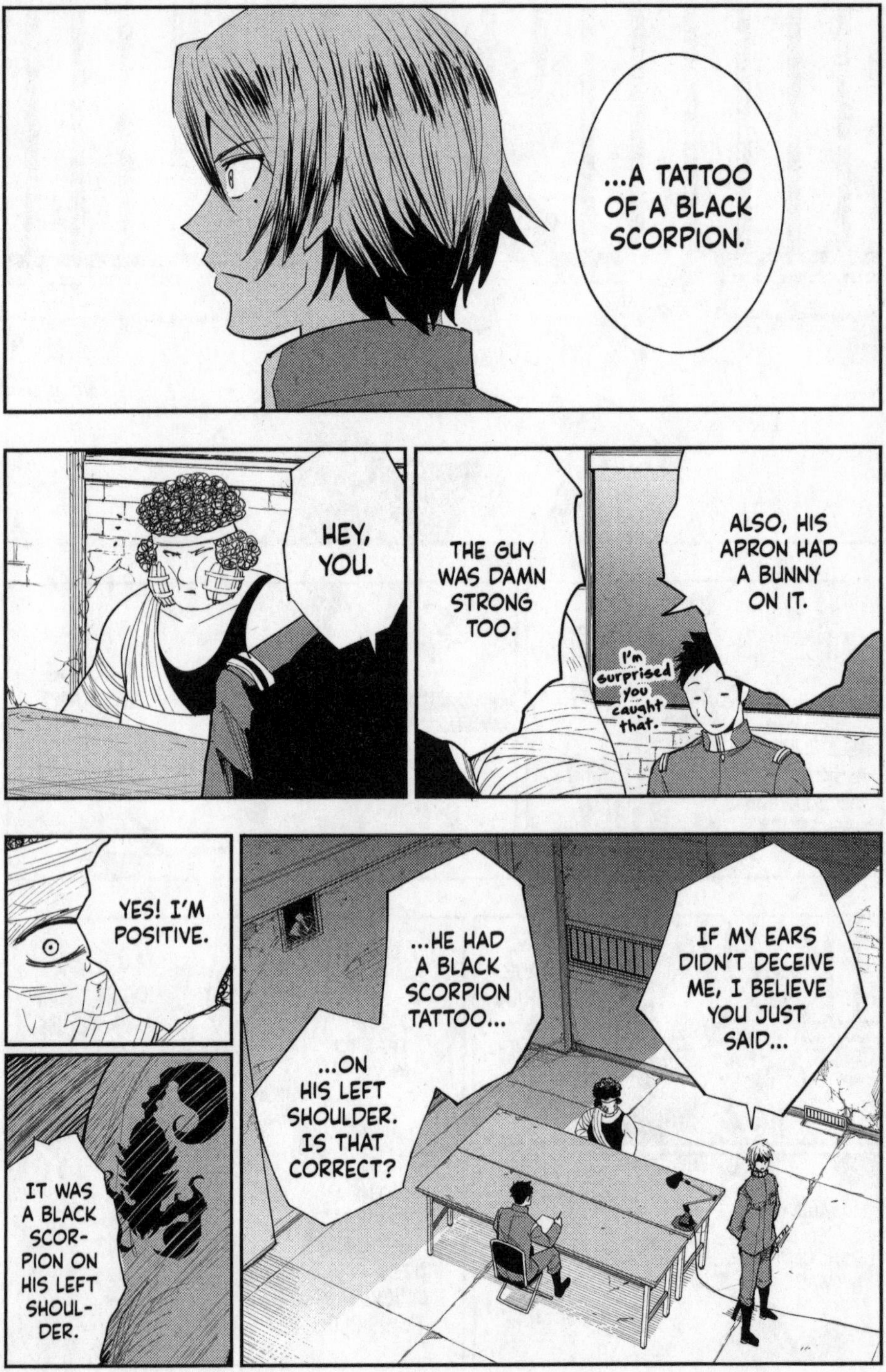
...A TATTOO OF A BLACK SCORPION.
ALSO, HIS APRON HAD A BUNNY ON IT.
I'm surprised you caught that.
THE GUY WAS DAMN STRONG TOO.
HEY, YOU.
IF MY EARS DIDN'T DECEIVE ME, I BELIEVE YOU JUST SAID...
...HE HAD A BLACK SCORPION TATTOO...
...ON HIS LEFT SHOULDER. IS THAT CORRECT?
YES! I'M POSITIVE.
IT WAS A BLACK SCOR-PION ON HIS LEFT SHOUL-DER.

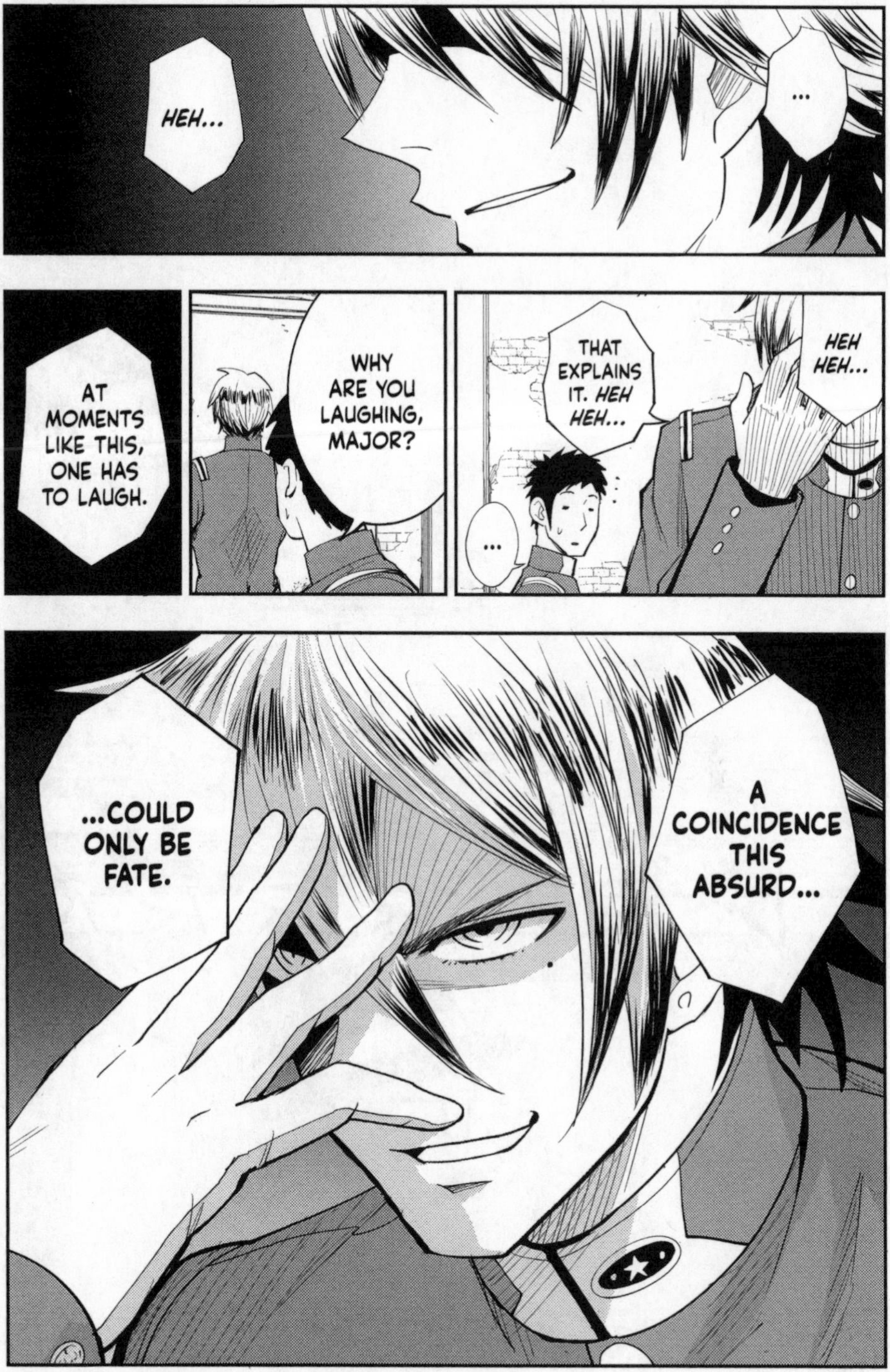
...
HEH...
HEH HEH...
THAT EXPLAINS IT. HEH HEH...
...
WHY ARE YOU LAUGHING, MAJOR?
AT MOMENTS LIKE THIS, ONE HAS TO LAUGH.
A COINCIDENCE THIS ABSURD...
...COULD ONLY BE FATE.

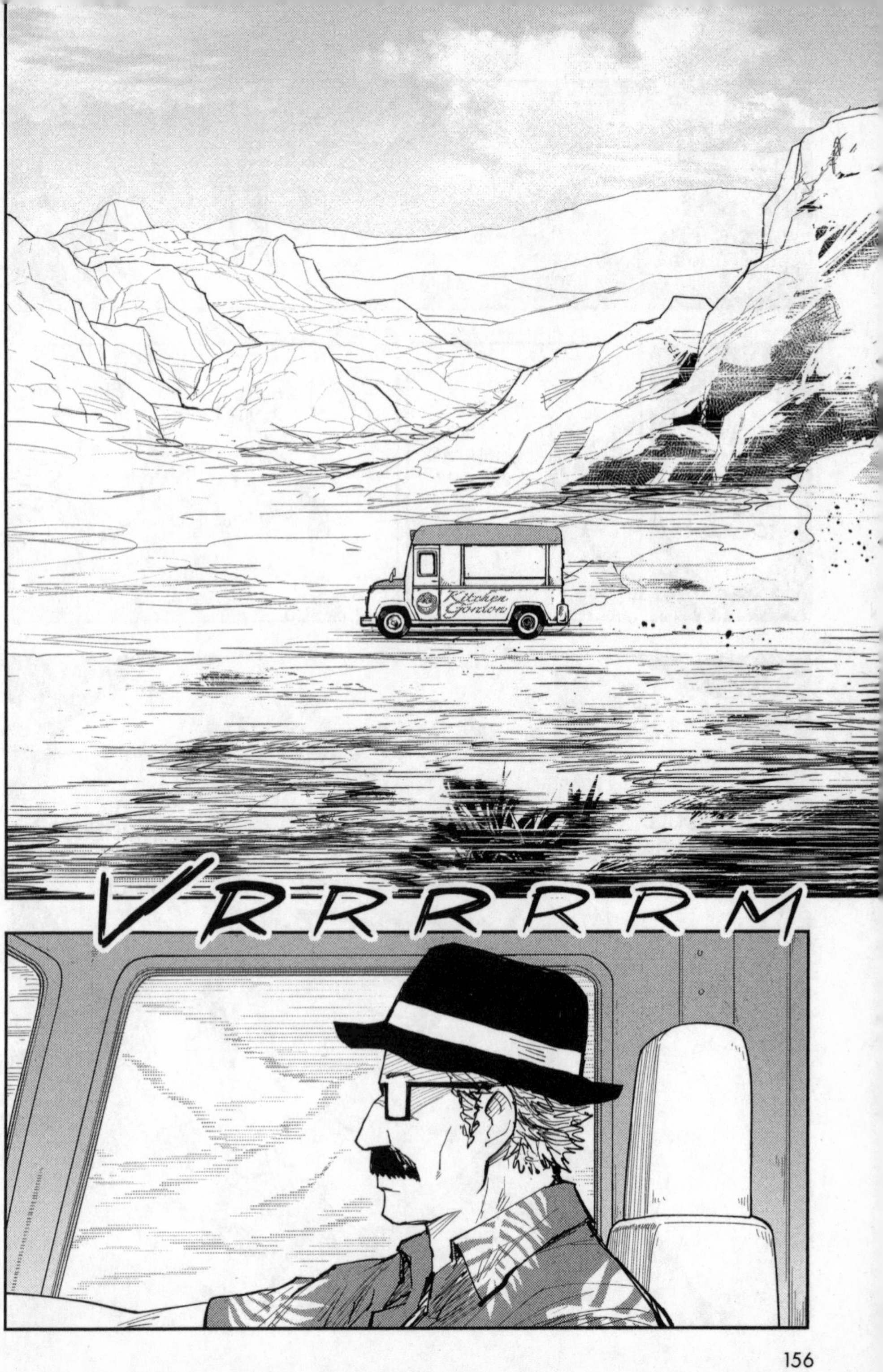
Kitchen Gordon
VRRRRRM

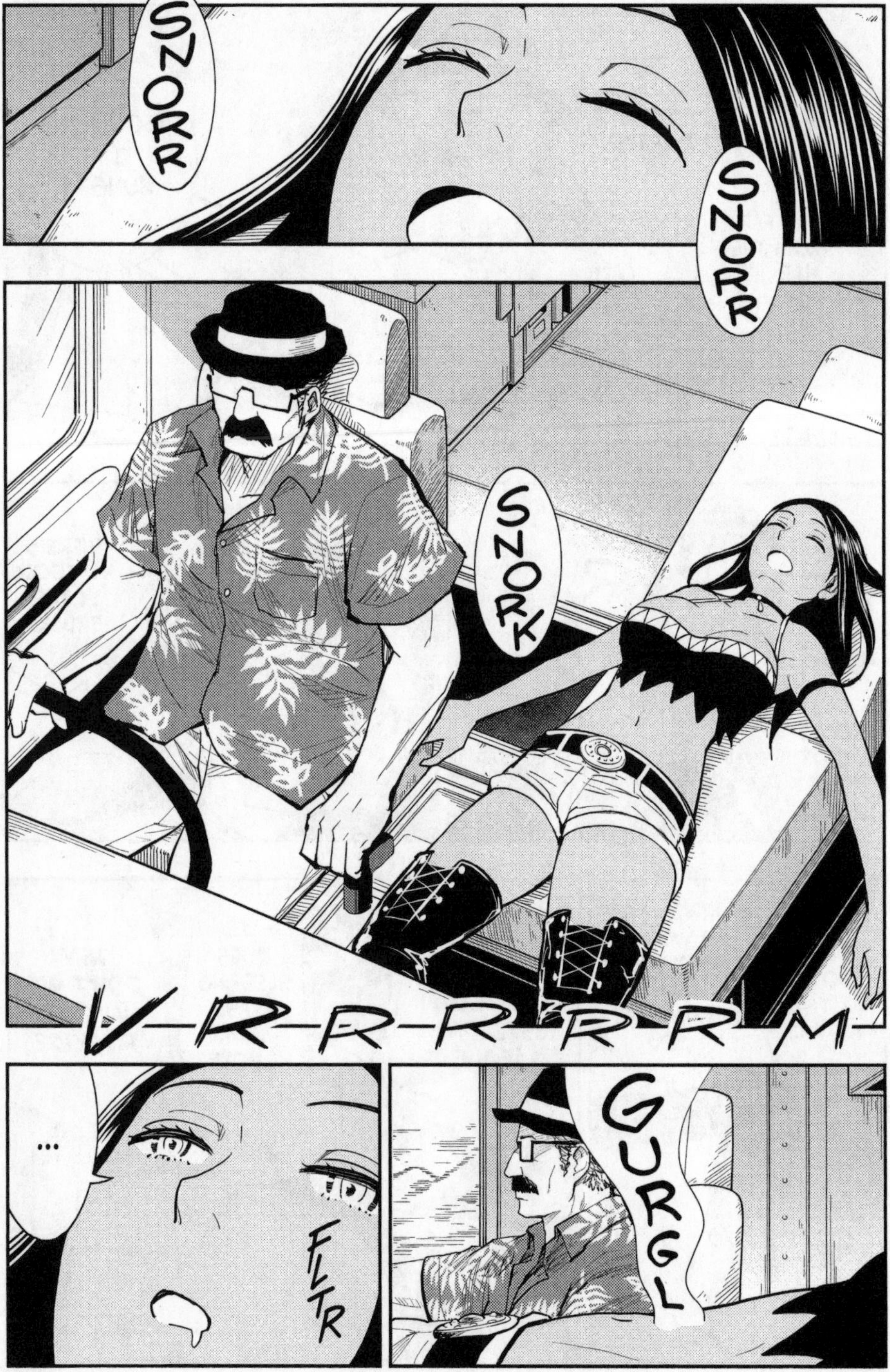
SNORR
SNORR
SNORK
VRRRRRRM
GURGL
...
FLTR

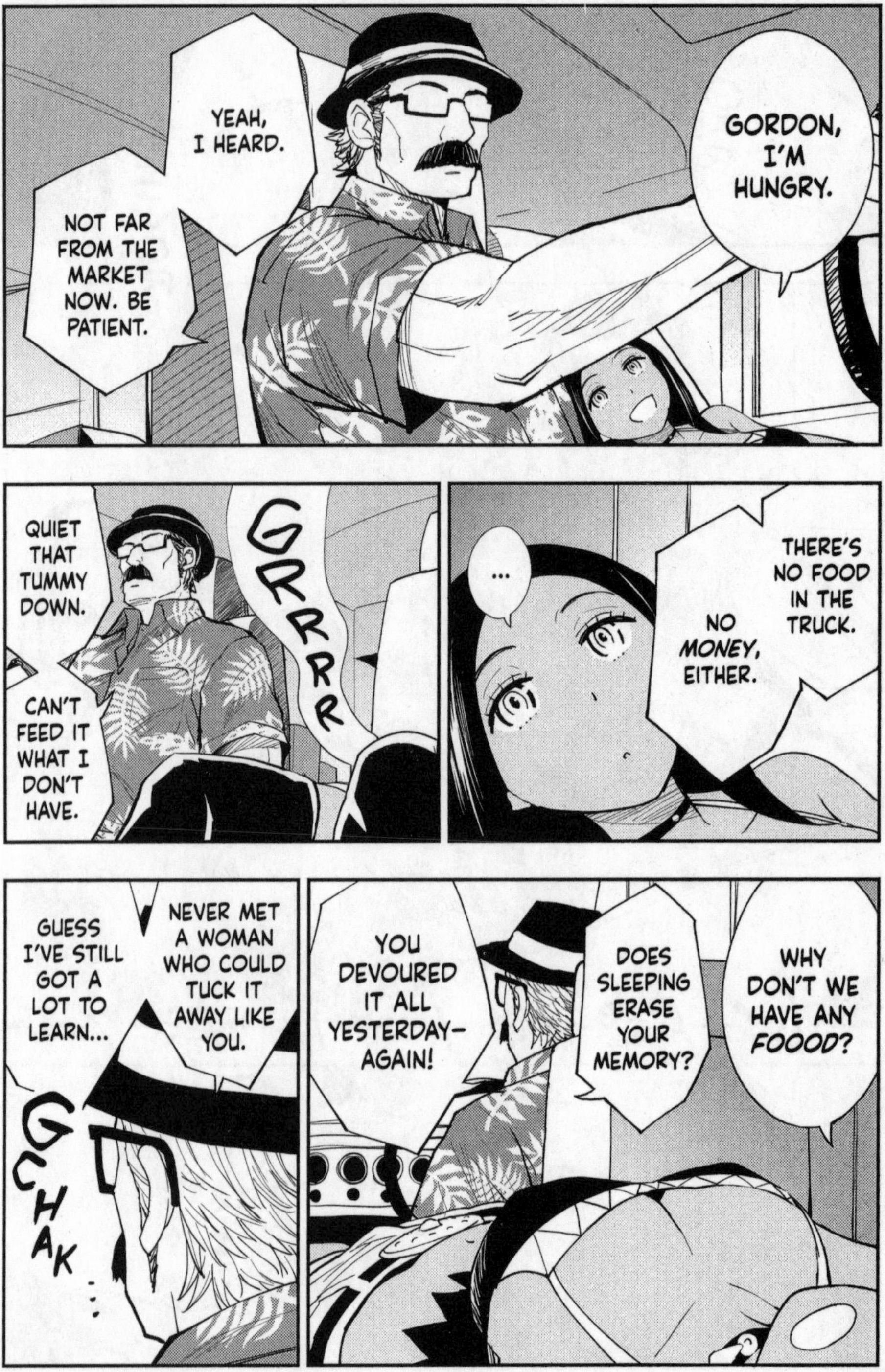
GORDON, I'M HUNGRY.
YEAH, I HEARD.
NOT FAR FROM THE MARKET NOW. BE PATIENT.
THERE'S NO FOOD IN THE TRUCK.
NO *MONEY*, EITHER.
...
GRRRR
QUIET THAT TUMMY DOWN.
CAN'T FEED IT WHAT I DON'T HAVE.
WHY DON'T WE HAVE ANY *FOOOD*?
DOES SLEEPING ERASE YOUR MEMORY?
YOU DEVOURED IT ALL YESTERDAY—AGAIN!
NEVER MET A WOMAN WHO COULD TUCK IT AWAY LIKE YOU.
GUESS I'VE STILL GOT A LOT TO LEARN...
GCHAK
...

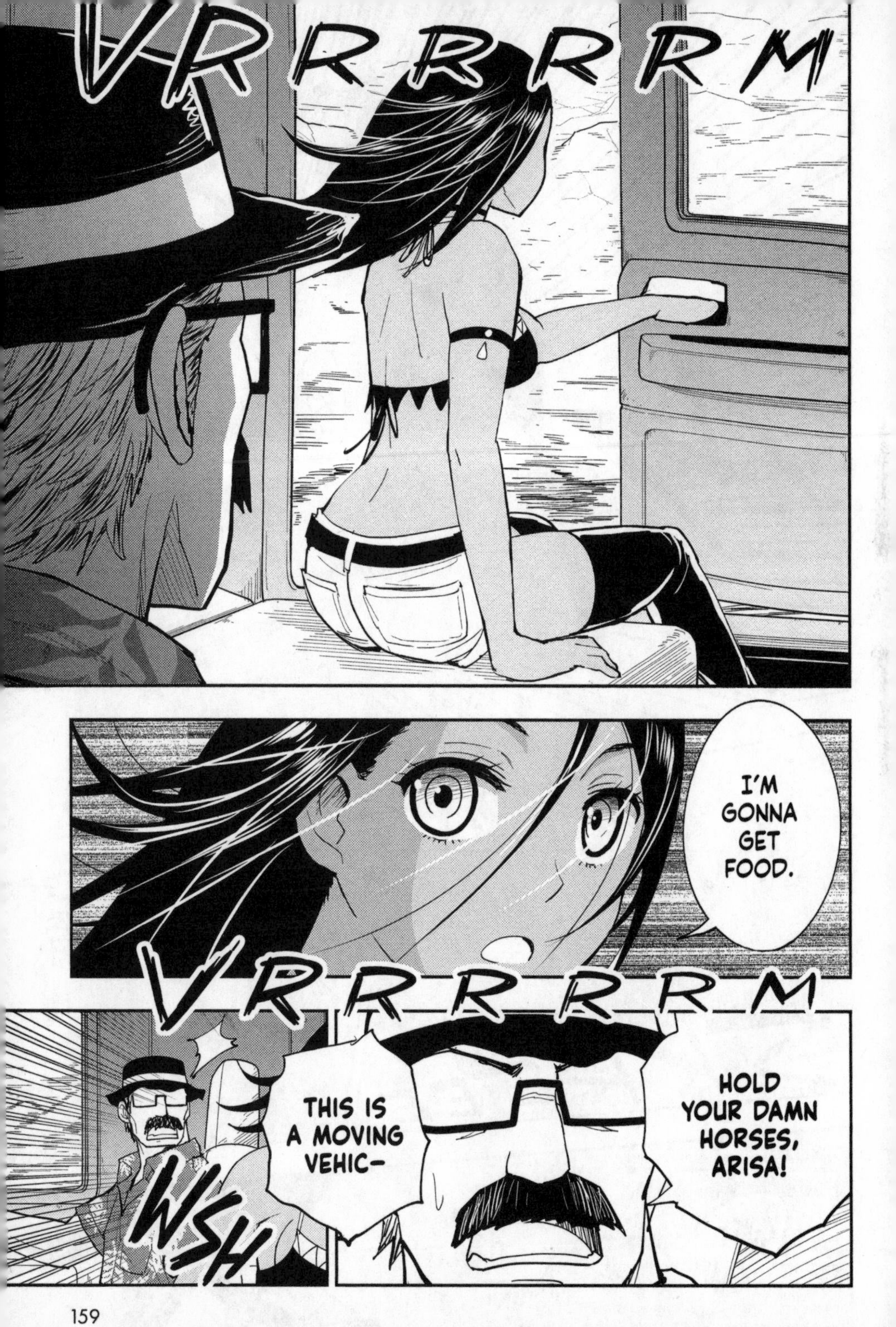
VRRRRRRM
I'M GONNA GET FOOD.
VRRRRRRM
HOLD YOUR DAMN HORSES, ARISA!
THIS IS A MOVING VEHIC-
WSH

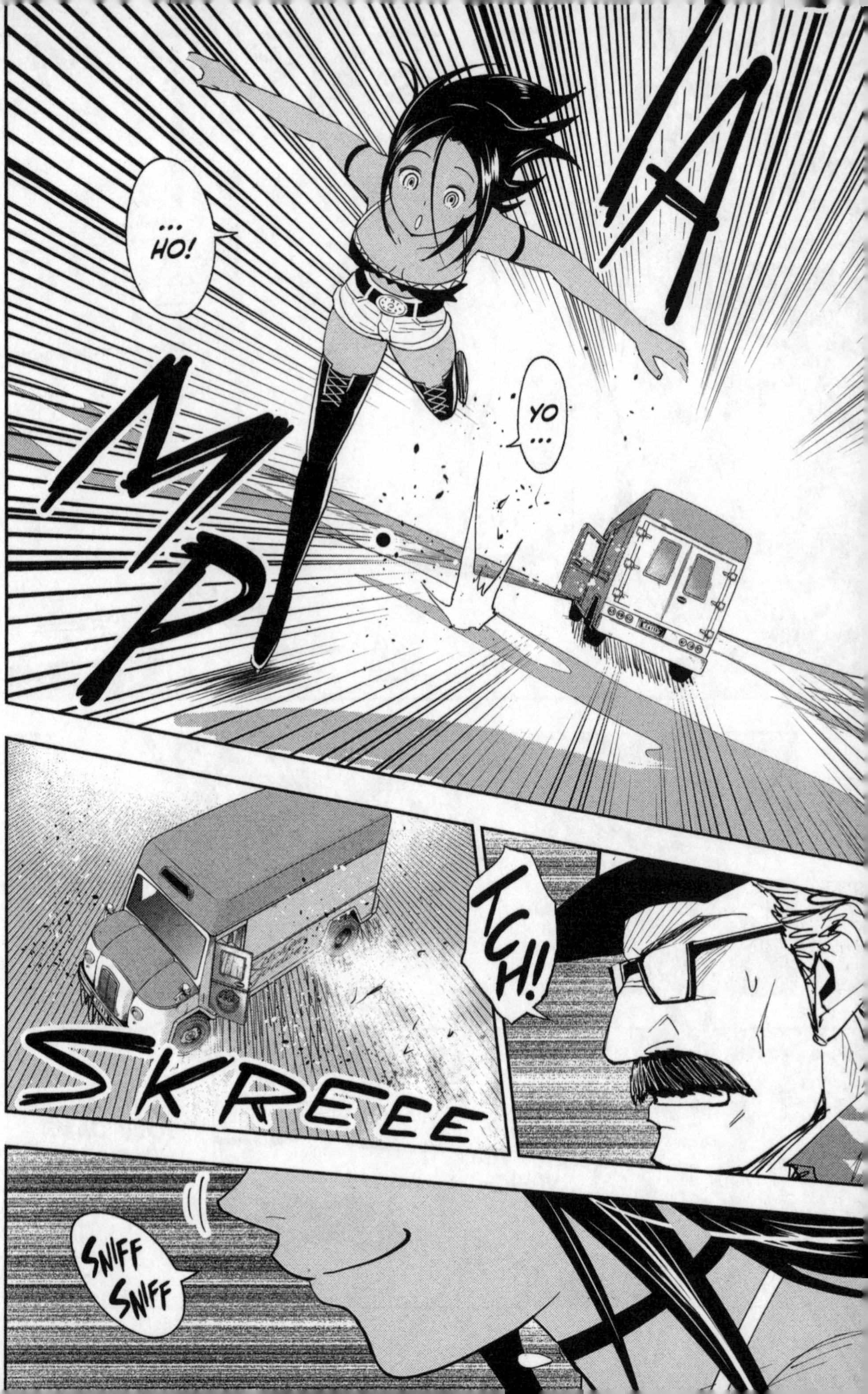
YO...
...HO!
TCH!
SKREEE
SNIFF SNIFF

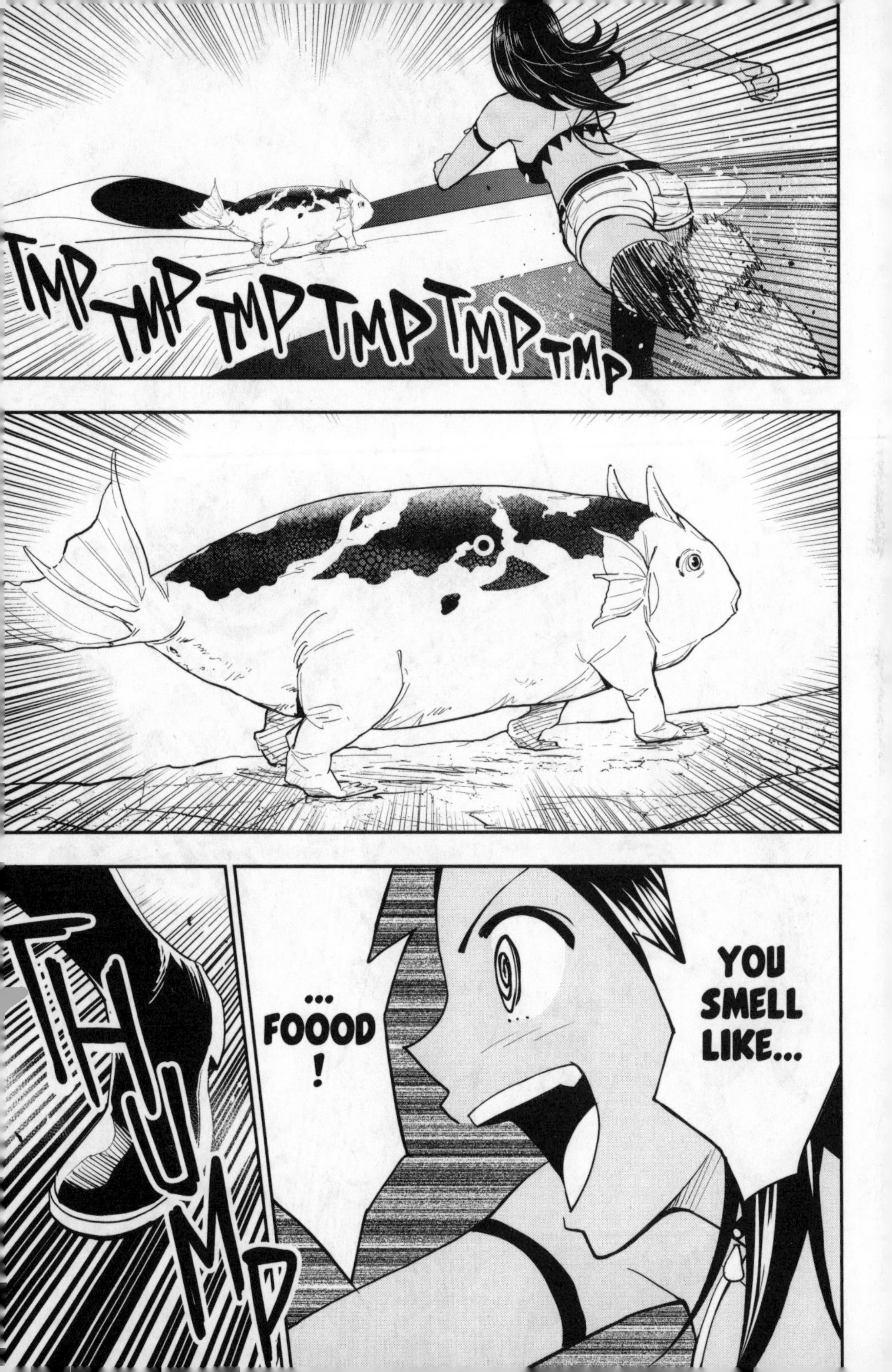
TMP TMP TMP TMP TMP TMP
YOU SMELL LIKE...
...FOOOD!
THUMP

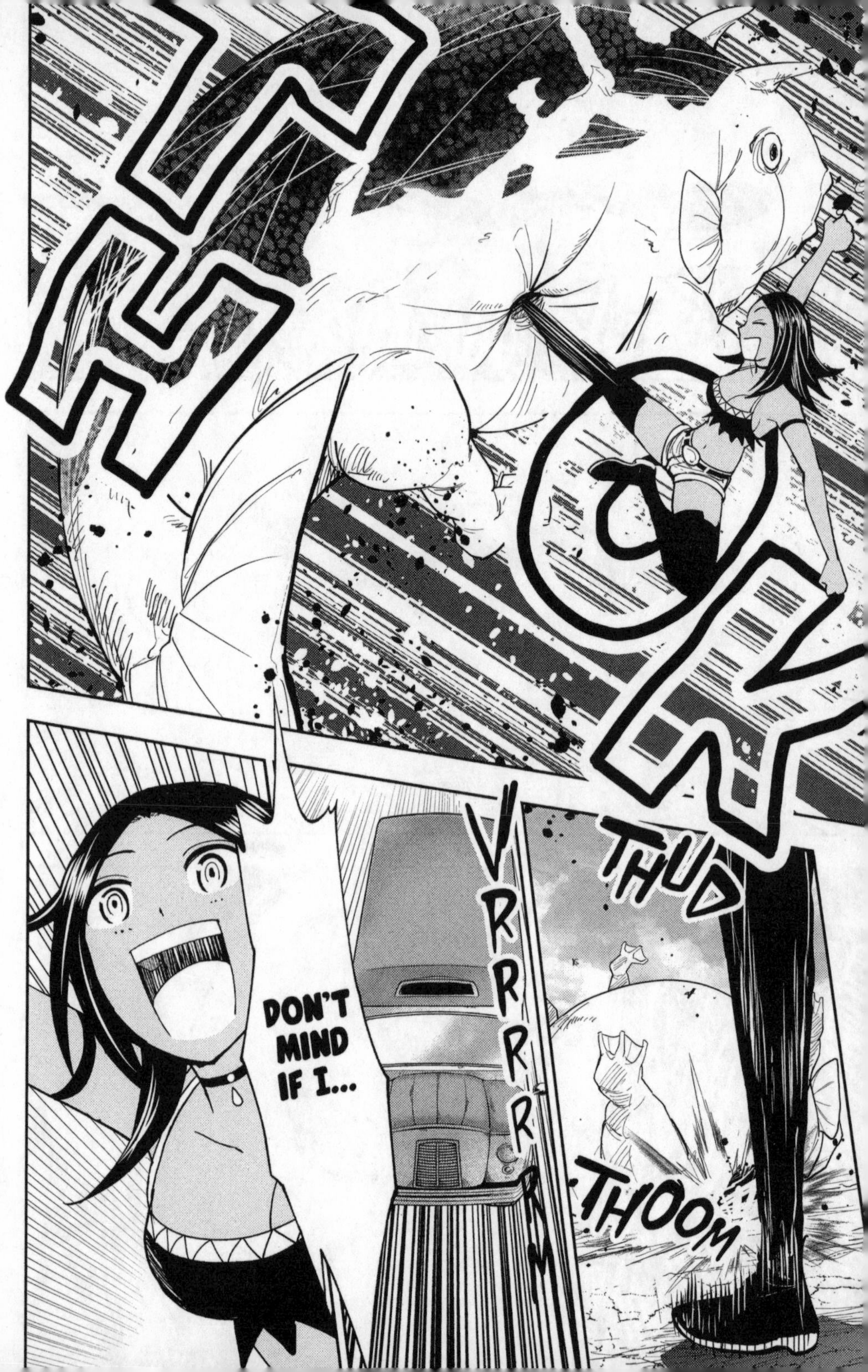
THUD
THOOM
VRRRRRM
DON'T MIND IF I...

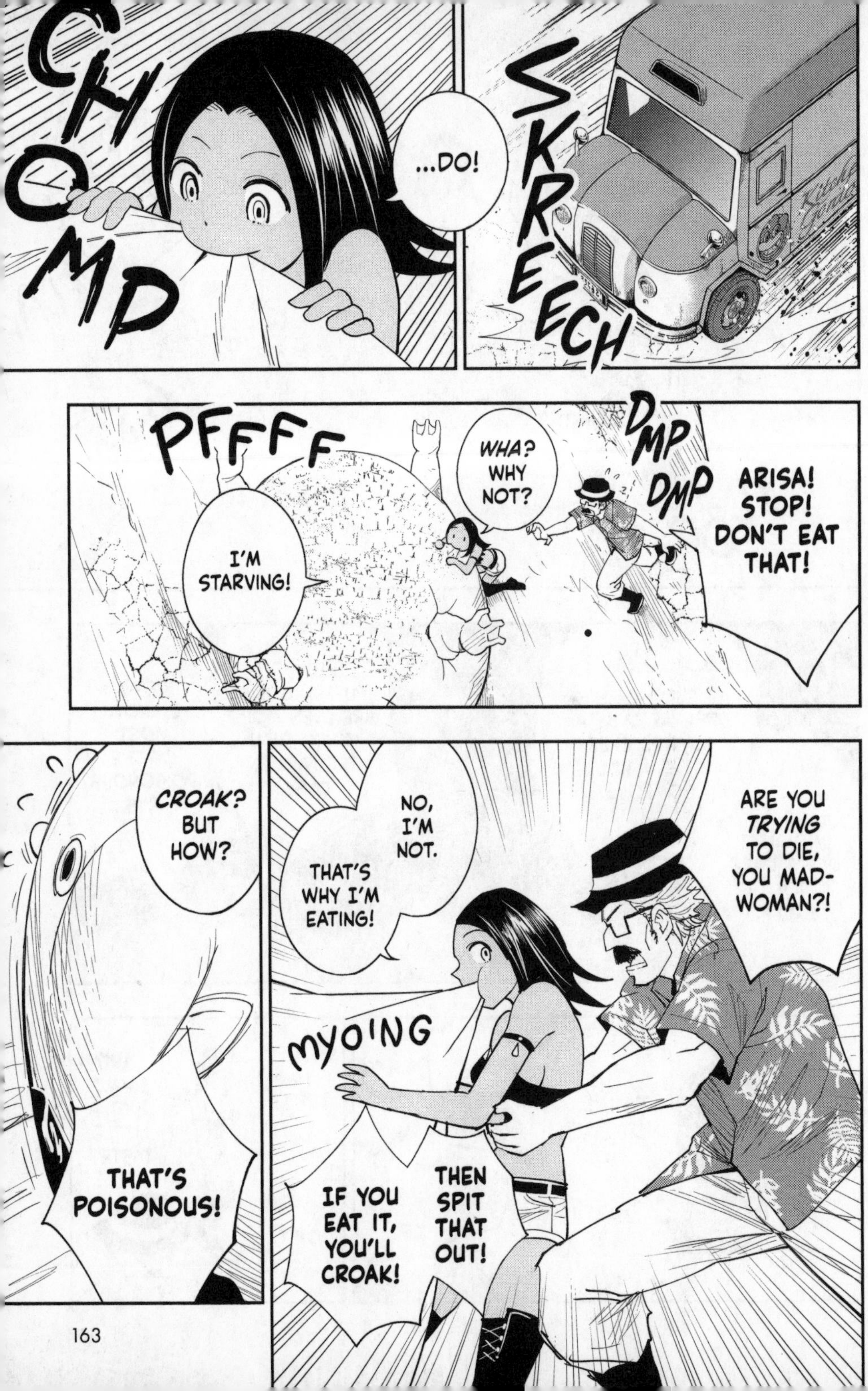
SKREECH
...DO!
CHOMP
ARISA! STOP! DON'T EAT THAT!
DMP DMP
WHA? WHY NOT?
PFFFF
I'M STARVING!
ARE YOU *TRYING* TO DIE, YOU MAD-WOMAN?!
NO, I'M NOT.
THAT'S WHY I'M EATING!
MYOING
THEN SPIT THAT OUT!
IF YOU EAT IT, YOU'LL CROAK!
CROAK? BUT HOW?
THAT'S POISONOUS!

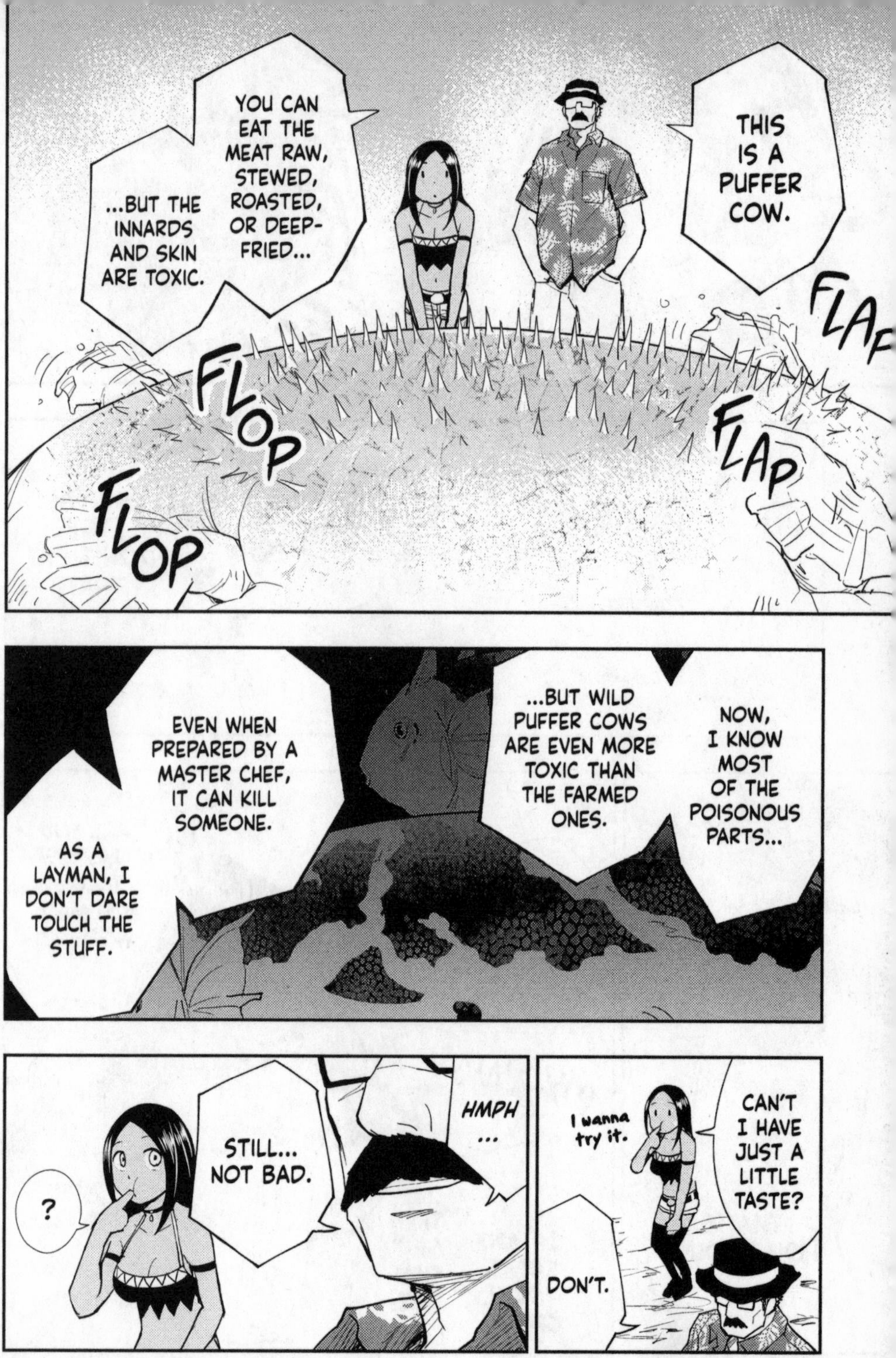
THIS IS A PUFFER COW.
YOU CAN EAT THE MEAT RAW, STEWED, ROASTED, OR DEEP-FRIED...
...BUT THE INNARDS AND SKIN ARE TOXIC.
FLA
FLAP
FLOP
FLOP
NOW, I KNOW MOST OF THE POISONOUS PARTS...
...BUT WILD PUFFER COWS ARE EVEN MORE TOXIC THAN THE FARMED ONES.
EVEN WHEN PREPARED BY A MASTER CHEF, IT CAN KILL SOMEONE.
AS A LAYMAN, I DON'T DARE TOUCH THE STUFF.
CAN'T I HAVE JUST A LITTLE TASTE?
I wanna try it.
DON'T.
HMPH...
STILL... NOT BAD.
?

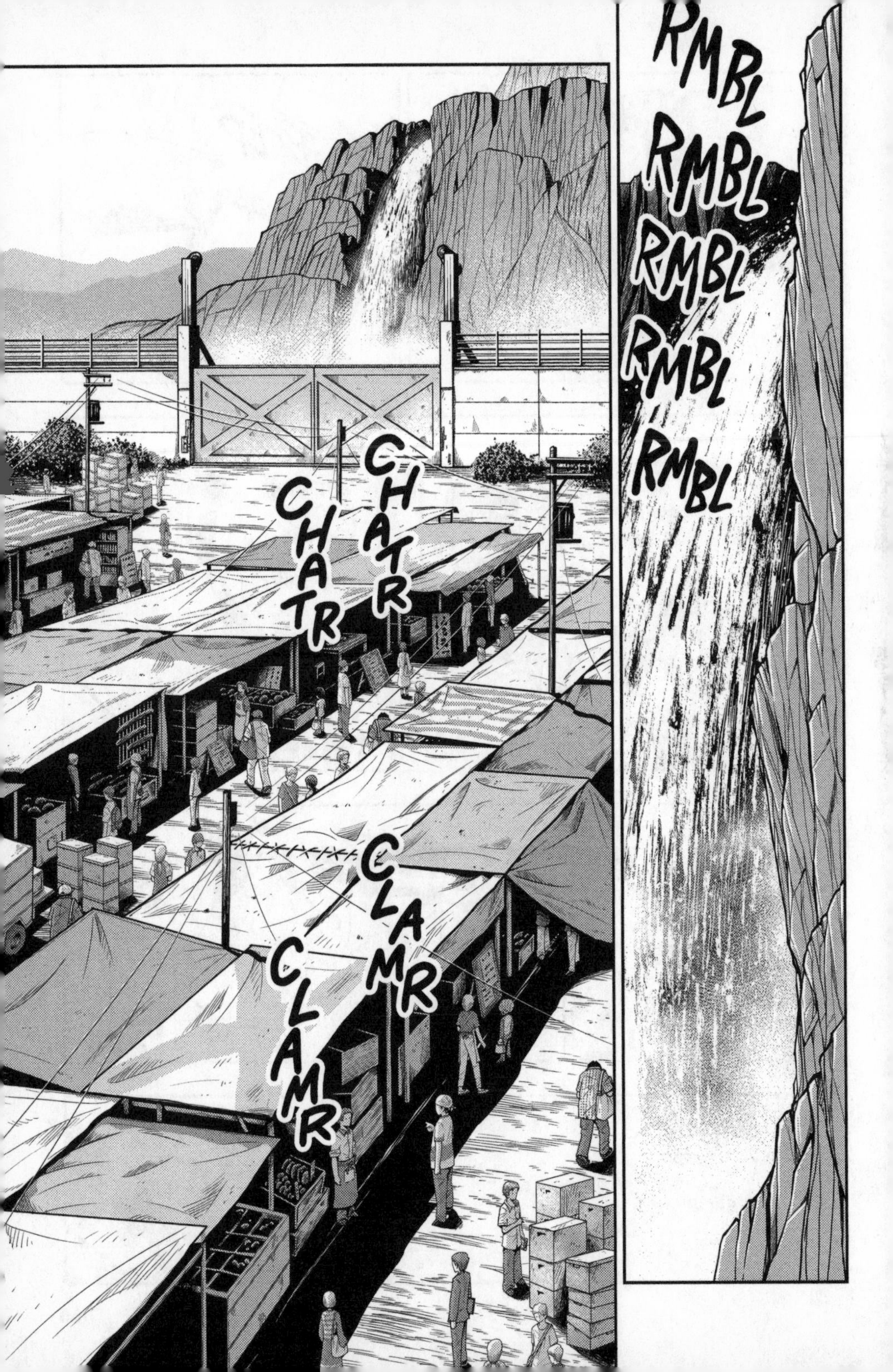
RMBL
RMBL
RMBL
RMBL
RMBL
CHATR
CHATR
CLAMR
CLAMR

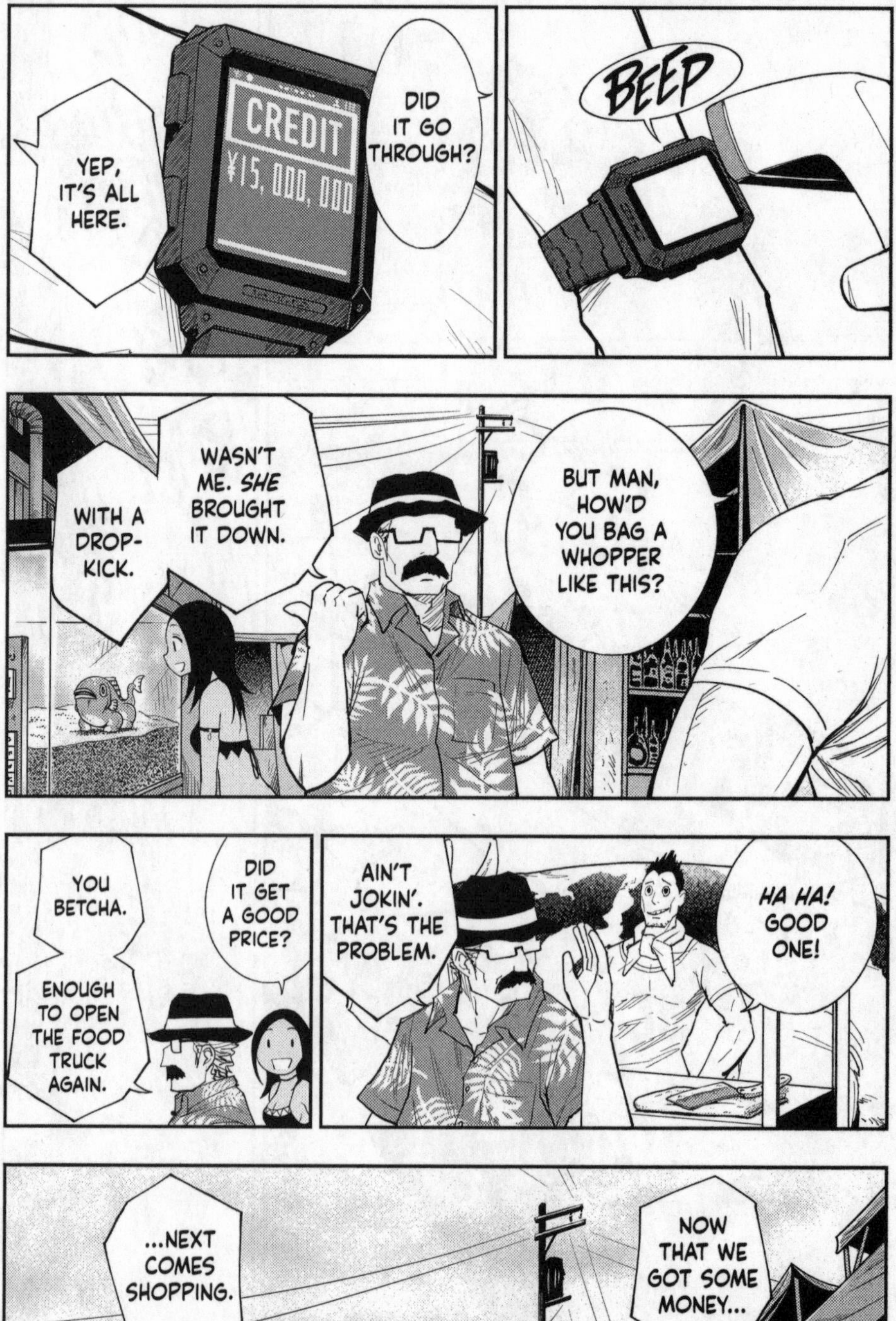
BEEP
DID IT GO THROUGH?
CREDIT ¥15,000,000
YEP, IT'S ALL HERE.
BUT MAN, HOW'D YOU BAG A WHOPPER LIKE THIS?
WASN'T ME. *SHE* BROUGHT IT DOWN.
WITH A DROP-KICK.
HA HA! GOOD ONE!
AIN'T JOKIN'. THAT'S THE PROBLEM.
DID IT GET A GOOD PRICE?
YOU BETCHA.
ENOUGH TO OPEN THE FOOD TRUCK AGAIN.
NOW THAT WE GOT SOME MONEY...
...NEXT COMES SHOPPING.

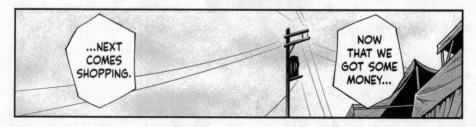

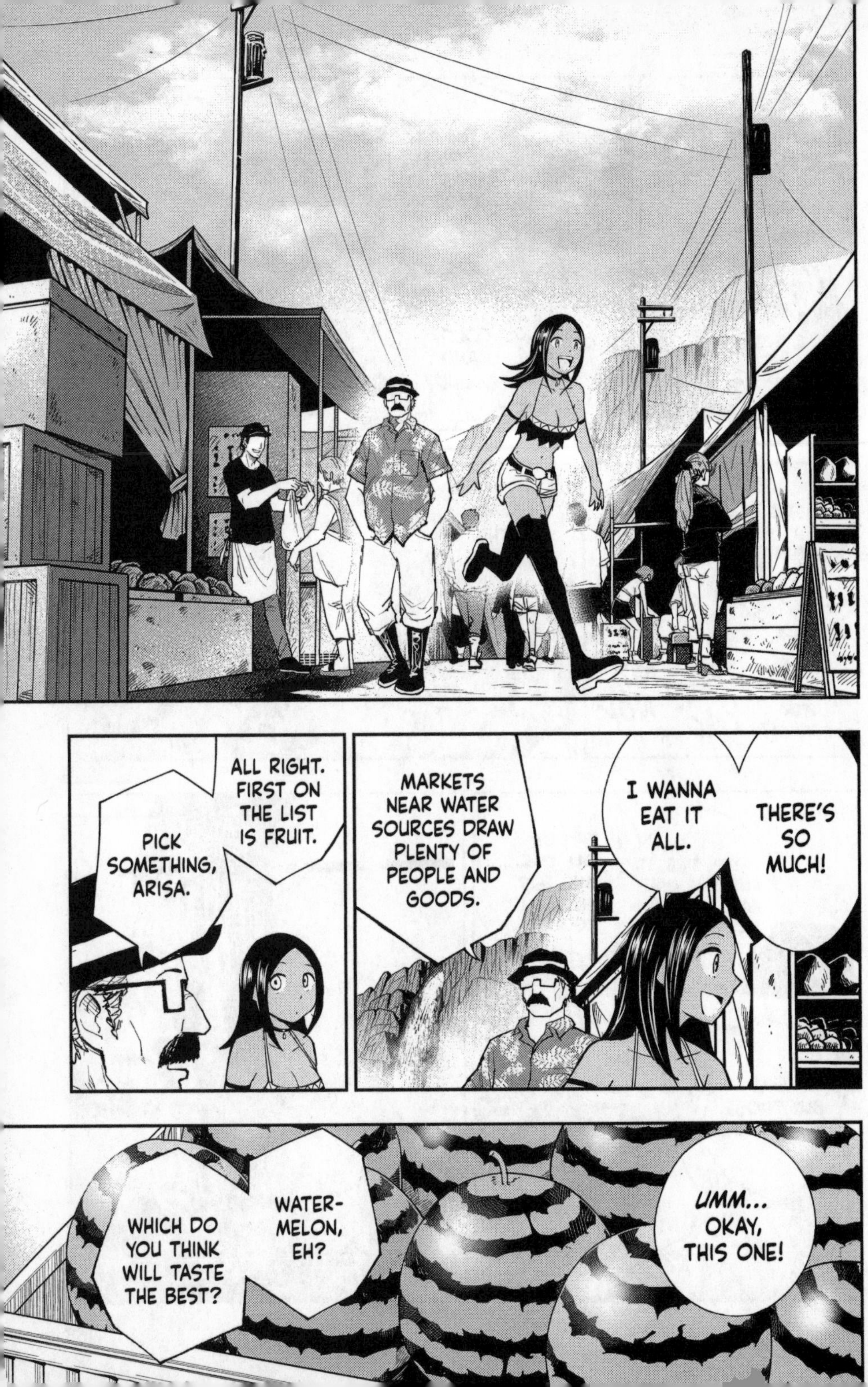
THERE'S SO MUCH!
I WANNA EAT IT ALL.
MARKETS NEAR WATER SOURCES DRAW PLENTY OF PEOPLE AND GOODS.
ALL RIGHT. FIRST ON THE LIST IS FRUIT.
PICK SOMETHING, ARISA.
UMM... OKAY, THIS ONE!
WATER-MELON, EH?
WHICH DO YOU THINK WILL TASTE THE BEST?

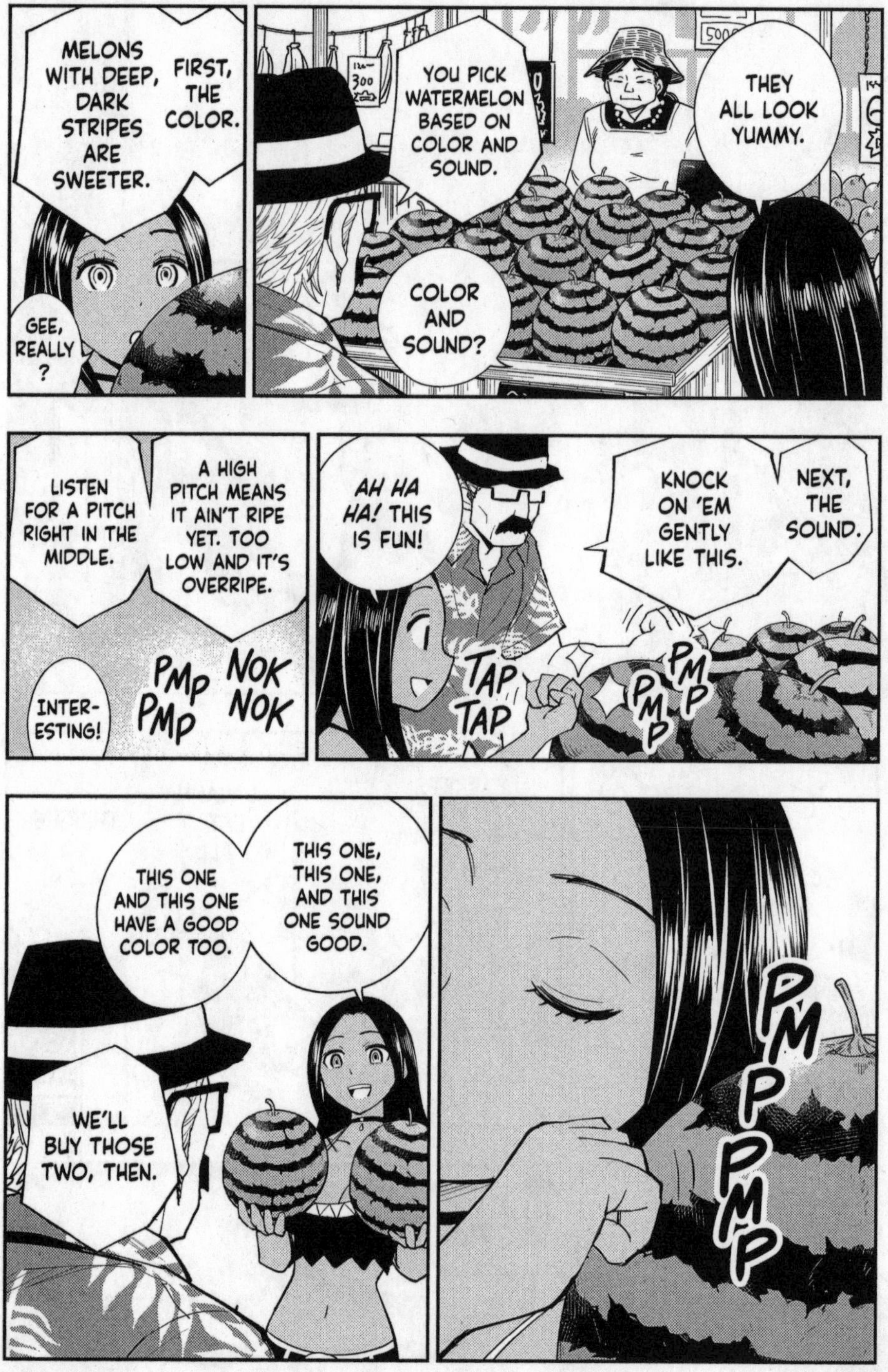
THEY ALL LOOK YUMMY.
YOU PICK WATERMELON BASED ON COLOR AND SOUND.
COLOR AND SOUND?
FIRST, THE COLOR.
MELONS WITH DEEP, DARK STRIPES ARE SWEETER.
GEE, REALLY?
NEXT, THE SOUND.
KNOCK ON 'EM GENTLY LIKE THIS.
AH HA HA! THIS IS FUN!
PMP PMP
TAP TAP
A HIGH PITCH MEANS IT AIN'T RIPE YET. TOO LOW AND IT'S OVERRIPE.
LISTEN FOR A PITCH RIGHT IN THE MIDDLE.
NOK NOK
PMP PMP
INTER-ESTING!
PMP PMP PMP PMP
THIS ONE, THIS ONE, AND THIS ONE SOUND GOOD.
THIS ONE AND THIS ONE HAVE A GOOD COLOR TOO.
WE'LL BUY THOSE TWO, THEN.

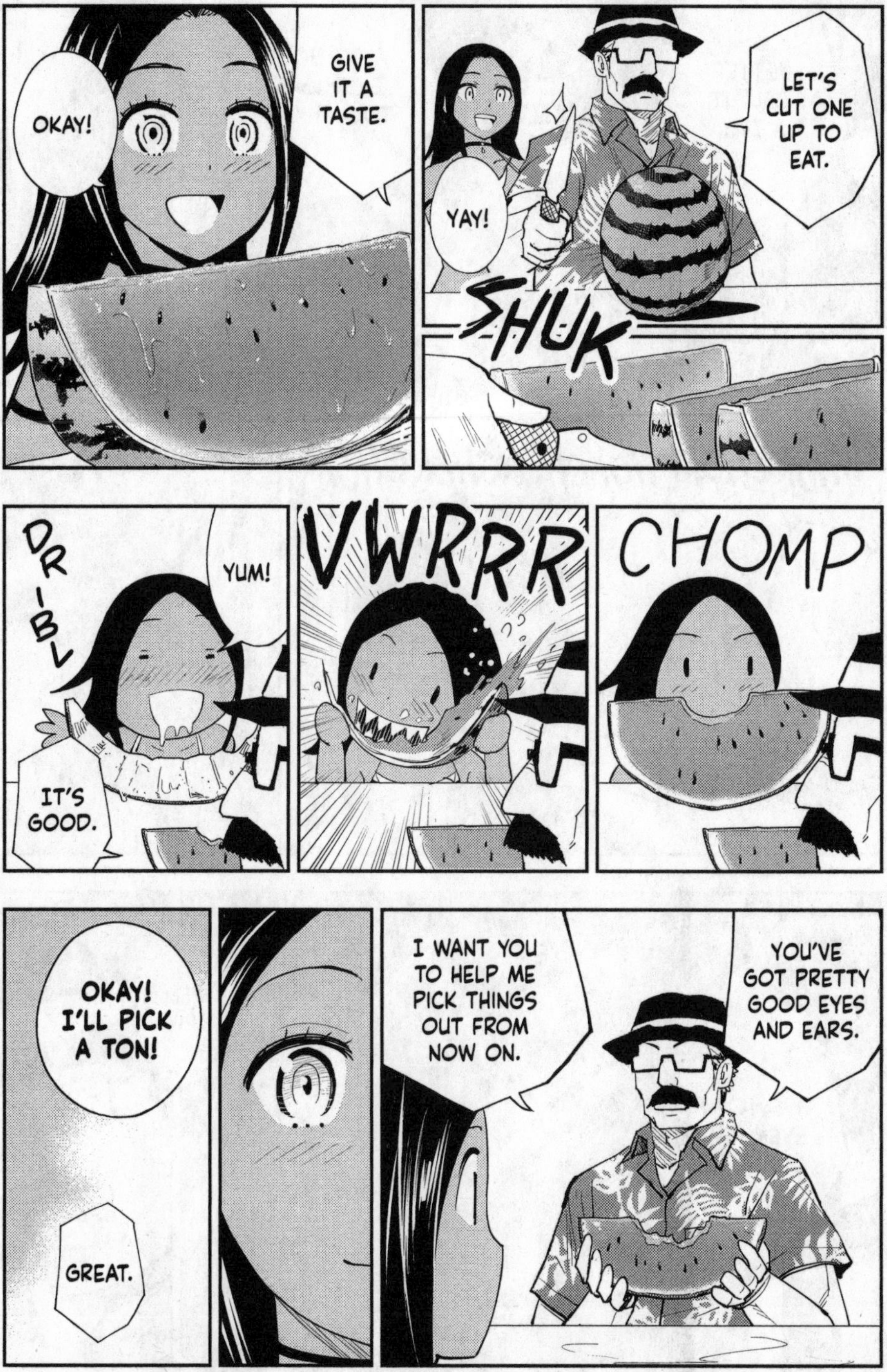
LET'S CUT ONE UP TO EAT.
YAY!
SHUK
GIVE IT A TASTE.
OKAY!
CHOMP
VWRRR
YUM!
DRIBL
IT'S GOOD.
YOU'VE GOT PRETTY GOOD EYES AND EARS.
I WANT YOU TO HELP ME PICK THINGS OUT FROM NOW ON.
OKAY! I'LL PICK A TON!
GREAT.

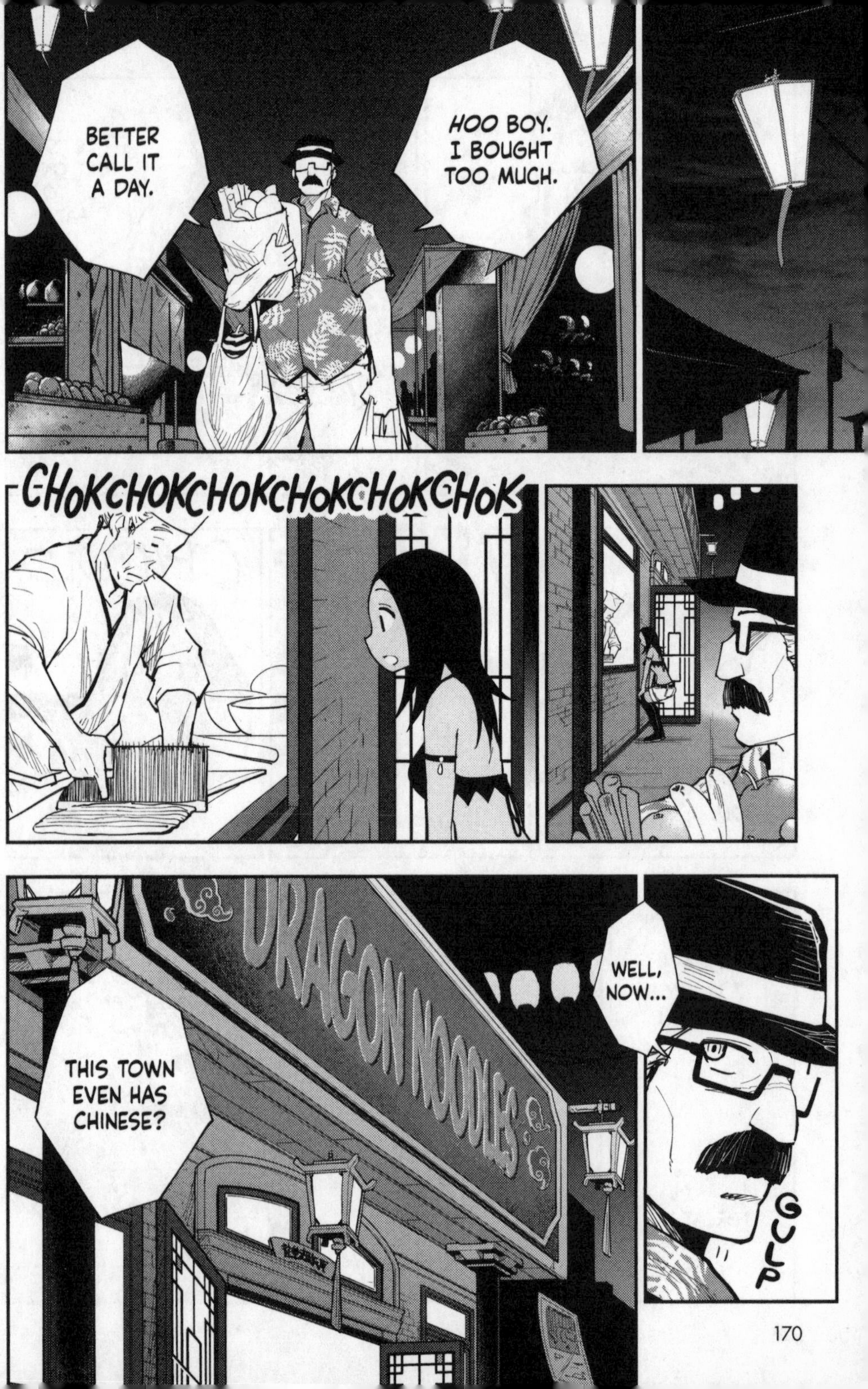

HOO BOY. I BOUGHT TOO MUCH.
BETTER CALL IT A DAY.
CHOKCHOKCHOKCHOKCHOKCHOK
WELL, NOW...
GULP
DRAGON NOODLES
THIS TOWN EVEN HAS CHINESE?

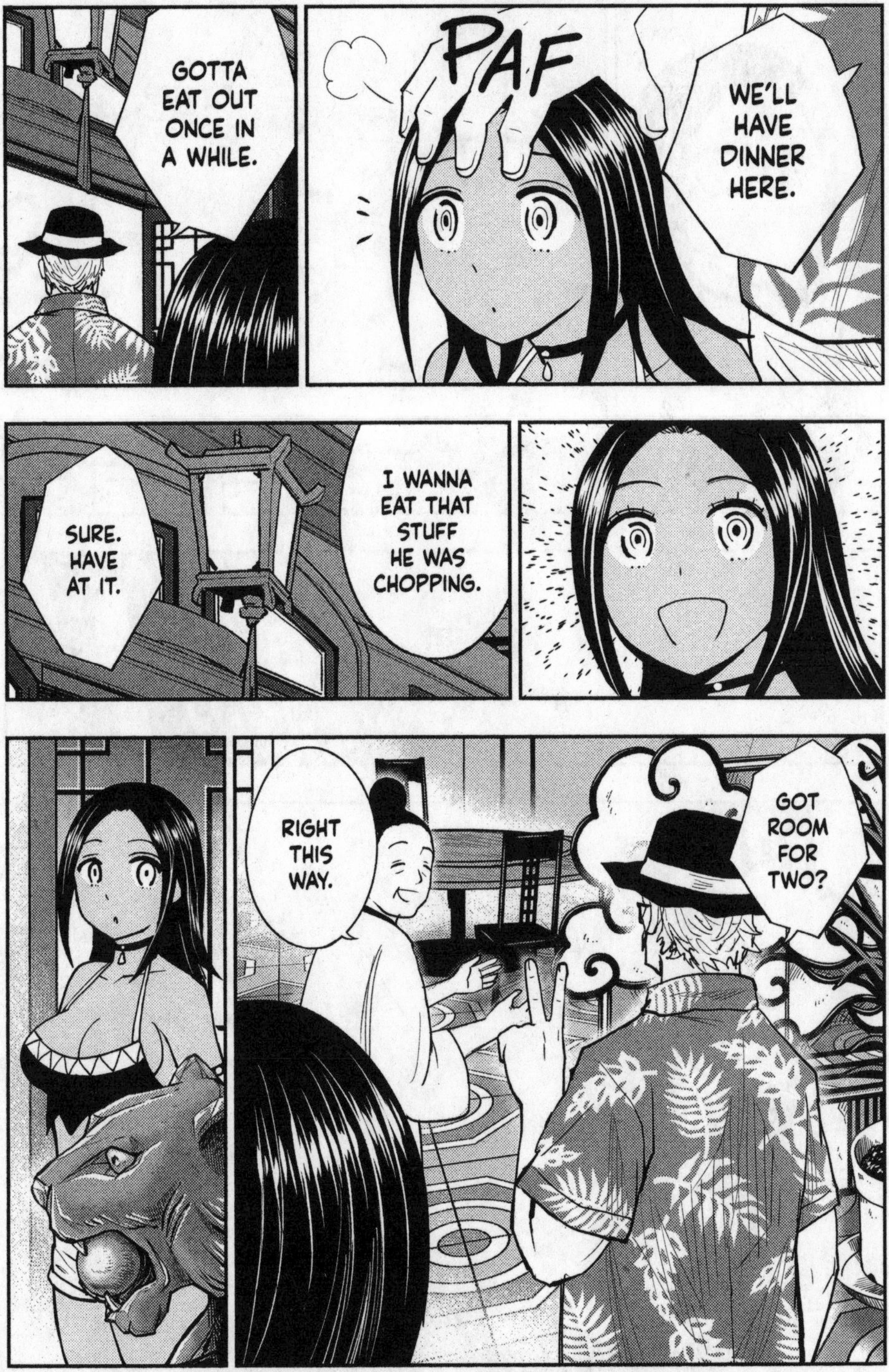
PAF
WE'LL HAVE DINNER HERE.
GOTTA EAT OUT ONCE IN A WHILE.
I WANNA EAT THAT STUFF HE WAS CHOPPING.
SURE. HAVE AT IT.
GOT ROOM FOR TWO?
RIGHT THIS WAY.

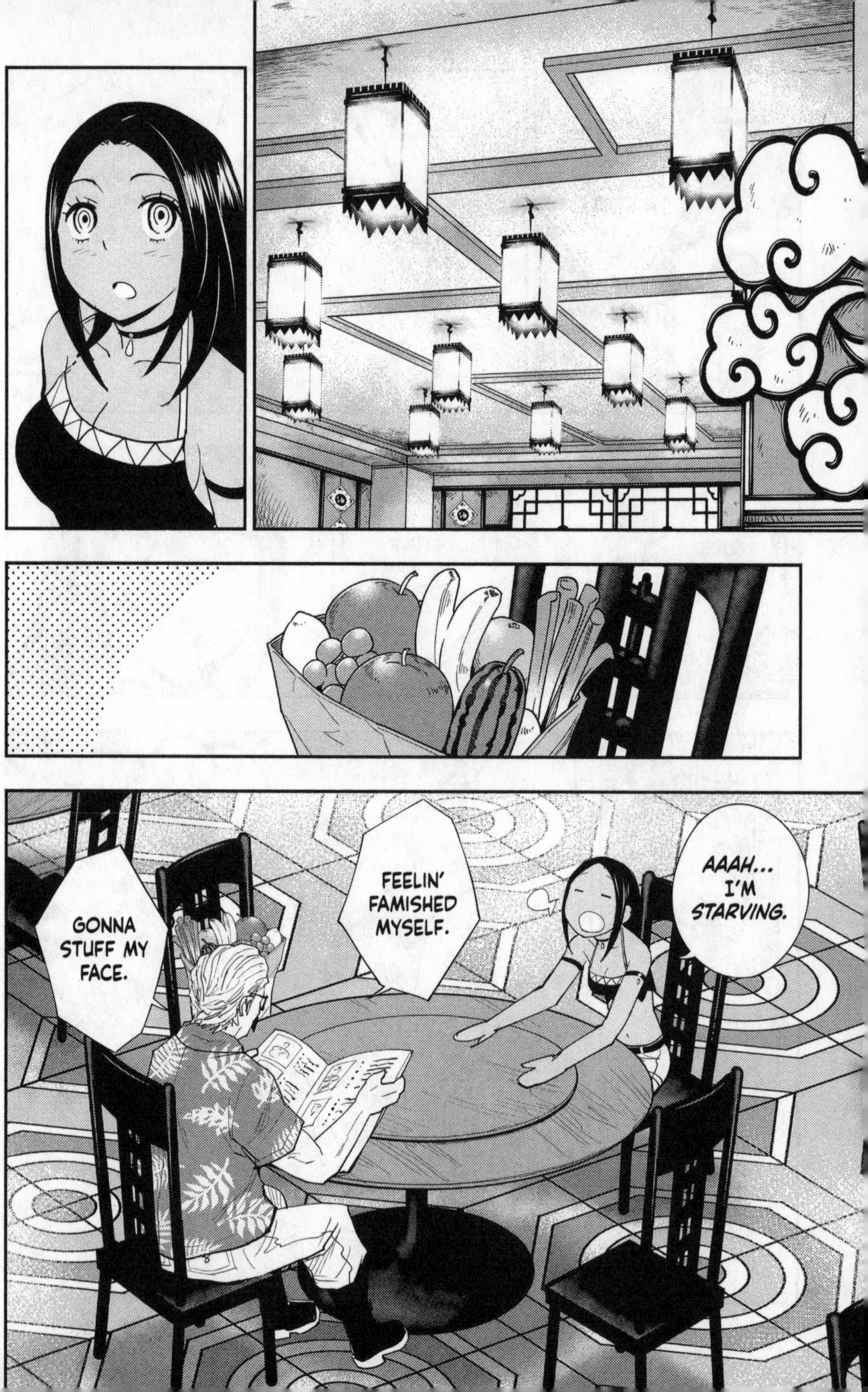
AAAH... I'M STARVING.
FEELIN' FAMISHED MYSELF.
GONNA STUFF MY FACE.

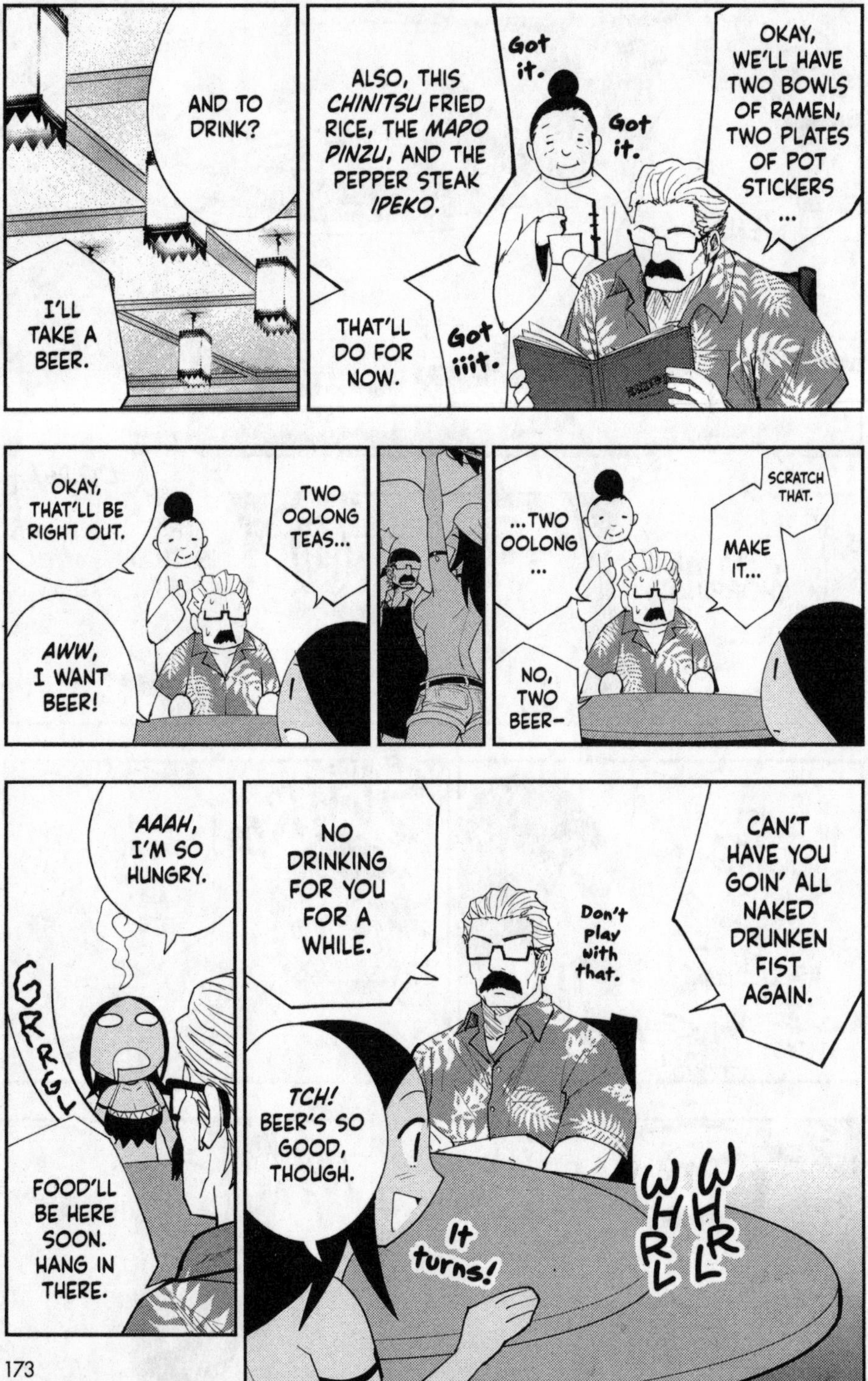

OKAY, WE'LL HAVE TWO BOWLS OF RAMEN, TWO PLATES OF POT STICKERS ...
Got it.
Got it.
ALSO, THIS *CHINITSU* FRIED RICE, THE *MAPO PINZU*, AND THE PEPPER STEAK *IPEKO*.
Got iiit.
THAT'LL DO FOR NOW.
AND TO DRINK?
I'LL TAKE A BEER.
SCRATCH THAT.
MAKE IT...
...TWO OOLONG ...
NO, TWO BEER—
TWO OOLONG TEAS...
OKAY, THAT'LL BE RIGHT OUT.
AWW, I WANT BEER!
CAN'T HAVE YOU GOIN' ALL NAKED DRUNKEN FIST AGAIN.
Don't play with that.
NO DRINKING FOR YOU FOR A WHILE.
WHRL WHRL
TCH! BEER'S SO GOOD, THOUGH.
It turns!
AAAH, I'M SO HUNGRY.
GRRGL
FOOD'LL BE HERE SOON. HANG IN THERE.

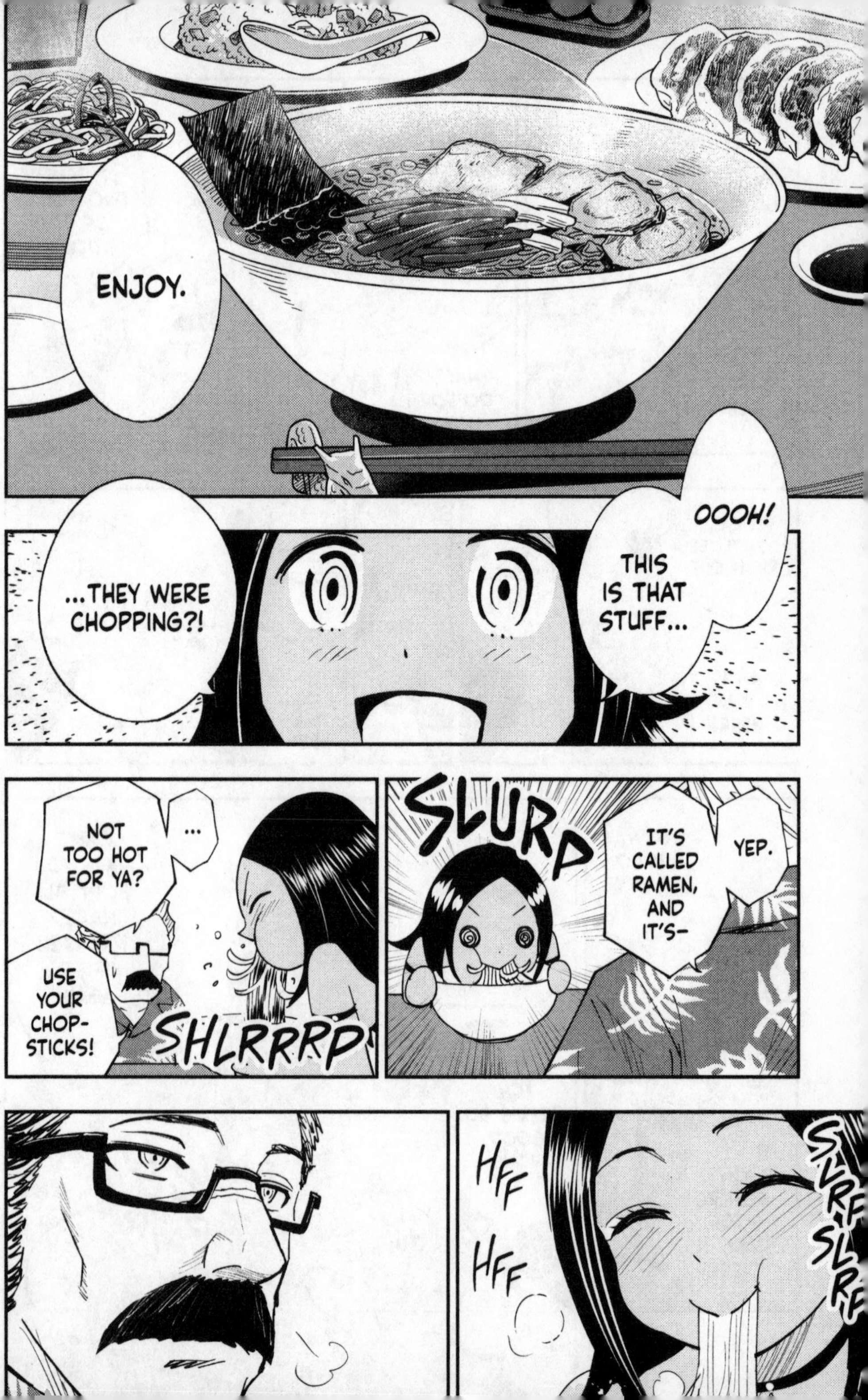

ENJOY.
OOOH!
THIS IS THAT STUFF...
...THEY WERE CHOPPING?!
SLURP
YEP.
IT'S CALLED RAMEN, AND IT'S-
...
NOT TOO HOT FOR YA?
USE YOUR CHOP-STICKS!
SHLRRRP
SLRP SLRP
HFF
HFF

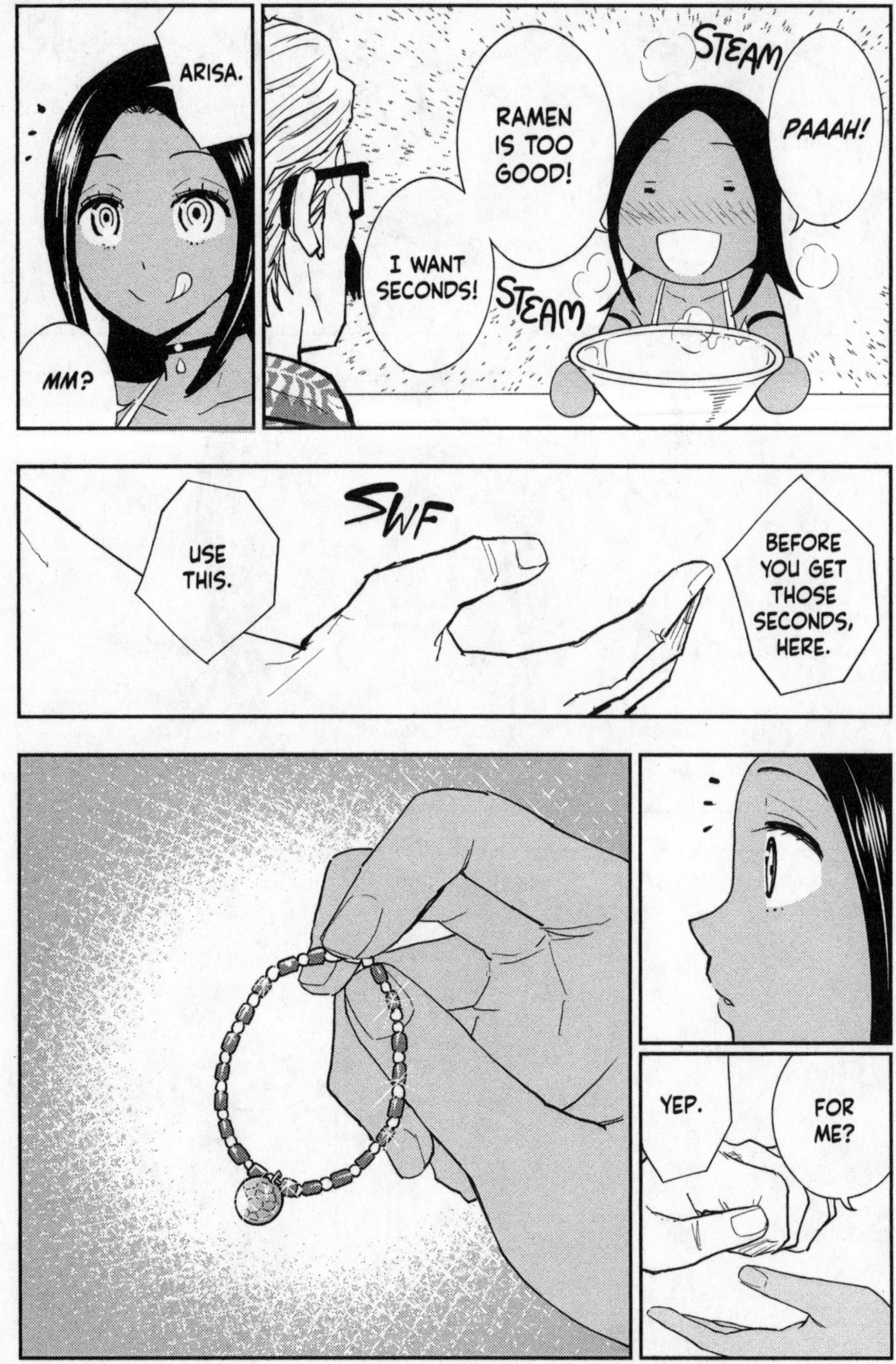
PAAAH!
STEAM
RAMEN IS TOO GOOD!
I WANT SECONDS!
STEAM
ARISA.
MM?
BEFORE YOU GET THOSE SECONDS, HERE.
SWF
USE THIS.
FOR ME?
YEP.

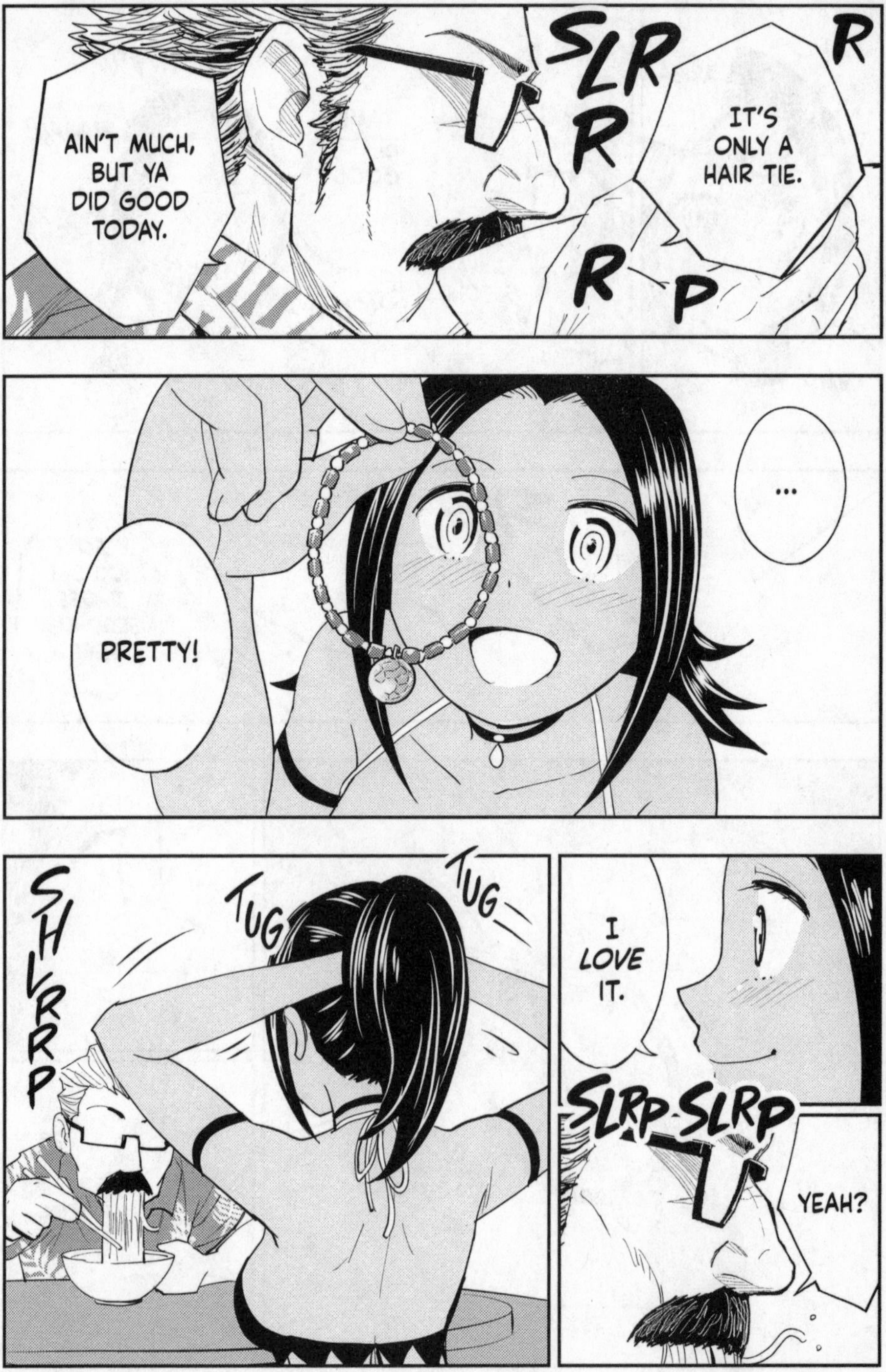
SLRRRRP
IT'S ONLY A HAIR TIE.
AIN'T MUCH, BUT YA DID GOOD TODAY.
...
PRETTY!
I LOVE IT.
SLRP SLRP
YEAH?
TUG TUG
SHLRRP

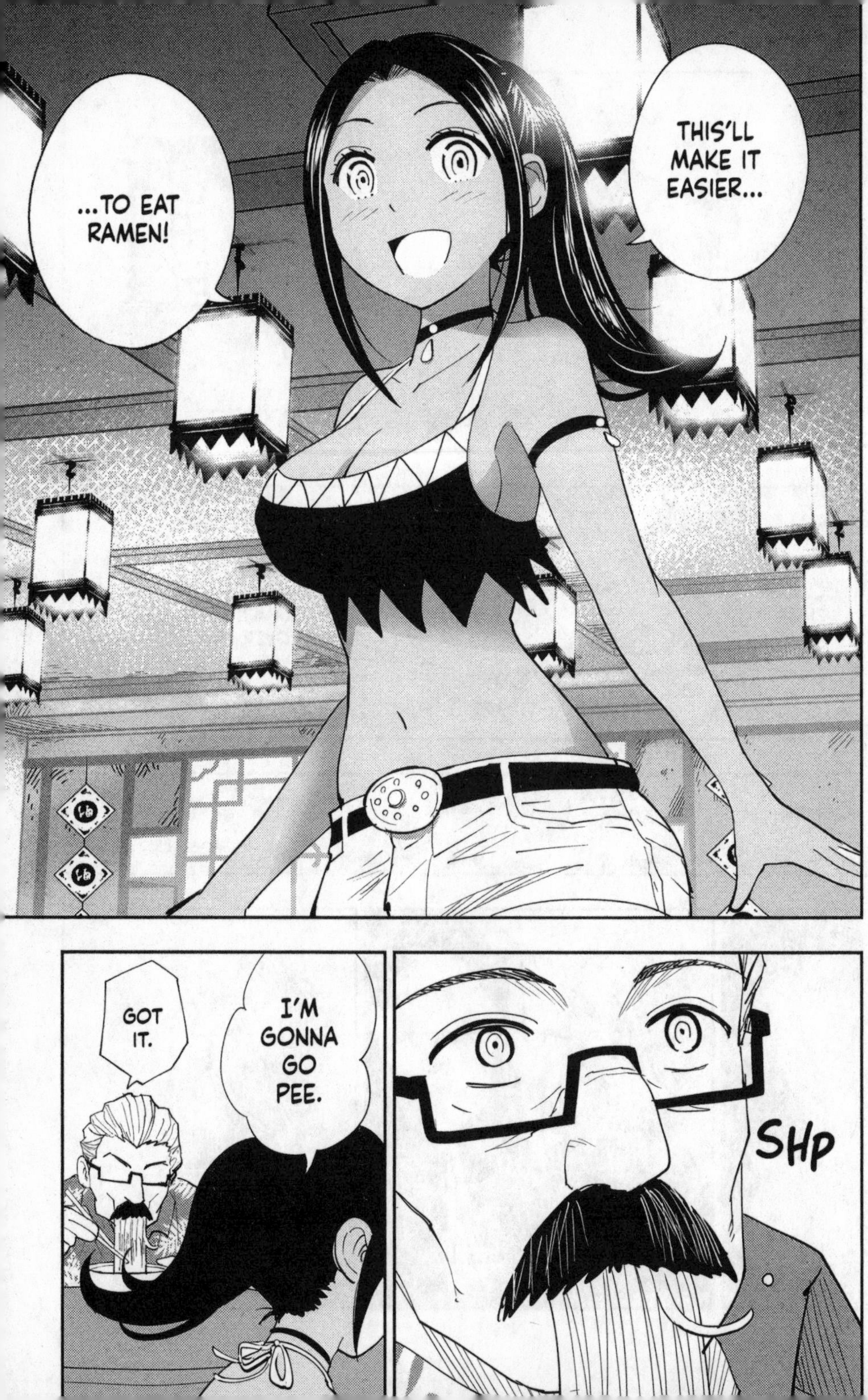
THIS'LL MAKE IT EASIER...
...TO EAT RAMEN!
SHP
I'M GONNA GO PEE.
GOT IT.

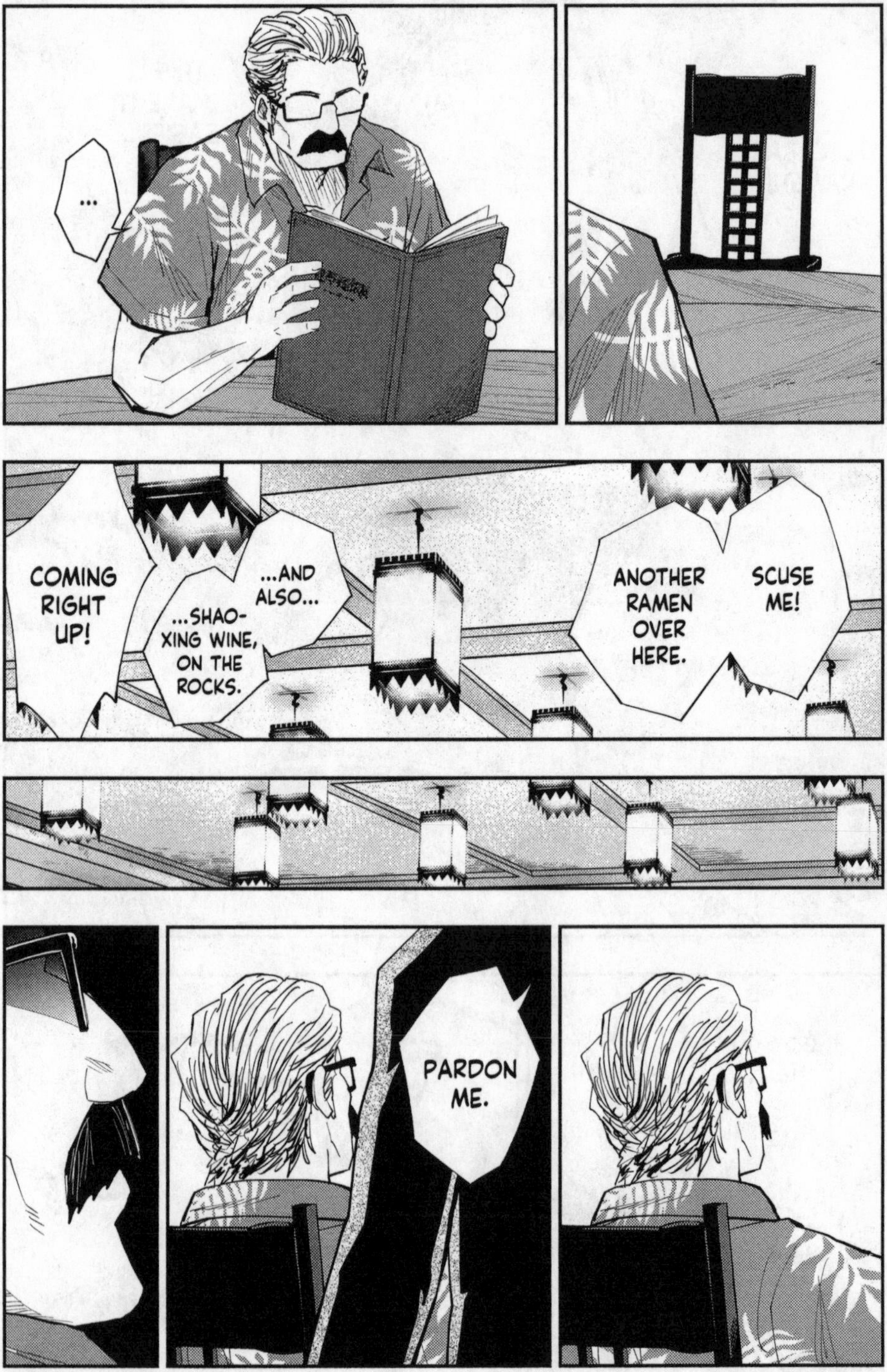
...
SCUSE ME!
ANOTHER RAMEN OVER HERE.
...AND ALSO...
...SHAO-XING WINE, ON THE ROCKS.
COMING RIGHT UP!
PARDON ME.

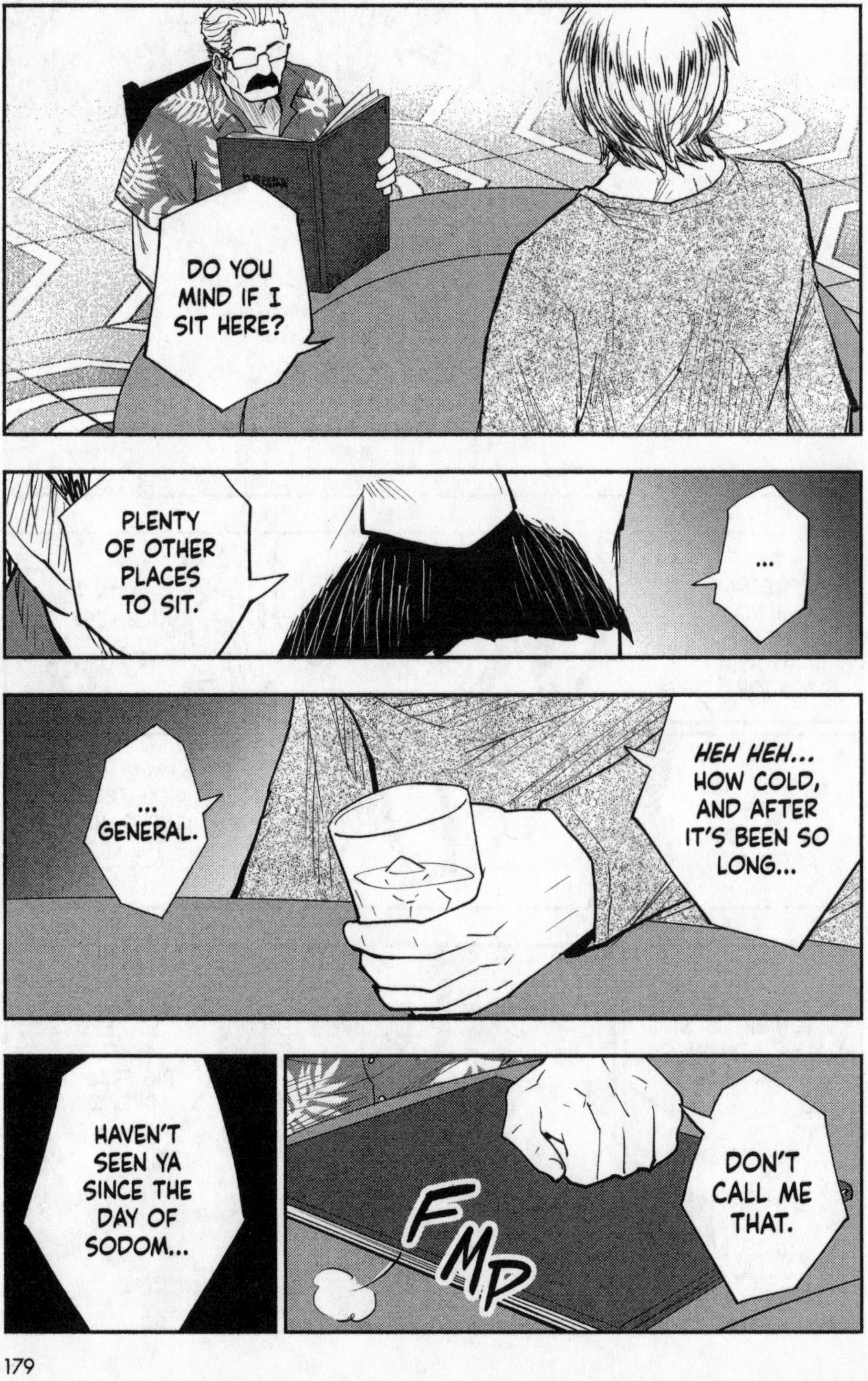
DO YOU MIND IF I SIT HERE?
...
PLENTY OF OTHER PLACES TO SIT.
HEH HEH... HOW COLD, AND AFTER IT'S BEEN SO LONG...
... GENERAL.
DON'T CALL ME THAT.
FMP
HAVEN'T SEEN YA SINCE THE DAY OF SODOM...

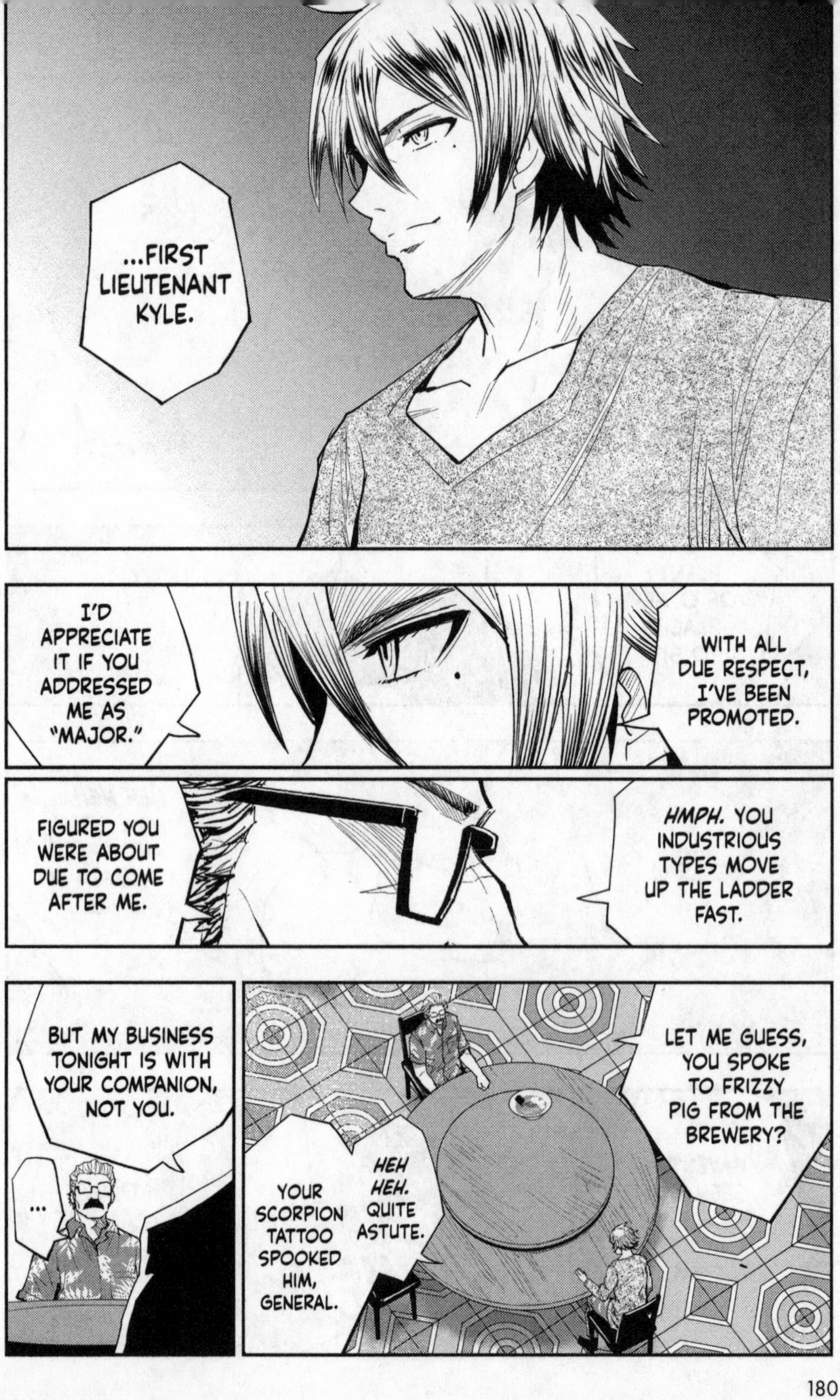
...FIRST LIEUTENANT KYLE.
WITH ALL DUE RESPECT, I'VE BEEN PROMOTED.
I'D APPRECIATE IT IF YOU ADDRESSED ME AS "MAJOR."
HMPH. YOU INDUSTRIOUS TYPES MOVE UP THE LADDER FAST.
FIGURED YOU WERE ABOUT DUE TO COME AFTER ME.
LET ME GUESS, YOU SPOKE TO FRIZZY PIG FROM THE BREWERY?
HEH HEH. QUITE ASTUTE.
YOUR SCORPION TATTOO SPOOKED HIM, GENERAL.
BUT MY BUSINESS TONIGHT IS WITH YOUR COMPANION, NOT YOU.
...

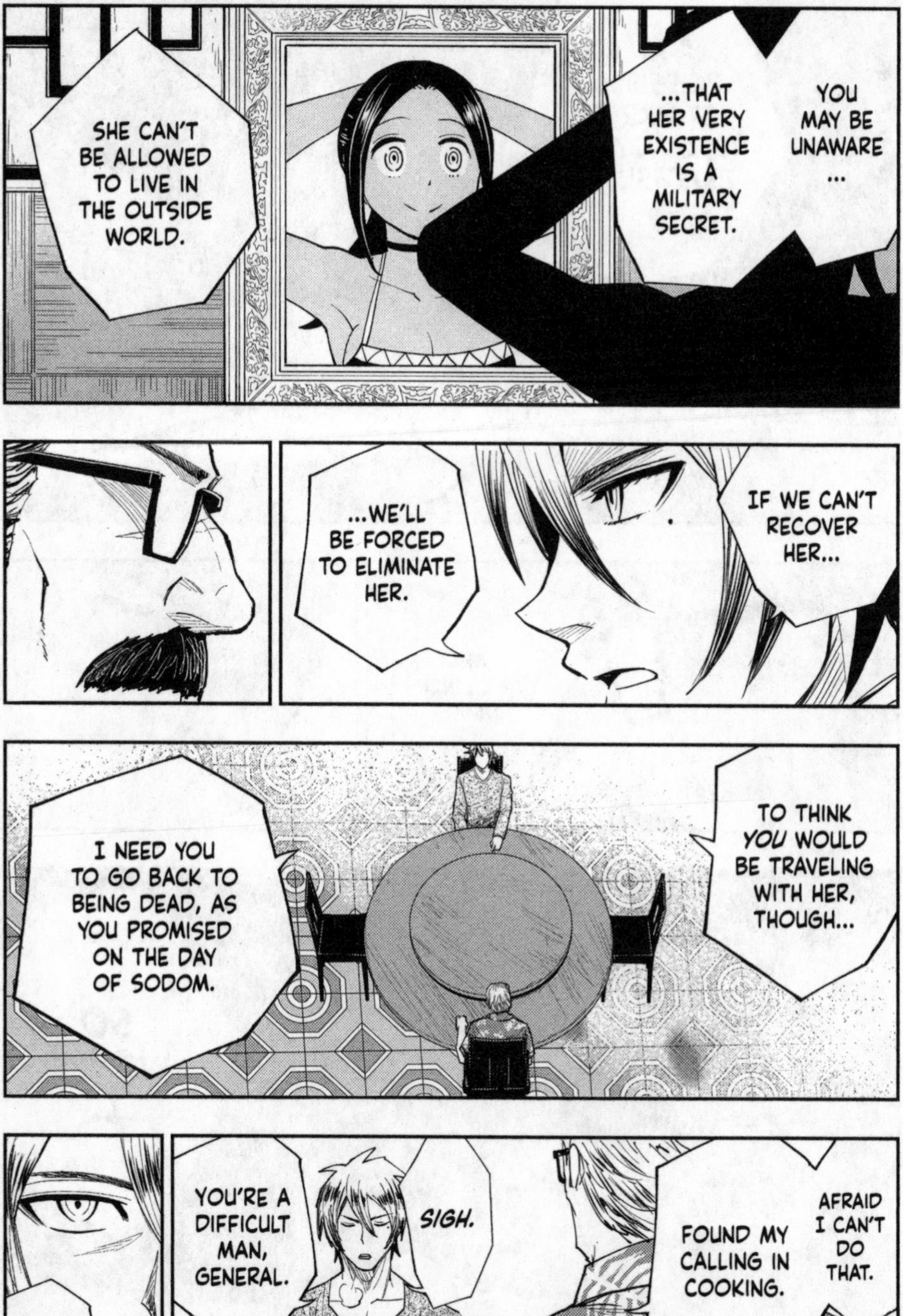
YOU MAY BE UNAWARE ...
...THAT HER VERY EXISTENCE IS A MILITARY SECRET.
SHE CAN'T BE ALLOWED TO LIVE IN THE OUTSIDE WORLD.
IF WE CAN'T RECOVER HER...
...WE'LL BE FORCED TO ELIMINATE HER.
TO THINK *YOU* WOULD BE TRAVELING WITH HER, THOUGH...
I NEED YOU TO GO BACK TO BEING DEAD, AS YOU PROMISED ON THE DAY OF SODOM.
AFRAID I CAN'T DO THAT.
FOUND MY CALLING IN COOKING.
SIGH.
YOU'RE A DIFFICULT MAN, GENERAL.
PERSON-ALLY...

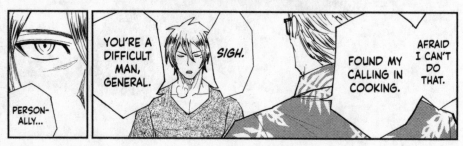

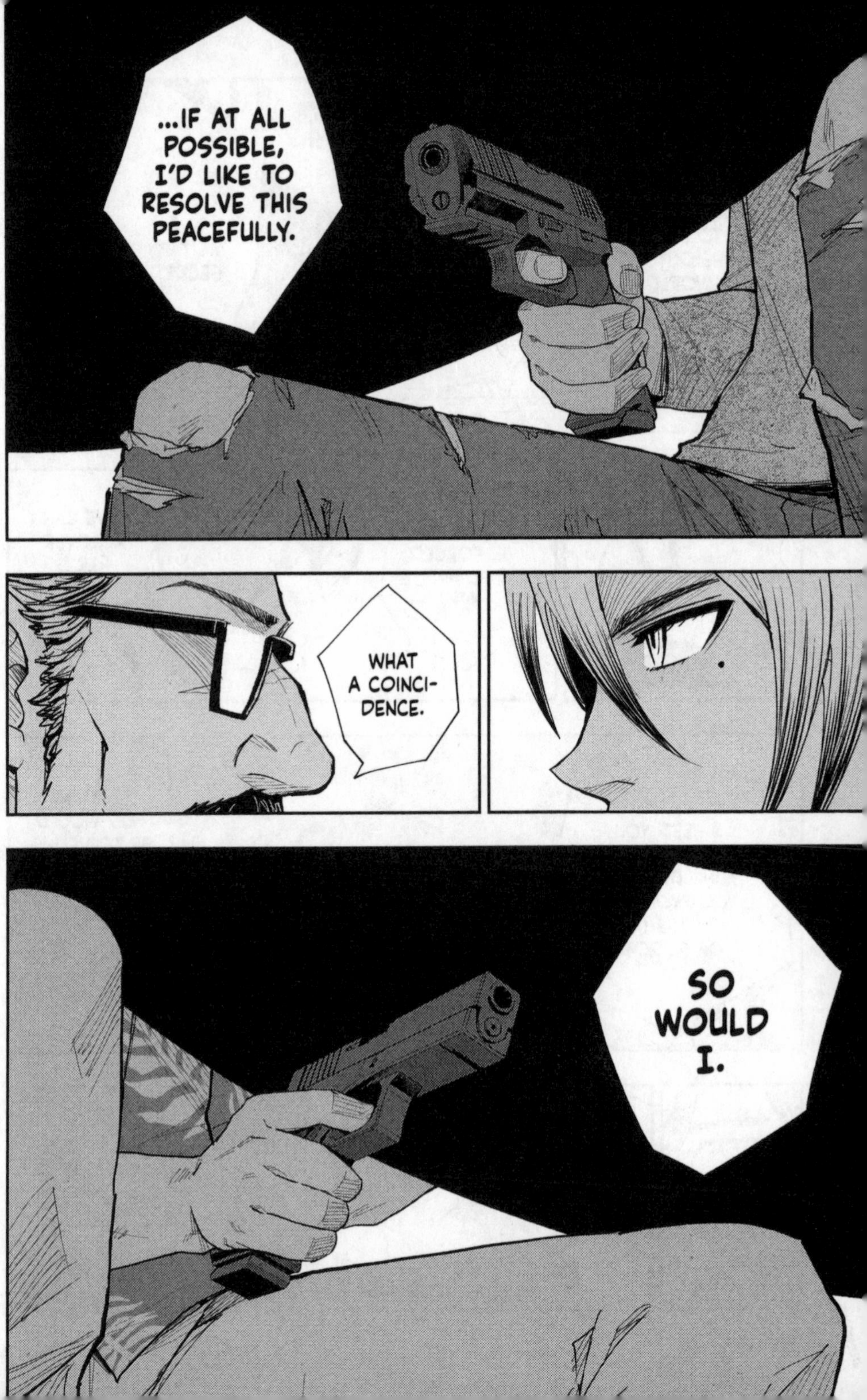
...IF AT ALL POSSIBLE, I'D LIKE TO RESOLVE THIS PEACEFULLY.
WHAT A COINCI-DENCE.
SO WOULD I.

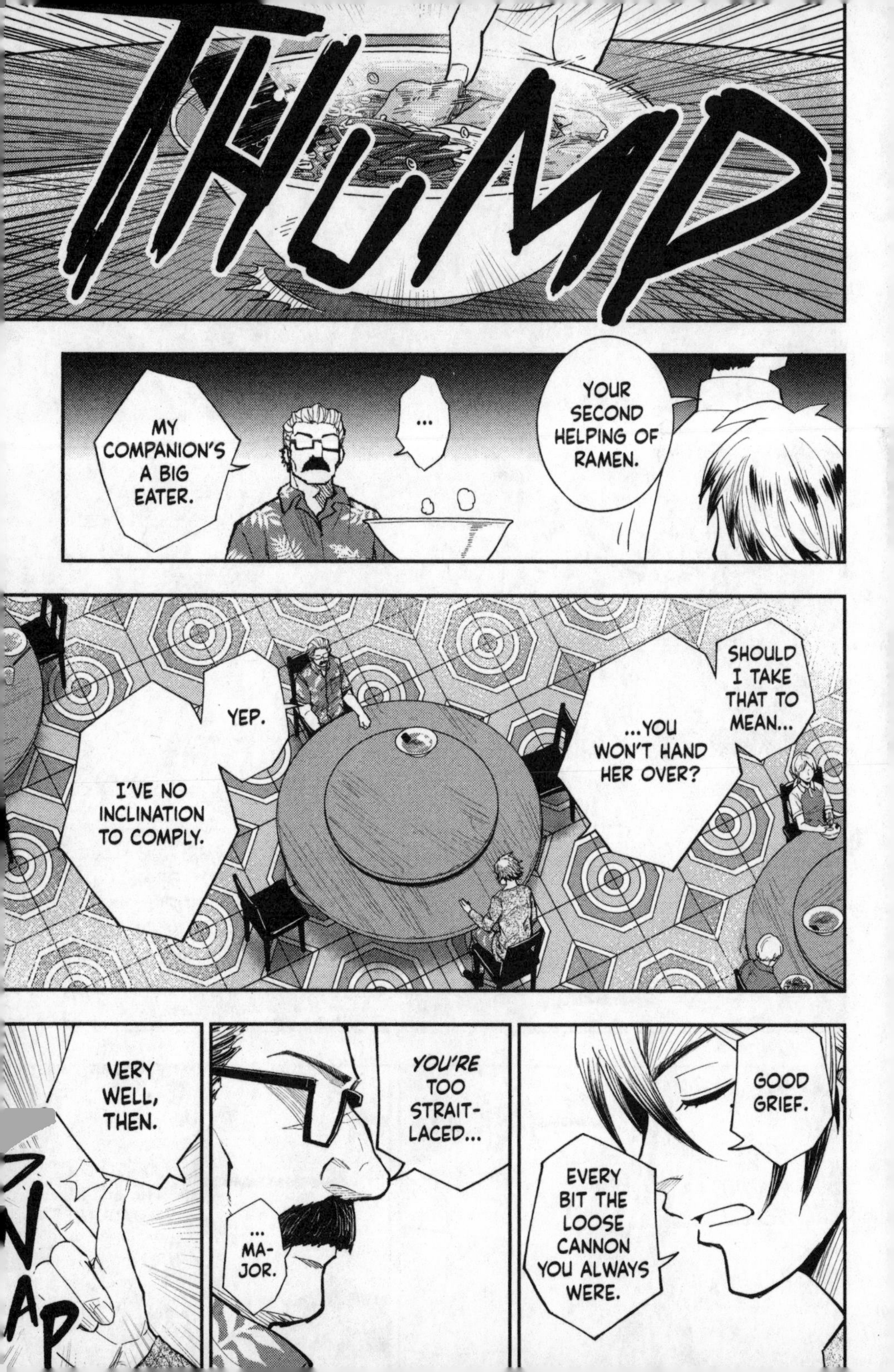
THUMP
YOUR SECOND HELPING OF RAMEN.
...
MY COMPANION'S A BIG EATER.
SHOULD I TAKE THAT TO MEAN...
...YOU WON'T HAND HER OVER?
YEP.
I'VE NO INCLINATION TO COMPLY.
GOOD GRIEF.
EVERY BIT THE LOOSE CANNON YOU ALWAYS WERE.
YOU'RE TOO STRAIT-LACED...
...MA-JOR.
VERY WELL, THEN.

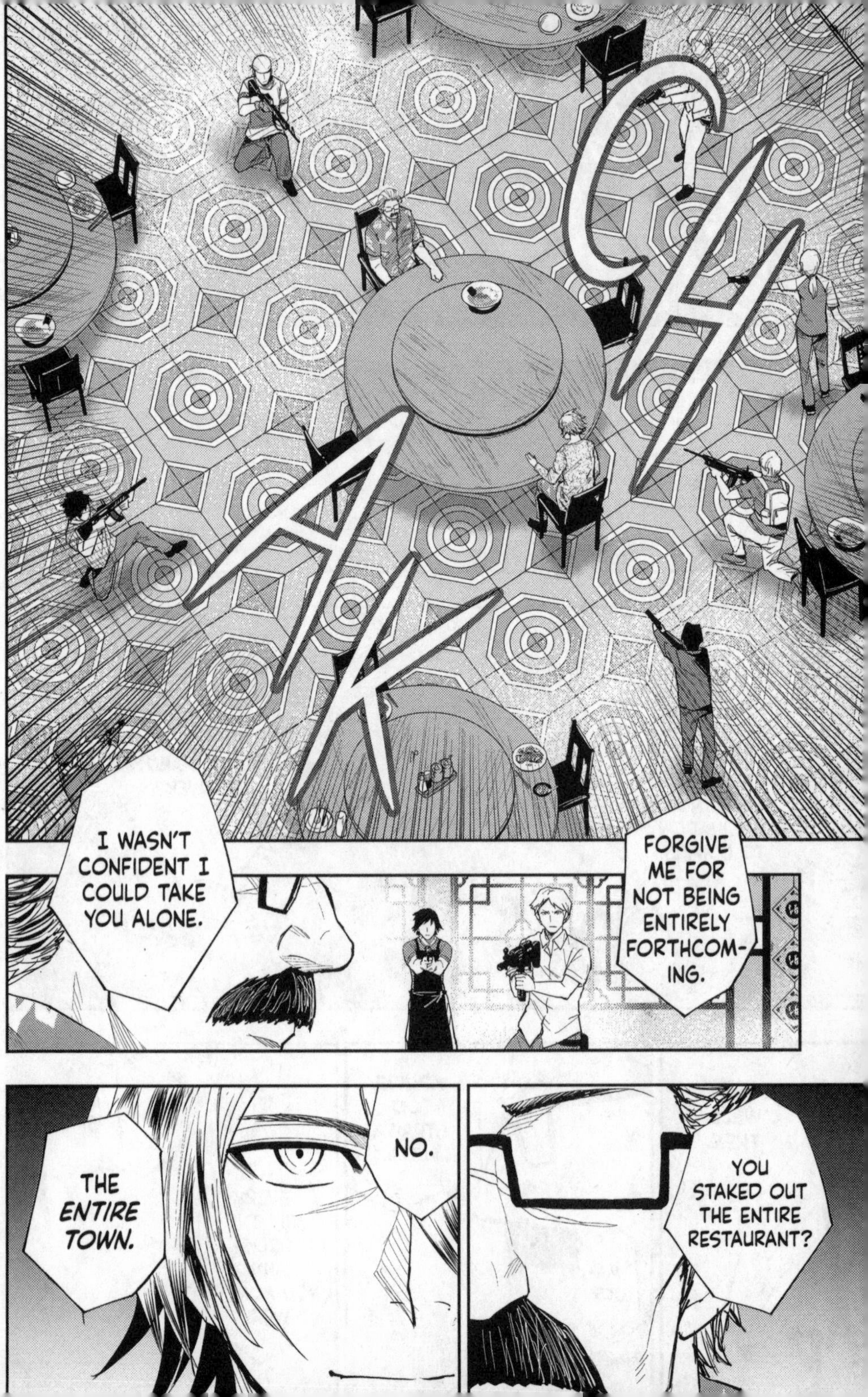
CHAK
FORGIVE ME FOR NOT BEING ENTIRELY FORTHCOMING.
I WASN'T CONFIDENT I COULD TAKE YOU ALONE.
YOU STAKED OUT THE ENTIRE RESTAURANT?
NO.
THE *ENTIRE TOWN.*

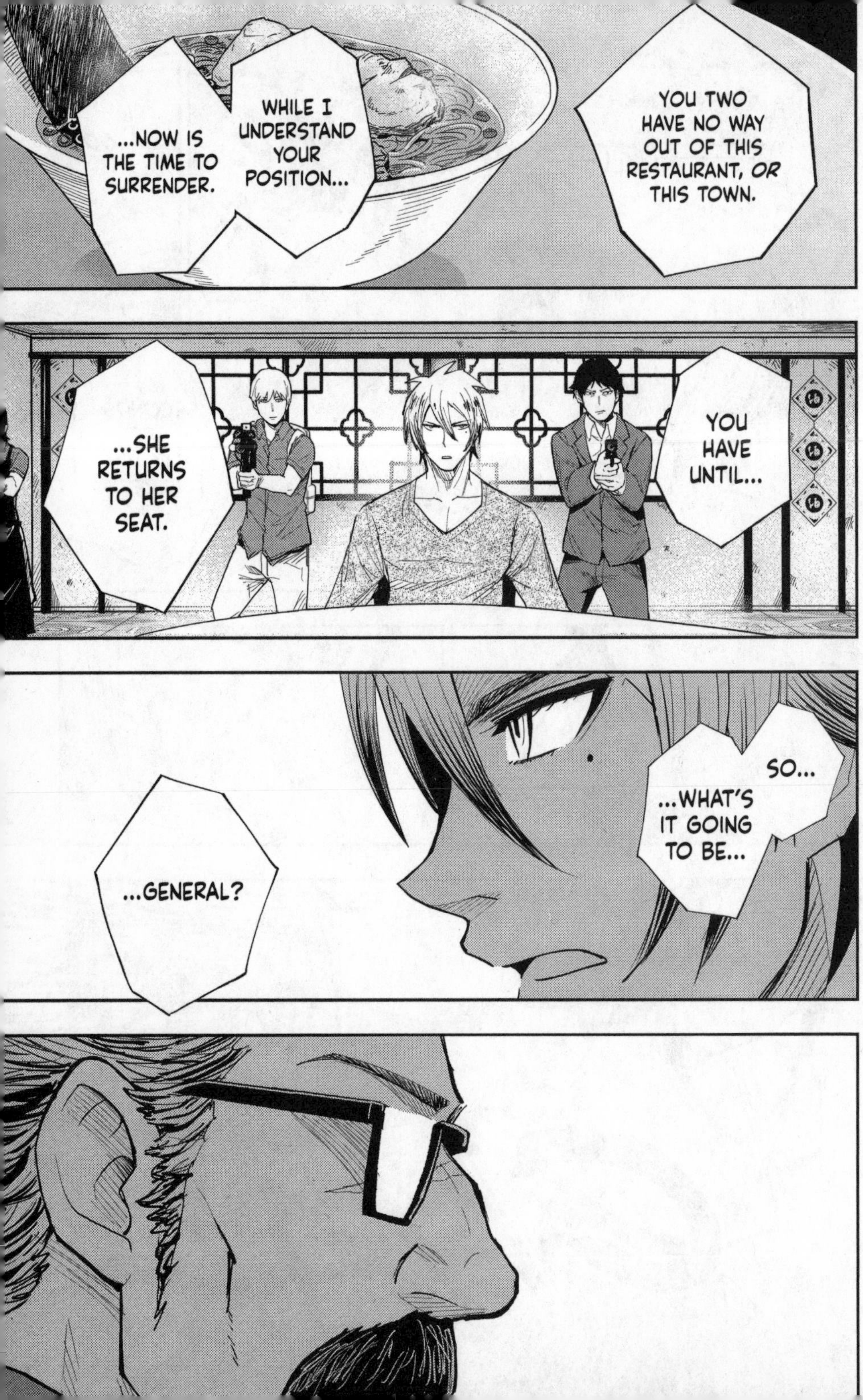
YOU TWO HAVE NO WAY OUT OF THIS RESTAURANT, *OR* THIS TOWN.
WHILE I UNDERSTAND YOUR POSITION...
...NOW IS THE TIME TO SURRENDER.
YOU HAVE UNTIL...
...SHE RETURNS TO HER SEAT.
SO...
...WHAT'S IT GOING TO BE...
...GENERAL?

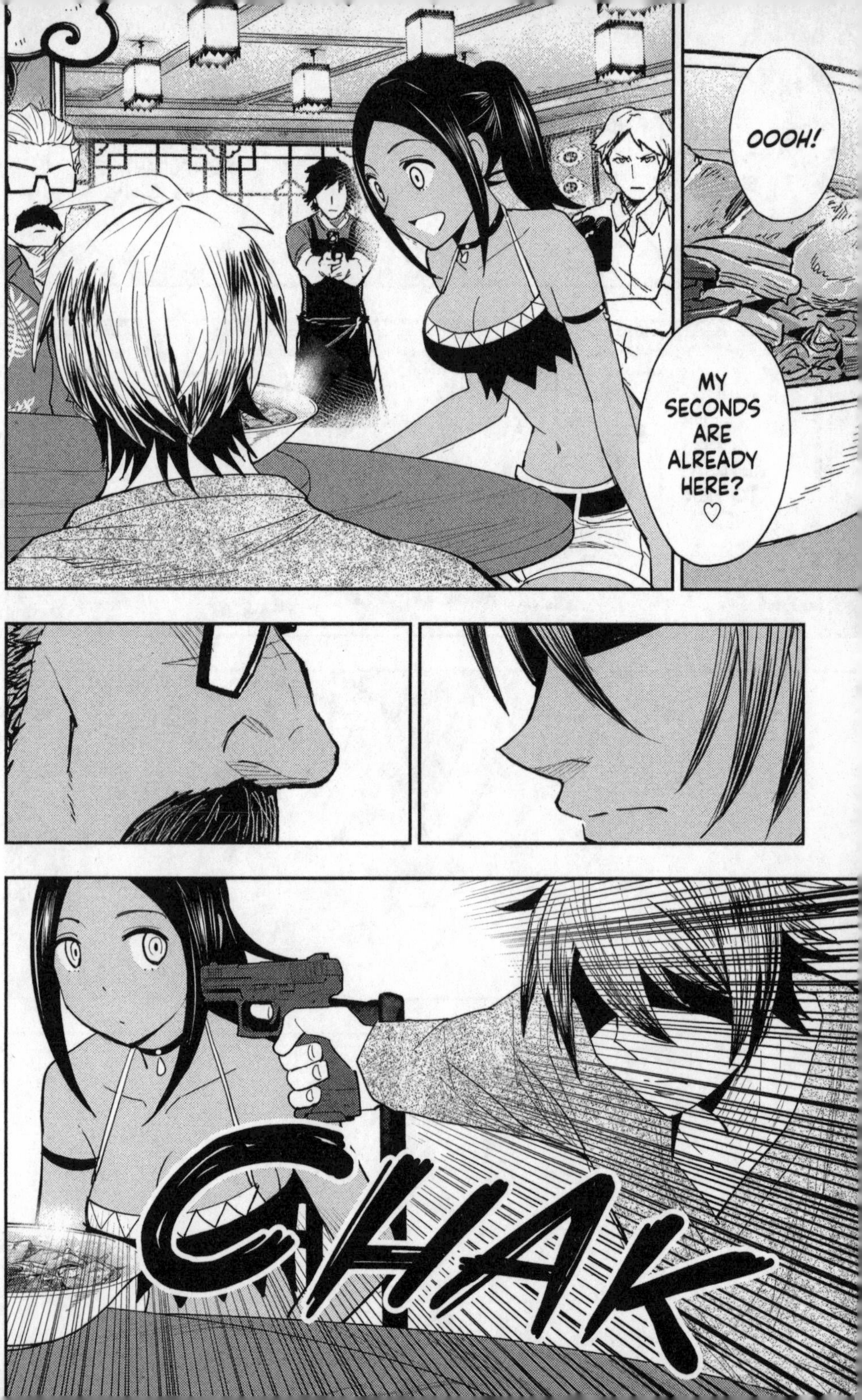
OOOH!
MY SECONDS ARE ALREADY HERE? ♡
CHAK

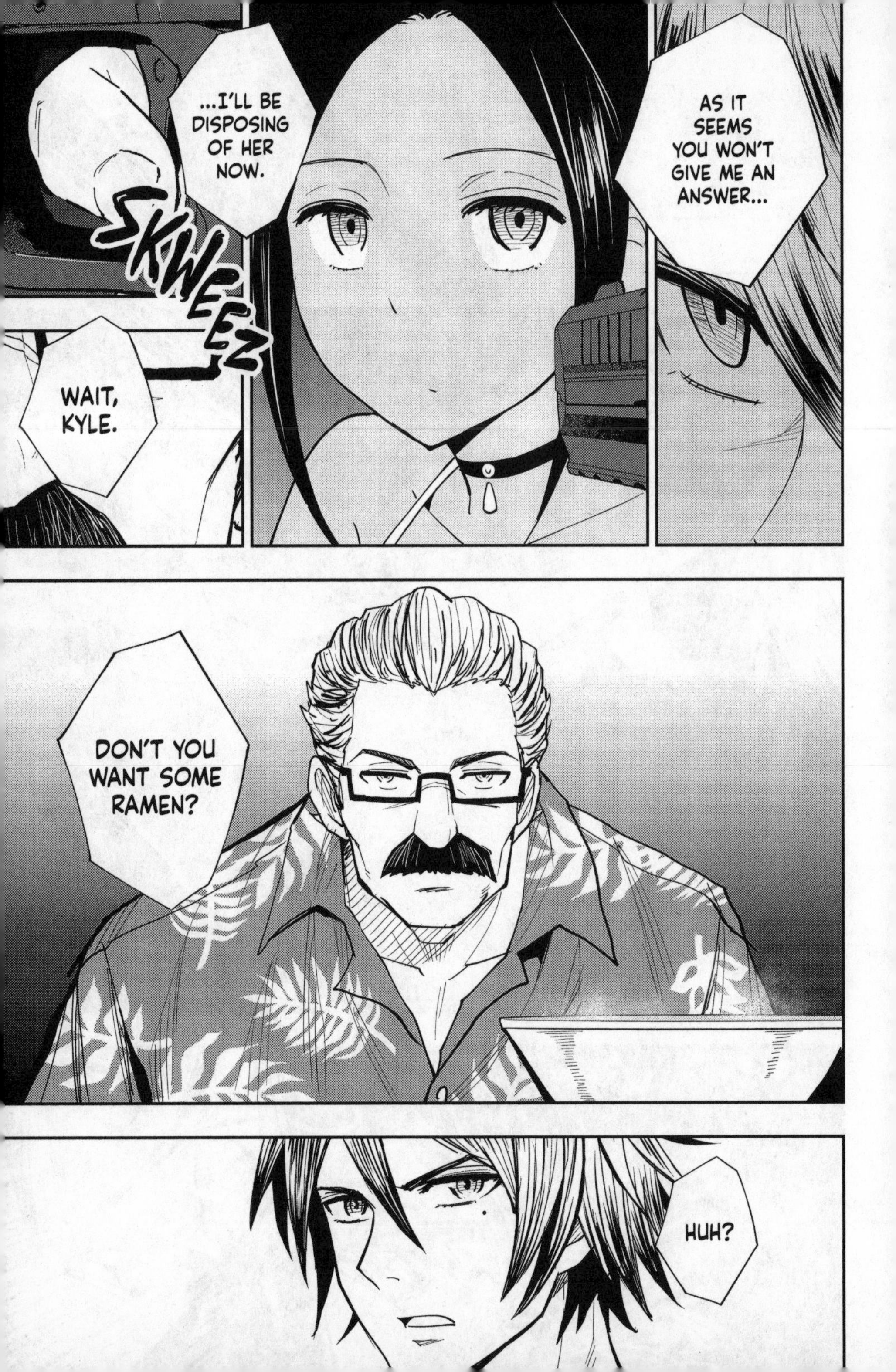
AS IT SEEMS YOU WON'T GIVE ME AN ANSWER...
...I'LL BE DISPOSING OF HER NOW.
SKWEEZ
WAIT, KYLE.
DON'T YOU WANT SOME RAMEN?
HUH?

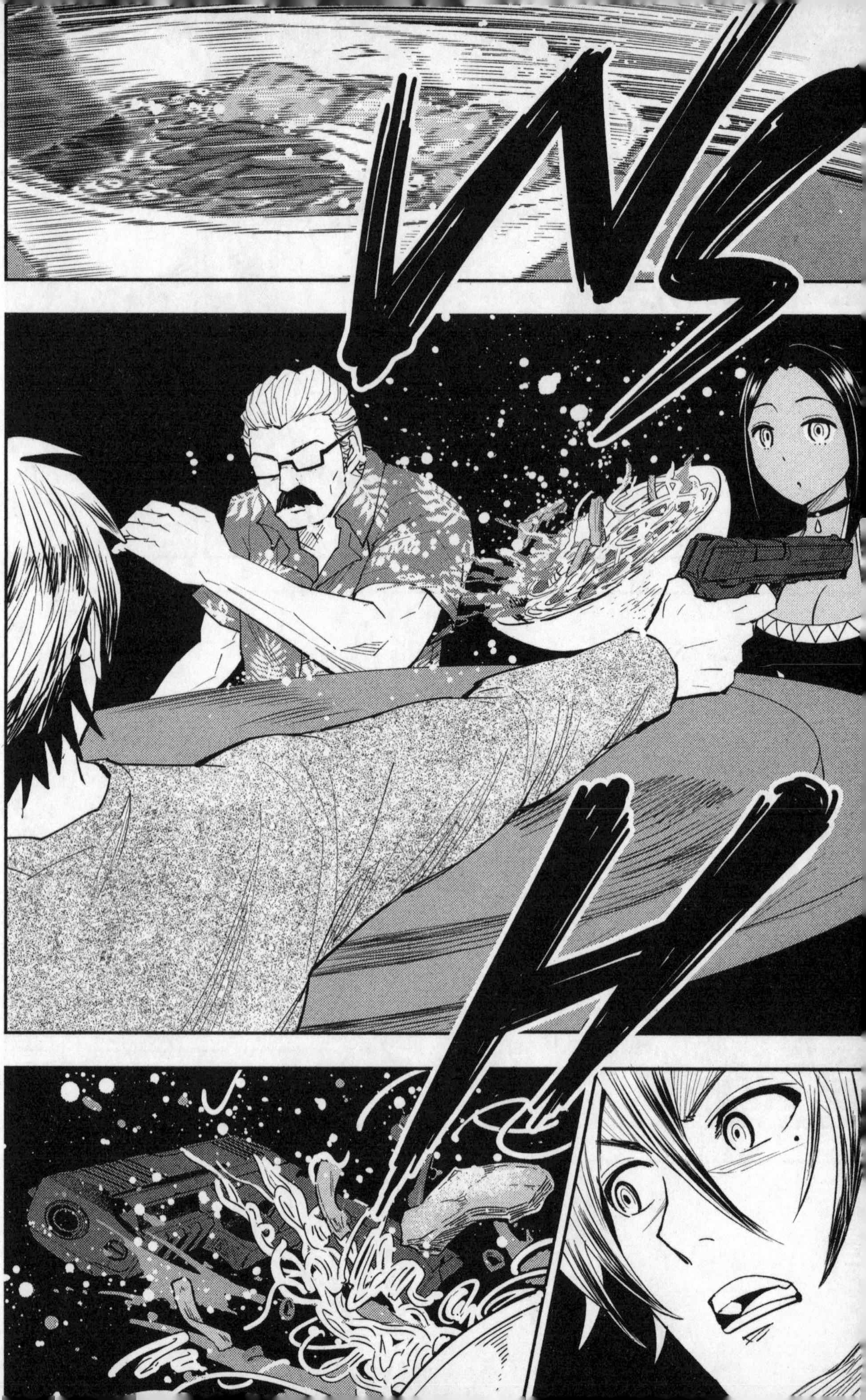
WSH

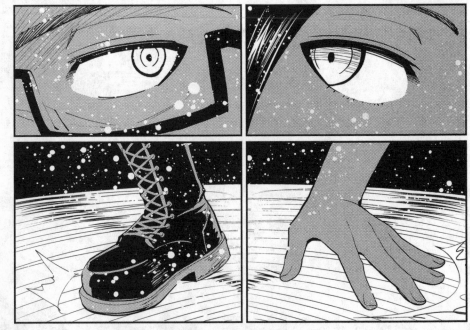

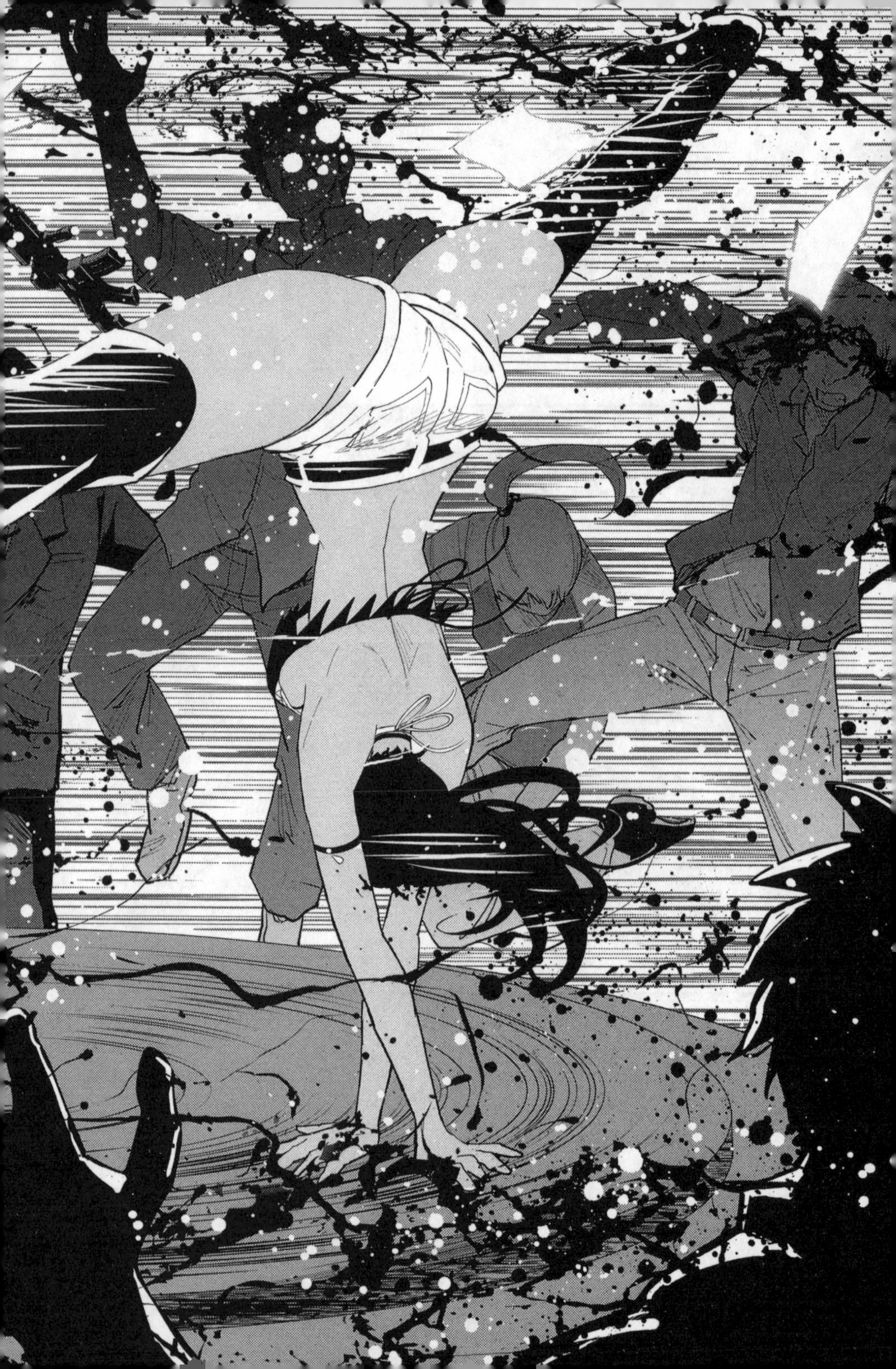

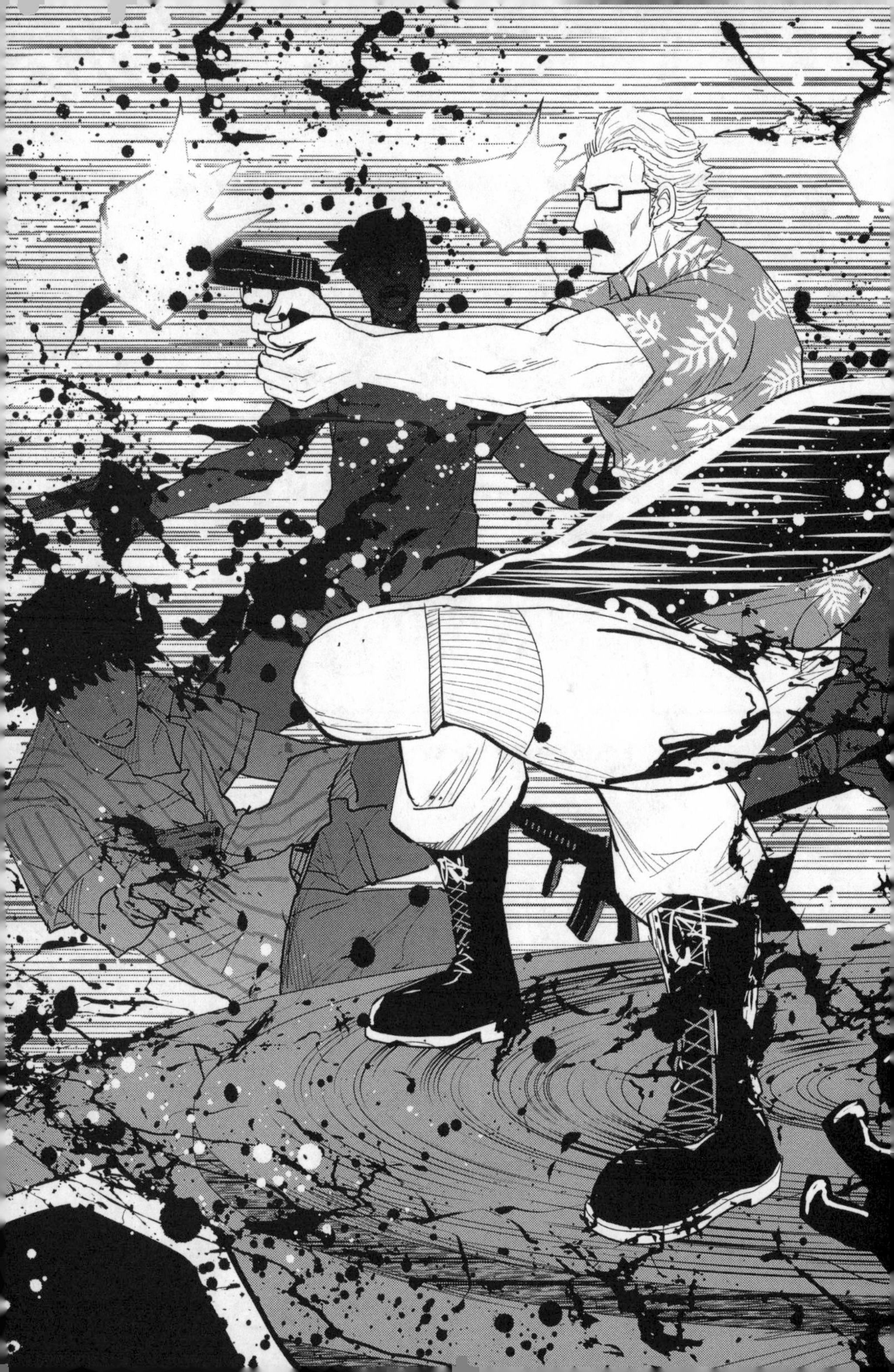

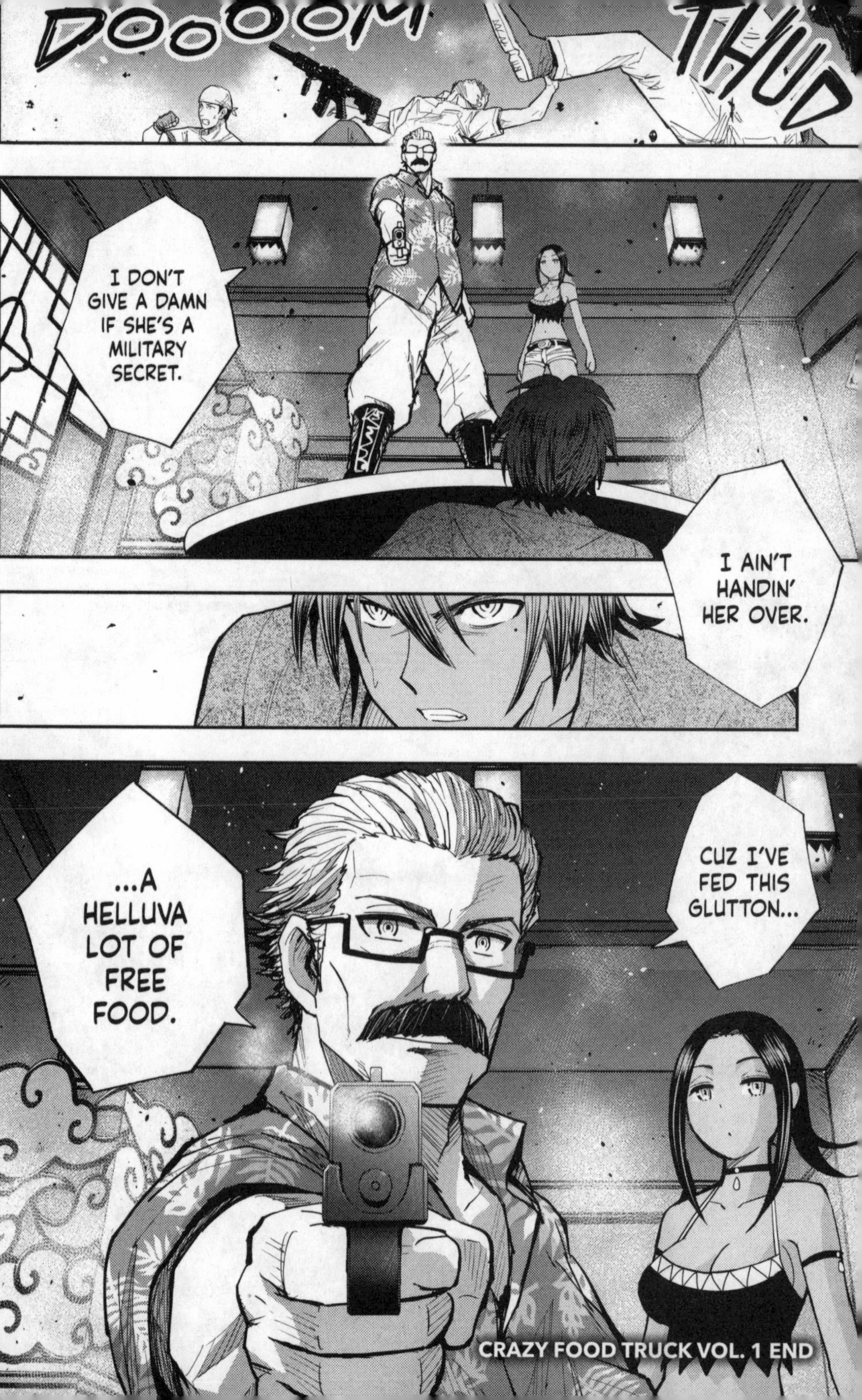
THUD
DOOOOOM
I DON'T GIVE A DAMN IF SHE'S A MILITARY SECRET.
I AIN'T HANDIN' HER OVER.
CUZ I'VE FED THIS GLUTTON...
...A HELLUVA LOT OF FREE FOOD.
CRAZY FOOD TRUCK VOL. 1 END

CRAZY FOOD TRUCK
TO BE CONTINUED
NEXT STOP VOL. 2.

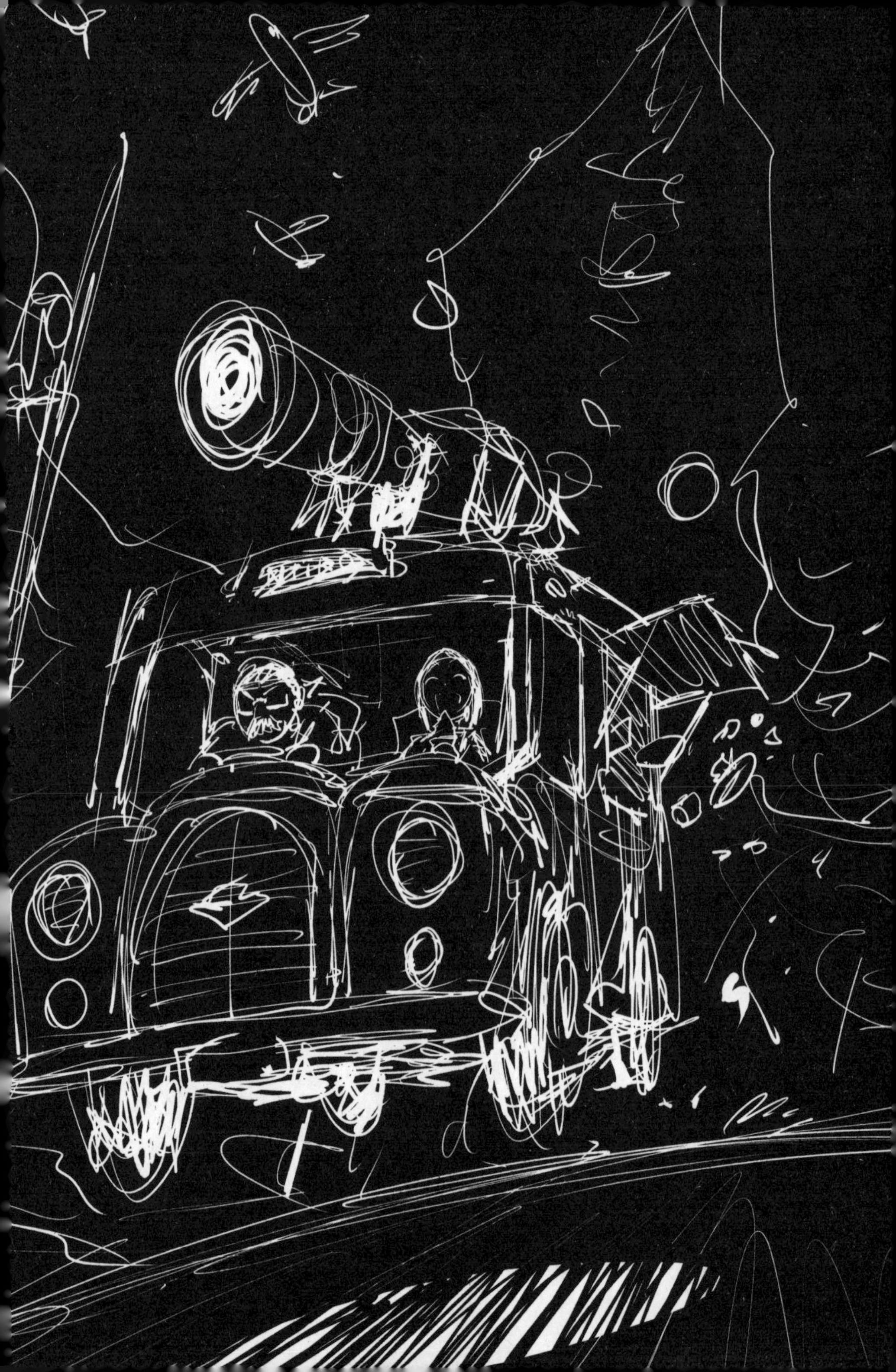

CRAZY STAFF

MANGA
ROKUROU OGAKI

ART
KAKU NINOMIYA
TATSUYA HAINOKI
SEI FUKUI

EDITING
YOSHINOSUKE SUMINO
MASAKADO KUNISAWA

COVER DESIGN
RYOUSUKE TAKEUCHI [CRAZY FORCE]

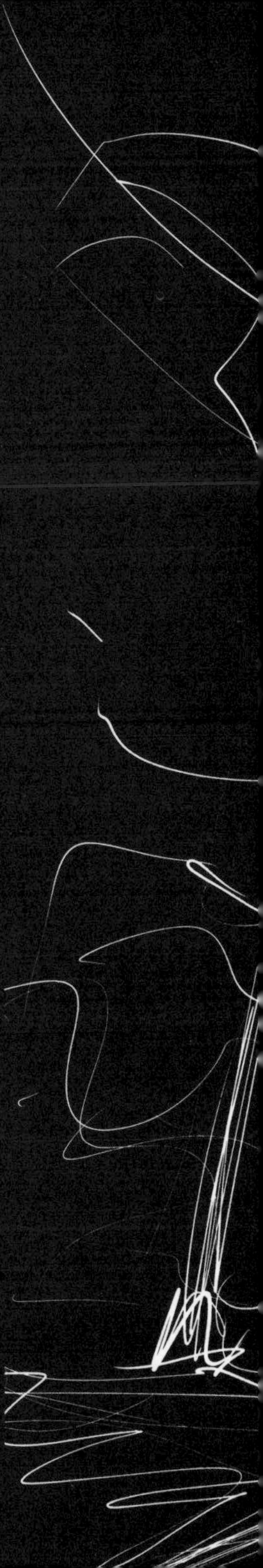

GORDON'S RECIPE 01

BLT SANDWICH

Ingredients (Serves 2)

Baguettes: 2.

Bacon: Plenty. 4 to 6 slices per sandwich.

Lettuce: Plenty. Stuff in as much as you want.

Tomatoes: 2. Skip 'em if you don't have 'em.

Onions: A good amount.

Mustard: Plenty of this.

Directions

1. Cook the bacon until it's crispy.
2. Slice baguettes in half. Butter the open faces and toast.
3. Spread plenty of mustard on the baguettes.
4. Load 'em up with as much as you like, then take a big bite.

If preferred, cheese and scrambled egg go good on it too!

GORDON'S RECIPE 02

SAND SQUID SASHIMI

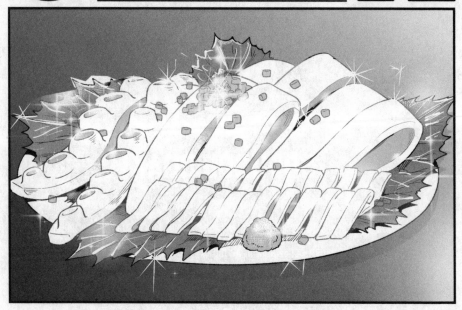

Ingredients (Serves 2)

Sand squid: As much as you can eat.

Perilla leaves: Even better if you have them.

Grated ginger: Even better if you have it.

Green onions: Even better if you have them.

Wasabi: Even better if you have it.

Soy sauce: This you gotta have.

Directions

Cut it up. Eat it while it's fresh.

Cleaning sand squid is a complicated process, so if you want to know how, I'll show you when we meet!

ROKUROU OGAKI

Cooking, traveling, a strong middle-aged man, an innocent beautiful girl, a world turned to desert wasteland, and a food truck—this is the manga I cooked up when I crammed in all my favorite things. I hope you'll enjoy this crazy world as if you're traveling right along with Gordon and Arisa. Also, a warning: reading this might leave you hungry!

Before his 2013 debut in *Shonen Sunday S* with *Unlimited Psychic Squad*, Rokurou Ogaki worked as an assistant for manga artists Junpei Goto and Kenjiro Hata. In addition to *Crazy Food Truck*, he's also the manga artist of the *Akudama Drive* anime's manga adaptation. Fun fact: Rokurou Ogaki's pen name is a reference to "rock and roll"! Rock on!

CRAZY FOOD TRUCK

VOLUME 1
VIZ SIGNATURE EDITION

STORY AND ART BY
ROKUROU OGAKI

TRANSLATION: **AMANDA HALEY**
ENGLISH ADAPTATION: **JENNIFER LEBLANC**
TOUCH-UP ART & LETTERING: **E.K. WEAVER, JEANNIE LEE, SARA LINSLEY, JAMES GAUBATZ**
DESIGN: **JIMMY PRESLER**
EDITOR: **JENNIFER LEBLANC**

CRAZY FOOD TRUCK volume 1
© Rokurou Ogaki 2020
All Rights Reserved
English translation rights arranged with SHINCHOSHA PUBLISHING CO.
through Tuttle-Mori Agency, Inc, Tokyo

Printed in the U.S.A.

Published by VIZ Media, LLC
P.O. Box 77010
San Francisco, CA 94107

10 9 8 7 6 5 4 3 2 1
First printing, May 2022

viz.com
vizsignature.com

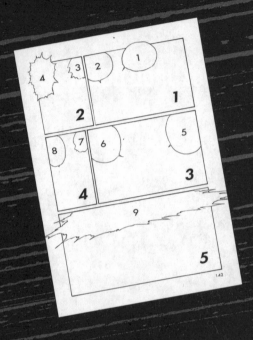

YOU'RE READING
THE WRONG WAY!

CRAZY FOOD TRUCK reads from right to left, starting in the upper-right corner. Japanese is read from right to left, meaning that action, sound effects, and word-balloon order are completely reversed from English order.